OUR POISONED LAND

LIVING IN THE SHADOWS OF ZUMA'S KEEPERS

JACQUES PAUW

TAFELBERG

Tafelberg
An imprint of NB Publishers, a division of Media24 Boeke (Pty) Ltd
40 Heerengracht, Cape Town
www.tafelberg.com

Cover design: Fuel Design
Book design: Wilna Combrinck and Marthie Steenkamp
Editing: Russell Martin
Proofreading: Riaan Wolmarans
Index: George Claassen

First edition, second impression 2022

ISBN: 978-0-624-09053-3
Epub: 978-0-624-09054-0

Printed by **novus print**, a division of Novus Holdings

Table of content

Departing Zumageddon

I WANT YOU to journey back to the end of 2017, the fading days of the fourth administration of the African National Congress and a time of great anticipation and uncertainty. The once-glorious liberation movement is at a crossroad. It is about to cavort down a steep and perilous slope where lurks a T-junction. Its 4 708 delegates, elected from branches across the country, are assembled at Nasrec on the outskirts of Johannesburg to choose which road to take. The one leads to Dlamini-Zumaville, an enclave that is poisoned with the skeletons and corpses of state capture and which sports a sculpture of the goddess Justitia, holding the scales of justice high, standing on Gupta Square with a sword in her back. The rand languishes in the junkyard, Air Myeni has been grounded, the trains have long been derailed, the Saxonwold shebeen has closed, and raw sewage is running down the potholed streets of sullied suburbs with names like Marikana, Nkandla and Kwezi.

Or will the delegates venture down another uncharted route, which leads to Phala Phala Park? They are promised an orderly settlement surrounded by green fields where legions of contented hands toil, white fumes billowing from the spinning turbines of shipshape power plants, a working courthouse, a well-resourced police station and a jail brimming with state looters.

Our beautiful land is in turmoil. Unemployment has risen to 27 per cent of the working population, the gross domestic product is growing by less than two per cent, the price of 95 unleaded fuel is a whopping R14.49 at the coast, and almost 19 000 people have been butchered and 37 000 raped in the previous year. The state-owned companies have been eviscerated and, although residents were spared loadshedding in 2016 and 2017, they were reminded of the 852 hours of blackness they had had to endure in 2015.

The delegates at Nasrec have just sat through uBaba's swansong as ANC president, a two-hour-long, intellectually indolent plod that could have inflicted irremediable brain trauma on anyone who listened to his ramble. Here is a president who inherited a functional democracy and turned it into a weapons-grade thiefdom of mass looting. Yet his supporters carry him into infamy with the words of "Umshini Wami", just as they had a decade earlier when they winched him from his rape trial towards the presidency of South Africa.

It is now time for the dynastic handover from one Zuma to another to ensure the continuation of the gangster republic and the state-capture project. Clambering onto the RET Express are Free State warlord and Zuma emissary Ace Magashule; gogo Bathabile Dlamini, who has to be dragged to her seat before passing out; a sobbing Carl Niehaus, whose mother has passed away yet again; superspy David Mahlobo, who heads straight to a cubicle for a Thai massage; and Mosebenzi Zwane, who is on a mission to bring the last remaining Vrede dairy cow to Dlamini-Zumaville to populate uBaba's deserted cattle kraal. An ebullient Fikile Mbalula assures delegates that they have fokkol to fear because he crushes balls and fixes everything. Nobody pays him any attention. Malusi Gigaba was in two minds as to which of his 200 tailored suits to wear and almost misses the bus. Smoking and drinking are banned, which makes Bathabile a venerated emissary.

There are fewer kleptos and sticky fingers aboard the CR-17 Express, but like the rest of the leadership they all harbour smallanyana skeletons. Gwede Mantashe is slumped in a corner reading *The Rise and Rise of King Coal* while Ronald Lamola has yet again bunked kindergarten. Tito Mboweni boards with a pot of his famous tinned pilchard curry but Thandi Modise says she cannot eat while her pigs are starving on the farm. The last on board is Zweli Mkhize, who has a jingle in his step and a smile on his face while listening to Digital Vibes on his earphones. There are few surprises, except for Bheki Cele, who crawls out of a red

Lamborghini driven by a drug dealer. Sporting a fedora, he leaps onto the CR-17 Express while hollering at hecklers on the RET Express to shut the fuck up.

It is early evening on a Sunday in December 2017 and the two factions are racing towards the T-junction with war cries filling the air. There is no clear winner in sight. As the delegates ready their wagons to take the corner, David Mabuza leans out of a window and sticks a spanner into the spokes of the RET Express. He will forever be known as the ultimate backslider, but he rescues the nation from a doctor president who exudes the verve of a mortuary keeper on Valium.

His intervention enables the CR-17 Express to screech around the corner and onto the road to the promised land. As the RET Express flattens the stop sign and veers off the tarmac, a mob of smallanyanas crawls out and scrambles onto the once-dreaded CR-17 Express. Among them are Nathi Mthethwa, David Mahlobo and Mr FearFokkol himself. Maite Nkoana-Mashabane also makes it, despite the hole in her head. As uBaba, Magashule, Gigaba and Niehaus retreat to lick their wounds and plot their revenge, the Ramabuza presidency is born.

True to form, the ANC's elective conference is nothing but a gangster jamboree where anything and anyone is tradeable and for sale.

The run-up to this crackpot era in South African politics served as the backdrop to the publication of *The President's Keepers*. It was a time of backroom conniving, dubious trading and deals, discrediting smears and ravaging the state coffers.

I said five years ago that South Africa was at a crossroads. We had to revive law enforcement, imprison the state looters, bring down the crime rate, find employment for our people and fix Eskom and the other state-owned companies. It didn't happen. In fact, the CR-17 Express had hardly arrived at Phala Phala Park or the comrades were at each other's throats as they scrambled for a spot at the new administration's feeding trough. Five years on, Phala Phala Park resembles Dlamini-Zumaville and suffers from the same disease that laid Jacob Zuma's kleptocracy to waste.

How did it happen? And is there a way out of this mess?

CHAPTER 1

Sunday, bloody Sunday

🐦 **Times LIVE** @TimesLIVE, 29 Oct. 2017
"He is a gangster like us": New book reveals Zuma's "darkest secret"

This is the tweet that thrust *The President's Keepers* into the public realm. Across the country's bigger cities, newspaper vendors stood at traffic lights brandishing the *Sunday Times* with a front page that bawled: GANGSTER REPUBLIC. Elsewhere, subscribers of the newspaper fired up their smartphones, tablets or laptops to be confronted with a picture of President Jacob Zuma surrounded by a plethora of those who kept him in power and out of prison.

I'd spent days, weeks and months scouring classified intelligence files and tax documents, meeting whistle-blowers in obscure Wimpy bars, and getting up in the early hours of the morning to write. Now the horse had bolted. This was the metaphor our lawyers used to illustrate that it was too late for the president himself, law-enforcement agencies or any of Zuma's keepers to try to prevent the book from being published.

🐦 **Tshifhiwa** @BishopRams, 29 Oct. 2017
Tell me this is a movie script for Tsotsi 2?

🐦 **Realeboga Mashiane** @Toscallo, 29 Oct. 2017
Initially I thought Jacques Pauw ke Jack Parow. Was thinking he's ditched a singing career 4 writing

🐦 **Thabiso** @m11_thabiso, 29 Oct. 2017
This book has dangerous information. Jacques Pauw must just go into hiding.

By ten that morning, my phone started ringing. It didn't stop for the next two months. By eleven, the book was headline news. An hour or so later, the Presidency took to Twitter to deny that Zuma's tax affairs were a mess and that he had received a monthly salary from KwaZulu-Natal security entrepreneur Roy Moodley while he was president.

The first full-on attack on the book came later that afternoon from Nkosazana Dlamini-Zuma's spokesperson Carl Niehaus. He described the front page of the *Sunday Times*, which carried an excerpt from the last chapter of the book that exposed self-confessed cigarette smuggler and fraudster Adriano Mazzotti as a benefactor of the Dlamini-Zuma campaign, as sewer journalism and a "fake-news pigsty" that was "wallowing in the mud of embedded advocacy journalism, fabricated news and downright lies".

Mazzotti responded that he had only met Dlamini-Zuma once briefly. He was lying. A week later, the *Sunday Times* produced two more photographs of Dlamini-Zuma, Mazzotti and his business associates. The photographs were taken in London and Sandton. A third photograph showed an associate of Mazzotti embracing the ANC presidential candidate in Greece.

On 30 October, one day after the book was launched, the first print run was sold out. I was perplexed as the events played out in front of me like a movie. If anyone had told me beforehand that *The President's Keepers* would outsell braai manuals, diet books, Harry Potter and Deon Meyer in South Africa, I would have scoffed at them.

🐦 **NB Publishers** @NBPublishers, 30 Oct. 2017
The initial print run was 20,000 books, but they sold out in the first day!

The publishers printed another 10 000 copies, and a few days later another 20 000. They then ordered another 30 000. They were at one point printing on two machines simultaneously. Then South Africa ran out of the matt paper on which the book was printed. One of the editions was printed on a brilliant white paper. On the second day after publication, I received 30 requests for interviews, ranging from *Huisgenoot*, *Fair Lady* and *Rooi Rose* to a host of newspapers and radio and television stations.

🐦 Abdullah bin Maisela'ad @ArthurMaisela, 30 Oct. 2017
Got me a copy this morning and I am beyond shook. This is Movie material. Thriller for that matter.

🐦 Musa Marawu @Musa160477, 1 Nov. 2017
Horror of horrors!!! What is really going on in this country? Suddenly i am very afraid!

* * *

The most valuable contribution of *The President's Keepers* was a blow-by-blow account of how the State Security Agency (SSA) spent far more time ring-fencing Jacob Zuma and his cabal of looters, plotters and connivers than guarding the integrity of the state. The agency ran a parallel intelligence network, the Principal Agent Network (PAN), which bought 293 cars for 72 agents, purchased properties which they registered in their own names, and employed family and friends. Agents ran cigarette-smuggling scams, plotted the wholesale dismantling of the revenue service, shielded criminals from prosecution and looted the agency's secret account.

Lurking in the centre of this intelligence cesspool was a soft-spoken and bespectacled man whom few South Africans had heard of before the publication of *The President's Keepers*. Arthur Fraser was not appointed as spy boss because of his sterling managerial skills or his devotion to the Constitution, but because of his usefulness to the president and his cabal. Why else appoint someone who engineered and commanded a parallel intelligence network that wasted around a billion rand of taxpayers' money?

On 1 November, the SSA said the book was "replete with inaccuracies" and amounted to "fake information". It alleged that the book contravened the Intelligence Services Act, which resulted in the SSA demanding that we remove *The President's Keepers* from the shelves of bookstores. Fraser gave us five days to do this, failing which he said he would bring a High Court application to compel us to do so.

For the first time in democratic South Africa, the state had attempted to ban a book. Did Arthur Fraser think that in a constitutional democracy that guarantees freedom of speech and the public's right to know, he was going to prohibit a book that exposed criminality and corruption? The attempt illustrated the parallel spook universe and cuckoo Fraserland that he lived in. To start with: you cannot give someone five days and then go to court to apply for an urgent application or interdict. If it's urgent, you do it right away; you don't wait five days. So, this was not urgent.

Fraser had inadvertently confirmed the truth of the content relating to the SSA in the book. I could only have contravened intelligence legislation if the allegations against him and the spy agency were true. If they were false, as he claimed, the book was fiction and didn't contravene any legislation. Fraser and, to a lesser extent, former SARS commissioner Tom Moyane became the best publicists I have ever had. Did Fraser have any idea how many books we would sell in the five days he gave us?

Constitutional law expert Professor Pierre de Vos said that there was nothing in the Intelligence Services Act that prohibited me from publishing revelations about corruption in the SSA. He said that the sections in the Act which prohibit disclosure of information about the SSA are unconstitutional as they limit the right to freedom of expression guaranteed in section 16(1) of the Constitution.

In response to Fraser's inanity, attorney Willem de Klerk told him: "Your generalised statement that the book is 'replete with inaccuracies' is not backed up by a single reference to any specific statement in the book. Your demand for a retraction 'of all those parts which are inaccurate' is therefore incongruous. It is furthermore unclear how you reconcile an allegation of falsity, on the one hand, with an alleged violation of statutory provisions on the other."

De Klerk said that exposing criminality in the SSA could not compromise the agency's legitimate operations or the security of the state. The book did not violate the "relevant intelligence statutes", as Fraser alleged. We also warned the spy boss: if you pursue your threat of going to court to seek an interdict to effectively ban the book and you lose, which you will, we will seek a punitive cost order against you personally.

Public Protester @Pasco_e, 3 Nov. 2017
Dear state security agency, please fuck off! We will read and analyse #thepresidentskeepers so we get to add more charges to the 783. Tsek!

Keith Levenstein @keithlevenstein, 3 Nov. 2017
I've read it on my kindle. Should I return the entire kindle to you, or just try to forget what I read?

Floyd Shivambu @FloydShivambu, 3 Nov. 2017
All South Africans should buy #ThePresidentsKeepers book and read about the Zuma led Mafia State. The book stores must print more copies.

GODFATHER @LetHeard, 3 Nov. 2017
This is going to be the first book I own.

Max du Preez @MaxduPreez, 3 Nov. 2017
I'd be keen to hear the SSA lawyer tell the court next week how the book can be banned from Amazon.

The unavailability of *The President's Keepers* in bookstores and the fear that the SSA threats could lead to a ban made people desperate to lay their hands on the book. PDF copies started circulating on the internet and became freely available. The shortage turned the book into an overnight global bestseller.

Eusebius McKaiser @Eusebius, 4 Nov. 2017
Wow. #ThePresidentsKeepers is the 8th fastest selling book on Amazon's kindle editions. That is 8th fastest seller GLOBALLY. Tell the SSA!

Ismail Akhalwaya @ismailak7, 5 Nov. 2017
#ThePresidentsKeepers now number 2

Karin April @KarinApril2, 5 Nov. 2017
Book is now #1 worldwide on Amazon Kindle in category "General Elections & Political Process"

* * *

HuffPost SouthAfrica @HuffPostSA, 3 Nov. 2017
A Snarling, Growling Jacob Zuma Goes On The Offensive #ThePresidentsKeepers

As we took legal advice about Fraser's threats, the Democratic Alliance (DA) leader Musi Maimane stood with *The President's Keepers* in his hand in Parliament and waved it at Zuma. He asked him if he had received a salary from Moodley while in office. The former president smiled before embarking on a sluggish and indolent duck-and-dive, his hands karate-chopping in the air in front of him. About the alleged payments from Moodley, he said: "I did not receive payments from private individuals or companies during my tenure as president, other than those which have been disclosed or reported to the necessary authorities." Evidence before the State Capture Commission would later reveal that Zuma lied to Parliament.

✈ Evita Bezuidenhout @TannieEvita, 2 Nov. 2017
Shame! You can't expect President Zuma to read the
#ThePresidentsKeepers – he's still colouring in the book I gave him
last year.

I received numerous reports afterwards of ANC members of Parliament who were seen surreptitiously reading *The President's Keepers* and carrying it in folders, files and plastic bags. Members of the opposition took great delight in exposing ANC MPs who attempted to hide the book.

✈ Leaky Tweets @Citizen_WatchZA, 7 Nov. 2017
Deputy President Cyril Ramaphosa has told Parliament that he is
reading veteran journalist Jacques Pauw's book.

* * *

✈ POWER987News @POWER987News, 3 Nov. 2017
#SARS Sandile Memela: We are speaking to our lawyers trying to
pursue criminal case and a civil claim against The Sunday Times and
Jacques Pauw

Not to be outdone, the South African Revenue Service (SARS) also threatened criminal charges and said in a statement that it was "seeking legal advice on what steps to take, including but not limited to criminal and civil investigation against Mr Pauw into the circumstances pertaining to the unlawful disclosure of confidential taxpayer information". Political commentator Stephen Grootes said in the *Daily Maverick*: "This surely has the consequence of proving that Pauw's claims are correct. Either Pauw published information which is true, and thus broke the law around taxpayer confidentiality, or he published information that is false. If it is false, that is not really SARS's problem, it is Zuma's. But now, by taking this action, SARS has confirmed that the information is possibly true, which in turn must surely also mean that Zuma has lied."

🐦 **Exclusive Books** @ExclusiveBooks, 4 Nov. 2017
EB is now OUT OF STOCK of #ThePresidentsKeepers. We anticipate receiving more stock on Monday, 06 Nov.

🐦 **Stage 6 Moferefere** @CJSteyl, 5 Nov. 2017
Just finished #ThePresidentsKeepers and fok if only half of it is true, SA is thoroughly fucked under another ANC term of government.

🐦 **Kwagga Robertse** @Afieplaas, 5 Nov. 2017
(Zuma to Atul) . . . Hallo Atul?! What's this book about President Scheepers? I'm still president right?

🐦 **Motaung Oa Ramokhele** @LebonaMoleli, 7 Nov. 2017
Is there anything that Jakop Zuma paid out of his pocket? Jesus Christ, what a looter.

* * *

It was time to emerge from my hideout in Riebeek-Kasteel and face the world. In the first week, hundreds of people had descended on the Red Tin Roof to have their books signed, take selfies or ask who would win the ANC presidential election in December. I mostly took cover in my study while my wife, Sam Rogers, had to make feeble excuses about my whereabouts. Undeterred, some admirers flung open the door of my study and forced their way in. An elderly woman hurled her arms around me while another brought me a milk tart. A male reader traced me to a corner table in a Riebeek restaurant and presented me with six bottles of Klipdrift brandy, while others insisted on paying for my meal. Lawyers offered their services *pro bono* (for free) and people presented their holiday mansions in Hermanus and on the Vaal to me as hideouts. I cringed in my seat when the captain of a South African Airways flight from Cape Town to Johannesburg announced my presence on board and upgraded me to business class.

I realised on my way to Johannesburg for the launch that airports are the worst place to be if you do not want to be seen. There is no place to hide, nowhere to go. I soon came to detest selfies, the self-portrait of the digital age. I learnt from the avid generation of selfie-bugs that a smartphone tilted at 45 degrees just above your eyeline is generally deemed the most forgiving. Not for me. I stared with horror at some of the results. I looked fatter, my eyes bulged and my complexion was a rosy red. Obsessively taking selfies is now a real mental disorder, called "selfitis". Its worst sufferers awaited me at every airport. Click, click, click. Please smile, they ordered. Smile about what? I snarled back. Didn't matter. Click, click, click.

A bodyguard by the name of Jabu awaited me in Johannesburg. A block of a man, he came with a big smile and a gun. The publishers had decided that I had pissed off too many people and received enough death threats to warrant a minder.

🐦 **eNCA** @eNCA, 7 Nov. 2017
[ON AIR] #ThePresidentsKeepers author, Jacques Pauw, and Former SARS Spokesperson, Adrian Lackay, LIVE in studio on #DStv 403

The eNCA interview with Joanne Joseph on the eve of my Johannesburg book launch attracted a year-best 132 000 viewers. When the Gupta-run ANN7 interviewed Jacob Zuma days later, they achieved 54 000 viewers.

🐦 **Team News24** @TeamNews24, 8 Nov. 2017
Jacques Pauw book #ThePresidentsKeepers will be officially launched this evening at Hyde Park corner

I dread book launches. I detest being the focus of attention and am beset by the fear that no one will pitch up. With my first book launch in 1992, for *In the Heart of the Whore*, I kept Nelson Mandela waiting for more than half an hour because I was overcome by a bout of angst and sat at home sipping brandy and Coke. In the end, I agreed to launch events for *The President's Keepers* in Johannesburg, Pretoria and Cape Town, where there were two. This time round, there wouldn't be a problem in accommodating enough people, as Exclusive Books in Hyde Park moved the event from the bookstore to the mezzanine level of the shopping centre. The SABC broadcast the event live on YouTube.

The roads around Hyde Park Corner were lined with supporters from the Ahmed Kathrada Foundation and Future SA, among others, with placards that said: "State Capture Is Real: We've Joined the Dots", "Wanted: President's Keeper Arthur Fraser" and "Wanted: Kept President Jacob Zuma".

I have only a vague memory of the launch – and not because I was pissed. I was simply overwhelmed. My minder, Jabu, had delivered me hours beforehand to the innards of Hyde Park Corner where I sat in a back room of Exclusives signing books. The bookstore had an extra thousand copies on the shelves, which sold out within an hour.

I took to the stage. A sea of people greeted me; they cheered, waved their hands. There were journalists, photographers, television cameras. I was blinded by the lights. Someone put a glass of wine next to me. I gulped it down. Exclusives CEO Benjamin Trisk said it was the biggest audience ever for a book launch. Political commentator Peter Bruce was the facilitator for the event. My brain was on preset and words tumbled impulsively out of my mouth – which can be dangerous.

🐦 **Ranjeni Munusamy** @RanjeniM, 8 Nov. 2017
#ThePresidentsKeepers @Bruceps says he was terrified when reading the book – it never stops! Commends Pauw's courage

🐦 **Franschhoek Lit Fest** @FranLitFest, 8 Nov. 2017
@Bruceps asks @Jaqqs if there were things he was too nervous to write about. Short answer: "no".

And then we were plunged into darkness, just thirty minutes into the launch. An eerie silence descended on the mall while everyone waited for the generators to kick in. For the first time ever, they failed to do so. A section of the crowd started chanting "Zuma must fall! Zuma must fall!" while a woman jumped onto the stage to sing "Nkosi Sikelel' iAfrika". They mercifully got her down again. Trisk announced that the launch was over. Spurred into action, Jabu grabbed me and yanked me through a maze of back alleys to Exclusive Books. I signed books by candlelight until my hand quivered and lost all feeling. When Jabu fetched me the next day for my book launch in Pretoria, he was armed with a pistol and a torch.

"Why the torch?" I asked him.

"This time," he said, "I'm not taking any chances."

Many believe to this day that the SSA sabotaged the Hyde Park book launch, especially because the generators at the centre seem to have been tampered with.

*　*　*

"So, the Jacques Pauw book launch . . . the book is so important for democracy and for South Africa. His investigations are superb and he needs to be celebrated. But I cannot ignore what I saw at the launch . . . There was another level of white privilege using the contents of the book to justify their racism and anti-black sentiment. I was in the back and there was a smug sense of 'you see what happens when you put blacks in charge'. Within five minutes of being there, I was pushed to one side, told to shut up and spoken down at." With this Facebook posting, political journalist and author Qaanitah Hunter ignited a fierce debate about issues of "whiteness" surrounding the book, its readers and those attending the launch.

🐦 **Temnotfo** @CMagagz, 9 Nov. 2017
Exactly what my husband and I were speaking about this morning. White people feel justified by this book hence I will not purchase it no matter how true it is.

NtsikiWethu @ntsikimazwai, 9 Nov. 2017
At what point as an African are you gonna be in this crowd and expect us to take you seriously as a thinker?

Author Sisonke Msimang said in the *Mail & Guardian*: "For some of the white South Africans who attended Pauw's book launch, the state of governance is emblematic of the failure of black people to manage the affairs of the country. They see Zuma's scandals and the allegations of corruption that trail him as a function of his race: Jacob Zuma is corrupt, because he is black." But she went on to argue that *The President's Keepers* did not imply this racial connection at all. The book was meticulously documented and joined the dots using available public information and bolstering it with new evidence, and it did so without resorting to stereotype. "Still, it would be foolhardy to suggest that discussions about corruption in South Africa – which have spiked in volume as the excesses of President Zuma and his friends and family have become more and more outrageous – are race neutral," she said.

Palesa Morudu @palesa_morudu, 10 Nov. 2017
#JacquesPauw is a journalist. He wrote a book, a very good one. Anyone who thinks he is a "white savior" gives whiteness too much power and/or wants us to care less about a criminal syndicate that passes for government.

Redi Tlhabi @RediTlhabi, 11 Nov. 2017
Starting debate about Pauw's race but not perturbed at the billions that could have funded free education but instead were looted in dubious intelligence operations? This pseudo black nationalism is going to be the death of us.

sam mashiloane @sam_mashiloane, 11 Nov. 2017
Some of us have read the book. No amount of race attack will get us to "unread" the book.

* * *

🐦 **EWN Reporter** @ewnreporter, 9 Nov. 2017
#PresidentsKeepers Jacques Pauw is holding the second leg of the
launch of his book at Brooklyn Mall Pretoria today.

I will remember the Pretoria launch – packed but well organised and
brightly lit – for two reasons. As I sat at a table in Exclusive Books
signing copy after copy with a quaking right hand, I saw from the corner
of my eye someone walking past me and dropping a small, white plastic
bag at my feet. I didn't look at it and didn't dare to pick it up until
much later that night when the long line of people winding out of the
bookshop had been reduced to nothing. In the bag was a computer
flash drive that contained two investigative reports of inspector-general
of intelligence Faith Radebe into Fraser's PAN. I did not have Radebe's
top-secret reports when I wrote *The President's Keepers* and eagerly
scrutinised them because Fraser had always maintained that they
contained "no criminal findings" against him.

Radebe was reportedly a Zuma supporter and former SSA employee,
which raised doubts about her independence and commitment to
holding former colleagues to account. But even Radebe could not ignore
the malfeasance at PAN. In her 174-page main report, she set out the
extent of the covert work of PAN, how it operated as a law unto itself
and conducted illegal operations without proper authorisation. Fraser's
outfit flouted Treasury regulations and squandered public money on
an enormous scale.

The second reason I remember the book launch was the presence of
Pravin Gordhan and Ivan Pillay. It was the first time I had met either
of the two. Former acting SARS commissioner Pillay is an introverted
man who kept to himself, but the forceful Gordhan was cheered to
the front, where he took the microphone and said: "What we need in
South Africa is more Jacques Pauws in government, in civil society, in
business, in the labour movement, so that we can bring the truth out
and can show the minority that want to bring the country to its knees

16

that the majority don't want that." As the crowd waited for me to sign their books, some walked over and asked Gordhan – and in some cases Pillay – to autograph their copies as well. They happily obliged.

A friend warned me afterwards: you are going to have years of shit, what with Pravin signing books at your launch. He was so right.

* * *

🐦 **Sunday Independent** @SundayIndy, 8 Dec. 2017
Who really wrote #JacquesPauw's book? Read about these exclusive revelations in #TheSundayIndependent this coming Sunday

Once a thriving and respected media house, Independent Media under its new owner Iqbal Survé has ripped the heart out of its newspapers by interfering with their independence and turning them into his personal mouthpiece. He expelled experienced and respectable journalists and replaced them with praise-singers who sugar-coat his diminishing empire.

Although the circulations of his papers are plummeting, he has weaponised them to fight his own battles, to shame his detractors, and to boost the radical economic transformation (RET) faction of the ANC. Survé and his army of discredited hacks backed Dlamini-Zuma as candidate for the ANC presidency in 2017 and led a dirty-tricks campaign against Ramaphosa and his closest confidant, Pravin Gordhan.

On Thursday, 7 December 2017, *Sunday Independent* editor Steve Motale sent me a list of questions about an "exposé" that he planned to publish. Motale said he had "sources" that revealed that Pravin Gordhan, Ivan Pillay, Johann van Loggerenberg and former spy boss Moe Shaik were the real authors of my book. He said I was facing "multiple lawsuits" and was demanding financial assistance from the "real authors". Motale's "exposé" followed Pravin Gordhan's signing of copies of *The President's Keepers* at the Pretoria book launch. Since then, trolls and bots of the pro-Zuma campaign have inundated Twitter with claims that Gordhan had a sinister hand in the book.

🐦 Thabang Theo @thabang16360834, 10 Dec. 2017
@Jaqqs was forced to write this. It was not his personal motive. This book was written to defame #Zuma and make #Ramaphosa win 2019 elections.

A former editor of *The Citizen*, Motale has had – to put it mildly – a colourful journalism career. In August 2015 – incidentally, on the third anniversary of the Marikana massacre – he penned an open letter in his newspaper to Jacob Zuma entitled "I'm sorry, Mr President". It was a most bizarre act of journalism. Motale said in his letter: "I've been party to the sinister agenda against Zuma and can only apologise for that. The media is as much to blame for the current parlous state of this country's politics and economy as the politicians and economists who have brought us here." Motale argued that Zuma had never been found guilty of fraud and corruption, yet had been vilified by the media as if he had been. Motale's crapology was lapped up by the SABC – then led by the jester Hlaudi Motsoeneng – and ANN7, which hauled him in front of the cameras and labelled him a brave visionary.

After emerging from the closet, Motale went on the attack and ran a series of stories that implicated former finance minister Trevor Manuel in criminality during a contract to upgrade systems at SARS. He said the Hawks were investigating the matter; they denied it. He then published what he said was a recording of Manuel telling a reporter to "stop fucking bothering me". It later emerged that the recording was manufactured from several recordings that were spliced together.

If Motale had intended to butter up Iqbal in this way, it worked. In May 2017, he was appointed as *Sunday Independent* editor, presumably to continue his attacks on the pro-Ramaphosa faction of the ANC. It was a grave mistake. As far as journalistic skills and integrity are concerned, Motale is a walking lobotomy.

With the ANC's elective conference looming in three months, the season of smear, slander and kompromat (a borrowing of a Russian term that means "compromising material") was open. In the first days of September 2017, a series of questions from Motale to Ramaphosa circulated on Twitter. He said he was in possession of a string of e-mails that Ramaphosa had sent to young women. Motale asked Ramaphosa if he had had intimate affairs and unprotected sex with them and if any of the women had fallen pregnant. In an article titled "Ramaphosa the Player", the *Sunday Independent* alleged that the deputy president was using his wealth to sexually prey on women. Motale said one of the women had had a miscarriage.

Ramaphosa replied in a statement afterwards that he and his wife supported 54 young people busy with their academic studies. He accused Motale of invading the young people's privacy and said that his article represented "an escalation of a dirty war against those who are working to restore the values, principles and integrity of the ANC and society". One of Ramaphosa's alleged "sugar babies", who was engaged and was studying towards a theology doctorate in Germany, said afterwards she had never even met Ramaphosa.

I have little doubt that the intelligence services, most probably the Special Operations Unit (SOU) of the SSA, hacked Ramaphosa's e-mails and gave copies to Motale. We know today that the SOU was Jacob Zuma's personal dirty-tricks troop. In choosing Motale as the messenger, however, they made a terrible blunder.

Following "Ramaphosa the Player", Motale promised more revelations about the deputy president's saucy private life. But his great unmasking of Ramaphosa seemed to have backfired, and a few days later he declared he had received death threats and was under tremendous pressure. The *Sunday Independent* backtracked on the story and apologised to its readers "for any inconvenience caused".

The *Sunday Independent* revealed that I had never intended to write *The President's Keepers* until Gordhan approached me "with tons of information", and that a prominent Stellenbosch businessman had given me the go-ahead to write the book. I was apparently concerned about lawsuits to come but was assured that I would be furnished with "sufficient budget" to cater for litigation. Motale wrote: "Sources say the book has indeed backfired and, as expected, Pauw is now facing multiple lawsuits and is demanding that Gordhan and co honour their promise to back him financially."

🐦 Max du Preez @MaxduPreez, 8 Dec. 2017
Perhaps we should also ask Sunday Independent editor Steve Motale a few questions, like: whose bidding are you doing, State Security or the Guptas? Who is your handler? Why would you want to identify whistleblowers in a state capture story rather than cover the story itself?

* * *

SARS announced that the revenue service had laid a criminal charge against me and said the book was based on "gossip, innuendoes and malice" and created a "misleading impression insinuating that [its head] Mr Moyane is immoral, corrupt, negligent, unprincipled, undermines the law and/or conducts himself in a manner that contravenes the law" – which was, of course, all spot-on.

Somewhere towards the end of December 2018, a sheriff of the court pitched up at my restaurant in Riebeek-Kasteel and insisted on seeing me personally to deliver a court summons issued by SARS. I also had to sign his book. Tom Moyane had brought an application in the High Court to obtain a declaratory order that I had contravened the Tax Administration Act by divulging confidential taxpayers' information.

Moyane's action made no sense. A declaratory order merely assists in clarifying issues of law. So what if he had obtained an order that I had contravened the Tax Administration Act by publishing the tax affairs of Zuma and his cronies? But it did confirm my allegations were true.

🐦 Rob Rose @robrose_za, 19 Dec. 2017
So from Tom Moyane's most recent ridiculous act, we get de facto confirmation from SARS that what Jacques Pauw said about Zuma's tax affairs is entirely correct. Moyane can't claim it's not true if he's going to court saying the info was "confidential" . . .

🐦 Redi Tlhabi @RediTlhabi, 19 Dec. 2017
So revelations in Jacques' book are true? Paragraph by paragraph, Moyane doesn't dispute veracity of Pauw's claims. Inadvertent admission.

Tom Moyane's nonsensical and cowardly action did not make it to court, and I never heard anything about a criminal charge. The application was withdrawn later in 2018.

* * *

🐦 Justice Malala @justicemalala, 28 Feb. 2018
They are going for #JacquesPauw. Exactly as they went for #PravinGordhan. Rage, rage now. And rage loud for tomorrow they will come for you.

🐦 AndrewM @SurferSilverza, 1 Mar. 2018
And everyone is walking around thinking Buffalo is the greatest thing since sliced bread. Just more kak in a better suit.

I now know how crooks feel when the Hawks raid their premises: relaxed and at ease unless the evidence is stacked on the dining-room table and marked with a sticker. Otherwise, they will never find whatever they are looking for. Where are the days when the cops raided the homes of activists and found banned material hidden under floors and in roofs, flower beds and sewage pipes?

Following Cyril Ramaphosa's election as president on 15 February 2018, I assumed that the commotion around my book would subside and eventually die down. This was not to be.

🐦 Annika Larsen @AnnikaLarsen1, 28 Feb. 2018
#Breaking News: Hawks have arrived at journalist Jacques Pauw's house in Riebeek Kasteel. His wife Sam sounds frightened and says she doesn't know if they want to arrest Jacques or search the house.

Late in the afternoon of the last day of February 2018, a man dressed in black with a matching hat and a pistol sauntered into my guesthouse and restaurant in Riebeek-Kasteel and introduced himself as Col. Johannes Ngaka Makua from the Crimes against the State (CATS) unit of the Hawks. This was an elite unit of the Hawks that was supposed to investigate crimes like terrorism, extremism, treason and insurrection. But Hawks head Berning Ntlemeza used the unit to help dig up dirt on enemies of the state-capture project, like Pravin Gordhan and Ivan Pillay.

Two Hawks captains accompanied Makua. A police veteran who started his career in blue in 1985 in the apartheid police, Makua presented me with a search-and-seizure warrant in relation to contraventions of the Protection of Information Act and the Intelligence Services Act. The warrant gave Makua the right to seize documents, notes, manuscripts, laptops, cellphones, flash drives, DVDs and any material relating to the book.

I had admitted early on that I was in possession of classified material, from which I quoted extensively in *The President's Keepers*. I got rid of most of the documents before publication by scanning them and storing them in the cloud. The originals were in safekeeping. To protect my sources, I told them on the eve of publication that they had to erase any traces of contact with me on their computers or cellphones. We also stopped communicating.

I said to Makua that I had to confirm the authenticity of the warrant by scanning it and sending it to attorney Willem de Klerk in Johannesburg. I was only playing for time. There were no documents in the office, but my two laptop computers were on my desk. Although I had cleaned the computers before and after the publication of *The President's Keepers*, I wasn't sure if I had left any traces.

I had prepared my staff for a moment like this. The chef, well-proportioned and with a don't-fuck-with-me demeanour, marched like a battle tank past Makua into the office, shoved one computer under her chef's jacket and went back to the kitchen. She deposited the laptop onto the neighbour's compost heap. A waitress chucked computer number two through the adjoining bathroom window. After De Klerk confirmed the warrant's authenticity, the search and seizure commenced. By then, news of the raid had spread like a veld fire through Riebeek-Kasteel, and villagers descended on the Red Tin Roof to witness the spectacle.

𝕏 **Annika Larsen** @AnnikaLarsen1, 28 Feb. 2018
#Hawks raiding #PresidentsKeepers Jacques Pauw's house in Riebeek Kasteel.
@eNCA see video below.

The raid coincided with the evening English news on eNCA, and we fed the channel footage as the raid progressed. This was priceless publicity, and if the sales of the book had dipped after the new year and the appointment of Ramaphosa, they were sure to pick up again.

Makua wanted to inspect the business computer and asked me to log him in. I refused. He fiddled a bit and then relented. His female colleague was on her knees, combing through files on the ground like a bloodhound. The raid was going nowhere. The third raider, a white male captain, was nowhere to be seen and had no interest in finding anything. He was idling in the lounge and looking utterly bored. He was about 55 years old and had clearly reached the pinnacle of his police career. He had no prospect of any further promotion. He longingly stared at the bar and I asked him if I could get him a brandy and Coke. "No, thank you," he said. "I'm still working. But while you are here, don't you quickly want to sign my book for me?"

A few days after the raid, Makua sent an e-mail to NB Publishers. It's so off the wall that it deserves to be quoted uncorrected: *I hereby requesting your office to draft a witness statement whereby your company "NB Publishers" to clarify the following as discussed telephonically: i. Whether Mr Jacque Pauw is the publisher of the book? ii. That the book was actually published and sold to the public? iii. That authorization has been received from the relevant authorities to publish the book or not?*

Makua also threatened to subpoena NB's publicist and drag her before the court. We told him we were not going to answer his questions and never heard from him again.

CHAPTER 2

The snake that eats other snakes

IT IS A balmy Saturday morning in December 2017 in the leafy and hilly Pretoria suburb of Waterkloof, home to embassies and their emissaries, top civil servants, captains of industry, a lush golf course and a handful of ministers.

In crafting his ineptocracy, Zuma stuffed his Cabinet with so many of his chommies that less than half fitted into the ministerial compound at the 107-hectare Bryntirion Estate next to the Union Buildings. He increased his executive to 73 ministers and deputy ministers, compared with former presidents Kgalema Motlanthe's 45 and Thabo Mbeki's 50. In doing so, he made sure that he employed more than half the ANC's national executive committee (NEC) and that he could rely on their undying support.

There are only 28 ministerial properties in Bryntirion, including the presidential residence Mahlamba Ndlopfu (it means "new dawn" and was previously known as Libertas), so most of the other ministers are scattered around upmarket Waterkloof. One of those that had to make do with a walled and guarded double-storey mansion was newly appointed state security minister Bongani Thomas Bongo. Just two months previously, Jacob Zuma had elevated an obscure backbencher to a prime portfolio in the Cabinet.

🐦 **Ngwato M. Thobejane** @TsipaA, 4 Nov. 2017
That Bongani boy isn't the sharpest tool in Zuma's toolbox.

🐦 Justine Limpitlaw @JustineLimLaw, 5 Nov. 2017
#GlynisBreytenbach – "My German shepherd is smarter than State Security Bongo"

🐦 Butch van Blerk @van_butch, 5 Nov. 2017
German shepherds are indeed VERY SMART – don't compare them.

Zuma had dispatched Bongo's predecessor and South Africa's de facto prime minister during his reign, David Mahlobo, to the energy portfolio, ostensibly to oversee a trillion-rand nuclear deal with the Russians. It was a transaction that could have bankrupted the country.

Nothing in Mahlobo's political career had qualified him to be a minister, never mind occupy such powerful portfolios as energy and state intelligence. He was a regular customer at an Asian massage parlour, owned by an alleged rhino-horn smuggler. The parlour was suspected of specialising in happy endings. He smeared public protector Thuli Madonsela as a CIA agent and under his watch intelligence operatives jammed cellphones in Parliament in 2015.

Mahlobo also showed the Constitution his broad backside when he received several forensic investigation reports that former State Security Agency (SSA) deputy director-general Arthur Fraser had established a useless spy network that was looted by top intelligence officials. One investigation concluded that Fraser may have acted treasonously by setting up the alternative intelligence network, yet Mahlobo recommended to Zuma that he appoint Fraser as SSA director-general. With a stroke of Zuma's poisoned pen in August 2016, he appointed a man who lacked managerial skills and was implicated in possible criminality as one of the most powerful civil servants in the country. Fraser became an ultimate Zuma keeper.

Bongo was the perfect successor to Mahlobo. He was a devoted Zuma shoeshine boy – a prerequisite for a portfolio that oversaw the omnipotent SSA with its seemingly bottomless budget and its machinations involving surveillance and intelligence gathering. He publicly backed Zuma, praised the lamentable rulings of public protector Advocate Busisiwe Mkhwebane, and was a vociferous critic of Thuli Madonsela, accusing her of behaving exactly like the Democratic Alliance.

Zuma appointed Bongo just two months before the ANC's elective conference at Nasrec in Johannesburg. At the time, Zuma relied on a criminal and unaccountable parallel intelligence structure within the SSA to serve his personal and political interests. The Special Operations Unit (SOU) had positioned its agents in crucial state institutions like the South African Revenue Service (SARS), Transnet, the Passenger Rail Agency of South Africa (Prasa), Eskom and South African Airways, and was Zuma's eyes and ears during his state-capture exploits.

With Mahlobo off to attend to the nuclear deal, Zuma needed a stooge to maintain the status quo. Bongo was his man.

* * *

It is the first half of December 2017. Sitting in his car in front of Bongani Bongo's Waterkloof residence is the inspector-general of intelligence (IGI), Dr Setlhomamaru Dintwe. He is parked under one of the city's jacaranda trees that flaunt the last remnants of their blossoming season. In October and November, the iconic jacarandas turn the city's upmarket eastern suburbs into carpets of mauve, lavender and violet.

Bongo has called for a reconciliatory meeting between Dintwe and Fraser after tensions between the spy boss and the intelligence oversight head turned into an ugly feud. This is centred partly on revelations in *The President's Keepers* in which Fraser was fingered for setting up PAN.

There were a host of investigations into PAN, including one by an internal SSA audit team headed by an advocate, as well as the Radebe report. The reports buried Fraser and his cronies in a morass of alleged wastage and exposed a host of irregularities.

In early 2017, the DA got wind of the fraud and corruption committed at the SSA and the alleged complicity of Fraser in the depravity. In May, then chief whip John Steenhuisen lodged a formal complaint with Dintwe to investigate the role of Fraser in PAN.

Faith Radebe, a former SSA manager that was branded a Zuma acolyte, had left the IGI's office in 2015 to become South Africa's ambassador to Sweden. For almost two years, the IGI office barely functioned, which meant that in practice the country's intelligence agencies accounted to no one. Only two bodies have oversight of the intelligence agencies: the IGI and Parliament's joint standing committee on intelligence. The latter proved itself ineffectual during the Zuma years and was dominated by party hacks. It seldom met and failed to produce annual reports.

The IGI is constitutionally mandated to protect the public from abuses by the intelligence services. He or she can enter any building belonging to or occupied by the SSA, police crime intelligence and defence intelligence, and open any file and attach any computer or other piece of evidence. It is a criminal offence to obstruct the IGI. Its activities, however, are cloaked in secrecy. Its reports are not made public and it does not engage the media. It accounts only to Parliament.

Following a series of public interviews, Parliament recommended to Zuma that he appoint the 40-year-old Dintwe as the new IGI. The president did so in March 2017. Little was known about Dintwe. Once a senior lecturer in Unisa's law department, he held qualifications in police science and forensic investigations. He described himself during his interview as an "all-in-one" when it came to matters dealing with the criminal justice system. He said to members of Parliament that to excel at his new job, he would have to become "the snake that eats other snakes".

A slender, unassuming and soft-spoken man, Dintwe would show by his handling of the Fraser matter whether he was a harmless brown house snake or a lethal black mamba.

* * *

Dintwe is early for his appointment with Bongo and waits outside his mansion in his car for the minister's first visitor of the day to leave.

After the guest has left, Dintwe drives in and is received by a security guard who ushers him into the residence and up the stairs where Bongo and Fraser are waiting for him in a small and intimate lounge.

The bald Bongo, a man with a reputation for not mincing his words, is casually dressed in shorts and sandals. After the men exchange niceties, a staff member enters with a tray with soft drinks, beer and cider. Bongo pushes a cider towards Dintwe, who declines and says: "No thank you, minister, I drink whisky and it is still too early to take alcohol."

The men make small talk.

The bald and bespectacled Fraser, who has a reputation for being tedious and not exactly the fun guy at a party, tells Dintwe about his plan for the spy agency, which he calls Vision 2035.

Says Dintwe: "You are already planning for 2035? But government doesn't plan that far ahead?"

You can cut the tension with a knife.

It is days before the ANC's elective conference, and much is at stake for Bongo and Fraser. The minister's continued habitation of his plush residence and Fraser's survival as the Zuma administration's stalker-in-chief are linked like an umbilical cord to the president's camp emerging triumphant at Nasrec. Both must know they are on Cyril Ramaphosa's hit list and will probably not survive his ascendency to the highest office.

The SSA under Fraser has been invaluable to the president. Remember the bogus intelligence report that Zuma used to fire then finance minister Pravin Gordhan and his deputy, Mcebisi Jonas, in March 2017? Or the "tremendous foreign and local threats" that David Mahlobo identified following Fraser's appointment? It was all concocted in the machinations and dirty-tricks laboratories of the SSA's headquarters at the Musanda complex on the banks of the Rietvlei Dam outside

Pretoria. The last thing Bongo and Fraser can afford now is an upstart and party outcast like Dintwe causing trouble by demanding answers about Fraser's train wreck of a spy programme. The allegations should have been encased in a Musanda strongroom years ago. But along came *The President's Keepers*, which dusted off Fraser's skeletons and exposed them for the world to see. Fraser then scrambled around like a headless chicken and, with the support of Bongo, fired off threatening letters demanding the removal of the book from the shelves. It turned out to be idiocy in overdrive.

Fraser is a troubled man. His attempt to ban *The President's Keepers* has backfired. His face and name were splashed all over, there were calls for a criminal investigation, the author mocked him as the best publicist he'd ever had, and his hot-headedness resulted in a deluge of book sales and copies circulating on the internet.

Just after the publication of the book, Fraser accused Dintwe of possessing classified information that he claimed Dintwe got from the Democratic Alliance. His threat to the IGI was as nonsensical as his attempt to ban my book. It violated the provisions of the Intelligence Services Oversight Act, because the IGI was legally entitled to receive and possess classified information and to use it in an investigation. He was under no obligation to declare it to the SSA.

A few days later, Fraser was at it again, claiming the SSA had received "disturbing information" impacting upon the IGI's security competence and demanding that he submit himself for re-vetting. No reasons were given.

The relationship further deteriorated at the end of November 2017 when Dintwe notified Fraser on a Friday morning that he needed a top-secret document for his investigation. When the IGI and his team arrived at the complex, Fraser had gone to Cape Town to consult Bongo. Dintwe was denied entry.

While the IGI waited for the document to be retrieved, he received a call from Bongo. The minister summoned him to an urgent meeting at his office in Cape Town. He wanted him to board a plane within an hour or two. He said he had spoken to Fraser and the tension between the two had to be resolved.

Dintwe stood firm. "I am sorry, minister, but I am doing an investigation. I cannot come to Cape Town. And what is more, I don't report to you."

Bongo mumbled that he would be in Pretoria the next week and would set up an engagement between the three of them.

* * *

"And so, doctor, on whose side are you?"

Bongo's dark and brooding eyes bore into Dintwe as he asks the question, while Dintwe mulls the question before answering: "Nobody. I am on nobody's side. I'm just doing my job."

"Because I serve the president," responds Bongo. "I serve at his pleasure and as such I support him. I support President Zuma. I make no apology for that."

Bongo speaks again: "And who do you drink with?"

"Excuse me, minister?" answers Dintwe. "How do you mean?"

"Well, you are not drinking with us. And if you are not drinking with us, it means that you are drinking with them."

Dintwe is confused. Who is Bongo referring to? The Ramaphosa camp? The DA? Journalists? He says: "I don't drink with anyone, minister."

Fraser, who has up to now been silent, speaks: "That book, *The President's Keepers*, have you read it? And what do you think of it?"

Dintwe has read the book but says to Fraser: "No, I haven't. I must still read it."

Fraser launches into a diatribe that lasts several minutes. That book is full of lies. It has tarnished my reputation and that of the intelligence agency. It has damaged the good name of my family. But I am taking steps to rectify the situation. The record must be set straight. I will not take it lying down.

The spy boss pauses for a moment before saying: "And that man Jacques Pauw, I am going to take him out."

As he utters those words, Fraser slowly slides his fingers across the side of his neck. Dintwe notices that Fraser did not use the common way to threaten someone with death by sliding his index finger across his throat. His gesture is more reminiscent of slashing someone with a machete, as happened in the Rwandan genocide of 1994.

Nobody says a word. Bongo pretends that he did not hear what Fraser said and clears his throat. Dintwe eventually says: "Director-general, I find it utterly disturbing that you, as a top government official, can use those words."

Fraser dismisses Dintwe with a gesture of his hand. Bongo attempts to steer the conversation in a different direction, but neither of his guests responds. The meeting is over, and the IGI is ushered out of the house and back to his car.

The expression on Fraser's face when he uttered those words is etched in Dintwe's mind. He thought he saw hatred. But then, could the spy boss have meant something else, like suing the pants off Pauw or getting him in prison? He was not going to take any chances.

*　*　*

I was at the time bogged down in challenging a *Sunday Independent* "exposé" that alleged that former finance minister Pravin Gordhan was the real author of *The President's Keepers*. I was also facing a legal blitzkrieg by SARS and the SSA. Then a staff member at my restaurant and guest house in Riebeek-Kasteel in the Western Cape handed me a small envelope that someone had left for me at reception.

"Who left it?"

"He went just a few minutes ago but didn't say who he was. I had to promise that I would personally give it to you. And that I would see to it that you read it."

31

Inside the envelope was a printed note: "I have to see you very urgently. It can be a matter of life and death. I will meet you at 11 am tomorrow on the stoep of the Royal Hotel."

The grand and iconic Royal, one of the oldest hotels in the country, was almost empty when I arrived. I sat down in a corner of the veranda – apparently the longest in the country. A few minutes after eleven, a man approached and sat down next to me. He greeted me courteously but didn't introduce himself or offer his name.

"Do you have a name?" I asked him.

"I can give you one, but it will not be my real name."

"And why are you here?"

"I work for the state. I've been sent to warn you."

"By whom?"

"I cannot tell you, but it comes from very high up."

"Warn me about what?"

"Arthur Fraser has threatened to take you out."

I did not respond and was neither surprised nor shocked. It was not as though a chill ran down my spine either. I was numb, weathered, eroded. The publication of *The President's Keepers* and the subsequent six weeks had felt like I was trapped at the bottom of a tsunami.

"You know what it means, don't you, to take someone out?"

"Of course. What else do you know?"

"He said it in front of a minister. And another top government official."

"Who was the minister."

"Can't tell you either, but the other government official sent me to warn you."

"What should I do?"

"I don't know but look after yourself. Do you have Telegram on your phone?"

"Yes, I have." Telegram is a free and instant messaging app that protects its users from the prying eyes of the intelligence services. It uses end-to-end encryption, making it nearly impossible for a third party to gain access to communication between two users without their consent.

After we befriended one another on Telegram, he said: "If there is a problem, send me a self-destructing message. If there is a crisis, call me on Telegram."

We spoke for no more than three or four minutes. Afterwards, I told my wife, Sam Rogers, about the meeting. Apart from that, I continued with my life as though the meeting had never happened. But I did glance nervously over my shoulder every now and then.

* * *

Following Bongo's abortive attempt to reconcile Dintwe and Fraser, their relationship descended into internecine warfare. I got caught in the middle of the feud when, on 5 March 2018, I received a cellphone call from the intelligence oversight head. He called me about two IGI investigation reports on PAN that Faith Radebe had written in 2014 and which were leaked to me just after the publication of *The President's Keepers*. I did not have the reports when I wrote my book and assumed that, because of Radebe's apparent loyalty to Zuma and the ANC, they would be a whitewash. But even Radebe could not turn a blind eye to the aberrations committed by the PAN commanders and agents. She found that agents were tasked with conducting illegal activities and identified a host of irregularities and acts of criminality.

On the same day that I wrote an exposé on the reports, Fraser informed Dintwe of an impending investigation regarding the leakage of the IGI reports. The spy boss suspected the oversight head of leaking the reports to me. Fraser also took the opportunity to accuse Dintwe of being uncooperative with his re-vetting.

Dintwe asked me for a letter confirming that I had not received the IGI reports from him or his office. It was an unusual request, but the next day I sent Dintwe an e-mail confirming that I had received the two reports "from sources that have absolutely no link with your office".

Somewhere in the bowels of the SSA's headquarters at Musanda, the call was recorded. In a transcript of the conversation, the SSA referred to me as "The Target" – in other words, the subject of their probe – and to Dintwe as "Dr". The transcription was leaked two months later to *City Press*, which published the story. The transcription was accurate and the time given to the conversation spot-on. It was clear that the SSA had bugged my phone.

Fraser pinned the leaking of the reports on Dintwe. The transcript was supposedly confirmation that the two of us were in cahoots. On 28 March 2018, Fraser revoked Dintwe's security clearance, making it impossible for the IGI to fulfil his duties. He couldn't enter Musanda or his own office and was blocked from accessing any intelligence files or documents.

Dintwe applied for a High Court application to set Fraser's ruling aside. He said the spy boss had intimidated him and tried to prevent him from investigating PAN, Fraser's rogue intelligence unit. Dintwe stated: "Mr Fraser is alleged to have established PAN . . . by allegedly copying the signature of the then-minister Ronnie Kasrils; Mr Fraser is alleged to have improperly influenced the awarding of contracts to his family members and other individuals . . . and Mr Fraser is alleged to have created an alternative intelligence capacity, which constitutes a criminal offence."

Fraser hit back in his replying affidavit and said he was safeguarding national security by acting against Dintwe and denied that he had acted unlawfully in any manner. He said the state faced "real harm if its classified documents and information continue to be exposed to a person whose security clearance may be questionable".

Two days before the court showdown loomed, Ramaphosa axed Fraser as spy boss but inexplicably redeployed him to the lesser position of correctional services commissioner. Although Fraser made the drive from Musanda to the Correctional Services headquarters in the Poynton's Building in Pretoria Central on the same day, he left behind his brethren in key positions throughout the agency. Ramaphosa might have cut off the SSA's malignant head, but the cancerous body remained.

Under Fraser's watch, the Special Operations Unit (SOU) and the remnants of PAN had monsterbated into an intelligence reprobate with access to vast amounts of money, safe houses and surveillance equipment – all in the service of Zuma and his cronies. It was ludicrous that Ramaphosa redeployed Fraser to a similar position in government when he ought to have been probed for malfeasance and, probably, treason against the Republic.

* * *

When I sat down to write this book, I thought about "Fraser Man" and scrolled through my Telegram contacts. I sent him a message and tried to phone him. He did not respond.

I called again later, and this time he answered. I thought I recognised the voice of the person I'd met at the Royal Hotel. I said who I was, and he responded: "Yes, I remember you. And your number is still on this phone."

"Is there any possibility I can meet with you? Confidentially and off the record?"

"About what?"

"About what you told me in December 2017. I need more detail."

"I'm not in that business any longer. I have left. And I'm not allowed to speak to you."

"Nobody will ever know. Please, it is important."

We met a week later at a coffee shop in Centurion, south of Pretoria. Previously called Verwoerdburg and named after apartheid engineer Hendrik Verwoerd, this is where I spent part of my childhood. After 1994, the ghost of the slain former prime minister was eradicated from the suburb as street names were changed and statues removed.

"Fraser Man" was far more forthcoming than at Riebeek-Kasteel two years earlier. The fact that he was a "former" made a big difference.

People who have left an agency or organisation are usually more willing to talk. He was also pissed off at the treatment he had received from the state, which made him an even better source.

I still do not know who "Fraser Man" had exactly worked for. He had skulked somewhere in the shadows of the intelligence world because he used intelligence jargon.

"So, who sent you to me?" I wanted to know.

He thought for a while and asked: "Why do you want to know?"

"I want to write it in a book. I cannot publish it with what I have. It is too vague. I don't even know who you are."

"So, you would go and speak to the person that sent me?"

"Yes, I have to."

"He's going to know it comes from me."

"Who else knows?"

"He has written a report about that meeting. He gave it to me to read before I met you."

"A report? Do you still have a copy?"

"I think so, yes, but I have to check."

"Will you give it to me?"

*　*　*

Protea's Fire & Ice Hotel in Menlyn, Pretoria, is, with its walls of graffiti, milkshake bar, dedicated location for snapping selfies and half-a-metre-long pizzas on the pool deck, a sanctum for the well-to-do of the capital's eastern suburbs, hipsters and senior civil servants. It is also my meeting place with the man who tasked "Fraser Man" with warning me: then inspector-general Setlhomamaru Isaac Dintwe. I arrive early and wait for him in the bar, thinking that it is not wise of him to meet me at a place with so many prying eyes.

I have hardly sat down when a man walks up to me and introduces himself as Joseph, the IGI's protector. He tells me to follow him. As we walk through the bar and out onto the patio, I ponder when body-guards became "protectors" – a bit like school pupils who morphed into "learners" or personnel officers who are now "human resources practitioners".

Dintwe sits at the end of the patio with his back towards other patrons. I had earlier texted him on Telegram, but he refused to speak to me, saying that he didn't engage the media or appear in public. As a result, he has acquired the image of a reclusive and reticent public servant. It was only when I told him that I wanted to talk to him about a meeting with Bongo and Fraser in December 2017 that he agreed to see me.

A reserved man with a soft handshake, he makes it clear at the outset that he feels uncomfortable meeting me. Sipping tea, he asks me to get to the point.

I tell him about the meeting with "Fraser Man" and that I know about his meeting with Bongo and Fraser, what what was said and what transpired. He glares at me as he sucks on his cigarette.

"And what now?" he wants to know.

"I am going to write about it."

"No, you can't."

"Yes, I am going to. I also have knowledge about the report you wrote."

"I should never have sent him to warn you."

"Who else did you give the report to?"

"I cannot talk about that."

"So, you can confirm that everything is true?"

"Let my silence be an answer," he says as he gets ready to leave.

As we part ways, I say: "Thank you for warning me. It was a brave thing you did."

CHAPTER 3

Sewer rat with a badge

THERE WAS A time when you crossed swords with security tycoon Roy Moodley at your peril. His swagger and omnipotence came from his access to the top; the very top where a ravenous parasite was perched, wolfing down the handouts from a wide range of altruists. The hawk-nosed and moustached Moodley had long been suspected of being a major Zuma benefactor alongside powerful KwaZulu-Natal business people like power and property mogul Vivian Reddy, who financially assisted Zuma to build the first phase of Nkandla; his financial adviser Schabir Shaik, who went to prison for his complicity in bribing Zuma; and cigarette tycoon and tax dodger Yusuf Kajee. Kajee was a regular visitor to Nkandla and boasted Zuma's son Edward as one of his associates. Stinking-rich businessman Thoshan Panday also counted Edward as one of his shareholders while allegedly having two police generals in his pocket too. When billion-rand tax evader and convicted killer Robert Huang ran an alleged import scam from Durban's harbour, Zuma's nephew Khulubuse was a close business associate. Huang also accompanied Zuma on a business trip to China. Zuma's reign in KwaZulu-Natal was a spectacular display of entitlement and moral depravity.

In *The President's Keepers*, I revealed that Moodley paid Zuma huge sums of money before he became president and during the first months of his presidency. Moodley concealed the president's stipends by registering Jacob Gedleyihlekisa Zuma as an employee of his company Royal Security and placing him on the payroll. Zuma wasn't just a kept president – he literally had a boss for a month or two while occupying the highest office in the land. This was not just illegal, it was unconstitutional. He didn't declare the income to Parliament, an omission that could have cost him his job.

🐦 Pieter Du Toit @PieterDuToit, 29 Oct. 2017
The Presidency denies reports about tax evasion . . . but says nothing about being on Roy Moodley's payroll.

🐦 News24 @News24, 2 Nov. 2017
"Corruption done by who?" – Zuma

🐦 News Africa Internat @News_AfricaNow, 19 Nov. 2017
Moodley says Pauw's book is "a sham".

Days after the launch of my book and its damning revelation of Moodley's role as Zuma's benefactor, Moodley moved like one of his racehorses out of the blocks. Most of those aggrieved by allegations in a book turn to the courts to sue for defamation. But Moodley may have realised this was a risky route because it would have allowed the defendants – NB Publishers and me, as the author – to discover evidence to refute his claim. We would, for example, have requested access to Zuma's and Moodley's bank accounts and the Royal Security payroll. But this was, after all, KwaZulu-Natal, where politics and business are done differently.

So, instead of approaching the courts for relief, Moodley turned to his pet cop at the detective section of the Durban North police station to have me arrested and dealt with. Colonel Reuben Govender is a disgrace to the SAPS. My own experience would confirm that he is no policeman but a criminal with a badge, who has allegedly diligently performed Moodley's dirty work for him for years. He persecuted, bullied and incarcerated those who dared to lock horns with the security tycoon.

When he unleashed Govender on me, Moodley had been awarded multibillion-rand contracts at various state institutions, among them Prasa and the eThekwini metro in KwaZulu-Natal.

*　*　*

Roy Moodley has for years been one of the top business people in the province, an outpost that accommodates a muddle of mafias in the taxi, construction and trucking industries, among others. Although not unique to the region, they are highly organised and efficient, making KwaZulu-Natal more violent, turbulent and lawless than any other province. It remains an outpost where Jacob Zuma, deploying his skills as a savvy streetfighter and an intelligence chief, had reigned supreme for almost a decade and continues to hold enormous sway from his stronghold at Nkandla.

A mutually beneficial relationship with Zuma and the ANC holds the key to tenderpreneurial success in the province. Under Zuma's incumbency, local politicians, business people, criminal networks, taxi bosses and law enforcement had cast a web of kleptocracy (the word means "rule by thieves" in ancient Greek) over KwaZulu-Natal and looted the provincial and municipal government coffers with impunity.

These are the dons of KwaZulu, who skulk almost exclusively in mansions of stone, glass and steel in gated estates on the Ridge in Umhlanga Rocks. It's a place where crystal chandeliers and infinity pools sparkle in the morning sun rising over the Indian Ocean and where snaps of themselves with Nelson Mandela, Jacob Zuma or Thabo Mbeki are on display in their bars, always stocked with every shade of Johnnie Walker. In their garages, some lined with marble, are the quintessential Ferraris, snapped up from the dealership on Meridian Drive on the Ridge and paid for in cash. They have contributed greatly to transforming Umhlanga, home to the iconic Beverly Hills and Oyster Box hotels, into one of the most desired addresses in the country. In 2019, it surpassed Sandton as South Africa's most expensive suburb (after Cape Town's Bantry Bay and Clifton). Durban and Umhlanga now boast 3 400 high-net-worth individuals with net assets worth more than R15 million.

By the mid-2000s, Roy Moodley was perfectly positioned for a monetary assault on several municipalities, state-owned companies and government departments, not just because of his bromance with the president, but also because of his ANC connections and credentials. In the decade between 2003 and 2013, he was ANC chairperson of the eThekwini metro's influential and wealthy ward 35 in Umhlanga, perched on Durban's northern coastal edge.

It was during this time that Moodley scored lucrative contracts worth hundreds of millions of rand, several within the eThekwini municipality. Central to any tenderpreneur's success in the metro is his or her relationship with the most powerful politician in eThekwini, regional chairperson and former mayor Zandile Gumede. She was also the ANC's provincial treasurer between 2007 and 2015. Sometimes referred to as the "gangster mayor", Gumede and her cronies controlled economic networks in the city through lines of patronage, nepotism and greed. No project could go ahead without their approval. According to the *Mail & Guardian* and amaBhungane, Moodley's company Royal Security had lucrative contracts with several municipalities and government departments in KwaZulu-Natal, among them an R85-million-a-month security tender with the eThekwini municipality, which was declared unlawful but has been extended month to month since 2017.

Gumede, also a close confidante of Zuma and aligned with the ANC's radical economic transformation (RET) faction in KwaZulu-Natal, has also allegedly been on the take. She and a string of co-accused, including the former chairperson of eThekwini's bid adjudication committee, the former city manager and several councillors, are facing 2 793 charges of money laundering, fraud and corruption amounting to R320 million. Gumede was suspended as mayor but staged an enormous comeback in April 2022 when she was elected as the ANC's eThekwini chairperson. Her Unity Slate made a clean sweep as five of her cronies were elected with her. It was a devastating blow for President Cyril Ramaphosa's renewal faction in the troubled province.

Less than ten days later, the ANC deputy branch secretary for ward 67 in eThekwini, Mfundo Mokoena, was gunned down. Although the motive for the murder is still unknown, Mokoena was a vocal opponent of Gumede and her slate. More than 25 councillors in the province have been assassinated since 2020 and many more political office-bearers have been murdered. By the time you read this, that figure will be outdated, following a spate of killings in the first six months of 2022.

KwaZulu-Natal's biggest metro is a prime example of how the ANC's elected leaders and the predatory elite of the province feast on one another to become fabulously rich while the populace continues to live in squalor. The most classic example of this greed is that of social butterfly Shauwn Mpisane, also known as the "Tender Queen". Her mother was an ANC councillor in eThekwini and her father a renowned activist. They passed their impeccable struggle credentials on to her and, like many business people with the right ANC connections in the city, Mpisane amassed a multimillion-rand fortune from building low-cost houses for the municipality and other construction projects. Her tenders amounted to more than R1.1 billion and were awarded despite her criminal conviction for tax fraud. ANC tenderpreneurs often have a common trait: the substandard level of their work. In her case, impoverished occupiers of dwellings she built have reportedly claimed that the houses are falling apart. Mpisane has denied this.

Mpisane and her former metro-cop husband, Sbu Mpisane (he drove to work in a Lamborghini), were once the bling couple of Durban as Cabinet members, celebrities and government officials flocked to the extravagant bashes at their La Lucia mansion, north of Durban, where their obscene wealth was on full display to all. At one of their parties, they ascended to golden thrones for the unveiling of their new Rolls-Royce Silver Ghost. Among their guests were reportedly Bheki Cele and Khulubuse Zuma. Cele and Shauwn Mpisane were particularly close.

In 2012, Cele's spokesperson said the police commissioner regarded Mpisane as a "foster daughter".

Following a lengthy police investigation into tax evasion and fraud, the Asset Forfeiture Unit (AFU) swooped on the couple's R25 million mansion in Addison Drive in La Lucia, Durban's millionaire avenue, in 2013. The AFU had a court order to seize assets worth R140 million. They found a fleet of 60 cars, including two Rolls-Royces, two Porsches, a Ferrari, an Aston Martin, a Lamborghini and assorted bulletproof vehicles. What the AFU didn't take, the South African Revenue Service (SARS) did, claiming that the couple and their companies owed the service more than R200 million in unpaid taxes. It seized the La Lucia mansion and several other properties with a combined value of R68 million.

Shauwn Mpisane was charged with 53 counts of fraud and forgery, but in 2015 the state dropped all the charges against her after the National Prosecuting Authority (NPA) failed to provide her defence with certain documents as required by the Criminal Procedure Act. Shauwn then left Sbu, got divorced, took back her maiden surname of Mkhize and reinvented herself as a philanthropist, reality television star and football club owner.

Unlike Shauwn Mkhize, Roy Moodley is an elusive man who doesn't give interviews and avoids the media – except when he appears with Jacob Zuma in public to flaunt his former "employee". In 2013, another former employee of Royal Security accused of fraud testified in court that he had often delivered large amounts of cash and alcohol to Edward Zuma and to Lucas Ngobeni, husband of then KwaZulu-Natal police commissioner Mmamonnye Ngobeni. Both Ngobenis are currently on trial with the connected businessman Thoshan Panday on unrelated charges of fraud and corruption. Both Moodley and the Ngobenis have denied the allegations.

There are many Shauwn Mkhizes and Roy Moodleys in KwaZulu-Natal and the political tentacles of greed are spread across the province. They and others like them have accumulated wealth at the direct expense of ordinary people, who remain desperately poor, mostly unemployed and deprived of proper services.

* * *

After the publication of my book, Moodley laid charges of fraud, forgery and uttering, crimen injuria and criminal defamation against me. You don't have to be a policeman to know that there was only one way to investigate the charges and determine whether the allegations in the book were substantially true. The investigator, at the very least, had to obtain or subpoena Royal Security's payroll and Zuma's bank statements, take affidavits from the implicated parties and approach SARS to obtain their tax records. But not Colonel Govender. Moodley gave him a four-line affidavit denying that he had paid Zuma a "salary" while he was president. That appeared to have been enough for Govender.

Moodley, at his devious best, seemingly decided to use the opportunity to kill two birds with one stone. He added investigative journalist Pieter-Louis Myburgh, author of *The Republic of Gupta: A Story of State Capture* and *Gangster State: Unravelling Magashule's Web of Capture*, to his Machiavellian plot. In August 2016, Myburgh had penned an exposé for News24 about a tender-rich IT security company making mysterious payments of more than R500 million to Moodley. The company had scored billion-rand contracts with the Passenger Rail Agency of South Africa (Prasa).

Again, Moodley seemed to be unwilling to sue for defamation. Perhaps this was because Myburgh's information was spot-on. He therefore laid similar charges – fraud, forgery and uttering, crimen injuria and criminal defamation – against Myburgh. In an obvious but highly revealing error, Govender claimed in a subsequent affidavit that Myburgh's alleged offences had also occurred on 29 October 2017, the date when *The President's Keepers* was published. So, with a stroke of Moodley's pen, I acquired a co-author.

Armed with only Moodley's affidavit of denial, Govender embarked on a mission to arrest me and Myburgh. His jurisdiction was confined to Durban and he therefore had to find a way to lure us to his lair. Govender made affidavits and completed applications for warrants of arrest for the two of us. But in his affidavit for my warrant, he misspelt my name, gave the wrong age and said I lived in Alice Lane in Sandton, which was also wrong. If the good colonel had done a shred of homework and read even the first paragraph of my book – which one would have thought he had, seeing that it was at the centre of his investigation – he would have known exactly where I lived.

Govender also gave two erroneous cellphone numbers and said in his affidavit: "Numerous attempts were made telephonically to reach Jacques Pauw, but to no avail. His cellphone numbers would ring and there was no answer."

When I later called one of the cell numbers, a man answered on the other side: "Pauw speaking."

"Pauw who?" I wanted to know.

"Who do you want to speak to?"

"I'm not sure," I said. "This is Jacques Pauw speaking and the police have given this number in a statement as belonging to me."

"This is also Jacques Pauw speaking," said the voice on the other side.

We both burst out laughing. It turned out there were two of us. In his hapless search to trace me, Govender had obviously conducted a company or credit search and confused me with another Jacques Pauw.

In the application for Myburgh's arrest, Govender misspelt his name too and said he lived in Greyville in Durban and was about fifty years old. Again, a load of rubbish. Myburgh was much younger and lived in Johannesburg at the time, where he worked for News24. Said Govender: "I have even been to the Durban branch of his place of employment, but this was to no avail." Govender gave Myburgh's work address as 18 Osborne Street in Greyville, which was the office address of Independent Newspapers.

Armed with his applications and affidavits, Govender went off to obtain warrants for our arrests. A Durban magistrate sent him packing. A Pietermaritzburg magistrate gave his paperwork one look and refused to sign anything. Govender then headed towards Ntuzuma, about 25 kilometres north-west of Durban, where he engaged magistrate N. Rai. Ntuzuma was outside Govender's jurisdiction, but he got around this difficulty by spinning another fable: that Myburgh and I were in the area attending a Democratic Alliance meeting. Govender said in his affidavit: "It is evident that Mr Jacques Pauw is evasive and would not respond to our calls for him to report to the police. Notwithstanding the above, this is High-profile [sic] matter also involving our Honourable State President Jacob Zuma of the Republic of South Africa." Govender's brazenness is stupefying; Rai's lack of inquisitiveness staggering. Perhaps the magistrate got the fright of his life when he saw Zuma's name, but he signed both warrants for our arrest.

Armed with his warrants, Govender called our attorney Willem de Klerk and said Myburgh and I were suspects in a criminal matter and that he wanted to see us. He refused to say what the charges were or who the complainant was. De Klerk told Govender we were not going to say anything or make statements, which was our constitutional right, but Govender insisted that we travel to Durban and tell it to him face to face. He said that he was being "nice" to us and that he would note our "lack of cooperation" in his docket. In a follow-up e-mail, he said it was clear that we had no intention of cooperating with him and that he would have to "resort to the necessary legal avenues unless they present themselves to me at my office at Durban North police station".

Did Govender think we were morons who didn't see through his antics on behalf of Moodley? A simple Google search revealed that he was up to his old tricks. We managed to identify five cases in which Moodley, or someone close to him, was the complainant in criminal matters where Govender or those who report to him were the investigating officers and had made several arrests without warrants.

In fact, as Govender was conniving to effect our incarceration, the Durban Regional Court ruled in favour of a Durban woman who had been terrorised by Durban North detectives in a case in which Roy Moodley was the complainant. Shanaaz Ally successfully sued the minister of police after she claimed she had been arrested at the behest of Moodley. In her evidence, detailed in the court's judgment, she said she had told Moodley's wife that he was having an affair. Moodley arrived on the scene and threatened her with arrest, saying he was "going to show her". Moments later, she was arrested by two officers from the Durban North police station, bundled into a car, taken to their police station, and charged with attempted murder, crimen injuria and extortion. She was detained for five days at Moodley's behest before the charges were withdrawn. The cops never had a case against her.

CapeTalk on 567AM @CapeTalk, 11 Dec. 2017
"We don't know what the charges are, he hasn't said to us who the complainant is and we don't know why we must report to Govender."
– Jacques Pauw

Farieda Khan @FaredaVandeKaap, 13 Dec. 2017
It's terrifying to think that morons like #ReubenGovender, who routinely contravene lawful procedures are allowed to remain in #SAPS & no action is ever taken against them!

In the days that followed Govender's demand that we present ourselves, he grew increasingly belligerent. We then agreed to meet him in Johannesburg, though he insisted that we come to Durban. When NB Publishers went public about the spat, Govender accused us of abusing the process by issuing indiscriminate media releases. He said to De Klerk: "You have left us as the police with little alternative but to use the available legal processes to secure their presence in order to face the criminal charges levelled against them."

Although we were out of reach of Govender's grubby paws, the possibility remained that he could ask his police friends in the Western Cape or Gauteng to execute the arrests on his behalf and transport us to KwaZulu-Natal. De Klerk informed police commissioner Khehla Sitole, who had been appointed in his new position just days before, that we were applying for an urgent court order to remove Govender from the case and cancel the warrants of arrest.

We laid a complaint against Govender with the Independent Police Investigative Directorate (IPID) and acquired the services of a top legal team in Durban. As our legal team headed to the Durban High Court for an urgent court application to remove Govender, the police responded as though we had ignited a bomb under their bottoms. Within an hour, Govender was gone and the dockets handed to Brig. André Holby, head of the KwaZulu-Natal commercial crimes unit. He rushed to the Durban magistrate's court to have the warrants cancelled. Bizarrely, the proceedings became a matter of the police versus the police. Magistrate Irfaan Khalil found that his counterpart in Ntuzuma had no jurisdiction to issue the warrants and requested that the chief magistrate in Durban investigate Rai for irregularities. He said there was no case against us, cancelled both warrants and ordered police command to investigate Govender.

* * *

With Reuben Govender riding off into the sunset, I thought the docket would be closed, especially after Cyril Ramaphosa was elected as ANC president at the party's elective conference in December 2017. But the docket landed up with Maj.-Gen. Jones Qhobosheane, deputy provincial commissioner of police in the Free State. He said he had been ordered from "very high up" to take over the investigation, because he was seen to be "neutral".

Shortly afterwards, I met Qhobosheane in De Klerk's office in Johannesburg. An affable and gentle man, he said that he was doing everything by the book. He described the investigation as one of the most difficult of his life. I got the impression Roy Moodley was leaning on him and that he felt the Durban tycoon was treating him like an underling. He also mentioned that he still needed to travel to Nkandla to get a statement from Zuma, but said he was having a tough time arranging it.

I urged Qhobosheane not to be misled by either Zuma or Moodley. I asked him to request and subpoena Zuma's and Royal Security's bank accounts and the company's payroll. The general looked at me as though I had hauled a KwaZulu-Natal mamba from its nest and hung it around his neck. Months later, the NPA announced that it refused to prosecute Myburgh and me.

I received a visit in March 2022 from IPID investigator Takalani Maphosho, who was finalising the criminal case against Reuben Govender. There is a host of charges against him, ranging from transgressions of the South African Police Service Act to fraud and intimidation.

* * *

In 2020, the State Capture Commission heard evidence that confirmed the allegations made in *The President's Keepers* about Roy Moodley's payments to Jacob Zuma. Between July 2007 and June 2009, a month after Zuma was sworn in as president, Moodley's company Royal Security paid some R64 000 a month to Zuma. The total amount paid over came to more than R1.5 million. From 2010, Moodley began to reap the rewards of his friendship with the man who now headed the South African state. As the commission revealed, he became one of the principal state capturers of Prasa's lucrative procurement process.

CHAPTER 4

South Africa's own Guptas

🐦 **OUTA** @OUTASA, 12 Mar. 2020

Roy Moodley was like Prasa's own Gupta, Zondo commission hears

IN MARCH 2020, State Capture Commission evidence leader Advocate Vas Soni told Judge Raymond Zondo that Chockalingam "Roy" Moodley was one of the principal state capturers at the Passenger Rail Agency of South Africa (Prasa). He was joined by several other politically connected businessmen and companies that bagged billions of rands of taxpayers' money from the state entity after the government promised to refurbish South Africa's rail system and bring cheap and safe public transport to the poorest in the nation. Just four entrepreneurs – Moodley, Auswell Mashaba, Mario Ferreira and Makhensa Mabunda – were the beneficiaries of two irregularly awarded contracts worth R8 billion. In return, Prasa did not get much more than thirteen oversized and unusable locomotives and security upgrades that have since been destroyed.

To understand state capture at Prasa, we must journey back to the state of rail transport during the apartheid era. Old-timers from South African Railways still reminisce about an era when you could set your watch according to the time your train arrived. In 1994, the new ANC government inherited an extensive rail transport system of just more than 20 000 kilometres – the thirteenth biggest in the world. But there was much work to be done as black urban areas had been starved of public transport under apartheid. New railway lines had to be brought to the previously disadvantaged.

For the next decade and a half, the railway system slowly deterio-rated as stations, routes and destinations were closed. To rejuvenate the system, the government announced in 2009 the formation of Prasa, formerly known as the South African Rail Commuter Corporation. Assets like Metrorail and Shosholoza Meyl were transferred to Prasa from Transnet, which would in future concentrate on its core business of rail freight. The rail agency's mandate included the fixing of the country's passenger trains and Metrorail system through a moderni-sation and upgrading programme to the value of R172 billion over twenty years. With the inception of Prasa, the government promised South Africans a return to a rail system that would move millions of people safely, efficiently and cheaply between their homes and places of work or to destinations across the country.

The first chairperson of Prasa was the deployed ANC cadre Sfiso Buthelezi, a former uMkhonto we Sizwe combatant who had spent eight years on Robben Island. After his release in 1991, he served for five years as an adviser to Jacob Zuma, then MEC for economic development in KwaZulu-Natal. The first group chief executive of Prasa was Lucky Montana, a former deputy director-general of the Depart-ment of Transport, who was part of the task team that devised the strategy for the restructuring of Transnet.

There was initially much promise. On the eve of the 2010 Soccer World Cup, Prasa opened fourteen kilometres of new rails as well as an elegant concrete and steel bridge that linked central Johannesburg with the FNB Stadium at Nasrec. It efficiently ferried more than 20 000 passengers during the soccer tournament.

Over the next decade, Prasa spent billions of taxpayers' money on refurbishing and modernising its ageing fleet of metro and passenger trains, acquiring new locomotives, renovating and securing stations, introducing a new ticketing system, installing new signalling systems and expanding routes. Today, the utility has nothing to show for it. The Nasrec station is closed and has been stripped of its former grandeur. Some of the rails have been removed and sold as scrap metal, the cables snatched, and the infrastructure demolished. On Cape Town's central line, running like an artery through the Mother City, the homeless have erected shacks. The story is repeated across the country where many stations have fallen into total disrepair.

The billions that were earmarked for the resuscitation of Prasa have been stolen and wasted. And nobody has been held accountable for this. By 2022, more than 80 per cent of South African train commuters – about 550 000 people – had abandoned the rail system which they had used daily a decade before. Prasa now relies on state grants to run its trains because its income from commuters has declined so drastically. In January 2020, transport minister Fikile Mbalula, for once talking sense, admitted that Prasa "has suffered blows from many years of mismanagement and deteriorating corporate governance. Today, it is a broken organisation." His predecessor, Blade Nzimande, described the rail agency as "an ATM".

The looting at Prasa was almost identical to that at Transnet. As both enterprises embarked on massive and lucrative modernisation programmes, the government placed top management in the hands of Zuma zombies – Brian Molefe as chief executive of Transnet and Lucky Montana as headboy of Prasa – after which the ministers of state-owned enterprises appointed boards with state-capture majorities. Under their watch, a host of contracts were then manipulated to siphon off billions of rand to the looters and their cronies. The greed-fest was enabled by top Prasa officials who manipulated supply and procurement processes to facilitate the flow of funds; a board that rubber-stamped the irregular contracts; a lame-duck parliamentary portfolio committee on transport that pretended not to see or hear anything; transport ministers who were intent on keeping the lid on the malfeasance at Prasa; apathetic top-ranking ANC politicians; and Hawks officers who were given the evidence of criminality at Prasa on a plate but ignored it. The looting continued for years, condemning those who depended on affordable, cheap and safe public transport to even greater hardship.

*   *   *

The Prasa state-capture cabal butchered and devoured the rail agency until there was nothing left but a scattering of bare bones. The looting was so comprehensive that even after more than two weeks of evidence at the State Capture Commission, Judge Zondo felt that a separate commission of inquiry was needed to reveal the full picture of plunder at Prasa. I don't agree with the judge. Who the looters are and who enabled them has been public knowledge since 2015 when public protector Thuli Madonsela published her *Derailed* report. This was followed by a host of forensic investigations by the firm of attorneys Werksmans and the Treasury and, ultimately, evidence presented before the State Capture Commission. We don't need another commission; we need those who captured Prasa to be put in the dock. Some should already have been convicted while others – who employed lawyers like Dali Mpofu to embark on a Stalingrad defence for them – should have been close to the day that the steel doors of Kgosi Mampuru prison clattered shut behind them.

Unlike in the state capture at Transnet, Denel and Eskom, or in the Free State provincial government, no member of the Gupta family was implicated in the looting of Prasa. It was home-grown South Africans who had laid waste to the rail agency. But, at the same time, a true hero of state capture emerged at Prasa: Popo Molefe, who was appointed as chairperson of the board in August 2014 and who held the reins for more than three years. He was supported by a handful of senior Prasa officials who resisted the allocation of manipulated tenders to ANC cronies.

Molefe is an ANC stalwart with impeccable struggle credentials. He was a former secretary-general of the United Democratic Front (UDF), a mass organisation campaigning for freedom during the apartheid years. He was convicted of treason and served jail time on Robben Island. He was the first post-apartheid premier of the North West province, a position he held for ten years.

At Prasa, Molefe took the reins of an enterprise in turmoil. Its rail services were in serious decline and the agency in a dire financial state with an accumulated loss of R4.4 billion from 2010 to 2012. The irregular, fruitless and wasteful expenditure at Prasa was highlighted by the auditor-general in his reports to Parliament. Within months of their appointment, Molefe and the new board members declined to approve two contracts worth altogether R4 billion, despite a previous board committee having okayed the deals. Many Prasa departments were dysfunctional, and controls were weak or nonexistent. The agency had, for example, 65 executives but needed only 20. Soon, Molefe and CEO Lucky Montana were at loggerheads.

From early on in his tenure, Molefe had become aware of attempts by connected business people to capture Prasa's procurement processes. He later told the State Capture Commission that he had hardly arrived at Prasa when Roy Moodley attempted to schmooze him. He first bumped into the KwaZulu-Natal entrepreneur in early 2015 at an international rail show in Berlin, Germany, where Prasa had an exhibition stand. Moodley, who was coincidentally booked into the same hotel as the Prasa chairperson and on the same floor, persistently courted him during the visit to Berlin. It was clear to Molefe then that Moodley had a close relationship with Montana, a favourite Zuma poster boy. According to evidence given at the commission, Montana had facilitated Moodley's capture of Prasa.

Molefe thought it was unhealthy for the rail agency's top administrator and a service provider to be so close. Upon returning to South Africa, Molefe made enquiries about Moodley, and he later described to the State Capture Commission what top Prasa officials told him: "One of them said: 'Look, this is Mr Prasa. He owns Prasa.' Another one says, 'Prasa is his farm. From time to time if it is harvesting time, you come to harvest.' So, that is how they put it." Molefe said he told Moodley he thought he was too close to Prasa management: "I do not think it is good for you. Keep your distance because you do not want suspicions when procurement is done or tenders are issued because you might be winning some of them."

Moodley's company Royal Security had contracts of almost R500 million with the rail agency. Moodley was also linked to several other companies with lucrative contracts with Prasa. These were mostly entities managed by Moodley's sons, along with other close associates. But Moodley himself played a crucial role behind the scenes and raked in hundreds of millions of rand from questionable deals.

Allegations of wrongdoing against Moodley have persisted for years. The *Mail & Guardian* reported that Royal Security had a contract with Telkom in 2001 to guard the parastatal's copper network. An internal investigation found that a top Telkom executive irregularly favoured Royal Security and authorised payments for work that it did not do. The executive resigned to avoid a disciplinary hearing, while Telkom reportedly instituted fraud charges against Moodley and Royal Security and cancelled the contract. However, nine years later, in 2010, another internal probe reported on by the *Mail & Guardian* accused three Telkom officials of "colluding with security companies who are hired to protect and monitor Telkom's copper cable network". Royal Security was again one of the implicated companies.

🐦 **TimesLIVE** @TimesLIVE, 20 Mar. 2020
Roy Moodley tried to capture me six times, Popo Molefe tells state capture commission

When Moodley heard that Molefe and his wife regularly attended the prestigious American Masters golf tournament at Augusta in Georgia, he not only decided to go himself but also offered to pay for the couple's first-class air tickets, plush accommodation and vouchers to attend the iconic event. When he made the offer, Moodley suggested that they could discuss future business deals during the trip. Molefe declined Moodley's "sweetener", which would have cost an estimated

R1.5 million. Molefe heard afterwards that Moodley had solicited money from a European service provider to Prasa to pay for the proposed golf trip to the United States.

Moodley then invited Molefe to be his VIP guest at the Durban July. Molefe once again declined, though President Zuma and some of his Cabinet members took up the invitation and were wined and dined by Moodley at South Africa's premier horse race. A triumphant and chortling Jacob Zuma was photographed clutching what was reported to be R15 000 after Moodley had advised him to bet on a winning horse.

Moodley flaunted his good relationship with Zuma and told Molefe that the president had personally invited him as a VIP to his state of the nation address in Parliament.

Moodley asked Molefe: "Are you going there?"

Molefe: "No, I have not been invited."

Moodley: "Look, I will get you an invitation."

Molefe: "I do not want you to ask for an invitation for me."

There were several other occasions when Moodley would invite Molefe to functions, saying things like "Come to dinner, the president will be there", or "Minister Jeff Radebe will be there" or "Zweli Mkhize [premier of KwaZulu-Natal] will join us".

Molefe and the Prasa board discovered huge irregularities in contracts awarded to Moodley-linked companies, among them Strawberry Worx, which managed advertising boards at all Prasa stations. Said Molefe: "The terms of that arrangement were that 60 per cent of the proceeds of advertisements will go to Prasa, 40 per cent will go to Mr Moodley's company. And then I asked, is it happening? Are we making money out of it? I was told: 'No, he has stopped paying to Prasa its 60 per cent. He is not paying it.'"

Those who questioned Moodley's business dealings with Prasa faced the wrath of CEO Lucky Montana, whom Judge Raymond Zondo later identified as a "significant role player" in the capture of Prasa. At one stage, the general manager of Prasa's legal services, Fani Dingiswayo, objected to a R82 million training contract between Prasa and a Moodley-linked company, Prodigy, of which Moodley was a director until 2012. The contract, which was supposed to have run from 2011 to 2014 but was later extended, bypassed the procurement processes and was entered into at the insistence of Montana, despite the exorbitant cost of the training scheme: 3 000 employees at R24 000 per person for a five-day customer service course.

Montana fired Dingiswayo for querying the lawfulness of the contract. The next day, his superior in the legal department, Martha Ngoye, asked Montana to explain the dismissal. Ngoye took the witness stand at the State Capture Commission and said: "Mr Montana would have nobody challenge him, nobody, it was unheard of. I was not even five minutes in his office, it is because I dare to challenge Mr Montana for having fired Mr Dingiswayo without having spoken to me as Mr Dingiswayo's boss. He said grand, grand, Martha, you are fired!" A week later, when Montana realised their dismissals were unfair, he requested Ngoye and Dingiswayo to return to work. He then suspended both for misconduct. They sat at home, returning to work only when Montana left Prasa.

The chief executive for strategy at Prasa, Tiro Holele, told Judge Zondo that he was called to a meeting about the Prodigy contract. There was a dispute about its lawfulness, based on the issues raised by Dingiswayo. Although a host of irregularities in the awarding of the contract had emerged and it was already the subject of court action, Prodigy and Moodley were still attempting to wring money out of a depleted Prasa.

When Holele entered the Prasa boardroom, a stern-faced Moodley awaited him. The evidence leader for the State Capture Commission, Vas Soni, asked Holele: "What was your reaction?"

Holele: "Well, it was – it was fear."

Soni: "Fear?"

Holele: "Because of the talk of how important he is, and now here he was."

According to Holele, Moodley bragged that he was "one of the top fifteen decision-makers in this country" and warned that "big changes were coming". He presumed that the "big changes" involved the transport minister or portended a Cabinet reshuffle.

Judge Zondo: "And what else did he say?"

Holele: "And then he said, and you must be on the right side of those changes."

Judge Zondo: "And what did you understand that to mean?"

Holele: "We don't want to be on the wrong side of whoever may come in."

Soni: "Did he say anything about any possible changes?"

Holele: "He said when those changes happen, the young man will come back."

Soni: "What did you understand that to mean?"

Holele: "We understood it to mean Mr Montana would recur as group CEO."

Soni: "Now you did not agree to pay Prodigy at that meeting?"

Holele: "No, we did not. Because it was a simple matter and here is a legal dispute. The matter is in court. The papers are before court."

Judge Zondo: "How did your meeting with Mr Moodley end?

Holele: "Was a dead end. A stalemate. He just insisted that the payment must be done."

During the testimony against Moodley at the commission, his attorney, Ravindra Maniklall, told Judge Zondo that not only would his client deny all the allegations against him, but he would also apply to cross-examine the witnesses to "easily dispel" the notion that he had been one of Prasa's main capturers. It was all bluster. Moodley never applied to testify or cross-examine any witness. Instead, he submitted an affidavit in which he denied the evidence against him. In his final report, Judge Zondo said that, after he had listened to the witnesses, "the probabilities are that what they said is true and correct".

*   *   *

🐦 **City Press** @City_Press, 5 July 2015
Prasa's R600 million blunder: Imported trains too high for SA rails

🐦 **News24** @News24, 6 July 2015
Our locomotives are best in the world – Prasa

The acrimony between Popo Molefe and Lucky Montana came to a head when investigative journalist and author Pieter-Louis Myburgh revealed in the Sunday newspapers *Rapport* and *City Press* that Prasa's new locomotives were too tall for South Africa's tracks. But Prasa flatly denied this. Montana held a press conference where he introduced the nation to Prasa's "doctor of trains", head engineer Dr Daniel Mthimkhulu, who was appointed in March 2010 as the executive manager of engineering services at a salary of R230 000 per month. Mthimkhulu was never interviewed for the position but claimed to be a qualified engineer with a doctorate from a German university. He signed off on the train specifications.

Montana said: "Daniel Mthimkhulu is our top engineer on rolling stock in the country. He is Dr Mthimkhulu. We invested in him. Many companies in the world want his services, want to employ him. He has been spending half of his time in Spain in the design of these locomotives. But maybe because he's black, isn't it, that his authority cannot be taken seriously?"

A few days later, News24 reported that Mthimkhulu's qualifications were fake. He had only matric and was neither an engineer nor a doctor. Prasa fired him and at the same time the board announced that Montana had been "released from servicing his notice period". Although Montana's contract only expired in December 2015, the board wanted him out as soon as possible.

After Montana left Prasa, he said publicly that he was still available to serve as Prasa chief executive. On 20 August 2015, Molefe was invited to a meeting with Zuma at the presidential guesthouse in Pretoria. Montana, transport minister Dipuo Peters and minister in the presidency Jeff Radebe were also in attendance. According to Molefe, Zuma said he had invited "that boy, Lucky Montana", because he was knowledgeable about rail matters and should not be lost to the country. Zuma attempted to get Montana reinstated at Prasa, but the meeting ended because Zuma fell asleep. Molefe told the State Capture Commission that he found it shocking that the president had interfered in the agency's internal affairs.

The extent of the rot emerged later in the year when public protector Thuli Madonsela uncovered in her 391-page report, *Derailed*, that Prasa had illegally awarded tenders worth billions of rand and failed to comply with supply-chain policy. She specifically fingered Montana in a host of irregularities and, as part of her remedial action, instructed Treasury to conduct a "forensic investigation" into all Prasa contracts valued at more than R10 million since 2012.

Madonsela found the appointment by Prasa of Moodley's Royal Security to be improper. At some point, Prasa had terminated the contract because of the company's underperformance, but year after year Montana simply instructed the head of security to extend the contract. This was "highly irregular" and might constitute criminality under the Public Finance Management Act.

"Shocked and perturbed" at the level of malfeasance exposed by Madonsela, Molefe and the board instructed attorneys Werksmans to set up a team consisting of almost three dozen lawyers, eleven IT experts and thirty forensic auditors to probe 142 dodgy tenders worth R24 billion at the rail agency. These investigations unearthed R14 billion in irregular expenditure – amounting to 90 per cent of Prasa's annual expenditure. Treasury, in compliance with Madonsela's recommendations, investigated 216 contracts worth around R15 billion awarded by Prasa between 2012 and 2015. Only 13 contracts and tenders were found to be above board.

* * *

Roy Moodley was a major beneficiary of a multibillion-rand contract that Prasa awarded to Siyangena Technologies in 2011 to install an integrated security system at selected Prasa stations. The initial cost of the tender was R517 million, but, like many other Prasa contracts, it was irregularly extended in 2013 and 2014 and ballooned to R4.5 billion. The State Capture Commission heard evidence of a host of wrongdoings that accompanied the awarding of the contract. Among other things, the minutes of the corporate tender procurement committee had been forged. All the forensic investigations found that there was an absence of record-keeping and documentation. Information, documents and data were missing altogether, misplaced, possibly destroyed or not made available to the auditors.

It is unclear what had qualified Siyangena for the massive contract. This is how the company described itself on its website: "Siyangena Technologies is positioned as a Systems Integrator, providing formulated value added concepts for client base and sourcing of products with the analogy of instating cost effective solutions in hand with quality emphasis." Would you have chucked R4.5 billion at this outfit to carry out your security upgrades?

The State Capture Commission heard evidence that after Prasa had awarded the contract to Siyangena, the company transferred R500 million to Hail Way Trading, an entity of which Moodley was the sole director. The company had no website and was set up just six months after Siyangena's first Prasa contract. There is no evidence that Hail Way Trading did any work for either Prasa or Siyangena. According to News24, Moodley and Siyangena co-owner Mario Ferreira were more than just business partners; they were also co-owners of the local racehorses One Man's Dream and Hi Societi.

One of the other main capturers of Prasa was the little-known businessman Makhensa Mabunda, who was a major beneficiary of another huge and irregular contract that Prasa concluded. In 2011 the German rail giant Vossloh inspected Prasa's locomotive fleet and recommended that Prasa purchase 100 locomotives at a cost of about R5 billion. In

November 2011, Prasa published a request for proposals for the loco-motive contract. Vossloh and its Spanish subsidiary, Vossloh España, were the preferred suppliers, but under South African law the company had to be compliant with the Broad-Based Black Economic Empower-ment Act and therefore needed a local empowerment partner.

Enter Mabunda, a former colleague of Lucky Montana and chair-person of the Siyaya group of companies. Siyaya was already a major beneficiary of Prasa's procurement processes, having won a R862.5 mil-lion contract to supply fuel and oil as well as a R98.5 million contract to give technical assistance to the upgrade of the rail signalling system in Gauteng. Mabunda acted as an agent on behalf of Montana and Prasa to locate a front company for the locomotive contract. He approached Auswell Mashaba, a former senior civil servant in the Mpumalanga provincial government and chairperson of AM Investments, to act as the middleman between Prasa and Vossloh. Mabunda told Mashaba that he knew Montana and could set things up.

Mashaba formed Swifambo Rail for the purposes of the deal. The name was chosen to give the impression that the company had exper-tise in railways. It didn't. It was an empty shell with no employees, no business record and no website. Its bid documents did not comply with Prasa's tender regulations, it didn't submit a tax clearance certificate or VAT number, and it failed to show it had experience in the rail industry. The purchase was never budgeted for and Prasa failed to obtain approval from either the minister of transport or the Treasury.

The procurement process circumvented multiple bodies – like the Railway Safety Regulator – that had to ensure that the locomotives were financially and technically suitable for Prasa. This was deliberate, because Vossloh's Afro 4000 locomotives, built in Europe and designed for that continent, were too tall for South Africa's railways.

The entire procurement process was manipulated and rigged to favour Vossloh and Swifambo. Yet, in July 2012, the Prasa board under Sfiso Buthelezi inexplicably approved the R3.5 billion contract with Swifambo Rail as the locomotive supplier. In turn, Swifambo entered into a subcontracting agreement with Vossloh for the purchase of 70 diesel-electric and hybrid locomotives. Judge Zondo said in his final report: "The process was so flawed that it must have been clear to any reasonable person acting with the requisite diligence and integrity that something was seriously amiss. The procurement process was designed to achieve a predetermined outcome – awarding the contract to a company which had little or no knowledge of the rail industry but was just a front for a foreign company."

Prasa paid an initial R2.65 billion in several tranches to Mashaba's Swifambo, which in turn transferred R1.87 billion to Vossloh. Swifambo paid around R450 million to a network of companies, trusts and businessmen with no links to the contracts. According to forensic evidence presented at the State Capture Commission, Swifambo passed on R56.6 million to Mabunda – obviously his sweetener for putting the deal together.

Vossloh also greased Mabunda's palm – making him ten tranches of payments totalling a staggering R89 million. The kickback, identified in the books as "management consulting services", was deposited into the accounts of his companies Siyaya and S-Investments. Asked to explain its payments to Mabunda, the company said it was meant for an "independent sales representative" for introducing them to Swifambo.

Makhensa Mabunda pocketed altogether R144 million for setting up an unlawful and wasteful contract between Swifambo, Prasa and Vossloh. Mashaba's cut of the loot was R103 million. He moved the money to a series of companies and trusts under his control, among them AM Investments and AM Consulting Engineers. For its part, Prasa received 13 oversized locomotives at a bewildering cost of R203 million each – despite being technically unusable. Although the rail agency had paid for 70 locomotives, it did not receive the remaining 57 engines.

Several other connected business people were blessed with Prasa contracts. Among them were controversial former spy bosses Arthur Fraser and Manala Manzini, respectively deputy director-general and director-general of the National Intelligence Agency. They bagged a

R87.8 million contract based on confinement to perform a "risk threat and vulnerability assessment". Confinement refers to contracts that are awarded without a tender but are allowed when an unforeseeable emergency arises, the company has a proven track record or secrecy is needed. Treasury found that in this case confinement was unjustifiable as there was no urgency, no emergency, no need for secrecy and no expertise that was unique. There was also no budget, not even after Lucky Montana had signed the deal. The contract was awarded irregularly, tender processes were flouted and the company might have submitted a false tax compliant certificate.

Confinement has become a merry tool in awarding state contracts. A look at the list of confinement contracts awarded by Prasa's top management between 2014 and 2017 makes for scary reading. Some of these tenders may have been legitimate, but enormous amounts of public money were spent on contracts that never went out for public tender. Baran Projects got a R91 million confinement contract to provide artificial intelligence; Ebcont, a R68 million confinement project to implement a software tool; KG Media, a R51 million confinement contract for a commuter newspaper; and Isiphikeleli Senyoni, a R1 billion confinement contract for supplying stock and infrastructure.

Lucky Montana @MontanaLucky, 29 Nov. 2017
The investigators were not interested in the truth but were given a mandate to bring down Lucky Montana

GroundUp @GroundUp_News, 29 Nov. 2017
Leaked @TreasuryRSA reports show that when @MontanaLucky was CEO of PRASA, it descended into grand-scale corruption, mismanagement and incompetence.

Lucky Montana @MontanaLucky, 29 Nov. 2017
I was born and grew up in the dusty streets of Mamelodi. I have fought far bigger battles. Never shall I be conquered.

* * *

Team News24 @TeamNews24, 26 Aug. 2016
EXCLUSIVE: ANC implicated in Prasa "bribes"

In Prasa's application to the High Court to have the Swifambo loco-motive contract set aside, Popo Molefe released a bombshell. He declared that the ANC had perhaps benefited from this irregularly awarded and possibly corrupt contract. He also revealed that very senior leaders in the ANC knew about the looting at the rail agency but did nothing to stop it.

Molefe said in an affidavit that Auswell Mashaba approached him during the board's forensic investigations "to come clean" about money he had paid to the ANC. Mashaba said that after Swifambo won the contract, the Angolan businesswoman Maria Gomes, known to be a fundraiser for the ANC and a close friend of Jacob Zuma, informed him that 10 per cent of the value of the contract must be paid to the ANC. Mashaba's partner-in-crime, Makhensa Mabunda, instructed him to make payment of R79 million to a company of which Gomes was a director and another that belonged to a business partner of one of Zuma's sons. Mashaba also made two cash payments to Gomes: one of R2 million and another of R90 000. Mashaba later confirmed the payments in an affidavit to the State Capture Commission but said he didn't know if the ANC had received any of the money. The ANC said it hadn't.

Lucky Montana later testified that he was at Gomes's home in Atholl, Johannesburg, when ANC treasurer-general Zweli Mkhize came looking for money for the party's 2014 general election campaign. He allegedly gave Gomes details of bank accounts into which she was asked to deposit money for the benefit of the governing party. Mkhize denied this.

After learning of Mashaba's alleged party contribution, Molefe approached the ANC's "top six" leadership in 2016. He was granted an audience with the six leaders, who included Jacob Zuma, Cyril

Ramaphosa, Gwede Mantashe, Jessie Duarte and Zweli Mkhize. Chairperson Baleka Mbete was not present. Molefe explained to them the rot at the rail agency, the R79 million party donation and the attempts to scupper his mission to clean up Prasa. He said that in response the leadership did nothing.

Molefe also wrote a letter to Ramaphosa about the critical challenges he faced at Prasa and implored him to help get things back on track. He also alerted Ramaphosa to attempts by transport minister Joe Maswanganyi to make the board dysfunctional. Again, nothing.

Parliament's portfolio committee on transport, which was supposed to provide oversight of Prasa, ignored Molefe's pleas for a parliamentary inquiry into malfeasance at the rail agency. While Molefe and his board attempted to restore good financial governance at Prasa, the committee slammed them for getting involved in "dispute after dispute". On the same day that Molefe asked for a parliamentary inquiry, he learned that transport minister Dipuo Peters had fired him and dissolved the board.

Molefe then filed an urgent court application to declare the dissolution unlawful. The High Court found that Peters's decision was irrational and arbitrary, and ordered her to reinstate Molefe and all the board members. Peters mercifully retired and left politics. She was succeeded by another Zuma acolyte, Maswanganyi, who turned out to be even worse and eventually rendered the board ineffectual.

🐦 EWN Reporter @ewnreporter, 3 July 2017
The South Gauteng High Court today ruled that Prasa's R3.5 billion contract with Swifambo Rail Leasing for new locomotives be set aside.

In July 2017, Judge Ellem Francis of the South Gauteng High Court set aside the Swifambo contract because it was tainted by serious irregularities and corruption. According to the court, "the discovery of corruption was impeded by the tyrannical manner in which Prasa was controlled by Montana". Judge Francis said: "Corruption should not be allowed to triumph. Harm will be done to the laudable objectives of our hard-fought freedom if I was not to set aside the award. Harm will be done to all the hardworking and honest people of our land who refrain from staining themselves with corruption. Harm will be done if the beneficiaries of the tender were allowed to reap the benefits of their spoils. Corruption will triumph if this court does not set aside the tender."

Swifambo appealed against the judgment, but the Supreme Court of Appeal confirmed Judge Francis's judgment and order. The Constitutional Court denied Swifambo the right of any further appeals. The company declared itself insolvent, and the High Court then appointed liquidators to find out what had happened to the money. Six years later, only 13 of the 70 oversized locomotives have touched South African soil in return for the R2.65 billion that Prasa transferred to Swifambo. Only an estimated R63 million has been recovered so far.

Prasa launched an application in March 2018 to set aside the Siyangena contract as well. By then, much of the documentation relating to the contract had disappeared or been deleted from official computers. One of Prasa's IT specialists was found to have deliberately deleted information from Lucky Montana's computer – allegedly on Montana's instruction. He was dismissed.

In October 2020, a full bench of the High Court declared the contract null and void and found Siyangena to be complicit in the corruption, impropriety and maladministration at Prasa. The three judges ordered that an independent engineer be appointed to evaluate the cost of the work done by Siyangena. This evaluation will then be set alongside the money already paid to the company.

* * *

In June 2022, Cyril Ramaphosa took his seat at the State Capture Commission to account for, among other things, his inaction and that of the top ANC leadership and their failure to address the looting at Prasa. Ramaphosa said he remembered that Molefe "raised the challenges" at the rail agency, especially in relation to corruption. He claimed that Molefe had received "nothing but support from the top six", who told him to use "various structures afforded by legislation to deal with these matters".

Judge Zondo didn't buy this story. He said in his final report: "South Africans would not have been surprised if President Zuma did not give Mr Molefe support for his fight against corruption, but they would have expected deputy president Ramaphosa's reaction and attitude to be different from that of Mr Zuma." He added: "Neither the ANC leadership, the national executive nor the portfolio committee on transport wanted to assist this board in its fight against corruption. The board was on its own. Jacob Zuma gave it no support. Ramaphosa gave it no support. The portfolio committee was openly hostile."

Judge Zondo concluded that the ANC's top leadership owed the country a "profound apology" because they had "allowed a state entity that is required to provide an essential service to the most vulnerable among us to be incapable to fulfil its duty".

CHAPTER 5

The Prasa Nostra

🐦 **AM Lodge** @amlodge_za, 16 July 2020
. . . Big 5 sightings. Spa treatments in the bush. Amazing sunsets in the heart of Limpopo. Lunch in the wilderness, surrounded by the wild. Song and dance to the bold sounds of the African drum.

WHAT BECAME OF the money that was looted from Prasa? One answer to that question may be found tucked away in a forest of green in the vast expanse of the Limpopo bushveld. Here lies AM Lodge, a place where the echoes of the wild hug you in the lap of luxury. With its five-star rating and string of international awards, AM Lodge houses just 22 guests in the utmost comfort. It is a hideaway that caters only for the discerning. To stay in the Ngala (Shangaan for "lion") suite, where "the roars of Ngala echo through the AM Lodge landscape as mother nature calls", costs a cool R30 000 per night for a couple. There is also a free-standing villa with its own chef and butler for R35 000 a night.

AM Lodge is supposedly testimony to the business acumen of its founder and owner, Auswell Mashaba, executive chairperson of AM Investments and founder of AM Consulting Engineers. But in fact, AM Lodge is nothing but an obscene shrine to a state capturer, a monument to one of those who gobbled up billions of rand of public money and gave the country back just thirteen oversized locomotives.

Auswell Mashaba seems to have no shame in flaunting his spoils. Five days after Prasa made its first payment of R460 million to Swifambo in

2013, a Mashaba company purchased three parcels of land and a lodge near Hoedspruit in Limpopo for R27 million. This became AM Lodge.

🐦 Nsovo Mashaba @sovo_m, 4 May 2021
Also, the argument about my father and corruption is tired, find something else man.

Mashaba's playboy son, the bearded and gym-sculpted Nsovo Mashaba, is the face of AM Lodge. Famous for dating celebrities and mingling with the rich and famous, he introduces himself on Instagram as enigmatic, blessed and the "capo di tutti capi" – the boss of all bosses, or the godfather. His photographs show him in various poses of deep contemplation while flaunting his new Louis Vuitton attire, sipping Dom Perignon champagne with a cigar dangling from his mouth, driving his R3 million Porsche Cabriolet, posing with his R2 million Mercedes-AMG, getting into AM Lodge's helicopter, or navigating a Bentley through the dense African bush.

Since its inception, AM has expanded its luxury portfolio across South Africa. It now operates spas throughout the Kruger National Park, an upmarket restaurant in the Manyeleti Game Reserve in Limpopo, a R14 000-a-day villa at the Zimbali coastal resort in KwaZulu-Natal, and a Provençal-style boutique hotel in Pretoria. Auswell Mashaba has further diverted R24.5 million from the locomotive contract to his trust to acquire a majority shareholding in the Orange Grove farm outside Robertson in the Western Cape. Nestled in the spectacular Breede River valley, the wine and olive farm is marketed as a luxurious retreat with a 200-year-old manor house and a collection of cottages, each offering private plunge pools and verandas overlooking the vineyards.

After Swifambo went into liquidation in December 2018, the High Court appointed liquidators to wrap up the company and find out what had happened to the money. According to their findings, the company's collapse was caused by the "reckless" and "fraudulent" diversion of funds from the Swifambo accounts. The company became "unable to perform its contractual obligations towards Prasa and/or unable to pay its creditors, suppliers and/or sub-contractors". The liquidators found prima facie evidence of criminality by Mashaba.

The State Capture Commission subpoenaed Mashaba to appear before Judge Zondo, presumably to explain his questionable gains. Just days after Jacob Zuma had refused to appear before the commission in February 2021, Mashaba followed suit and said his subpoena was unlawful – which was the same reason that Zuma had given. Judge Zondo said that if the behaviour of Zuma and Mashaba spread, it could result in chaos in the commission and the courts. He ordered the commission secretary to lay a criminal charge of contempt against Mashaba. That was early in 2021. How difficult can it be to prosecute Mashaba for snubbing the commission?

Roy Moodley and Makhensa Mabunda were more circumspect than Auswell Mashaba in flaunting their dirty money. However, the *Daily Maverick* reported that by mid-January 2015, when Prasa transferred the sixth instalment of R444.5 million to Swifambo, Mabunda was constructing a palatial villa in the exclusive Waterfall Equestrian Estate between Johannesburg and Pretoria. Prasa had by then paid R2.2 billion to Swifambo – without having yet received a single locomotive. Mabunda's pad in Waterfall covers a staggering 3 200 square metres under roof space – the size of half a soccer field. Houses of a similar size on the estate sell for around R70 million.

Mabunda is clearly a man who demands the best. According to the Swifambo liquidator's court findings, Swifambo transferred R5 million of the R444.5 million payment from Prasa to Sterlings Living, a company installing Italian kitchens and bathrooms for a rich and discerning clientele.

So, we know about the hundreds of millions that Roy Moodley, Makhensa Mabunda and Auswell Mashaba bagged from the smash-and-grab at Prasa. But what did Lucky Montana get, he who toiled hard to sidestep Prasa's procurement and tender regulations, spun fables and bullshit about the resuscitation of the railways, installed donuts like Daniel Mthimkhulu in key positions, and sacked and intimidated those who opposed his nefarious enterprises? State capture must be hard work. Montana certainly didn't do it for the millions of rail commuters who desperately depend on Metrorail, because he left the rail agency in a far worse state and the fiscus much poorer than when he was appointed as group chief executive in 2009.

🐦 **Lucky Montana** @MontanaLucky, 29 Nov. 2017
I have many weaknesses like all human beings but corruption or looting has not been one of them.

The State Capture Commission heard that Montana purchased several properties in upscale Waterkloof in Pretoria and Sandhurst in Johannesburg on the eve of Prasa awarding the security contract to Siyangena. Although Montana purchased the properties, he didn't pay for them. The money came from a Pretoria attorney, Riaan van der Walt, who was also director of the company Precise Trade and Invest. His firm had acted for Siyangena in the past. Commission investigators found that millions of rand had been transferred from entities controlled by Siyangena co-owner Mario Ferreira to Van der Walt's Precise Trade.

In May 2014, Precise Trade also bought a house from Montana in Johannesburg for R6.8 million, although it was valued at R3 million less. There are several other examples. When Montana bought the Sandhurst property for R13.9 million, he said he would pay a R5 million deposit. Instead, the money was paid from the trust account of Van der Walt's law firm. By the time the State Capture Commission sat, Van der Walt had sold his shares in his firm to his partners and relocated to the United States.

When Montana testified before the commission, he didn't volunteer any explanation save to say that he was in business with Van der Walt. Montana said he didn't drink or smoke and added: "If there's one activity I do in my spare time, I go look at land." He then attacked evidence leader Vas Soni for being biased and brought an application for his recusal.

The *Daily Maverick* reported that the value of the properties owned by or associated with Montana was just under R52 million, mostly covered by cash transactions effected during Montana's time in charge of Prasa. Referring to the properties, Judge Zondo found in his final report that there was a "reasonable basis for concluding that Mr Montana received an undue benefit from a Siyangena-linked entity".

Armed with a 447-page submission to the commission, Montana was a bundle of bravado and bluster at his various appearances before Judge Zondo. He swaggered into the commission and lamented Judge Zondo's alleged bias against him. He claimed that someone from the Hawks had attempted to extort R500 million from him, that witnesses were threatened to get them to testify against him, and that the attorneys Werksmans had conducted unlawful surveillance on him, broken into his house and nearly killed his son.

Montana has been particularly savage in his attacks on the judiciary. In November 2020, he sat down for a two-and-a-half-hour ramble with *Insight Factor*'s Thabo Makwakwa and Modibe Modiba. The programme, broadcast intermittently on YouTube, is dedicated to the cause of the radical economic transformation faction of the ANC. Besides reminiscing about Israeli and Mozambican hitmen whom a criminal gang (undoubtedly headed by his nemesis, Popo Molefe) had deployed to silence him, he said that judges were used as political instruments to destroy him. They hunted like a pack, acted improperly, manipulated facts and created their own laws. He claimed that finance minister Pravin Gordhan was a member of a criminal enterprise and that Molefe had begged him for money. "At Prasa, he got companies to pay money into the Popo Molefe Development Trust. He says it's for charity. Companies that are contracted to Prasa pay money. I have seen some of the statements. There is no charity. Money laundering at its best!"

Montana's response to the State Capture Commission's final report was predictable. He lashed out at Judge Zondo and announced that he intended to lay criminal charges against the newly appointed chief justice for "deliberate violation of the law, abuse of power, criminal conduct and disgraceful conduct". Good luck to you, Lucky.

* * *

South Africans have a right to be very angry about the failure of the state at every level to stop the derailment of Prasa and save our trains. Nobody, not the president or the deputy president, not Parliament, the government or the ruling party, and not the Hawks, gave a damn about the plight of those who counted on the state to provide them with the most basic of services: public transport. Prasa was strangled, throttled and left to die in front of their very eyes, and nobody lifted a finger.

As we have seen, Popo Molefe at one stage pleaded with the ANC's top six to help him end the thievery and nepotism at Prasa. Instead of assisting him, the ANC's bigwigs ogled Molefe in disbelief, shook their heads, clicked their tongues and spoke of their disappointment that cadres were plundering a state-owned entity. Sadly, one wouldn't have expected anything else. Many ANC politicians are nothing but brown-nosed apparatchiks who mindlessly shadow their leaders in their quest to get a spot of their own at the feeding trough. And once they've tucked in, they morph overnight into corruptocrats who quickly forget that they have been elected to improve the lives of those who voted them in.

There is no better example of this than Dikeledi Magadzi, chairperson of the parliamentary committee on transport during the capture of Prasa. Appearing before the State Capture Commission, she praised herself for a job well done during her tenure. Her committee decided twice to investigate fraud and corruption at Prasa but never got the probes off the ground. It also didn't think it necessary to bring the Hawks to Parliament to explain their inaction. Magadzi attempted to explain her vote against a motion in Parliament to investigate state capture and the Guptas by saying that the ANC had instructed its

74

members not to support the submission. "I'm not in Parliament as myself, I represent the African National Congress, and I will always ensure that I toe the party line."

Judge Zondo found that ANC members on the committee had cared little about their obligations and were not worthy to serve on an oversight body. They were so far removed from reality that when Molefe told them about Mashaba's monetary contribution to the ANC, they demanded to see the receipts.

Despite her failure to be accountable to the public, Cyril Ramaphosa awarded Magadzi richly when he appointed her as deputy transport minister in 2019, complete with a handsome pay rise, protectors, a blue-light brigade, a ministerial mansion and an array of underlings at her disposal. Commenting on her promotion, Judge Zondo said: "Is it in the public interest to appoint as a deputy minister someone who has not covered herself in glory in performing important oversight functions?"

* * *

The failure of the Hawks to bring the looters and enablers of Prasa to book must count as one of the police's biggest betrayals ever of the people of South Africa. The Hawks had had evidence of the wrongdoing at Prasa since the end of 2015. Subsequently, year after year, testimony of more criminality piled up. The proverbial mountain of evidence against the looters and capturers of Prasa included several forensic investigations that unearthed corruption and fraud, an investigation by the public protector that uncovered widespread wrongdoing, various successful court applications to set aside unlawful contracts, an insolvency investigation that highlighted the criminality committed by Swifambo, two weeks of evidence at the State Capture Commission that detailed the most notorious episodes of state-sponsored looting in our recent past, and the final report by Judge Raymond Zondo.

Makhensa Mabunda's palatial mansion at the Waterfall Equestrian Estate in Gauteng and Auswell Mashaba's portfolio of five-star properties around the country have for years been hanging like ripe plums on Prasa's tree of iniquity. They are easy pickings for the Asset Forfeiture Unit and should have been seized and preserved years ago. Will that happen soon? Don't get your hopes up.

Only one criminal conviction has stemmed from the loot-fest. In January 2022, the specialised commercial crimes court in Johannesburg convicted former Prasa chief engineer Daniel "Tall Trains" Mthimkhulu on three counts of fraud for falsifying his qualifications. Lucky Montana rushed to his defence during the trial and assured the court that Mthimkhulu was good at his job and had played an important role in modernising Prasa's archaic rolling stock and rail infrastructure. He was awaiting sentencing at the time of the writing of this book.

* * *

State capture at Prasa was vast, brutal and ravenous. You cannot steal so many millions without leaving a trace of your fatty fingerprints. And none of the monetary marauders ever imagined that a deployed cadre like Popo Molefe would stand up and demand accountability, institute forensic investigations and ultimately spoil their pillaging escapade. Towards the end of August 2015, Molefe filed 43 criminal complaints with the Hawks arising from a host of forensic investigations into corruption and fraud at Prasa. All the evidence from the investigations was transferred to the crime-fighting unit. Prasa and the Hawks reached an agreement that the rail agency would pay for the services of expert forensic accountants to assist the police in their probe. Although Prasa footed the bill, the forensic team reported directly to the Hawks.

Maj.-Gen. Senaba Mosipi was then commander of the Hawks' commercial crime unit. He appointed forensic accountant Ryan Sacks, a director at Horwath Forensics (now Crowe Forensics), to conduct a cash-flow analysis of irregular, wasteful and fraudulent expenses relating to the Swifambo locomotive contract, followed by a similar exercise for the Siyangena contract. Sacks already possessed extensive knowledge of the two contracts because Werksmans had appointed him to assist in its earlier investigation.

On 14 January 2016, Prasa, the Hawks, the Asset Forfeiture Unit (AFU) and the National Prosecuting Authority (NPA) agreed on an investigation plan for Swifambo. The alleged crimes, the suspects and the witnesses had been identified, Sacks had commenced his financial analysis of the contract, and the AFU was poised to seize and preserve the assets of suspects under the Prevention of Organised Crime Act. But this was the Hawks of the nightmarish Berning Ntlemeza, unlawfully appointed as commander of the elite unit in September 2015. If it had been his mission to make sure that the Hawks did not disrupt the state-capture project or safeguard the looters against prosecution, he could hardly have done a better job. And the Hawks' investigation of Prasa was not going to be any different.

At the end of January 2016, Ntlemeza fired Mosipi as the head of the commercial crime unit and banished him to the dark innards of the Hawks. He then appointed an incompetent puppet, Maj.-Gen. Alfred Khana, as the new head of the unit. Khana replaced the whole investigations team and put a deployed cop from the North West province, Brig. Mmeli Makinyane, in charge of the probe. According to Popo Molefe testifying before the State Capture Commission: "Our experience with this case is that there were a number of professional police officers, but every time those professional officers put their teeth on the cases, they would be removed and cronies would be appointed in their place, clearly with the instruction to do nothing."

To find a way forward, Molefe and several Prasa executives, among them the head of legal risk and compliance, Martha Ngoye, and the general manager of legal services, Fani Dingiswayo, met Khana, Makinyane and the forensic investigators in April 2016. Khana assured Prasa that the Hawks had identified the main suspects, that subpoenas had been issued in terms of section 205 of the Criminal Procedure Act, and that the AFU was preparing to seize and preserve assets.

It didn't appear as though Khana intended to arrest any state looter. The Hawks stonewalled further, saying Prasa had not provided them with the necessary evidence to compile a prosecutable docket. It was a tired old trick used time and time again during the state-capture years to prevent politically connected cases from moving forward. In fact, Prasa provided the cops with all the documentation they needed – the contracts, correspondence, bank accounts, financial records, minutes of meetings, and subsequent forensic investigations with all their supplements and attachments. What the Hawks had to do was trace the flow of money (which Sacks was doing for them and which Prasa was paying for), subpoena the bank accounts and documents they needed, track down the beneficiaries, secure witnesses, take statements, do lifestyle audits, liaise with prosecutors, compile a prosecutable docket and ultimately execute arrests.

But that did not happen. In her evidence to the State Capture Commission, Ngoye said: "It has been so frustrating dealing with the Hawks because they come back with the same issues all the time and you just do not understand what they want. We have given information and they come back and they say we have not given information."

Judge Zondo: "They are not up to the job?"

Ngoye: "No, they are not up to it, Chairperson. In that meeting, Khana told the chairperson of the board that we had provided no information to them about Swifambo and Siyangena."

In July 2016, Molefe supplied the Hawks with an additional sixteen lever-arch files of documentary evidence relating to the Swifambo matter. Dingiswayo was tasked with providing the Hawks once again with all the other evidence, which he hand-delivered to the offices of the directorate in Pretoria. He told Judge Zondo that a Hawks investigator ushered him through security out of the building. They started talking about the investigation. Dingiswayo wanted to know why the Hawks had not yet interviewed prime suspect Auswell Mashaba. In reply, he later testified, the policeman told him: "What you are telling me is something that we have asked from our superiors. I was instructed not to touch Mr Mashaba."

Khana reiterated that the documents provided to the Hawks were not useful in a criminal investigation. He said in a letter to Ngoye in January 2017: "This office has already placed investigators across the country on alert so that we can tackle the matter head-on. It is however dependent on us to get the requisite documentation so that we can sit with the prosecutor on case planning."

Outraged, Molefe wrote to Hawks commissioner Berning Ntlemeza a month later and said it was clear that Khana had failed to familiarise himself with the available evidence and information. Molefe commented: "Recent correspondence from Major-General Khana makes it clear that DPCI [the Hawks] has done very little to date to progress and finalise these matters, despite Prasa's ongoing assistance and cooperation. The DPCI had failed its constitutional and statutory obligations. There is a serious risk that the ability to recover significant public funds is or may soon be compromised."

The irony is that while Ntlemeza and Khana stalled on Prasa and allocated scant resources to the investigation, a Hawks task team, commanded by the head of the unit's organised crime unit and supported by senior NPA prosecutors, was diligently hounding former finance minister Pravin Gordhan and SARS's Oupa Magashula, Ivan Pillay and Johann van Loggerenberg. They had no case and ultimately humiliated themselves by attempting to charge Gordhan and the others.

Forensic accountant Ryan Sacks, who testified for two days before the State Capture Commission, told Judge Zondo that he'd had a meeting with the Hawks in Pretoria in April 2017 and presented to them the results of his money-flow investigation of the Swifambo locomotive contract. At the meeting, Sacks handed his preliminary report to Makinyane. Sacks's investigation exposed a web of corruption within and outside Prasa and showed how hundreds of millions in taxpayers' money had been diverted to Auswell Mashaba, Makhensa Mabunda and a host of other entities, high-ranking public officials and beneficiaries connected to them.

The essence of Sacks's findings was confirmed three months later when the Johannesburg High Court set aside the Swifambo contract and ruled that Prasa had awarded the contract through a "corrupt tender process" and that Swifambo had acted as a mere front for the locomotive manufacturer Vossloh. All the evidence and documentation from Prasa's application in this matter was also transferred to the Hawks.

In the second part of the Swifambo investigation, Sacks would have proceeded to forensically analyse the recipients of the money and what they did with it. For this, Sacks depended on the Hawks to subpoena bank statements and accounts on his behalf because he didn't have the authority to do so. After that, he would have tackled the Siyangena security contracts whose main beneficiaries were Roy Moodley and Mario Ferreira.

Sacks never heard from the Hawks again. They never asked any questions about his money-flow findings in the Swifambo matter. They didn't provide him with accounts and information to carry out the next phase of the investigation, and they never commissioned the Siyangena part of his forensic probe – despite Prasa paying Sacks. Judge Zondo said to Sacks at the commission hearing: "In a few weeks' time, it will be four years since you gave the Hawks your report, and they have never come back to enable you to complete the investigation?"

Sacks: "That is correct."

Judge Zondo: "And they have never said to you if there is any problem."

Sacks: "I have not heard one word regarding any problem."

Advocate Vas Soni: "And what impression did you get when you presented your report?"

Sacks: "A general lack of interest into what I was explaining in the meeting."

By the time Molefe took the Hawks' inaction to court, Berning Ntlemeza was gone. The High Court had found in March 2017 that he was unlawfully appointed. Deputy Hawks head Lt.-Gen. Yolisa Matakata was then acting in his position. She wrote to Molefe in May 2017, saying that the Prasa probe was continuing but that Khana and his unit were still waiting for the preliminary report from Horwath Forensics. This was either a blatant lie or she didn't know what was going on. Not only had Sacks already handed his report to the investigating team but they had also stopped him carrying out any further forensic probes.

By then, Molefe and the Prasa board had had enough. They took the unusual step of taking the Hawks to court to force them to investigate the R14 billion in irregular expenditure. The Hawks opposed Molefe's authority to bring the application, describing it as "fatally defective". Instead of dealing with the merits of the application, the Hawks raised two technical objections.

Judge Zondo remarked at the Prasa hearing: "Prasa goes to the Hawks and says, go and catch them. Here is the evidence. The Hawks do not seem to do much until Prasa says, let us go to court to force the Hawks to do their job, and what do the Hawks do? They oppose that, they fight with Prasa. What kind of thing is that?"

Molefe's term as well as that of his board had expired at the end of July 2017. The new transport minister, Joe Maswanganyi, appointed an interim board, which was unlawful because the relevant Act didn't make provision for such an appointment. The State Capture Commission heard how Maswanganyi deliberately rendered the interim board dysfunctional by persuading certain members to resign at the same time that the department withdrew its representative. This left the board without a quorum. Its court application to force the Hawks to investigate disintegrated.

While listening to the failure of the Hawks to investigate Prasa, Judge Zondo remarked: "Now, if so many years later still nothing has been done, the Hawks owe the country an explanation. Because if this inaction is connected with the weakening of law-enforcement agencies or the aiding and abetting of those who were pursuing state capture, then the Commission wants to know exactly what happened."

On 23 August 2021, Hawks head Godfrey Lebeya, appointed in May 2018 to resuscitate South Africa's premier crime-fighting unit from the devastating neglect of the Zuma administration, submitted an affidavit to the State Capture Commission. In it, he said that the Siyangena and Swifambo investigations were "delayed" because Prasa was uncooperative and failed to provide documentation and statements to his investigators. He specifically blamed Prasa executives Martha Ngoye and Fani Dingiswayo, and said: "The unsound relationship between the DPCI and Prasa between 2015 and 2018 contributed to the delay in completing the investigations." Lebeya had simply rehashed the bullshit that the Hawks and Alfred Khana in particular had been spinning for years. All the evidence suggests that, in doing so, he attempted to mislead a judge and lied under oath, which is, by the way, a criminal offence.

Judge Zondo said in his final report (albeit in nicer language) that Lebeya relied on nothing but hearsay. The judge said he had no reason to reject the evidence of Ngoye and Dingiswayo. He added: "The DPCI has scored an own goal in the way it has failed to act diligently to investigate the criminal complaints laid many years ago by Prasa. One possible reason why it has dragged its feet may be connected with the risk or fear that any proper investigation may well lead to the ANC or to certain figures within the ANC."

It is clear what happened. Compelled to provide answers to Judge Zondo, Lebeya asked Khana what had happened and swallowed his ludicrous explanation hook, line and sinker. The Hawks head didn't even have the courtesy to read some of the evidence presented to the State Capture Commission about the Hawks' failure to investigate. He was, after all, an advocate, and one would have expected more circumspection from him. Instead, he gave a fuck-you reply to the judge.

Lebeya offered a bizarre explanation as to why the Hawks rejected the Sacks and Horwath money-flow investigation into Swifambo. He said that Prasa looter Auswell Mashaba had complained to the Hawks about the Sacks investigation, and as a result police investigators withdrew Sacks's mandate (without informing him). Can you imagine that a suspect in a billion-rand fraud and corruption case who doesn't like the forensic investigator combing through his bank accounts and financial records would phone the general in charge and ask him to get the pesky investigator off his case?

But the story gets worse. Lebeya said the investigators then discussed Sacks's report with prosecutors, "who raised a concern and discomfort" about the "objectivity" of his work and advised that an "independent report" by another forensic investigator should be obtained. Lebeya didn't say who the prosecutors were (if they existed at all), what their problem was with Sacks's report and why they found him not to be objective. Judge Zondo rejected Lebeya's explanation and said there was no evidence that Sacks's report was not impartial. He remarked: "If this is what has happened and is genuine, the DPCI would have asked Mr Sacks's firm to comment on the allegation of bias, but they did not." Judge Zondo said that there was also no sign that the Hawks had then attempted to find another forensic accountant to conduct an "objective" report on the flow of money received by Swifambo. He concluded: "All this suggests that their explanation is false and there is something more to the DPCI's conduct. I reject their explanation."

Judge Zondo's devastating remarks about Lebeya are hidden deep within the almost 250 pages he devoted to Prasa's capture in his final report of more than 2 000 pages. As a result, nobody picked up on Lebeya's big lie, saving him public embarrassment and humiliation for trying to cover up the Hawks' investigation.

Lebeya further said in his affidavit that the Swifambo case was still under investigation though 90 per cent complete, while the Siyangena investigation was 75 per cent complete. Of the remaining eighteen cases of fraud and corruption at Prasa, fourteen were still being investigated. Only four had been completed. Judge Zondo did not buy this either. "Given that more than six years had passed since the complaints were lodged with police, his explanation does not stand scrutiny. What is disturbing is that, even after he [Lebeya] took over in 2018, not much has happened. The reluctance persists even now."

* * *

The name of ANC apparatchik Leonard Ramatlakane has cropped up in some of the most emblematic chapters of state capture as a devoted and deployed cadre who abused his position as a member of two vital parliamentary portfolio committees to shield and protect the ruling party at all costs. During the state-capture project, Ramatlakane served on the parliamentary portfolio committees on police and transport, which he also chaired following Dikeledi Magadzi's disastrous reign there. The transport and police committees dallied and procrastinated while the Hawks and Crime Intelligence were hollowed out and Prasa destroyed and robbed blind. Judge Zondo had harsh words for Ramatlakane's performance on the transport committee, which he described as "less than distinguished".

Despite Ramatlakane's lamentable performance and lack of business acumen, transport minister Fikile Mbalula appointed him as chairperson of the Prasa board in October 2020. It was probably payback time for Ramatlakane's sterling defence of the ruling party. As we shall see in a later chapter, the ANC veteran played a vital role on the police portfolio committee to prevent the renewal of Robert McBride's contract as head of the Independent Police Investigative Directorate (IPID). The police watchdog was investigating the national police commissioner and some of his top generals for allegedly attempting to siphon millions from the Crime Intelligence secret fund for the ANC in the run-up to the party's elective conference in December 2017. Mbalula, then minister of police, was implicated in the matter, which I explain in a later chapter in this book.

After years of turning a blind eye to state capture, a firecracker ignited under Ramatlakane's backside upon his taking office as chair of the Prasa board. He almost immediately announced that the board had terminated the employment contract of Martha Ngoye because she was allegedly a member of the bid adjudication committee which had recommended the appointment of Swifambo as the locomotive supplier in 2012. Another Prasa whistle-blower, head of strategy Tiro Holele, was fired for the same offence.

Ngoye emerged at the State Capture Commission as one of Prasa's heroes who had fought the looting of the rail agency tooth and nail. She led Prasa's legal campaign to have the Swifambo and Siyangena contracts declared invalid and was also instrumental in stifling a R1 billion Prasa "investment" in the doomed VBS bank. The authenticity of the document that Ramatlakane used to justify her firing – the minutes of the committee meeting – was disputed by the forensic investigators appointed by Prasa to investigate corruption. The minutes were not signed and were dated before the alleged meeting took place. The bid adjudication committee never met to discuss these bids.

Ngoye and Holele brought an urgent application in the labour court, which ruled that they had been fired without justification. The judge ordered their reinstatement, but Prasa refused to allow them back to work. This led to another court ruling compelling Prasa to reinstate them. In return, Prasa launched an appeal, which meant that they stayed suspended.

Ngoye said in her evidence to Judge Zondo: "Those like myself, regarded by the main actors as dangerous, have been pushed out of their jobs and rendered lepers. When I first came to testify at this commission, I was an employee of Prasa. But I was ultimately pushed out of the organisation by the board of Prasa, based on spurious reasons."

In his final report, Judge Zondo said he had hoped that the abuse of power by top officials like Lucky Montana to fire those he regarded as a problem or a threat had come to an end. Referring to Ramatlakane's reign as chairperson, Judge Zondo observed that "such unacceptable practices continue to plague Prasa".

In March 2021, Ramatlakane and the board announced the appointment of Zolani Matthews as Prasa group chief executive. Matthews has a master's degree from Harvard University and ample struggle credentials. His sister is Cabinet minister Naledi Pandor, and his grandfather was Z.K. Matthews, an ANC struggle hero and an architect of the Freedom Charter. This was Prasa's first full-time chief executive since Lucky Montana's departure in 2015. But the board suspended him just eight months later after he failed his security clearance because he didn't declare his dual citizenship. Matthews acquired British citizenship because his father, Joe Matthews, was an ANC activist in exile in the United Kingdom.

An arbitration hearing, chaired by retired Supreme Court of Appeal judge Robert Nugent, found that Prasa had acted unfairly and ordered that Matthews be reinstated. Prasa reportedly refused to allow Matthews to go back to work and seemed intent on firing him again – this time for poor performance. Judge Zondo said that even "after Prasa had had much instability for six years when it did not have a permanent CEO, that instability has continued even after a permanent CEO had been appointed".

The fates of Martha Ngoye and Zolani Matthews are just some of Leonard Ramatlakane's problems. In the most recent financial year (2020/21), Prasa suffered a R1.9 billion loss, while irregular spending of R1.3 billion was also reported. In February 2022, Ramatlakane told the media that Prasa might have paid salaries to about 3 000 ghost employees for years. That is almost 20 per cent of the rail agency's workforce. Such bad news has not prevented the minister from bursting with excitement and optimism:

🐦 **Fikile Mbabula: Mr Fix** @MbalulaFikile, 5 July 2022
100 TRAINS MANUFACTURED LOCALLY. More importantly, this is a practical demonstration of the progress we have made towards delivering a commuter rail system that is safe, efficient, affordable, reliable.

🐦 **Craig** @CraigGradidge, 5 July 2022
Are these ones going to run on air and fresh water? Where's the electricity, the railway lines? The stations?

In July 2022, Mbalula announced at a media briefing that an additional five railway corridors would be up and running later in the year. South Africa has forty rail corridors, which connect two metropolitan areas. Only five were operational at the time of the minister's announcement.

Questioned about the issue of the locomotives, Ramatlakane said at the same briefing that of the thirteen Afro 4000 engines that Prasa had received as part of the R3.5 billion Swifambo contract, seven had been auctioned. He said these seven locomotives were presently operating on South African tracks and were not too tall. "They are running in the country, and they don't break bridges. Bridges are still standing, they go under the bridges." Ramatlakane was lying.

🐦 **Pieter-Louis Myburgh** @PLMyburgh, 27 July 2022
More lies about those damned tall trains. If @PRASA Group chair Leonard Ramatlakane's dishonesty is anything to go by, SA's long-suffering rail commuters can expect yet more deceit from those currently leading the organisation.

In 2019, as the Swifambo liquidators attempted to wrap up the company's financial affairs, they sold the seven locomotives to a private rail operator, Traxtion, at a huge loss. The company transported the locomotives by truck to Zimbabwe, and they are currently running between Zambia and Tanzania. The remaining six locomotives are gathering dust in a Prasa warehouse. None of them has ever operated in South Africa.

We all know the saying "repeat a lie often enough and it becomes the truth". This is exactly what a coterie of discredited and implicated state-capture enablers like Lucky Montana and "Dr" Daniel Mthimkhulu have been doing for years. Every now and then, nameless trolls and bots on Twitter rehash the lie that the Afro 4000 locomotives are not too tall for South Africa's rails. Ramatlakane has swallowed the canard hook, line and sinker.

Both the State Capture Commission and the Supreme Court of Appeal have confirmed that the locomotives are in fact too tall for our rails. Prasa's own engineers concluded in a report that the "locomotive structure gauge does not fit in the infrastructure clearance envelope. It is evident that there is a compliance conflict." It said that the locomotives would be non-compliant for most of the rail network's electrified areas. In 2015, the Railway Safety Regulator (RSR) investigated the Afro 4000 locomotives and said that because of their height, the engines ran the risk of making contact with overhead power lines. They are not allowed to run on South Africa's 3kV lines, which make up a large part of the major long-distance railway system.

Yet Ramatlakane said at the briefing that the RSR had "dismissed" media reports that the trains were too tall. Why is the Prasa chairperson lying like an ANC politician on the eve of a general election?

He said there were an additional 23 Afro 4000 locomotives standing at a harbour in Spain that had to be shipped in the following six months to South Africa, where they would join the remaining six. The locomotives were part of the Swifambo contract and had been paid for. According to Ramatlakane: "We need to use those locos to transport long-distance passenger rail." So, Prasa sold seven of its Afro 4000 locomotives at a loss to get rid of them – just to get more of the same?

CHAPTER 6

Where lurks the mafia state

🐦 **Phumlani M. Majozi** @PhumlaniMMajozi, 14 Mar. 2021
There's a crisis in South Africa – a very serious crisis. It's a crisis of crime, and it's deadly crime. We're not dealing with this. We're not.

🐦 **Ricardo Mackenzie** @ricardomackenzi, 15 Mar. 2021
Indeed! We have a dysfunctional security cluster, from the Executive, to Police Commissioner, detective services, forensic services, prosecutorial services, crime intelligence, it's a big mess!

AT ONE OF the swankiest five-star addresses in Africa, a concrete and glass hulk that exudes elegance and style, I sit down in the saloon to meet a top police Crime Intelligence officer for breakfast. The hotel's interior is a fusion of Manhattan glitz and European opulence, a Johannesburg sanctuary that insulates its patrons from the inequality and ugliness a mere stone's throw away.

A few minutes after ten, a conspicuous-looking fella who looks out of place peeks into the saloon and sets his eyes on me before scuttling away. It is the scout, sent ahead to make sure there isn't a trap. Minutes later, my source plonks himself down next to me. His eyes stealthily scrutinise the space, although there is only one other couple in the furthest corner. We order poached eggs and ham on dark rye, the same breakfast we had in the same place several years ago when I did research for *The President's Keepers*. Halfway through the meal, he leans forward and mumbles from the corner of his mouth: "General Mfazi. I have seen the new post-mortem. He was poisoned."

"Really?"

"Yes, with resin."

"By whom?"

"I don't know, we now have to find out."

"Maybe a cop?"

"Might be; he had serious enemies."

Deputy national police commissioner Lt.-Gen. Sindile Mfazi died in July 2021 – from Covid complications, according to his family. The 59-year-old career cop oversaw Crime Intelligence as well as detective and forensic services. Two months after Mfazi's funeral, rumours circulated that he might have been poisoned and that his body had been exhumed. Police confirmed the exhumation and said that his death was being investigated.

At the time of his death, Mfazi was at the centre of internecine warfare within the upper ranks of the police. Instead of the police waging war against tik-infested and gun-toting Capeland mudda-fuckers or hitmen pumping slugs into their political targets in KwaZulu-Natal, this is a duel that is pitting blue against blue. As allegations, accusations and conspiracies echo through the service's top ranks, the police's ability to keep ordinary citizens safe has been at least partly paralysed.

You can justifiably ask: where is the thin blue line when AK-wielding cash-in-transit robbers with itchy trigger fingers attack armoured vehicles? And why has there been scant action against white-collar looters who fedex sickly amounts of public money to veiled accounts in that laundromat of international financing, Dubai? Nor have there been consequences for bent state officials who abet cronies in bagging lucrative tenders in return for their children's private school fees, a Milan shopping spree for the ol' lady, or a holiday on Turkey's Turquoise Coast.

While rumours and allegations abound about who is involved and on which side, it is difficult to distinguish fact from fiction and to separate that which carries credence from rubbish manufactured to smear an adversary. My meeting with my Crime Intelligence source is a case in point. After washing down our eggs and ham with cappuccinos, he pulls out a ledger and hands me a document. It is a 21-page letter, addressed to President Cyril Ramaphosa and Deputy President David Mabuza and sent by e-mail to the Presidency towards the end of 2020. The author calls himself "Proudly South African" and claims to have ten years of service in the Hawks.

"Mr President, I am writing this anonymously to express my concern over the issue of abuse of power and corruption in the DPCI [the Directorate of Priority Crime Investigation, known as the Hawks]. It is desperately in need of a clear direction and strong leadership. There has been outright and open corruption by senior management who have been placed to manage the affairs and develop this falling institution."

The e-mail is a direct attack on the integrity and ability of the head of the Hawks, Lt.-Gen. Godfrey Lebeya. Said the author of the e-mail: "It is no secret that Lebeya rules the DPCI with an iron fist. Many members have been targeted, suspended whilst others are increasingly opting to transfer to the mother body or other government departments."

Lebeya's appointment was hailed as bad news for organised crime and the beginning of the end for state capturers and their cronies. Not so. Three years after his appointment, Lebeya admitted to Parliament in March 2021 that the Hawks were operating at less than 50 per cent capacity and not firing on all cylinders. South Africans made a dire mistake in thinking that the appointment of just one man was going to shake up the Hawks. We underestimate the rot and decay that have infested the police. Some top cops appointed during the Zuma era were placed in strategic positions to shield the former president and his cronies from prosecution. Other loyalists, often useless or compromised, were shifted into key posts where they were supposed to see and do nothing. Many are still there and clinging to their jobs and their pensions. Although they are not necessarily intent on disrupting the new order, they are not suddenly going to morph into crime-busting machines.

The e-mail to Ramaphosa and Mabuza originated from within the ranks of the Hawks. After it arrived at the Presidency, it found its way back to the police and to Crime Intelligence to investigate and identify the author. They discovered the e-mail had been written by two Hawks brigadiers and a colonel – a staff officer of former Hawks head Lt.-Gen. Berning Ntlemeza, who was illegally appointed by Zuma's Cabinet and credited with wrecking the Hawks.

One of the brigadiers had been charged with corruption a month or two before authoring the letter. What is truly frightening is that their letter has now been widely distributed by a faction in Crime Intelligence to smear Lebeya. This faction wants Lebeya gone and would like to sink the Hawks yet further into a state of decline.

And if the Hawks are in turmoil, Crime Intelligence is shambolic. For more than a decade, this unit has betrayed South Africa on every level. It has failed to detect and combat serious crime. It has played a vital role in targeting and getting rid of law-enforcement officials who posed a threat to President Zuma. Its top echelons have looted its secret account, intended for covert crime-fighting operations. Jacob Zuma may be a president of the past, but his legacy still looms large in the police.

To his credit, Zuma's successor, Cyril Ramaphosa, has sought to build the capacity of some law-enforcement agencies like the South African Revenue Service (SARS) and the National Prosecuting Authority (NPA) by introducing new leadership in both entities. He also established the High-Level Review Panel to investigate the State Security Agency (SSA), although the agency remains in turmoil. Furthermore, he boosted the State Capture Commission with extra funds, agreed to extend its deadline and provided additional resources. He also established the Special Investigating Unit (SIU) Special Tribunal in 2019 to fast-track the recovery of state funds. Moreover, an Investigating Directorate (ID) was established within the NPA, a specialised unit consisting of Hawks investigators and special prosecutors, to bring to book the perpetrators of state-capture crimes. Many see the ID as a seedling of the old Scorpions that will hopefully sprout into a full-blooded and well-resourced new law-enforcement agency. But the president has done little to resuscitate the South African Police Service (SAPS). There has been no clean-out of rogue cops and there is no plan to rebuild the service. It is lurching from crisis to crisis.

*   *   *

You have seen the visuals: Vladimir Putin's cruise missiles and artillery ripping into Ukrainian apartment buildings, schools, hospitals, houses and train stations. Whole villages have been reduced to rubble in a matter of hours. Yet before the war, Ukraine was a haven of peace. It had a murder rate of 6 people per 100 000 of the population, compared with South Africa's 36 murders per 100 000. Ukraine had a rape rate of 1.5 cases per 100 000 of the population, compared with South Africa's 72. Then the Russian invasion of Ukraine changed everything. On 23 May 2022, exactly three months after the first Russian tanks crossed the border between the two countries, the United Nations High Commissioner for Human Rights announced that 4 031 Ukrainian civilians had died in the conflict and many more had been injured.

On 3 June 2022, South African police minister Bheki Cele took to the podium to release the crime statistics for the first three months of 2022. Between January and March 2022, 6 083 people had been murdered in the country. Ukraine is at war with a foreign nation while South Africans are massacring one another. When Cele released the crime figures, he admitted: "All in all, these statistics don't give us a good picture. The first three months of this year were violent, brutal and unsafe for many South Africans."

Wearing his customary black fedora with a black shirt and grey suit, and flanked by a host of his generals, including Hawks head "Doctor Advocate Lieutenant-General" Godfrey Lebeya, Cele said there had been an overall increase of 9.3 per cent in reported crime. Murder kept going up and up. For example, murders for the three months of

July to September 2021 increased by 20.7 per cent in comparison with the same period the year before. The murder rate for January to March 2022 increased by 22 per cent compared with the same period in 2021. Most shocking was the violent deaths of women and children, which showed an increase of 71 per cent and 37 per cent, respectively. Virtually every category of crime has increased. There were 41 000 residential burglaries in South Africa between January and March 2022. Every South African asks the same question: where is it going to end – with a gun against my head?

There is a plethora of things the ANC should be deeply ashamed and embarrassed about, but none more so than the sexual abuse of our women and children. A staggering 10 818 people were raped between January and March 2022 – an increase of almost 14 per cent over the same period in 2021. And remember that only about one in nine or ten rapes is reported to the police.

🐦 **Bantu Holomisa** @BantuHolomisa, 19 Aug. 2022
Crime stats: More than 6 400 people murdered in SA in just three months, over 40% killed by guns – Criminals are in charge.

When a sombre Cele faced the nation again three months later, another 6 423 people had been murdered between April and June 2022 – an increase of 11.5 per cent or 664 people more than in the same period in 2021. Although rape cases showed a small decline – from 10 006 between April and June 2021 to 9 516 between the same period in 2022 – there is nothing to celebrate.

The police are looking on as South Africans are increasingly butchered, raped and robbed in their beds, their homes, their streets, their communities, their towns and their cities. The service has seemingly lost the capacity to solve serious crime. According to the Institute for Security Studies (ISS), murder and armed robbery increased by 37 per cent and 43 per cent, respectively, in the eight years leading up to March 2020. In 2019/20, detectives were only able to solve 19 out of every 100 murders.

The record for aggravated robbery is worse, with only 17 per cent of cases solved. And yet, said the ISS, the police had no clear strategy to tackle murder and other serious crimes and reduce the numbers of incidents.

Several public opinion surveys have shown that the police, by far the largest government department with just more than 180 000 members, is one of the least trusted and most corrupt. The service has become a fossilised and rigid bureaucracy which citizens don't trust to combat crime or bring organised criminals to book.

🐦 **News24** @News24, 20 Apr. 2022
The thin blue line gets thinner as visible policing budget continues to shrink

So, what is the government's response to the increasing crime rate? It is cutting budgets. The police are hugely understaffed in relation to the crime threat that South Africa faces. We have about 400 police officials per 100 000 of the population, compared with Spain (530), Turkey (520), Serbia (635), Russia (515), Greece (500) and Italy (455) – all countries with a much lower crime rate. Moreover, the police budget for 2022/23 will decrease in real terms by more than R4 billion from the previous year. The most worrying decline has taken place in visible policing, which is the practice of deterring criminal activity by showing a police presence. Instead, the SAPS will spend more money on protecting politicians, dignitaries and national key points, like Parliament (or whatever is left of it), than on priority crimes like criminal syndicates, cash-in-transit heists and corruption.

One would think that a top priority for police management would be the strengthening of the Hawks to combat the rising tide of organised crime and the deluge of cases emanating from state capture. No so. The budget for the Hawks remains a paltry R2.167 billion – just more than 2 per cent of the total police budget. This is far less than the money allocated for protection and security services, which increased to R3.23 billion. Within this figure is the VIP protection unit's budget of around R1.7 billion to protect 209 dignitaries and officials. That is a staggering R8 million to protect each person.

Have you ever watched Cyril Ramaphosa's cavalcade go by? When he campaigned in Mabopane in northern Tshwane in October 2021, his procession consisted of eight traffic cops on bikes and ten BMWs, Mercedes-Benzes and Land Cruisers. The president was cocooned somewhere in the middle of his blue-light brigade. This was not unusual, and it happens wherever Ramaphosa goes.

A vast array of government officials is surrounded by firepower. Every one of Ramaphosa's 64 ministers and deputy ministers is heavily protected. So are provincial premiers and members of the provincial executive councils. Directors-general and many of their deputies have bodyguards. Every mayor and every council speaker in South Africa is eligible for municipal-funded bodyguards, although the only threat they probably face is from livid residents who don't receive services. Police top brass all have bodyguards, including the nine provincial police commissioners and the head of the Hawks.

Yet the South Africans who need protection most have been left to fend for themselves. Think of Charl Kinnear of the Western Cape anti-gang unit and Babita Deokaran, a chief director in the Gauteng department of health and a key witness in the Special Investigating Unit's probe into fraudulent Covid-19 contracts. They both died exposed, defenceless and without police protection as assassins mercilessly mowed them down when they arrived home.

With 200 generals and 600 brigadiers in the top echelons, police management waddle about like overfed ducks. Yet only 15 posts at general and brigadier level will be cut in the coming years.

When I wrote this book, I spoke to a host of top Hawks and Crime Intelligence officers to find answers to the dismal state of our men and women in blue. Although I encountered a host of deeply compromised cops, especially at Crime Intelligence, I also found dedicated and skilled policemen at units like the Hawks. They are heroes in our quest to

96

combat crime and wipe out state capture. But here lies the problem: they are getting fewer and fewer. There are far fewer of them left than when I wrote *The President's Keepers*. Many have retired, taken packages or joined private security companies. State capture may have stopped, but the hollowing-out of the SAPS continues unabated.

With the police in a state of paralysis, criminals must be rejoicing. More than four years after Cyril Ramaphosa was sworn in as South Africa's fifth democratically elected president, almost nothing has come of his promise of dire consequences for the state looters or to halve the crime rate in the next decade.

𝕏 **BusinessLIVE** @BusinessLiveSA, 24 Oct. 2021
SA "in danger of being a mafia state", says Momoniat

Towards the end of October 2021, the intergovernmental Financial Action Task Force (FATF), a global money-laundering and terrorist-financing watchdog, detected conspicuous shortcomings in South Africa's ability to counter and combat financial crimes and money laundering. The FATF gave South Africa eighteen months to take remedial steps to address these "significant weaknesses". In turn, Cabinet tasked Treasury with this job. Acting director-general Ismail Momoniat warned that the country would become a mafia state if it failed to deal urgently with these crimes. He said: "South Africa's doors are open to those who want to use the country for organised crime and terrorism. We are very exposed to that. We don't even know how much so. It seems to me that our intelligence about crime is almost non-existent."

* * *

𝕏 **Ferial Haffajee** @ferialhaffajee, 8 Aug. 2022
Must Read. Police in pockets of Zama-zama. Zama zamas just one part of a multibillion-rand organised crime economy that threatens SA

🐦 **City Press** @City_Press, 15 Aug. 2022
Government too incompetent to deal with zama zama cancer

Somewhere below us, 30 000 people are tunnelling into abandoned mineshafts and tunnels that dot the landscape along Johannesburg's eastern, southern and western edges and stretch as far as the Free State goldfields. Two decades ago, illegal miners, many from Lesotho and Mozambique, descended on disused mineshafts and started digging for leftover gold. It spread like wildfire and festered into a billion-rand organised crime industry. The zama zamas, as these illegal miners are called, are at the very bottom of a thriving illicit economy that goes all the way up to South African scrap-metal and gold dealers, gold refineries and precious metal exporters.

The zama zamas are heavily armed with assault rifles and explosives, live by their own code and have for years terrorised nearby communities with impunity because police have, once again, failed to address this cancer in our society. Residents can hear the machinery and see the illegal miners skulking about at dusk and walking around armed. Theft and rape in these areas have increased disproportionately in comparison with areas further away.

In 2019, a United Nations report showed that illegal mining cost South Africa's economy an estimated R41 billion in lost profits every year. Police have not just failed to stop the zama zamas from getting a foothold in affected communities but have also ignored repeated warnings about the dire effects of illegal mining on the industry. In March 2022, Auditor-General Tsakani Maluleke reported that there were 6 100 abandoned mines belonging to the Department of Mineral Resources and Energy. She warned the department that the mines "posed serious health, safety and environmental hazards for nearby communities". Nobody bothered to respond.

In early August 2022, South Africa woke up to the news that eight women who were taking part in a music-video shoot at a disused mine on Johannesburg's West Rand had been gang-raped, reportedly by zama zamas who attacked them in broad daylight. It was an atrocity so vile that the police couldn't ignore what was going on any longer. In a show of force, hundreds of policemen, among them members of the Special Task Force and tactical response teams, descended on the area and arrested more than a hundred illegal miners, many of them for allegedly participating in the rapes. They have appeared in court in an ongoing case.

We all know how this will end. Despite promises by Bheki Cele that the police will get to the bottom of the illegal mining industry in the country, the dust will eventually settle over the rape, the zama zamas will return and the illegal industry will continue unabated.

Said Cele in the aftermath of the rapes: "There are many victims of crime who need counselling. Some are dead walking. I am told that rape here has been turned into a hobby." And in a country in the clutches of a gender-violence pandemic, Cele had words of comfort for a 19-year-old victim who was allegedly raped by a zama zama during the Krugersdorp attack. He said she was "lucky, if it is lucky" to have been raped by one man while others were raped by several men at a time.

* * *

To understand how we got here, we must go back to the Zuma years, which spawned two terrifying police wreckers: Lt.-Gen. Richard Naggie Mdluli, the divisional commissioner of Crime Intelligence, and Berning Mthandazo Ntlemeza, the head of the Directorate for Priority Crime Investigation (the Hawks). These two were Zuma's guardians of the state-capture project, men he could trust to persecute and hound his enemies. They would ensure that politically sensitive cases and dockets disappeared, and they would appoint pliable cronies in key positions throughout the force.

🐦 **Max du Preez** @MaxduPreez, 16 Mar. 2016
Factoid: President JG Zuma's chief henchmen are both policemen from the nasty 1980s apartheid era: Richard Mdluli and Berning Ntlemeza.

99

There is a close nexus between Mdluli and Ntlemeza. When Mdluli was accused in the early 2000s of assaulting, kidnapping and killing his lover's boyfriend, Oupa Ramogibe, he appointed Ntlemeza to investigate the allegations against him. Ever heard of a suspect appointing his own investigator? After a five-month probe, Ntlemeza concluded that Mdluli was innocent. It was a lie, as almost a decade later, Mdluli was convicted of the kidnapping and assault of Ramogibe and sentenced to prison.

It was the departure of Hawks head Anwa Dramat that paved the way for Ntlemeza's appointment as acting head in December 2014. A few months later, police minister Nathi Nhleko reportedly ignored a shortlist of five selected cops and unlawfully appointed Ntlemeza as permanent Hawks head. Just six months earlier, Pretoria High Court judge Elias Matojane found that Ntlemeza had lied under oath in a matter involving a former Gauteng Hawks head. He said Ntlemeza was dishonest and lacked integrity.

The Constitution First @Spiwo, 10 Sept. 2015
A dishonest, lying crook who doesn't deserve to be close to that office. Ntlemeza appointed as Hawks head.

The buffoonery of South Africa's premier crime fighter soon became evident as he bumbled his way through parliamentary committee meetings where he had to explain a 60 per cent decline in Hawks arrests and an even greater drop in conviction rates under his command. When Ntlemeza was grilled in Parliament and was unable to reply coherently, he was forced to concede: "I am lacking . . . we are now swimming."

Ntlemeza's biggest contribution to trashing the Hawks was his appointment of sidekicks to top positions, thereby transforming the unit into his personal cronytocracy. These cops became his personal hit squad. They terrorised state-capture crime busters like Johan Booysen, Ivan Pillay and Robert McBride with trumped-up criminal investigations and charges.

Although Ntlemeza's reign at the Hawks came to an end in March 2017, these appointees survived the coming of Cyril Ramaphosa and continued to cause havoc. Some are inexplicably still clinging to their positions in the top echelons of the police.

One of Ntlemeza's first appointments was that of the commander of the serious organised crime unit of the Hawks. With the country staggering under the scourge of organised crime, this should have been a cop with vast experience and expertise who could hunt down the state looters and bring them to book. Instead, Ntlemeza plucked a police brigadier from obscurity in rural Sekhukhuneland in Limpopo where she was a cluster commander and appointed her as a major-general in one of the most crucial posts in the police. Ntlemeza knew her from the time when he was deputy provincial police commissioner in Limpopo because she reported to him.

There was no indication on her CV that Maj.-Gen. Sylvia Ledwaba knew anything about complex organised crime investigations, racke-teering, high-level corruption or the Prevention of Organised Crime Act (POCA). Not that this was in any way important, for her real role in the Hawks soon became apparent. In September 2015, about 12 national intervention unit policemen, decked out in riot gear and flaunting R5 assault rifles, descended on a Durban home. The squad was led by Ledwaba, dressed in white pants and a striped shirt. She demanded entry to see the owner, but he was away on work-related business in Pietermaritzburg. The cavalcade of cars and vans then made their way to the city centre to his attorney's office. CCTV footage shows Ledwaba and her procession strutting into the attorney's chambers, where she made a phone call before disappearing through a door.

As Ledwaba was the head of the serious organised crime unit, one would assume she was executing a warrant of arrest on a drug kingpin or a dangerous gangster. In fact, she was abusing taxpayers' money and probably flouting police regulations merely to serve Ntlemeza's notice of suspension on KwaZulu-Natal Hawks head Maj.-Gen. Johan Booysen. This was nothing but a show of force and an act of intimidation, executed at the behest of Ntlemeza. It didn't matter that Booysen had been acquitted in a police disciplinary hearing of all wrongdoing and the High Court had ruled there was no case against him. Ntlemeza was intent on nailing the Hawks major-general, allegedly to protect a Zuma associate from being prosecuted.

Ledwaba said in a media interview later that she was "born to be a leader". And that is exactly what she was during the Ntlemeza era at the Hawks. She led a pack of bloodhounds that hunted Booysen, former finance minister Pravin Gordhan, former SARS commissioner Oupa Magashula and former SARS executives Ivan Pillay and Johann van Loggerenberg. Gordhan, Magashula and Pillay were charged with fraud relating to Pillay's early retirement. When that failed, Ledwaba went after Gordhan for setting up a mythical SARS rogue unit. Pillay and Van Loggerenberg were eventually charged with offences relating to the alleged bugging of the offices of the NPA and the Scorpions in 2007. In all cases, there was no evidence against any of them. Much of the Hawks correspondence carried Ledwaba's signature.

Ntlemeza promoted several other cops from the Limpopo outback to crucial positions in the Hawks for which they were ill-qualified. At the end of 2015, he appointed the station commander of Makhado, previously known as Louis Trichardt, as the Western Cape head of the Hawks' organised crime unit. There is a great difference between being a uniformed cop and detective in a forgotten outpost in Limpopo and the chief investigator of organised crime in the Western Cape. Brig. Mushavhaduvha Ramovha had no experience or expertise in investigating organised crime. Ramovha was also implicated in racial incidents on several occasions by the local Makhado newspaper. When a white journalist from the *Zoutpansberger* questioned him about the rise of crime in the town in 2015, he reportedly shouted at her: "Your newspaper is racist! Isabel, your newspaper is racist! Whatever you want to write about black people you write in Afrikaans so that black people won't be able to understand. I am opening a case against you . . . I am not kidding!"

* * *

Ntlemeza replaced eight of the nine provincial Hawks heads with his own cronies. Several of them had limited or no policing experience. What is frightening is that every candidate was supposed to have undergone a rigorous selection process and approval by the Cabinet.

🐦 Radio 786 @radio786online, 4 Feb. 2016
The Western Cape has a new Hawks head. Major General Nombuso Portia Khoza has been appointed. Khoza worked as a senior prosecutor at the National Prosecuting Authority and would bring good leadership needed in the province.

In the gangster paradise of the Western Cape, Ntlemeza appointed the 38-year-old Nombuso Portia Khoza as Hawks head with the rank of major-general. She had no policing experience but promised to tackle serious corruption, organised crime, and drug and human trafficking. She quickly gained a reputation for not having a clue about police work, skipped meetings, lacked leadership and sat in her office sipping tea and watching television. Some colleagues referred to her as "The Bold and the Beautiful".

🐦 SAfm news @SAfmnews, 4 Feb. 2016
Hawks have confirmed that former NPA integrity head Prince Mokotedi has been appointed the head of the Hawks in Gauteng.

🐦 Mandy Wiener @MandyWiener, 13 Feb. 2016
Charges withdrawn against Jiba. Prince Mokotedi appointed Gauteng Hawks head. Breytenbach taken to court. That all tells a story.

In the crime hub of Gauteng, Ntlemeza appointed a former disgraced head of the NPA's integrity unit, Prince Mokotedi, as Hawks head.

He had resigned under a cloud of controversy from the prosecuting authority in 2014 after he was charged with gross insubordination and bringing the NPA into disrepute. The charges were dropped after his resignation. Mokotedi had, like his counterpart in the Western Cape, no policing experience, but that didn't matter. What mattered was that he once tweeted "I am 100% Zuma" (the tweet has since been removed) and he was therefore, in Ntlemeza's estimation, perfect for one of the most crucial positions in the police.

Mokotedi is a strong contender for the Dufus Moronicus in Gold award for his contribution to policing during the state-capture era. By the end of 2016, the Independent Police Investigative Directorate (IPID), with the assistance of forensic investigator Paul O'Sullivan, was investigating then acting police commissioner Lt.-Gen. Khomotso Phahlane for fraud and corruption. Mokotedi decided to bring an end to the investigation and net the whole rotten and unruly rabble in one devastating police swoop. He claimed in an affidavit that O'Sullivan, IPID head Robert McBride, former Gauteng Hawks head Shadrack Sibiya and members of the Democratic Alliance and AfriForum were plotting South Africa's own "Arab Spring", which would see the ousting of Jacob Zuma. Mokotedi described the alleged plotters in his Mad Max-like fantasy as the "Black Hawks". They laughed him off, with McBride saying that "Prince is hearing voices". He nonetheless laid charges against them of treason, espionage, conspiracy to commit murder, corruption, intimidation and harassment, defeating the ends of justice, and tax evasion. Said the *Mail & Guardian* of Mokotedi: "It looks more like a case of flinging as much kak [shit] as he can find and hoping some gobbets stick. We're bewildered. And we think Mokotedi may be, too."

🐦 **ECR Newswatch** @ECR_Newswatch, 14 Jan. 2016
Just in: Major General Jabulani Zikhali has been appointed the new head of the Hawks in KZN.

🐦 Pauli van Wyk @PaulivW, 20 Jan. 2016
Jabulani Zikhali was SAPS acting cluster commander of Durban Central.
No experience of specialised work the #Hawks should do.

In KwaZulu-Natal, shortly after suspending Johan Booysen on trumped-up charges of fraud, Ntlemeza rushed to appoint a new Hawks head for the province – an acting cluster commander with limited experience in organised crime. Maj.-Gen. Jabulani Zikhali soon showed his real colours when he attempted to protect and shield from arrest a Nigerian evangelist accused of rape, sexual assault and human trafficking. As a Hawks team got ready to pounce on Timothy Omotoso during a church service in a packed Mangaung city hall, they found Zikhali addressing the congregants. He identified himself as the Hawks head in KwaZulu-Natal and said that he was the "extension and the arm of the unit's national boss [Ntlemeza]". He referred to Omotoso, head of the Jesus Dominion International Church in Durban, as "Daddy" and said: "I was a brigadier, but Daddy prayed for me and I was upgraded to a major-general."

🐦 Xoli @Undlunkulu_Xoli, 4 May 2017
#TimOmotoso Nigerian pastor had senior Hawks member in his pocket, court hears

Omotoso was eventually arrested at an airport. A Hawks investigator told the court during the pastor's bail hearing that Omotoso knew the Hawks investigators' every move and evaded capture by being whisked away in vehicles with blue lights. He said the "entire operation was in disarray". The Hawks team that hunted down Omotoso laid a complaint against Zikhali with Frans Kgomo, judge at the Office of the DPCI, which was established to hear and investigate complaints against the Hawks.

* * *

It is hard to believe that Sylvia Ledwaba was not Ntlemeza's worst appointment in the Hawks. Neither was Prince "I am 100% Zuma" Mokotedi in Gauteng nor the tea-swigging Portia Khoza in the Western Cape. That honour may well belong to Maj.-Gen. Alfred Khana, appointed as head of the commercial crime unit of the Hawks in May 2018. You met him in the previous chapter as the general who oversaw the fraud and corruption investigation at Prasa and royally fucked it up. The police didn't announce his appointment, with good reason, because the incumbent had much to hide. He lurks to this day in the unit.

In 2013, Hawks head Anwa Dramat tasked his commercial crimes head, Maj.-Gen. Hans Meiring, to investigate charges of fraud against Khana, then a brigadier and head of commercial crimes in Gauteng. The brigadier had allegedly submitted false claims. During the investigation, Khana requested a transfer to the Gauteng provincial government, probably to avoid a disciplinary hearing.

Meiring says in an affidavit, submitted to the State Capture Commission, that the investigation against Khana showed prima facie evidence of fraud, and the docket was referred to the head of the NPA's specialised commercial crime unit in Pretoria, Glynnis Breytenbach. As Khana had resigned, the NPA declined to prosecute.

Following Meiring's retirement, Maj.-Gen. Senaba Charles Mosipi – by all reports, a competent fraud and corruption investigator – was appointed as head of the commercial crime unit. Upon his arrival, Ntlemeza shifted Mosipi sideways and advertised the post. Khana applied and was appointed.

Ntlemeza's nickname was "The Bulldozer", and it wasn't just a reference to his brash and boorish personality – he told a management meeting that when he was finished with the Hawks, "I will be the whitest man here". He bulldozed and buried politically sensitive and state capture cases. Khana played a key role in this.

𝕏 **Daily Dispatch** @Dispatch_DD, 6 Jan. 2018
Top cop told to give up R500m fraud dockets

According to the *Daily Dispatch*, Alfred Khana ordered a raid on the office of Eastern Cape Hawks investigator Capt. Luphumlo Lwana in August 2017 to remove 20 dockets he was investigating. Many of his probes implicated prominent Eastern Cape politicians, mayors, officials and councillors allegedly involved in fraud and corruption. This wasn't the first time that dockets were removed from Lwana's care. The State Capture Commission heard evidence that in December 2015 – less than three months after the appointment of Ntlemeza as the head of the Hawks – head office ordered Lwana to surrender a fraud investigation into the South African Social Security Agency (Sassa). The social security minister at the time was Zuma acolyte and convicted criminal Bathabile Dlamini, whose family members had allegedly scored a R49 million Sassa tender to distribute food parcels. Nothing came of the probe.

Khana was also implicated in evidence before the State Capture Commission in Berning Ntlemeza's persistent hounding of Johan Booysen. When the Hawks boss suspended Booysen on trumped-up fraud charges, it was Khana he appointed to investigate.

CHAPTER 7

Cabbage-patch kids

DRAPED IN BROWN with a white underbelly, a hawk is nature's perfect predator. As it soars on the hunt, its wings are spread wide with its wingtip feathers stretched like fingers. Hawks sweep the backwoods in silence with eyes that have the intensity of binoculars and with steely claws that can crush prey several times their size. And when they swoop on their target, they do so with fatal efficiency. This is what the men and women of the Directorate for Priority Crime Investigation (DPCI), or the Hawks, are meant to be: silent, aloof, efficient and lethal. Instead, we have ended up with a scrawny, bald-headed turkey that cannot catch a dead mouse or bag a roadkill.

I am not saying for a moment that DPCI head Berning Ntlemeza turned every Hawk into a cabbage-patch kid, but those who stayed true to their craft and honoured their mission were shafted and kept away from high-profile and politically sensitive cases. They were isolated and could forget about promotion. That was why so many left the service. Ntlemeza was the grim reaper of the Zuma era, a dour-faced wretch who turned a functioning outfit into a graveyard in less than three years. His legacy lived on in the likes of Ledwaba, Khana, Mokotedi and many others, and to this day the Hawks are burdened by his decisions and appointments.

🐦 **SABC News** @SABCNews, 17 Mar. 2017
#Ntlemeza | The high court in Pta has set aside the appointment of Hawks head Berning Ntlemeza, ruling it irrational.

🐦 **Aubzie** @Aubreychiibi, 17 Mar. 2017
So many unlawful appointments. What's South Africa coming to?

Then in March 2017, as the result of a High Court ruling, police minister Fikile Mbalula suspended Ntlemeza. For a person claiming to possess a law degree, Ntlemeza showed complete legal ignorance by insisting that the High Court had no authority to pronounce on his appointment. He claimed that the ruling was a "devastating blow to the country as a whole", but six months later the Supreme Court of Appeal dismissed his application for leave to appeal. It also meant that he left the police with a lower rank.

On his departure, Lt.-Gen. Yolisa Matakata, who had been Ntlemeza's right-hand person throughout his calamitous reign, was appointed as acting Hawks head. Despite going on to become the provincial police commissioner in the Western Cape, Matakata will not go down in policing annals as the Nancy Drew of South African law enforcement.

Days after her acting appointment, Matakata and Alfred Khana headed to Parliament to report back on various investigations, including that of Prasa. Khana said the serious commercial crime unit had a "large volume of cases", but he couldn't provide a list because it "was long". Khana reported no progress on Prasa because he claimed that the investigatory and forensic reports that Prasa board chairman Popo Molefe had provided to the Hawks lacked supporting documents and were therefore not useful. It was a lie he repeated time and time again.

* * *

Several other high-priority investigations perished under Khana's watch, most notably the fraud and corruption charges against former SARS deputy commissioner Jonas Makwakwa and his girlfriend. In 2016, amaBhungane reported that Makwakwa, a key player in the capture of SARS, was caught by ATM cameras feeding wads of cash into his personal account as well as receiving other deposits amounting to at least R1.2 million. The revelations against Makwakwa were made in a Financial Intelligence Centre (FIC) report, which found that payments were also made into his girlfriend's account. Former SARS commissioner Tom Moyane, the Zuma acolyte credited with ultimately breaking the revenue service, unlawfully disclosed the FIC report to Makwakwa and failed to report the alleged corrupt activities to the Hawks.

In December 2016, Corruption Watch lodged criminal complaints against Makwakwa, his girlfriend and Moyane. When the case landed on Khana's desk, he passed the docket to the same brigadier who "investigated" the Prasa matter. This case also disappeared, despite repeated efforts by Corruption Watch to determine if any progress had been made.

Despite Khana's dismal track record, Yolisa Matakata inexplicably entrusted him with the investigation into the biggest corporate fraud perpetrated in South African history. It all started in September 2017 when the international retailer Steinhoff, dual-listed in South Africa and Germany and operating in thirty countries, received an e-mail from its auditors, Deloitte, saying that they refused to sign off on the company's financial results because of "accounting irregularities".

Moneyweb News @Moneyweb, 6 Dec. 2017
Steinhoff CEO Markus Jooste quits. Amid a storm over the global retail giant's accounting irregularities.

Kim Heller @kimheller3, 7 Dec. 2017
#Steinhoff "accounting irregularities" = a code word for white corruption

Wesley Fester @wesleyfestersa, 7 Dec. 2017
When black people or companies are involved it's called corruption. When white people and companies are involved it's called "collusion" or "accounting irregularities".

Steinhoff's shares crashed and it almost immediately lost R282 billion in market value. This erased R15.6 billion of government workers' pensions and social savings that the Public Investment Corporation had invested in Steinhoff because of previously glowing asset and performance assessments. CEO Markus Jooste resigned immediately, and other executives followed.

Almost overnight, Jooste became the face of white monopoly capital and was labelled a kingpin in the so-called Stellenbosch mafia. Nicknamed "The Seagull" because he would "fly in and shit all over his subordinates before flying out again", he was used to flaunting his staggering wealth, extensive portfolio of high-end properties, and collection of racehorses on the front pages of South African newspapers. Jooste denied guilt and said on the day he resigned that he was not aware of any financial irregularities. Later, the Financial Sector Conduct Authority imposed a R122.9 million fine on him for insider trading, which is a criminal offence carrying a prison sentence.

🐦 **Mzi** @DezDelvekio, 13 Dec. 2017
Reading about Markus Jooste's mistress, her lavish lifestyle and numerous properties in her name. The line that killed me is: "She does not appear to work." Sure she does. A whole lot of work.

From the time it was first exposed, the Steinhoff case was almost guaranteed to become a symbol of South Africa's fightback against organised crime, corruption and judicial impunity. It was a major test of the ability of the Hawks to pursue and convict high-level white-collar crime. For crime fighters, it was important to show that the face of corruption was colourless and knew no racial, economic or social boundaries.

By the time the Steinhoff dockets landed on Alfred Khana's desk, Berning Ntlemeza was gone, Cyril Ramaphosa was president-in-waiting and the name of Godfrey Lebeya was being mentioned as the new Hawks head. The Steinhoff case was also Khana's opportunity to flaunt his investigative skills and, after the Prasa fiasco, redeem himself and his reputation. The vast majority of South Africans wanted to see a pale-skinned, billion-rand crook in the dock.

* * *

Ramaphosa's rise to the presidency ignited a firecracker under acting Hawks head Yolisa Matakata's bottom. She had to show the new commander-in-chief that the Hawks still had the ability to crush their prey and rip open the belly of grand corruption in South Africa. And what better way than to bag a Gupta?

Just a day before Ramaphosa's election in February 2018, the Hawks raided the Gupta family home in Johannesburg and arrested eight Gupta associates in connection with the Vrede dairy farm scandal. In Gupta terms, the R280 million farm project in the Free State, also known as the Estina case, was peanuts in comparison to the R49 157 323 233.68 (a figure quoted at the State Capture Commission) that the family nicked and extracted from the state's coffers. But the money came in handy to pay for the klepto-clan's lavish family wedding at Sun City in 2013.

While their glitzy guests, jetted in from India on a chartered Airbus, gorged themselves on French truffle chocolates and slumbered in rooms that cost up to R44 000 per night, 360 kilometres away on the 4 400-hectare Estina farm, eighty black emerging farmers saw their dream of becoming partners and beneficiaries in a dairy farm withering away. The Free State government entered into an agreement with Estina – a Gupta front company that was used in multiple criminal endeavours – to develop the farm and turn it into a laudable model of economic empowerment. The State Capture Commission heard that between July 2012 and May 2016, the provincial government paid R288 million into Estina's account. The Guptas laundered the money to a host of offshore companies and accounts.

Nothing illustrates the annihilation of the Hawks better than Estina. The *Mail & Guardian* had already linked the Guptas to the project in mid-2013. In 2016, the family started selling off their shares in a string of South African businesses – a clear indication that they were planning to leave. In the same year, the Financial Intelligence Centre (FIC) reported suspicious Gupta transactions amounting to R6.8 billion between 2012 and 2016. Still, the Hawks, constipated and wallowing in their own imbecility, did nothing. It was far more important to persecute Pravin Gordhan and the architects of the mythical SARS rogue unit.

🐦 **Sunday Times** @SundayTimesZA, 23 Feb. 2018
Atul Gupta "got the cream" of Vrede dairy project

There were early signs that the state's case was a hastily assembled shambles when the Bloemfontein High Court in May 2018 set aside a restraining order that the Asset Forfeiture Unit (AFU) had obtained against Gupta assets. This order froze R250 million of their goods and chattels – including 43 residential, business and farm properties and a host of luxury cars as well as a helicopter. Judge Phillip Loubser found there was not a reasonable basis to believe that Gupta family members, associates and businesses would be convicted on money-laundering and fraud charges linked to the Estina scam.

What happened next was utterly predictable. In a clear sign that the Hawks had botched another investigation, the NPA withdrew charges against the eight suspects accused of wrongdoing in the Estina project.

* * *

🐦 **Yusuf Abramjee** @Abramjee, 24 May 2018
Congratulations to General Godfrey Lebeya who has been appointed as the Head of the Hawks @SAPoliceService – General Lebeya has years of experience.

🐦 **Daily Maverick** @dailymaverick, 25 May 2018
Directorate for Priority Crime Investigation: Godfrey Lebeya, Hawks' new boss, is bad news for organised crime.

In May 2018, the pedigreed Seswantsho Godfrey Lebeya was appointed as head of the Hawks. This former deputy national commissioner, whose career had been cut short in the mid-2000s because he dared to stand up to Richard Mdluli, was the obvious candidate to resuscitate the Hawks in the post-Zuma era. The task he faced was immense and, on the face of it, almost impossible. Lebeya's biggest challenge was to rid the Hawks of the Ntlemeza cronies, who were hooked like listeria microbes to the intestines of the country's premier crime-fighting unit. If the president's men in the law-enforcement agencies failed to extract the state-capture enablers from their ranks, they would remain diseased, impotent and unstable, and organised and serious crime would continue to reign supreme.

People generally underestimate the challenge that Lebeya faced when he walked into the Promat Building in Silverton, Pretoria. Ntlemeza's devotees held, with rare exceptions, all the key positions in the unit. Most were not qualified or experienced enough, and this made it easy for Ntlemeza to control them. They were at his beck and call and, with rare exceptions, most were too thick to realise how useless they were. With the talent left behind by Lebeya's predecessor, there was no way the unit could successfully investigate big-time corruption, organised crime or state capture. Lebeya had to boot out the provincial Hawks heads that Ntlemeza had put in place and rejuvenate both the commercial crime unit and the serious organised crime unit with new commanders.

🐦 **Annika Larsen** @AnnikaLarsen1, 15 Aug. 2018
Top SAPS leadership here at Parliament. Hawks Head Gen Godfrey Lebeya and Police Minister Bheki Cele to discuss Steinhoff, Verulam, rail arson and restructuring of crime intelligence.

When the top SAPS leadership went to Parliament in August 2018 to report on Steinhoff and other cases, Lebeya told MPs that the Steinhoff investigation was at an early stage and that "no suspects have been identified as yet" but that the Hawks did have "an idea about who the possible suspects are". However, they had "not yet definitively concluded whether those persons are the correct suspects". This was ludicrous. Eight months after the rot in Steinhoff came to light and state pensioners lost investments worth billions, the Hawks had apparently not identified a single suspect. Any trainee constable in the police college could have done so.

Just a month later, Alfred Khana told the parliamentary police committee: "There are three cases, but with no substance to them. The three cases lodged were based on media reports and failed to contain details investigators required, such as who committed what offence in which way and at what cost. Without such details, the elements of a crime were not established." Khana said the Hawks were still waiting for a statement by Steinhoff that set out what went wrong. "There is not a shred of evidence under oath that will allow me to go to anybody to question them."

The inescapable conclusion is that Jacob Zuma had so successfully hollowed out the Hawks that they did not know how or where to start a legitimate investigation. Democratic Alliance (DA) finance spokesperson David Maynier said after Khana's presentation: "I now know why Markus Jooste is hanging out, looking very, very calm in Hermanus. It seems to me that the truth of the matter is that there is no investigation under way by the Hawks and, frankly, no capacity to investigate."

Khana's position in the Hawks had become untenable and plainly embarrassing. But what to do with the troop of devoted Ntlemeza henchmen that skulked in the unit? Consequently, Lebeya brought back to the Hawks the former head of the commercial crime unit, Maj.-Gen. Charles Mosipi. He appointed Mosipi in his previous post, occupied until then by Khana. What to do with Ntlemeza's puppy-in-chief? The Inspectorate Division of the police is generally known as the cemetery for top cops who have fallen out of favour and must be ensconced somewhere in the innards of the force. Its core function is the inspection and evaluation of police stations and specialist units. It also investigates complaints against the SAPS. It has become a dumping ground for rogue policemen because this is probably where they can cause the least damage. One would have thought that at the very least this should have been Khana's next stop. He should have been served with a notice of suspension pending an investigation into his gross incompetence. This was not to be. What happened next boggles the mind.

Organised crime head Sylvia Ledwaba was moved sideways to make space for a new incumbent: Alfred Khana. Yes, the undertaker of the Prasa investigation and the procrastinator of the Steinhoff case became head of the serious organised crime unit of the Hawks. Khana is still the country's chief organised crime fighter, although Ledwaba mercifully called it a day and resigned at the beginning of 2021.

* * *

🐦 Annika Larsen @AnnikaLarsen1, 11 Sept. 2018
Hawks Head Gen Lebeya: we are trying to fill 250 vacant posts and are resuscitating the Anti Corruption Task Team in order to try to deal with high profile commercial crimes.

Upon taking office, Lebeya embarked on a massive recruitment drive to draw back hundreds of officers who had left, to tackle corruption and to conduct more efficient organised crime investigations. These officers, many of whom had been purged, sidelined or forced into retirement during the tenure of Berning Ntlemeza, would staff and head specialised task teams that investigated organised crime.

The Hawks had more vacant posts (2 780) than actual personnel (2 552). The unit's 1 700 investigators were working on more than 18 000 cases, with over 15 000 accused on court rolls countrywide. Among the task teams, the Narcotics Enforcement Bureau had 143 members and 977 vacancies. The National Bureau for Illegal Firearms Control and Priority Violent Crime had 232 members and 926 vacancies.

To Parliament, Lebeya constantly stressed the need to recruit more and better investigators. The problem was always going to be where they would come from. The police service generally is a shadow of its former self, and talent is thinly spread across the investigative units. Where do you find forensic analysts or accountants to staff the commercial crime unit? Who would want to work for the Hawks after Ntlemeza's destructive reign? If you were a qualified accountant – especially if you were black – would you become a cop? The world is your oyster, and much bigger packages and opportunities beckon in the private sector. This means that the Hawks must rope in outside accounting and forensic firms to conduct complicated cases. This expertise comes at a huge cost to the fiscus and is no guarantee of success.

* * *

Lebeya had more success in getting rid of the most noxious provincial Hawks commanders that Ntlemeza had appointed. Gauteng Hawks head Prince "I am 100% Zuma" Mokotedi was the first provincial commander to leave when Lebeya transferred him to head office. He challenged his transfer in the labour court but lost. Mokotedi had shielded an East Rand colonel from facing a police disciplinary hearing into 21 serious charges, including extortion and kidnapping. He not only transferred the colonel to the Hawks but also gave him only a verbal warning and told him to sort out his personal matters. As a result, Mokotedi was found guilty on three charges of misconduct and ordered to forfeit one month's salary. He has since then skulked at the Inspectorate Division of the SAPS.

He has obviously used his downtime to plot his revenge. In January 2022, Mokotedi, acting as a whistle-blower, alerted the police minister and the SAPS top command to the fact that Lebeya had already reached the retirement age of 60 and was therefore occupying his position illegally. This is a ridiculous complaint because police management would have taken Lebeya's age into account when they appointed him.

Two Ntlemeza lackeys – the provincial heads in the Eastern Cape and KwaZulu-Natal – resigned upon facing disciplinary proceedings. Eastern Cape Hawks head Maj.-Gen. Nyameko Nogwanya, appointed by Ntlemeza in January 2016, was suspended in October 2017 for allegedly sexually assaulting a colleague. The suspension was lifted two months later, but he was reportedly ordered to stay at home while continuing to draw his R1.8 million annual salary.

As for KwaZulu-Natal Hawks head Maj.-Gen. Jabulani Zikhali, who shielded Nigerian pastor Timothy "Daddy" Omotoso from arrest in 2017, he had a complaint laid against him by an investigating team. It took the Hawks watchdog Judge Frans Kgomo more than two years to rule on Zikhali. Judge Kgomo recommended that Lebeya act against Zikhali for abusing his power and state resources to aid and abet a criminal suspect in evading arrest. However, Zikhali resigned in December 2019, probably to avoid disciplinary action.

The wheels of justice turn sluggishly, but they do turn. In August 2021, Western Cape Hawks head Maj.-Gen. Portia Khoza was charged with a host of offences. She had allowed a person with a "criminal history" to attend a meeting between the Hawks and the auditor-general, attempted to gain access to Parliament with a false accreditation card, and used a state vehicle without authorisation. She was found to have been dishonest and to have acted without integrity and was fired. The vacancy left by Khoza gave Lebeya the opportunity to appoint a competent and experienced Hawks head in the crime-ridden Western Cape where, in the shadow of Table Mountain, one of the most feared criminal gangdoms in the world flourishes. The Hawks have failed miserably to make any impact on organised crime in the province.

Upon the departure of Khoza, Lebeya promoted the head of the Hawks' serious organised crime unit in the province, Brig. Mushavha-duvha Ramovha, to the position of acting provincial head of the unit.

* * *

🦅 News24 @News24, 12 Nov. 2019
Hawks head: We need to move quicker. The honeymoon is over

After the hollowing-out of the Hawks, Lebeya had a limited pool of talent to choose from in appointing his new provincial heads. Unlike Ntlemeza, he chose mostly experienced cops with solid track records, although several had limited experience in organised crime and complex financial and forensic investigations. Most of Lebeya's provincial appointments went by almost unnoticed except for that of the so-called Porn Cop as provincial Hawks head in the North West. It was a faux pas of prodigious proportions, on the part of both Lebeya and Ramaphosa's Cabinet, which had to concur with the selection. The South African Police Service Act requires a provincial Hawks head to be a "fit and proper person" who serves with "conscientiousness and integrity". Patrick Mbotho is not that person.

Mbotho, then the Western Cape's deputy provincial commissioner, sent porn videos on his cellphone to an official police WhatsApp group in July 2017. Upon realising that he had dispatched smut to his underlings, Mbotho scrambled to message the group, group saying: "Sorry, guys, delete that" and "It's a bad joke to my friend".

Shortly before the incident, News24 reported that Mbotho was twice seen meeting notorious Western Cape underworld figure and murder accused Nafiz Modack, who is said to have high-ranking cops in his pocket. According to evidence given in a bail hearing, Mbotho is one of them. Mbotho, along with the Western Cape Crime Intelligence head, was also accused of running a "rogue unit" in the province, which colluded with the criminal underworld to infiltrate and undermine the police. The existence of the unit was later confirmed in an Independent Police Investigative Directorate investigation.

Mbotho was also accused by a top detective in the Western Cape, Brig. Sonja Harri, of conducting a campaign of harassment against her when he was her superior. According to the *Daily Maverick*, she claimed he humiliated, belittled and undermined her authority and, as a result, compromised her dignity and psychological well-being. Head of the Western Cape family, child and sexual offences unit, Harri is a career cop with an impeccable record and has successfully investigated some of the most high-profile cases in the province, including the brutal murder of Anene Booysen in 2013. Mbotho's harassment caused her "great psychological and emotional trauma" and, as a result, she had to take several months' leave. Her alleged tormentor brought spurious charges against her, but these were eventually withdrawn.

Instead of facing a disciplinary hearing, Patrick Mbotho was instead promoted to become the Hawks head in the North West province. This was not one of Lebeya's greatest achievements.

CHAPTER 8

An ignoramus

OVER JUST MORE than two weeks in June and July 2020, six police generals made their way to the Police Training Academy in Pretoria for a crucial one-on-one interview with Hawks head Godfrey Lebeya, deputy national commissioner Lt.-Gen. Fannie Masemola and a senior official from the Department of Public Service and Administration. They were all vying to become the national deputy head of the Hawks, the cop who would be Lebeya's right-hand person and drive the unit's operations and investigations nationally. The incumbent would be appointed as a lieutenant-general, the second-highest rank in the police service.

Various Hawks officers have described Lebeya to me as incorruptible, credible and administratively competent, but also as overcautious, circumspect and hesitant to make difficult decisions. Said a seasoned Hawks investigator: "Lebeya cannot make decisions. If he had to order toilet paper, it would take him a month to decide between one-ply or two-ply. Let him deal with administration, legal issues, the commissioner, the minister and Parliament. He's good at it. His 2IC must oversee investigations and make sure that dockets are built into prosecutable cases. It must be someone that knows POCA [the Prevention of Organised Crime Act], racketeering, money laundering and the PFMA [Public Finance Management Act]. Only a few cops understand this legislation." When the police advertised the post of deputy Hawks head, the notice required exactly that, a candidate with "applicable training and development in the operational policing of serious organised crime, serious commercial crime and serious corruption investigations".

At the top of Lebeya's list should have been former KwaZulu-Natal Hawks head Johan Booysen and former Gauteng Hawks head Shadrack Sibiya. They are widely regarded as warriors against state capture. Both are no-nonsense lawmen, among the most experienced organised crime fighters that South Africa has on offer. Indeed, I was told that police minister Bheki Cele urged Booysen to apply while Lebeya eyed Sibiya. There were in fact two Hawks posts going vacant at the time: those of national deputy head and provincial head in Gauteng. They both fitted Sibiya and Booysen like a glove.

This was Lebeya's opportunity to make good on his promise of bringing back the Hawks officers who had been lost during the state-capture years. Sibiya's demise in the police was directly linked to his overseeing the murder, kidnapping and assault investigation of Richard Mdluli. As for Booysen, his police career came to an abrupt halt when he investigated Thoshan Panday, a politically connected businessman with links to the Zuma family. Both men were ultimately isolated, targeted, victimised, humiliated, hauled before the courts on trumped-up charges, and forced to incur massive legal costs. Their careers were over.

The State Capture Commission heard evidence about the decimating crusade that Mdluli, Ntlemeza and their cronies in the National Prosecuting Authority (NPA) waged against Booysen and Sibiya to destroy their careers, extract them from the Hawks and have them criminally prosecuted on bogus charges. In the end, their adversaries had to manufacture murder, racketeering and kidnapping allegations against them. These they fed to journalists then employed by the *Sunday Times* to discredit Booysen and Sibiya and, eventually, to their co-conspirators at the NPA to charge the pair criminally. Ultimately, nothing stuck against either of them. Between the two, they left with sixty years of policing experience and irreplaceable institutional memory. In contrast, their replacements were muppets that snogged the state-capture project.

I don't want to put either Booysen or Sibiya on a pedestal and present them as lily-white and unblemished crime fighters. There have been allegations against both, mostly coming from compromised and dodgy characters implicated in wrongdoing or from colleagues with whom they crossed swords. When Zuma's cops hatched their plots to discredit and take out Sibiya and Booysen, they went with a fine-toothed comb through their careers to dig up dirt. There were formidable forces mustered against them and, if there had been a shred of evidence to haul them before a police disciplinary hearing for misconduct, they would have done so. Ntlemeza tried to nail Booysen on scurrilous fraud charges, but he was exonerated every time. So was Sibiya.

Both Sibiya and Booysen continued their crime-fighting careers after leaving the police. Three months after Herman Mashaba became mayor of Johannesburg in August 2016, he appointed Sibiya as the head of forensic investigations at the Johannesburg municipality. By January 2019, Sibiya and his team had uncovered 4 000 fraud and corruption cases involving R24 billion. Booysen became the head of investigations at the Fidelity Security Group, where he specialises in reducing and combating cash-in-transit heists.

After being fired by Ntlemeza in August 2015, Sibiya turned to the Labour Court to get his job back. Judge Mpina Mathebula ruled almost five years later that there had never been a case against him and that his dismissal had been procedurally and substantially unfair. He said that witnesses had "hopelessly lied". Sibiya had asked the court for both compensation and reinstatement to his previous position at the Hawks. The judge said he couldn't give Sibiya his job back but awarded him costs and one year's salary.

When the position of deputy head of the Hawks was advertised in 2020, there was another factor in their favour: their return would be an indication to their former colleagues on the outside that real change was at hand and that it was the appropriate time to return to the Hawks.

As it happened, the selection panel came up with a shortlist of six. Besides Sibiya and Booysen, the candidates were Eastern Cape provincial commissioner Lt.-Gen. Liziwe Ntshinga, the Hawks' commercial crime unit head Maj.-Gen. Charles Mosipi, divisional commissioner of the detective service Lt.-Gen. Tebello Mosikili, and none other than Alfred Khana. The shortlisting of Khana was ludicrous. Did nobody realise that he was a Ntlemeza appointee who had been exposed during the Prasa and Steinhoff investigations as not exactly the Sherlock Holmes of South African policing? He applied for the position, so he obviously rated himself as right up there with the best. His shortlisting cast aspersions on the whole process.

Booysen was by far the most experienced of the candidates. He holds two university degrees and several diplomas. He had attended no less than sixteen police courses and was trained by, among others, the American FBI and the German Federal Criminal Police Office. Before becoming the head of the Hawks in KwaZulu-Natal, Booysen was for thirteen years the head of organised crime in the province, where he dealt with a host of serious economic and organised crime cases. But on 28 August 2020, two months after he was interviewed, Booysen wrote to Lebeya, saying that he was withdrawing his application. He gave no reason for his decision. The Hawks head acknowledged receipt on the same day.

Booysen told me that he became suspicious when the announcement of the preferred candidate began to take so long. He said that when he was appointed as provincial head of the Hawks in KwaZulu-Natal in 2010, it took four months from the interview to the announcement because police minister Nathi Mthethwa meddled in the selection. Booysen disclosed to me that he had received a phone call just before he sent his e-mail to Lebeya withdrawing his application. "The person told me that my possible appointment as deputy Hawks head was a matter of contention at ANC headquarters in Luthuli House. There were two opposing factions: one that wanted me, the other was dead against me. I decided there and then that I don't need a second round of this stuff, and informed Lebeya that I am withdrawing."

I wanted to know: do you think your "whiteness" played a role?

Booysen said: "Why then was I shortlisted? Why did they waste their own time? There is not a single white general in the Hawks."

"Maybe they wanted a woman?"

"Why then shortlist four men? They must have looked at equity before compiling the shortlist."

"And what about your age, seeing that you are already over 60?"

"Again, why shortlist me? Lebeya is over 60. Yes, the retirement age in the police is 60, but this is a contract post for seven years. It would not have been unusual, and I am fit and healthy."

* * *

𝕏 TimesLIVE @TimesLIVE, 9 Sept. 2020
The Directorate for Priority Crime Investigation (Hawks) said on Wednesday Lt-Gen Tebello Constance Mosikili has taken over as its deputy national head.

Instead, the new deputy head who was appointed was the only candidate with no experience in the Hawks, who had never investigated priority economic crimes, and who had never built or compiled a winnable racketeering case. The unit's spokesperson lauded her as an "investigative solutionist" – whatever that is – bringing a "wealth of experience" to the Hawks, a term used with every announcement of every position being filled.

Tebello Mosikili holds the same policing degree as Sibiya and Booysen and has risen through the ranks – from station commander, cluster commander, provincial commander and deputy provincial commissioner for crime detection in Gauteng to national head of the family violence, child protection and sexual offences unit in 2016. Two years later, she became the national head of the detective service. She has also attended a host of courses, but none in the field of organised crime, money laundering or racketeering.

Mosikili's tenure as national head of detectives was, on the face of it, not one of efficiency and accomplishment. The May 2021 report of the parliamentary portfolio committee on police states: "The Detective Services Programme and the Protection and Security Services Programme show erratic performance over the past three financial years. While the Protection and Security Services Programme's performance increased from 79% in 2018/19 to 86% in 2019/20, the Detective Services recorded a significant decline in performance in 2019/20 compared to the previous financial year (2018/19)." Was the selection panel aware of this?

There is no question that Mosikili is highly experienced, but her expertise in fighting organised crime cannot compare with that of Booysen and Sibiya. In 2011, Sibiya joined the Directorate of Special Operations, also known as the Scorpions, as a senior special investigator. After the disbandment of the Scorpions, he was appointed as Hawks head in Gauteng. He has attended a host of courses on organised crime, money laundering, racketeering and asset tracking. Not only are the Hawks in dire need of experience and expertise in their higher echelons, but the SAPS also has a moral obligation to bring the likes of Shadrack Sibiya back into the fold. He is keen to return to the Hawks and has an unblemished police record, and the Labour Court, to which he turned after being dismissed, made it clear that his dismissal had been procedurally and substantially unfair.

In mid-2020, Lebeya was making a host of appointments in the Hawks, including that of provincial head in Gauteng, which was Sibiya's previous position. Why did the Hawks boss not at least offer it to Sibiya? When I prodded Sibiya about not getting the job, he initially said that Mosikili already held the rank of lieutenant-general and that Lebeya probably wanted a woman in the post.

Then, a few weeks later, a top Crime Intelligence officer whispered in my ear: "Bheki Cele doesn't like Sibiya. He doesn't trust him."

"And why not?"

"The minister was fed bullshit and he believed it. For as long as he is there, Sibiya will never get back into the Hawks."

"What bullshit?"

"It's about the death of Senzo, the soccer player. Cele believes that Sibiya is involved in a cover-up of the murder."

"Where does he get that?"

"He was fed that."

"By whom?"

"People who do not want him to come back to the police."

"Who? Crime Intelligence?"

"I don't know, but it's possible. There are still some old Mdluli people here."

* * *

On the night of 26 October 2014, Shadrack Sibiya rushed to Vosloorus on the East Rand to assist in securing the crime scene where Bafana Bafana goalkeeper Senzo Meyiwa had been shot dead. Although this was never a Hawks investigation, it was not unusual for the unit to assist in high-profile cases.

Two males, armed with a pistol and a knife, had burst into the house and demanded money and cellphones. A scuffle ensued between the soccer star and the robber with the firearm. A shot was fired, hitting Meyiwa in the chest. The incident had all the markings of a botched robbery.

When Sibiya arrived at the house, there were people everywhere and the crime scene had already been contaminated. He says he took control by cordoning off the scene and assisted the detectives with their preliminary on-scene investigation. This was his total contribution to the probe. He didn't carry the docket or take any statements, but Berning Ntlemeza suspended Sibiya less than three months after the murder.

As the police investigation dragged on, speculation and conspiracy theories abounded on social media about a planned hit on Meyiwa and a police cover-up that involved Sibiya. Much of it came from a parody Twitter account with the name Man's NOT Barry Roux (@AdvoBarryRoux), named after Paralympian Oscar Pistorius's advocate during his murder trial. In 2018, @AdvoBarryRoux published a slew of allegations against Sibiya. Although @AdvoBarryRoux is a purveyor of fake news and a social media gossipmonger, he has a staggering number of followers, mostly among Ramaphosa adversaries and radical economic transformation (RET) sympathisers like Julius Malema, Floyd Shivambu and Zweli Mkhize.

Man's NOT Barry Roux @AdvoBarryRoux, 25 Feb. 2018
Shadrack Sibiya is a very corrupt and dangerous individual who's no stranger to violent conducts and trust me this is not going to sit well with him until someone is six feet under.

Baba ka Nhlonipho @Nhlanhlalucan, 25 Feb. 2018
Advocate I just hope ur safe man!!!

Man's NOT Barry Roux @AdvoBarryRoux, 25 Feb. 2018
On the Senzo Meyiwa case, I was told by one of the investigating officers that they can not make arrests because the killer is protected also by Shadrack Sibiya and some people at Luthuli house.

Kanyisa M @kay_lunz, 25 Feb. 2018
Go on son, for it is the truth.

In January 2019, News24 exposed @AdvoBarryRoux as a 27-year-old Zambian who lives in a small town south-west of the capital of Lusaka. At the time of the exposé, he had 500 000 hangers-on, a number which has now grown to 1.4 million. He has never produced a shred of evidence for any of his allegations, yet his followers refer to his "exposés" as "dropping files". He is a classic disinformation peddler who takes a true incident and embellishes it with fiction, rumours and next-level bullshit.

𝕏 Julius Sello Malema @Julius_S_Malema, 18 Jan. 2019
Parody Acc of @AdvBarryRoux threatens Stratcom to the point of commissioning an investigation, hayi. Kill them Papa, go deeper.

You might well ask what a parody account on Twitter has to do with the appointment of the deputy head of the Hawks. According to Shadrack Sibiya, everything. I asked the cop if he was aware of Bheki Cele's resistance to his appointment. Days went by before he eventually explained that after Cele's appointment as police minister in February 2018, he spoke to him several times about returning to the Hawks. It seems to have been a done deal, but then, said Sibiya, things changed. "Then, to my surprise, the minister made a sudden 180-degree U-turn on me. I got feedback that he doesn't want me back any longer. I continued to try and engage the minister, but he avoided speaking to me at all costs. I sent him messages to try and understand what I did wrong, but to this day I haven't been able to speak to the minister again."

He said he was convinced that Cele was influenced by allegations that he was protecting Senzo Meyiwa's killer. According to Sibiya, elements in Crime Intelligence spread the rumours that reached the minister's ear. "When they realised that the rendition matter was failing and that I was coming back, they brought this one of Senzo and used it to influence my reappointment at the Hawks." Sibiya said it "pained him deeply" that Cele, whom he respects and trusts, would believe allegations like this.

I asked Johan Booysen if he was aware of this. He said he was, and that he has even discussed the rumours with Cele.

129

"What did you tell the minister?"

"My meetings with the minister are confidential, but I told him it is nonsense that Sibiya is involved in a cover-up. It's impossible because he never investigated the murder."

"And what did he say?"

"I don't want to go into that," he said.

In October 2020, Cele announced the arrest of five suspected killers of Senzo Meyiwa. Among them is a notorious KwaZulu-Natal hitman who has already been convicted of six murders. The case is under way in the High Court.

* * *

South Africans are mostly kept in the dark about appointments in the top echelons of the police. In the case of Godfrey Lebeya, we have no idea who else was on the shortlist to become Hawks head. We do know who was on the shortlist to become deputy head, but we still do not know why Mosikili was preferred over the other candidates. It is a process shrouded in secrecy, with no opportunity for civil society to scrutinise the incumbent or the other candidates.

The South African Police Service Act instructs the minister of police to appoint the head and deputy head of the Hawks in concurrence with the Cabinet. This leaves the process wide open for political abuse. As Judge Edwin Cameron of the Constitutional Court warned in 2014 in a minority judgment dealing with the formation of the Hawks: "The more the institution's mandate threatens political office bearers, the greater is the risk of political weight being brought to bear on its appointments. Where the institution's core mandate is to investigate crime committed by political office bearers, the risk may become severe."

The positions of head and deputy head of the Hawks are far too crucial and sensitive to leave in the hands of politicians. Said Judge Cameron in his minority judgment: "In my view, consolidating the powers to appoint the head [of the Hawks] in the [police] minister and Cabinet erodes the DPCI's independence to a constitutionally impermissible degree."

South Africans don't have faith in politicians, and their mistrust is exacerbated by the meddling of the ruling party in top-level appointments through its cadre deployment committee. This came under the spotlight at the State Capture Commission. During his testimony before the commission, Cyril Ramaphosa, who chaired the ANC deployment committee as Zuma's deputy president, suffered from amnesia and conveniently revealed that minutes of meetings held by him had gone missing.

The ANC furnished the commission with minutes of subsequent committee meetings under the chairmanship of Deputy President David Mabuza. After studying them, commission evidence leader Advocate Paul Pretorius SC presented the deployment committee as an authoritative and shadowy structure that overrode the legally prescribed appointment processes. In 2019, the committee had recommended the names of people to be appointed as Constitutional Court judges, as a judge of the Supreme Court of Appeal and as a judge president in one of the provinces.

ANC members serving on the deployment committee are mostly an odious lot. They lack not only the moral authority to support the appointment of certain judges, for example, but also the knowledge and insight to make any judgment about who should serve in any position in law-enforcement agencies. RET diehards like Lindiwe Sisulu and Nkosazana Dlamini-Zuma serve on the commission, and so does Sfiso Buthelezi, implicated in rampant mismanagement and corruption during his tenure as Prasa board chairperson. Another member, former higher education deputy minister Mdu Manana, is a convicted criminal after pleading guilty to assaulting three women.

Advocate Pretorius said: "Ministers seek permission to proceed, and the Deployment Committee grants permission. Ministers get called to account. Loyalty to the ruling party, party membership and compliance with party prescripts is an issue relevant to the appointment."

* * *

In July 2021, a stern-faced Godfrey Lebeya, accompanied by his deputy Tebello Mosikili, reported the progress of the Hawks' investigations to Parliament. It was more than three years since Lebeya had taken office with great aplomb and ten months since the appointment of his deputy. The advent of the new sheriff and his deputy was supposed to signal a dire day for organised criminals, the end of impunity for the politically connected, and the dawn of justice after an era of state capture and grand corruption. During these years, there had been much hype about the resuscitation of South Africa's premier crime-fighting unit, the appointment of skilled and credible investigators, the weeding-out of the scum that Ntlemeza had appointed, and the promise of widespread prosecutions of state-capture cases.

If anyone had thought that 2021 was going to be the year of putting grand corruption in the dock, Lebeya had a rude awakening for them. He told MPs that the Hawks had a total workload of almost 21 000 cases involving 76 000 charges. But they had to do this work with a staff complement of less than half of the approved posts. This was no different from two years earlier when the Hawks had embarked on a campaign to fill posts.

🐦 **Julian Rademeyer** @julianrademeyer, 15 July 2021
Steinhoff case: going nowhere slowly. The criminal-investigation process has been glacial. Markus Jooste hasn't so much as received a "please call me" from the Hawks, writes @robrose_za via @BusinessLiveSA

MPs also wanted to know from Lebeya why former Steinhoff CEO Markus Jooste had not been asked for a warning statement or even been contacted by the Hawks. It turned out that investigators were still identifying witnesses. The Steinhoff investigation has revealed a crucial faultline in the Hawks' armoury: a lack of money to conduct complicated forensic investigations into corporate fraud and state-capture corruption. The elite unit lacks the expertise to do its own forensic probes and must rely on outside audit companies and firms of attorneys. And that is hugely expensive.

🐦 eNCA @eNCA, 5 Mar. 2021
Retailer Steinhoff gave the Hawks and the NPA R30-million to investigate alleged fraud at the company. This because the state doesn't have funds. Steinhoff says it was approached to assist the state in order to probe the case.

According to the *Financial Mail*, the Hawks and NPA approached Steinhoff to ask if audit firm PwC – which did the original investigation – could assist the state because it lacked the resources to probe such a complex case. They further said they didn't have the money to pay PwC. Steinhoff chipped in. The Hawks and the NPA tried to fudge this peculiarity by pretending that it was not unusual.

In his attempt to build capacity to deal with serious organised crime, commercial crime and corruption, Lebeya appointed a chartered accountant as the head of forensic accounting investigations in October 2021.

Lebogang Matjeke must be one of the youngest generals in the police, having graduated from the University of Pretoria in 2012. She has just a handful of years of experience but was appointed at a salary of around R120 000 per month. It is ridiculous to appoint a civilian with no policing experience as a general, but Matjeke previously worked as an audit manager at Deloitte and the only way Lebeya could lure her to the SAPS was at the salary level and rank of a major-general.

🐦 Peter Armitage @peterarmitage, 8 May 2019
Enron, the world's biggest fraud, was R650bn. At R250bn of fraud related writeoffs, Steinhoff is right up there on the biggest ever ranking table.

I have no doubt that South Africa will see prosecutions in the Steinhoff matter, probably with Markus Jooste in the dock. The case is too big to go away. But if you think that you are going to see Jooste – or for that matter a Gupta, a Molefe or a Montana – in orange attire in the next year or three, dream on. Once the matter is on the court roll, it will consume massive resources from the prosecuting authority. Above all, the table has been set for the likes of Jooste and the state-capture looters to embark on a Zuma-like Stalingrad defence and frustrate justice for years to come.

🐦 **BusinessLIVE** @BusinessLiveSA, 17 July 2021
Forget Zuma, it was Gary Porritt who pioneered Stalingrad

Business tycoon Gary Porritt was arrested after the infamous Tigon corruption scandal in December 2002. Before Tigon imploded, it was, like Steinhoff, one of the top companies on the Johannesburg Stock Exchange. The state alleged that Porritt siphoned off R160 million invested in his scheme to his business entities. A company executive, Sue Bennett, was arrested a year later. The two eventually faced 3 160 counts involving contraventions of the Income Tax Act, the Companies Act and the Exchange Control Act, as well as racketeering and fraud.

Porritt and Bennett used every trick in the book and spent millions in legal fees to delay the trial. They dismissed their legal team, applied for legal aid, applied for the judge to be recused, applied for the prosecutors to be recused, missed court dates because of illness, and used the SARS "rogue unit" as part of their defence to derail proceedings. Over the past fifteen years, three trial judges have handled the case while seventeen judges have heard some element of it. The first witness in the trial only testified in September 2016 – and the state's case is still far from finished. In March 2018, Judge Ramarumo Monama described Porritt's tactics as "unjust, cruel and primitive" and said they deserved to be rooted out. The trial has cost the state millions. Because of the complexity of the matter, the state had to employ the services of an advocate in private practice to assist the prosecution.

The only justice in this case may be that Porritt's bail was revoked in June 2017 after he failed to appear for his trial. He has ever since languished in a single cell in the Johannesburg Correctional Centre, otherwise known as Sun City.

* * *

In 2022, Godfrey Lebeya and Cyril Ramaphosa celebrated the fourth anniversaries of their appointments as, respectively, the head of the Hawks and the president of the country. They both assumed office with great aplomb and personified the hope of a new dawn for the Hawks and the country, and the return of the rule of law. But few leaders have ever been dealt a worse hand than Ramaphosa and Lebeya. Ramaphosa inherited looted state-owned enterprises, entrenched corruption, broken law-enforcement agencies, failed service delivery, rampant unemployment and an unsustainable fiscal trajectory. And then, two years into his presidency, he was bombarded by Covid-19. As we have seen, Lebeya inherited a hollowed-out police unit where skilled and dedicated cops had been replaced by pliant and inept lackeys who were paid not to pursue certain prosecutions.

Both men did some things right. For his part, Lebeya brought a sense of professionalism to the Hawks. He managed to rid the unit of crucial appointments made by the state-capture command and brought back limited skills and expertise. It is not nearly enough, but it would be wrong to say that nothing has happened under his watch.

It was unthinkable during the Zuma era that Bongani Bongo, one of the president's state security ministers, would find himself in the dock, implicated in dubious land deals in Mpumalanga amounting to almost R124 million. Even more unimaginable was that ANC secretary-general Ace Magashule, once the second most powerful person in the ANC and the face of the RET faction's fightback campaign against

Ramaphosa and his administration, might have a possible future in orange uniform. Magashule faces 21 charges of fraud, corruption and money laundering linked to a R255 million tender to audit and eradicate hazardous asbestos roofs in the Free State during his tenure as premier. Magashule is joined in the dock by fourteen co-accused, who include top Free State government officials and a prominent businessman. The ANC suspended Magashule and eventually forced him to step down as secretary-general. Another Zuma crony and confidante, former eThekwini mayor Zandile Gumede, is also in the dock for money laundering, fraud and corruption.

🐦 **Carl Niehaus** @niehaus_carl, 30 Nov. 2021
Today uMama #ZandileGumede is again, for the umpteenth time, appearing in the Durban High Court, in the perpetually postponed & politically motivated trial against her. This harassment must end now! Together with many other outraged South Africans I say: #HandsOffZandileGumede!

Finally, South Africa managed to get several Gupta associates in the dock. Lebeya had to pick up the pieces left behind by his predecessor when the Hawks bungled the R288 million Estina farm scam and allowed the Guptas to slip through their fingers. Businessman Iqbal Sharma was nabbed in June 2021 in connection with a R24.9 million feasibility study in the Free State that formed a precursor to the Estina contract. He is among a group of 17 accused who, at the time of writing, were facing charges of contravening the Public Finance Management Act, fraud and money laundering. He was released on bail of R500 000.

Sharma's role in state capture stretches far beyond the Estina project. He joined former Transnet group chief executives Brian Molefe and Siyabonga Gama and chief financial officer Anoj Singh as the "primary architects" of state capture at the state-owned enterprise. Through the Guptas' influence over Jacob Zuma and public enterprises ministers Lynne Brown and Malusi Gigaba, the family ensured the appointment of Sharma to the board of Transnet, where he ultimately served as the chair of the acquisitions and disposal committee. This was a key moment in the Guptas' assumption of control over Transnet's board and top management while they weakened its internal controls and oversight structures to illegally siphon billions of rand to their companies. Transnet became the hub of the Guptas' looting frenzy as companies linked to them and their associate, Salim Essa, were irregularly awarded Transnet contracts worth a staggering R41.2 billion in total. This made Transnet the primary target of state capture, accounting for 72 per cent of all government and state-owned entity contracts linked to state capture.

The State Capture Commission heard evidence that Zuma insisted on the appointment of Gama as Transnet chief executive. Shortly before his promotion, Gama donated R500 000 towards the Jacob G Zuma Foundation on Transnet's behalf.

Following an investigation by the Hawks and the NPA's Investigating Directorate (ID), Siyabonga Gama, Gupta associate Eric Wood and three others, including two Transnet executives, were arrested and hauled before court on charges of fraud, corruption and money laundering amounting to R93 million. The alleged crimes were linked to Transnet's acquisition of 1 064 locomotives. Alongside them in the dock is alleged Gupta fixer Kuben Moodley, who was arrested in September 2021 as he was about to board a flight for Dubai.

The arrests of Brian Molefe and Anoj Singh were imminent in the case.

🐦 **Eusebius McKaiser** @Eusebius, 30 Aug. 2022
Life of Brian: Molefe's fall from executive darling to court room 10

More than seven years after Transnet had awarded the R41.2 billion in contracts to companies linked to the Guptas and their associate Salim Essa, state-capture kingpins Brian Molefe and Anoj Singh appeared in the commercial crimes court at Palm Ridge on Johannesburg's East Rand in connection with the R93 million corruption and fraud case linked to the procurement of the 1 064 locomotives. Two directors of the Gupta-linked firm Regiments Capital were charged with them.

Once one of South Africa's brightest financial stars and tipped as a future finance minister, Molefe cut a lonesome and dejected figure in the dock. He was by all reports a diligent civil servant and was before his appointment as Telkom CEO the chief executive of the Public Investment Corporation (PIC) where he oversaw the management of billions of rand in investments. Along came the Guptas, who ultimately dictated his career path at both Transnet and Eskom, where he later also became the CEO. Judge Zondo said that Molefe, Singh and Gama were at the centre of the "Gupta racketeering enterprise". Molefe played a pivotal role in helping the Guptas to "completely capture Eskom". The chief justice also found that there were "reasonable grounds" to believe that Molefe accepted bags of cash from members of the Gupta family.

Whether he is convicted or not, Molefe will be remembered for his award-winning performance in 2016 when then Public Protector Thuli Madonsela found in her state-capture report that Molefe and Ajay Gupta, the eldest of the three brothers, had made 58 telephone calls to each other at the height of the family's capture of Eskom. Cellphone tracking records indicated that Molefe had been at or near the Guptas' Saxonwold, Johannesburg, compound 19 times between August and November 2015.

Molefe broke down in tears and said: "There's a shebeen there, two streets away from the Gupta(s). I will not admit or deny that I've gone to the shebeen. But there is a shebeen there."

He had the same hangdog expression then as in August 2022 when he shuffled into the dock.

𝕏 **Mail & Guardian** @mailandguardian, 19 July 2022
Can the state deliver the Guptas?

There is one question on everyone's lips: will we ever see Ajay, Atul or Rajesh in the dock? State-capture linchpins Rajesh and Atul Gupta were arrested in Dubai on 2 June 2022, four months after Interpol issued a red notice for them on charges of fraud and money laundering linked to the R24.9 million feasibility study in the Free State. If they were to be extradited to South Africa, they would join their associate Iqbal Sharma and the others in the Bloemfontein High Court.

At the time of the writing of this book, the NPA was preparing the extradition request, which must be submitted within 60 days of the arrest of the Guptas. The prosecuting authority has also requested statements of Gupta bank accounts in the United Arab Emirates, which prosecutors hope will show that the final destination of the R24.9 million was a Gupta company in that country.

* * *

Not even the most diehard supporter of either Ramaphosa or Lebeya can claim that the past four years have fulfilled the promise or the euphoria of the first few months after their appointment. South Africa is more unsafe than ever, making a joke of Ramaphosa's pledge that violent crime would be halved in a decade. One of the president's biggest failures has been his inability to clean up the police and intelligence services. Most political analysts don't give the president a scorecard of much more than five out of ten.

Although Lebeya cannot be blamed for the soaring crime rate, he must take responsibility for failing to engineer the return of lost expertise and experience to the Hawks and for attempting to address state-capture crimes with half the posts at the unit vacant. He has, as we have seen, made some questionable appointments of old Ntlemeza lackeys to key positions in the unit and protected a policing ignoramus like Alfred Khana, whose contract expires in three years' time. One wonders who is going to take over from him.

In the case of Ramaphosa, South Africans are tired of the so-called long game. The nation wants results. And in the case of Lebeya, people have had enough of tough talk. They want action.

Was the arrest of Brian Molefe and Anoj Singh the spark that we had all been waiting for – one that will hopefully end in a reunion of the Saxonwold shebeen regulars at the Kgosi Mampuru prison?

CHAPTER 9

Blue boy in a pumpkin suit

🐦 **SowetanLIVE** @SowetanLIVE, 29 Sept. 2020
It took 22 years, but Richard Mdluli has gone from crime intelligence boss to jailbird

29 SEPTEMBER 2020 was a day that nobody thought would ever arrive: the chickens had come home to roost for the man who had once been perched like a noxious spider at the top of Jacob Zuma's septic web of deceit, delinquency and depravity. The president's pet cop had been untouchable and the swagger in his step had flaunted his omnipotence. But now it was payback time. Richard Mdluli's dirty tricks had ended the careers of straight-up policemen like Anwa Dramat, Shadrack Sibiya and Johan Booysen because they resisted the state-capture project. He turned Crime Intelligence into a family enterprise, circumnavigated the globe at taxpayers' expense and reduced the unit's crime-fighting ability to rubble.

But several years on, Judge Ratha Mokgoatlheng reduced Mdluli to a mere mortal in the Gauteng High Court when he found him guilty on four counts of intimidation, two counts of kidnapping, two counts of common assault and two counts of assault with intent to do grievous bodily harm. Mdluli begged the judge for mercy and to spare him jail time. I am a father and I don't want my children to grow up without me, he pleaded, and, besides that, I have a bad back that requires medical attention.

Mokgoatlheng was having none of it, and besides sending Mdluli to prison for five years, he denied him the right to appeal against his sentence. As the general prepared for his first night behind bars, he swore that the charges had been fabricated and that he hadn't received a fair trial. He was still suffering from delusions of grandeur.

🐦 **News24** @News24, 29 Sept. 2020
Richard Mdluli likens himself to Mandela, says he will petition SCA to appeal 5-year jail term.

The labyrinth of state capture always leads back to Richard Mdluli, one of the earliest Zuma keepers, who not merely captured Crime Intelligence but also played a major role in preparing the Hawks for its seizure. Much has been written about Mdluli over the past decade. He stands alongside Arthur Fraser, Berning Ntlemeza, Khomotso Phahlane, Prince Mokotedi, Nomgcobo Jiba, Lawrence Mrwebi, Shaun Abrahams, Thulani Dlomo, Tom Moyane and Jonas Makwakwa as Jacob Zuma's keepers-in-chief in the law-enforcement agencies. They were key players in the Zumatocracy who laid waste to their respective agencies to cast a legal shield around the president, his family and his cronies.

Mdluli was one of the earliest state-capture enablers and was almost secretly appointed as the divisional commissioner of Crime Intelligence just weeks after Zuma had come to power in May 2009. Normally, the heads of police divisions are selected by the commissioner of police, advised by an interview panel of top policemen. Politicians are for obvious reasons supposed to stay out of the process. But in 2009, police minister Nathi Mthethwa reportedly hijacked the process and convened a panel of pro-Zuma ministers, including state security minister Siyabonga Cwele and deputy minister of home affairs Malusi Gigaba, to interview Mdluli. There wasn't a single police official on the panel. This would become the norm for appointments to the law-enforcement agencies during the Zuma era.

Mdluli had hardly taken office when the *Sowetan* reported that he had been implicated in murder when commanding the Vosloorus police station in the late 1990s. He allegedly killed his girlfriend's lover and was complicit in kidnapping and assault. A case was opened but the docket disappeared. Following the *Sowetan* exposé, Hawks head Lt.-Gen. Anwa Dramat appointed his Gauteng Hawks head Shadrack Sibiya and Hawks colonels Kobus Roelofse and Piet Viljoen to investigate. They discovered the lost dockets gathering dust at the Vosloorus police station and reopened the case. In March 2011 Mdluli and his henchman, Lt.-Col. Mthembeni Mthunzi, were charged with the killing of Oupa Ramogibe, the husband of the woman with whom he had had an affair.

With Mdluli under siege, Crime Intelligence officers told the Hawks that their commander and his cronies had looted the unit's secret services account, then worth about R250 million annually. This account has been at the centre of instability in Crime Intelligence. It is supposed to fund covert operations and undercover agents, but it became nothing but a piggy bank for Richard Mdluli, his cronies and some of his successors. In May 2011 Mdluli was suspended and, four months later, charges of fraud, corruption, theft and money laundering were added to his docket – all linked to his alleged abuse of the Crime Intelligence slush fund.

It soon emerged that Mdluli was armoured and protected from the very top. He had a toxic and mutually beneficial relationship with acting prosecutions boss Nomgcobo Jiba, which dated back to the latter half of the 1980s. When Jiba's husband, also a senior National Prosecuting Authority (NPA) prosecutor, was suspended and charged with fraud, Mdluli had a hand in arresting the prosecutor handling the case on trumped-up charges. When Mdluli himself was charged, it was probably now her turn to refuse to prosecute him. In December 2011, Zumalinquents in the NPA withdrew the fraud and corruption charges against Mdluli as well as Maj.-Gen. Solly Lazarus, chief financial officer of the Crime Intelligence secret services account, and Col. Hein Barnard of Crime Intelligence supply-chain management. Prosecutors withdrew the murder charges two months later, and Mdluli was reinstated in March 2012.

🐦 Richard Mdluli @MdluliRichard, 16 May 2012
Johnnie Walker Blue after a hard day at work.

🐦 Max du Preez @MaxduPreez, 18 May 2012
I have a coded message for spook-cop Richard Mdluli: 37OH-SSV-O773H (don't get it, general? Try reading it upside down)

Two months later, however, the South African Police Service (SAPS) instituted disciplinary charges against Mdluli and, by the end of May 2012, he was suspended for a second time. He overturned his suspension in the Labour Court in June 2012. Mdluli insisted on going back to work, but the civil society organisation Freedom Under Law turned to the High Court to prevent him from returning to his position. Judge Ephraim Makgoba interdicted Mdluli from executing his duties as a policeman.

🐦 Nickolaus Bauer @NickolausBauer, 3 June 2012
#Mdluli suspended – reinstated – suspended – reinstated – suspended – reinstated – suspended.

In September 2013, Judge John Murphy ordered that the charges against Mdluli be reinstated and that police commissioner Gen. Riah Phiyega – another of Zuma's disastrous appointments in law enforcement – had to proceed with the disciplinary cases against him, which in the meantime had been aborted. When the Supreme Court of Appeal confirmed the High Court ruling, the NPA had to charge Mdluli and his co-accused, and in August 2014 they appeared for the first time in the commercial crimes court.

🐦 **eNCA** @eNCA, 17 Apr. 2014
BREAKING: Supreme Court of Appeal rules fraud & corruption charges against former crime intelligence boss Richard Mdluli must be reinstated

🐦 **News24** @News24, 6 July 2015
Mdluli walks free

Once again, Zuma cronies came to his rescue. Just days after Zuma had appointed Shaun Abrahams as the new prosecutions boss, the NPA struck all fraud and corruption charges against Mdluli and his co-accused off the roll because of "outstanding investigations". They blamed the fiasco on Phiyega, saying she was unwilling to declassify documents that the prosecutor needed to conclude the case.

In the meantime, an inquest court had found that neither Mdluli nor his co-accused could be conclusively linked to the death of Oupa Ramogibe. He was thus also off the hook for murder, though not for kidnapping and assault, as the court made no findings about those charges. By the time the kidnapping and assault case against Mdluli and Mthunzi got under way in the Johannesburg High Court in June 2015, the Crime Intelligence chief was on suspension, receiving his full salary. The SAPS never brought any disciplinary case against Mdluli. He sat at home throughout the Zuma years watching some of South Africa's top law-enforcement crime fighters perish in their quest to prosecute him.

* * *

In September 2019, a witness appeared before Justice Raymond Zondo at the State Capture Commission to testify about years of looting and nepotism at Crime Intelligence. A former accountant who dealt with Crime Intelligence's secret account, Col. Dhanajaya Naidoo spoke from an undisclosed location and from behind a screen. He also has a new identity and is no longer known by his original name and surname. Naidoo is a family member of Solly Lazarus and had access to the innermost secrets of the looting cabal. Naidoo himself nicked R100 000 from the secret account, but when confronted by Col. Kobus Roelofse in 2011, he decided to cooperate, turned state witness and ratted on his superiors. He and his family were whisked away under a witness protection programme, relocated and given new identities.

When giving evidence about Mdluli to the State Capture Commission, Naidoo and Roelofse painted a picture of a man no better than a tattooed and gun-toting Cape Flats ghetto gangster except that he flaunted three stars and crossed swords on the epaulettes of his blue uniform and had the ear of the highest authority in the land. Feared and untouchable, Mdluli was, according to former Hawks head Berning Ntlemeza, destined to become police commissioner.

Naidoo took the commission on a journey through Mdluli's debauchery. The general had hardly taken office when Lazarus stole R100 000 from the secret services account for Mdluli and his wife to buy two business-class air tickets to China to visit their daughter, who was studying in that country at the time. The secret fund paid for everything, including the couple's shopping spree and sightseeing.

On Mdluli's next overseas trip, this time to Singapore to buy surveillance equipment for the unit, he took his girlfriend, whom he later married. A host of Crime Intelligence cronies joined the junket, all at taxpayers' expense. They were in Singapore for nine days, four hours of which were spent in an electronics shop. Mdluli and his crew spent almost R1.2 million on international travel in just more than a year.

🐦 **Stoned Advocate** @MoSativa, 30 Sept. 2019
So Naidoo was General Mdluli's butler? Or maid? Or errand boy??

🐦 **Gaopalelwe Phalaetsile** @Gao_Phala, 30 Sept. 2019
Naidoo says after Mdluli was appointed as head of Crime Intelligence his work at the unit became minimal as he became their lackey, he says he was at their back and call.

Mdluli helped himself to an array of luxury cars – five of them at a cost of more than R3 million – while the secret account leased him and his family safe houses stocked with groceries. Crime Intelligence also rented one of Mdluli's properties as a safe house for the unit.

In January 2011, police commissioner Bheki Cele approved a request from Mdluli to appoint an additional 250 undercover managers and agents to infiltrate organised crime syndicates and gather evidence which "cannot be obtained through normal and conventional investigation methods". It also made provision for the appointment of an additional four brigadiers and thirty colonels. This was typical Mdluli bullshit – nothing more than a smokescreen for him and his cronies to appoint their wives, girlfriends, sons and daughters in senior positions in the unit. He handed Lazarus, who was responsible for the appointment of agents and informers from the secret fund, a list of family members who had to be employed. The Mdluli Seven had between them no knowledge or experience of the intelligence world. Both Mdluli's former wife and his new wife were appointed as colonels, his daughter as a lieutenant-colonel and his son as a captain. They all received cars, ranging from Audis to BMWs and Mercedes-Benzes.

🐦 **Team News24** @TeamNews24, 1 Oct. 2019
#StateCaptureInquiry: Naidoo has told the Commission that seven of Richard Mdluli's family members – appointed as agents – cost Crime Intelligence approximately R5 million in salaries, claims, vehicles, safe houses etc. between March 2010 & Oct 2011.

🐦 **State Capture Commission** @StateCaptureCom, 2 Oct. 2019
Naidoo is still talking us through cars that they (himself, General Lazarus, and General Mdluli) were fraudulently buying left, right, and centre.

Lazarus himself appointed twelve of his family members and friends as agents. Other top policemen followed suit. The most preposterous appointment at Crime Intelligence was that of convicted Durban drug dealer Panganathan "Timmy" Marimuthu and eight of his family members and girlfriends. None of them had any intelligence or policing background. The South African taxpayer forked out millions upon millions for the upkeep of the Marimuthu mob for just one reason: his closeness to police commissioner Bheki Cele.

Because of his criminal record, Marimuthu didn't qualify to become a police officer. That is why he was appointed as an informer at a salary of R50 000 per month. He was given a BMW X5 with blue lights while Crime Intelligence rented several of his properties – which were uninhabitable – for R250 000 monthly. Marimuthu's wife was appointed as a colonel, his daughter and son-in-law as lieutenant-colonels, his brother as a colonel, his niece as a captain and two of his girlfriends as clerks. The secret account paid R37 000 for the replacement of Timmy's dental crowns while his daughter claimed R50 000 for the delivery of her child.

The provincial head of Crime Intelligence in KwaZulu-Natal at the time, Maj.-Gen. Deena Moodley, wasn't told about the appointment of Marimuthu, his family or his girlfriends. He only discovered this when Marimuthu's son-in-law was arrested for driving around Umhlanga Rocks in a Crime Intelligence BMW X5 with blue lights flashing. He was taken to the Durban Central police station where he identified himself as a lieutenant-colonel in Crime Intelligence. He refused to show identification but was released after a call "from the top".

Moodley was astonished. The KwaZulu-Natal branch of Crime Intelligence was at the time conducting an extensive organised crime investigation into Marimuthu. He was allegedly still involved in drug smuggling and was suspected of importing so-called grey cars into South Africa. Marimuthu didn't have a licence to import these cheap second-hand cars.

Mdluli ordered Moodley to stop investigating Marimuthu. The one day he was a suspect in an organised crime investigation, the next day he was untouchable. None of Marimuthu's family members ever reported for duty or submitted any reports, yet they had access to top-secret intelligence.

Judge Raymond Zondo found in his final report that fraud, corruption, nepotism and theft at Crime Intelligence were so rife that these activities could be described as looting. He fingered Mdluli and Lazarus as controlling the criminal enterprise and said it was impossible to know why they had embarked on a "life of crime" because they chose not to testify. "Where secret state funds fall under the control of scoundrels, only strong oversight institutions can protect the public against the harm that such scoundrels can inflict." Judge Zondo said that NPA advocates Lawrence Mrwebi and Nomgcobo Jiba's withdrawal of charges against Mdluli "gives rise to a suspicion that there was something more sinister behind the decision than mere professional incompetence and ineptitude".

* * *

Crime Intelligence has over the past decade performed not even the most basic of its obligations and duties: identifying and infiltrating crime syndicates, surveilling and tagging their members and mapping organised crime trends. A unit of 7 000 men and women with an annual budget of around R4.5 billion, Crime Intelligence has for more than a decade been so compromised, politicised and captured that it has descended into a dysfunctional muddle where there is little honour, no moral compass and zero integrity.

Crime Intelligence, alongside the State Security Agency (SSA) and the Hawks, inexplicably failed to act against the Guptas ravishing South Africa's state-owned enterprises. As state capturers laundered billions to accounts around the world, Crime Intelligence members did bugger-all except to pillage and to plot one another's downfall. Their intelligence operations were designed as disinformation campaigns in favour of Jacob Zuma and against his perceived enemies.

If Berning Ntlemeza bulldozed the Hawks, Richard Mdluli sledge-hammered Crime Intelligence into rubble. Under him, Crime Intelligence descended into a pro-Zuma dirty-tricks unit while the incidence of organised crime, cash-in-transit heists and robberies skyrocketed.

In the nine years after Mdluli was suspended, he was succeeded by more than ten heads and acting heads of Crime Intelligence. Every one of them, with perhaps the exception of Peter Jacobs, made a grand mess of their job and dragged the unit deeper into the gutter. Chris Ngcobo didn't last long because he lied about having a matric certificate – not that it affected his standing in the ruling party's deployment committee because he was shortly afterwards appointed as South Africa's ambassador to Mali. Ngcobo was followed by Maj.-Gen. Bongiwe Zulu, an educationist with no experience of intelligence. She was reportedly not fit for the position because she didn't have a security clearance. She held on until 2015 before she was sent to the police's research division.

✯ Allan Taylor @AllanTaylor2011, 22 Oct. 2013
So General Bongiwe Zulu is acting for the suspended acting Head of Crime Intelligence who was acting for the suspended original Head.

Disgraced police commissioner Khomotso Phahlane then appointed Maj.-Gen. Agnes Makhele, head of crime intelligence in the Free State, to command the unit. She was soon embroiled in controversy and accused of running a rogue counterintelligence campaign to derail the Independent Police Investigative Directorate's investigation into Phahlane. She was criminally charged in 2018.

✯ Team News24 @TeamNews24, 11 Jan. 2018
Head of Crime Intelligence in the Free State, Major General Agnes Makhele is now appearing in the Pretoria Mag Court. The matter will be remanded for disclosure.

Jacaranda News @JacaNews, 12 May 2021
#StateCaptureInquiry: Dintwe has told the commission that the nepotism practice was also rife in the Free State. He said Major General Agnes Makhele told him children and girlfriends of officials were appointed because they were "well-bred"

Next was Maj.-Gen. Pat Mokushane, appointed in June 2017 in an acting capacity. He lasted only a few months because he did not have a security clearance and allegedly tried to obtain one illegally. According to *City Press*, he also had a criminal record.

Team News24 @TeamNews24, 15 June 2018
BREAKING: Former acting Crime Intelligence boss Pat #Mokushane arrested for corruption, fraud and money laundering.

In August 2017, four months before the ANC's elective conference at Nasrec in Johannesburg, Zuma appointed his former chief body-guard, Maj.-Gen. Bhoyi Ngcobo, as acting Crime Intelligence divisional commissioner. The general allegedly played a pivotal role in attempting to siphon off millions of rand from the secret services account to pay for votes at the elective conference in December of that year.

At the beginning of 2018, four Crime Intelligence generals submitted a "collective grievance" to the inspector-general of intelligence (IGI) about the "victimization, intimidation, bullying and abuse of power" within the unit, which had resulted in a "breakdown of service delivery, discipline and the hampering of operations". The aggrieved parties included head of intelligence collection Maj.-Gen. Deena Moodley, head of intelligence support Maj.-Gen. Feroz Khan, head of the secret services account Maj.-Gen. Obed Nemutanzhela, and head of counter-intelligence Maj.-Gen. Dumezweni Zimu. They claimed that Bhoyi Ngcobo was a law unto himself and that the situation had become "unbearable".

Moodley and Nemutanzhela were at the time suspended for alleged fraud and corruption and were sitting at home. They claimed that police regulations stipulated that a disciplinary hearing had to be held within 60 days of an officer's suspension. According to their list of grievances, Ngcobo had failed to act against them. They then went back to work but were denied access to their offices. They were suspended once again.

In the meantime, Ngcobo had appointed acting commanders in their posts, in the case of Moodley the notorious Brig. Nkosana "Killer" Ximba, a close Mdluli ally, even though he had a criminal record. He was promoted from constable to colonel in one day.

The complainants also claimed that another Ngcobo ally, Brig. Leonora Phetlhe, had obtained a false security clearance for herself and former acting divisional commissioner Pat Mokushane. An amount of R50 000 was transferred to her bank account for organising refreshments for a three-day police conference. She didn't pay any of the money back.

The four generals demanded the immediate removal and replacement of Ngcobo and said he should return to protection services. He didn't have the "competency, skills and knowledge" required for the post of divisional commissioner. According to the complainants: "The majority of the senior officers are disillusioned with the current toxic environment of the division."

* * *

🐦 Min of Police: Mr Fearfokkol @MbalulaFikile, 17 Jan. 2018
I wish to announce that Lt. Gen Richard Mdluli who held the position of Divisional Commissioner will be relieved from his duties. CI has seen 12 Acting Divisional Commissioners, this alarmed me greatly when I resumed my duties at the Police. It's now fixed.

In an attempt to fix the rot at Crime Intelligence, and especially to deal with its problems of leadership, minister of police Fikile Mbalula (who then went by the name of Mr Fearfokkol on his Twitter account) announced in January 2018 that Richard Mdluli would be relieved of his duties. Most often when Fikile Mbalula holds a press conference, tweets or opens his mouth, he scores an own goal – such as saying that Crime Intelligence was "now fixed". This is why it boggles the mind that any president – even Jacob Zuma – could have elevated Mr Fearfokkol to police minister or, in the case of Cyril Ramaphosa, transport minister. But then, Mbalula is the ultimate political survivor: a Zuma-ite the one day, a Ramaphosa disciple the next.

Mbalula's negotiation of the early departure of Richard Mdluli probably counts as one of his rare achievements, even though the state paid the policeman just more than R8 million for the almost seven years he sat at home doing fokkol. Included in his package was a production bonus; moreover, he never faced a single disciplinary charge. Mbalula paid Mdluli an additional R4.2 million for leaving early, and the general galloped into the sunset with full pension benefits.

But the real hero of the story of Mdluli's comeuppance is Hawks colonel Kobus Roelofse, who held on to Mdluli's docket for the best part of a decade and refused to let go. After the NPA struck Mdluli's case off the roll in 2015 when police commissioner Riah Phiyega would not declassify documents implicating him in crime, Mdluli must have thought his prospects of being cleared were good. The evidence for the corruption and fraud charges was safely entombed in the bowels of police headquarters in Pretoria. As for the kidnapping and assault charges, these were moving at a snail's pace, and Mdluli always thought he had the political backing to beat them.

But Mdluli didn't count on the tenacity of the soft-spoken and unassuming Col. Roelofse. Testifying before the State Capture Commission, Roelofse told Judge Raymond Zondo that Berning Ntlemeza once summoned him for a briefing about the Mdluli matter. "He got very perturbed with me, very angry when I explained as to what we have uncovered. He asked, 'Why are we investigating? You didn't do this with [Vlakplaas death squad commander] Eugene de Kock. So, why are you doing this in our time to eat?'" Roelofse said it was clear that Ntlemeza didn't want him to continue, but "in the absence of him giving me a direct instruction, I was going to continue with the investigation".

It took Kobus Roelofse eight years to declassify the documents he needed to complete the docket that enabled the NPA to reinstate nineteen charges of corruption, fraud, theft and defeating the ends of justice against Mdluli, Lazarus and Barnard. The case revolves around the looting of the Crime Intelligence secret account for cash, cars, air tickets and travel expenses and the securing of jobs for pals, girlfriends and family. The extent of the debauchery knew no limits: the secret account also paid for jewellery, perfume, clothing, luggage and electronic gear. If convicted, Mdluli, who is now in his early sixties, will be an old man by the time he is released.

Roelofse said one after the other Zuma-appointed police commissioner and Crime Intelligence head ignored his requests to declassify the documents. But he kept on knocking on doors, and after 2 825 days (yes, he counted) police commissioner Khehla Sitole relented and released the evidence. Kobus Roelofse, a police veteran with more than three decades' experience in investigating complex commercial crimes, is a silent hero of state capture. In the face of threats and intimidation, he upheld law and order and vowed to bring a state plunderer to book.

* * *

𝕏 News24 @News24, 29 Mar. 2018
From suspended WC cop to top police spy – the rise of Peter Jacobs.

A month after Mbalula engineered the departure of Mdluli, Crime Intelligence acquired a new head in the person of Peter Jacobs, then the golden boy of South African policing. By this stage, Jacob Zuma was gone and the new administration could appoint its own man to clean up Crime Intelligence. Jacobs had all the credentials. A former political prisoner who spent several years on Robben Island – with Bheki Cele, incidentally – he joined the police in 1995 and rose rapidly through the ranks to become Western Cape deputy provincial commissioner. He was also a rare bright light at Crime Intelligence as provincial head in the Western Cape, where he participated in some of the biggest criminal investigations in that province. Jacobs holds a master's degree in corporate security from Cranfield University in the United Kingdom – a far cry from the incumbents with school-leaving qualifications who infested Crime Intelligence over the years.

Jacobs shot to fame when he and the Western Cape's most avid anti-gang crusader, Maj.-Gen. Jeremy Vearey, embarked on an investigation to find the source of the guns that were streaming into the Western Cape, fuelling the gang violence on the Cape Flats. They started sifting through thousands of ballistic shooting reports and discovered that as far back as 2010, guns that had found their way to the ganglands of the province had been altered by the same gunsmith. The hunt began to find the supplier of the guns.

Named Operation Impi, the investigation became a rare police success story and South Africa's biggest firearm smuggling investigation to date. It blew the lid off a criminal enterprise headed by the provincial head of firearms control in Gauteng, Col. Christiaan Prinsloo.

🐦 **News24** @News24, 21 June 2016
Ex-cop gets 18 years for stealing, reselling guns to Cape gangsters

He sold thousands of police and army guns to gangsters in the Western Cape, KwaZulu-Natal and Gauteng. By 2015, Operation Impi had linked the smuggled guns to 1 666 murders and 1 403 attempted murders. More than 260 children were shot in Cape gang hotspots between 2010 and 2016. Several of Prinsloo's accomplices were also arrested and police retrieved more than 800 firearms.

With Prinsloo in prison, Operation Impi morphed into a major national project investigating more cops implicated in gun-running throughout the country.

In 2016, police commissioner Gen. Khomotso Phahlane turned policing in the Western Cape on its head when he unexpectedly suspended Vearey and Jacobs. Phahlane, a Zuma acolyte, replaced both Vearey and Jacobs with pliable cronies. Vearey and Jacobs fought their suspension tooth and nail. They took their case to the Labour Court, which declared their demotion invalid and ordered that they return to their original posts.

Nevertheless, they were kept in limbo until Zuma's departure from office in February 2018, making way for Cyril Ramaphosa to become president of South Africa. Twelve days later, Ramaphosa reshuffled his Cabinet and appointed Bheki Cele as minister of police. At the end of March, Cele announced that Jacobs would be the new divisional commissioner for Crime Intelligence.

During his career, Jacobs had acquired the image of a no-nonsense and uncompromising policeman, but, as with Godfrey Lebeya, it is naive to believe that one person could turn the unit around. The rot simply went too deep. If Lebeya had marched into a beehive at the Hawks, Lt.-Gen. Anthony Peter Jacobs stumbled into a maximum-security nuthouse filled with berserk maniacs with carnage in their eyes and long knives in their hands. For the next days, weeks and months, Jacobs felt his way through the labyrinth of factions, conspiracies, collusions, intrigues, gossip and backstabbing at the Division Crime Intelligence (DCI) of the SAPS. Ultimately, he too succumbed.

🐦 **Mandy Wiener** @MandyWiener, 21 Dec. 2018
For years the police's Crime Intelligence unit has been a mess, marred by abuse and corruption. Now General Peter Jacobs is facing a standoff within his own unit. This is what insiders in CI are saying

* * *

As Peter Jacobs assumed office, he issued a general instruction to all Crime Intelligence personnel, including agents appointed in Richard Mdluli's agent programme and paid from the secret services account, to report for duty. The idea was to make them "formal" and to get them working. Out of the woodwork crawled the households, offspring and lady friends of Richard Mdluli, Solly Lazarus and other top policemen. Many of them were, despite seven or eight years of doing nothing, still employed at Crime Intelligence and had gobbled up millions from the secret account. Under Jacobs, they were given official tasks and told to report for duty daily and work from the office.

Timmy Marimuthu was by then no longer a Crime Intelligence informant, but the rest of his family were full-time policemen appointed from the secret services account. They ignored Jacobs's instruction, apart from Marimuthu's son-in-law, Lt-Col. Dennis Redhi, who did show up at the office. The rest refused to report for duty, saying they were "undercover".

Inspector-general of intelligence Dr Setlhomamaru Dintwe had investigated the non-performance of the Marimuthu clan and reported to Jacobs, advising him to act against those who refused to turn up for work. The divisional commissioner stopped the salaries of Marimuthu's wife, Neermala, his daughter Shantal Redhi and the rest of the mob. Marimuthu was furious and got on the phone to Jacobs, who refused to take his calls. He then sent a slew of messages threatening the divisional commissioner with legal action.

Although the salaries of the Marimuthu clan were stopped (apart from that of Dennis Redhi), Jacobs never concluded a disciplinary case against them. When he was suspended a few months later for using the wrong account to purchase Covid-19 protection equipment for his agents, the Marimuthu troop were still on Crime Intelligence's books and their pensions accumulating every month. They remain there to this day. What more must you do to get fired from the SAPS?

* * *

When Peter Jacobs arrived at Crime Intelligence, two of his generals – Obed Nemutanzhela and Deena Moodley – were sitting at home, both suspended for allegedly abusing the secret services account. One had sat at home for two years, the other for eighteen months. Police regulations demand that a disciplinary hearing be held within 60 days of suspension.

Some of the fraud charges against the head of the secret services account, Maj.-Gen. Nemutanzhela, dated back to 2013 when he authorised the payment of R563 000 for blinds that cost only R77 000. The company that supplied the blinds did not exist. Nemutanzhela, who succeeded the disgraced Solly Lazarus and carried on where the latter left off, is still under investigation for signing off on a R50 million cash budget for a Crime Intelligence rogue unit, beefed up by moonlighting Defence Intelligence operatives, who descended on the ANC's elective conference in Mangaung in December 2012. Although Jacob Zuma was then at the crest of his power and popularity, Crime Intelligence had to ensure that the president triumphed decisively. Nemutanzhela is also suspected of attempting to derail the IPID investigation into former acting national commissioner Khomotso Phahlane, now in the dock for a host of criminal charges relating to corruption.

Crime Intelligence veteran Deena Moodley was the other major-general sitting at home. He was implicated in 2013 in the illegal bugging of the phones of two *Sunday Times* journalists and of police commissioner Bheki Cele. Although he was exonerated, a Crime Intelligence captain was convicted of illegal phone bugging. During the Fees Must Fall campaign, Moodley headed a Crime Intelligence contingent that spent millions from the secret account to infiltrate the movement's leadership. He allegedly used taxpayers' money to stay in a luxury hotel, registered a Crime Intelligence luxury car in his own name, and fraudulently claimed for the use of a safe house.

Jacobs appointed a Hawks general to investigate the charges against Moodley. He completed his report just six days before Jacobs was suspended. With the Crime Intelligence head gone, the case against

Moodley never got off the ground, and he is back at work. The same happened in the disciplinary case against Nemutanzhela. It commenced in September 2020 but then the prosecutor, Maj.-Gen. Jeremy Vearey, was suspended. Everything ground to a halt.

Jacobs ordered an audit of all the electronic surveillance equipment purchased by Crime Intelligence. Much of it had been bought on paper and paid for but was nowhere to be found. Crime Intelligence had, for example, acquired social media encryption technology that was missing. Jacobs was also alarmed to find that around four out of every five projects funded by the secret account had yielded no results, and he concluded that they were registered for the sole purpose of channelling money.

Jacobs initiated a host of intelligence-gathering projects, among them one focusing on the construction mafia, also known as the Amadela Ngokubona. There was evidence that business people were in cahoots with organised criminals in demanding a share – usually 30 per cent – of construction projects. He also ordered his generals to gather intelligence on the All Truck Drivers Forum and Allied South Africa (ATDF-ASA), an organisation at the centre of violent action against the employment of non-South African truck drivers. Hundreds of trucks have been petrol-bombed, burned, shot at or stoned across the country.

* * *

In August 2018, Peter Jacobs presented Parliament's portfolio police committee with a renewal strategy for Crime Intelligence. He said police management was determined to "restore the trust and respect" of the unit by rendering a "professional, effective and efficient" service. In his view, Crime Intelligence needed to improve the application of technology, eradicate corruption, establish key information networks, enhance intelligence collection and revitalise its relationship with the Hawks.

Police commissioner Khehla Sitole admitted that the damage at the unit was severe, and that management was working on "the purification of the unit". He spoke about "rogue units" that had been closed and said that everyone had been ordered to "accept it or ship out". He warned Jacobs that should he fail to command the unit effectively, he would also "have to get out".

The parliamentary response to Jacobs's renewal plans ranged from praise to disbelief to the inane. One ANC MP mentioned media reports about the escape of two suspects through the roof of a police van in Limpopo. Although it had nothing to do with Crime Intelligence, she wanted to know how it had happened. An EFF MP wanted to know what had happened to the "high-level panel established by the president on Crime Intelligence". The panel had in fact investigated the State Security Agency, not Crime Intelligence. Another ANC MP expressed her concern about the "proliferation of expired food products being sold in the streets by foreign nationals". Nobody asked about the rogue units that were closed, who the rogue cops were and in what rogue activities they had engaged. Neither did the parliamentarians want to know how Jacobs planned to rid the unit of the dregs appointed during the Mdluli era and beyond.

I have no doubt that Jacobs was earnest in trying to turn the unit around. He wanted to do the right thing. It is, however, difficult to have faith in any government turnaround strategy. Think about strategies for local government and municipalities, youth job creation, direct foreign investment, corruption, Transnet, Prasa and South African Airways. They all failed. The SAPS has had several turnaround strategies, but the continued rot is an indication that the plans were destined for the rubbish heap. The Crime Intelligence turnaround plan would follow suit.

CHAPTER 10

When everybody does nothing

🐦 **Daily Maverick** @dailymaverick, 19 Sept. 2020
Editorial: Age of the Assassin: A man died for his country today – RIP
Charl Kinnear

19 SEPTEMBER 2020 was one of the bleakest days in the annals of the post-apartheid South African Police Service. For more than a year, Anti-Gang Unit (AGU) section commander Lt-Col. Charl Kinnear knew that some of the worst thugs spawned by the Cape ganglands were tracking him. He therefore never drove the same route home from the offices of the AGU. He tried to arrive home at different times, and he kept his service pistol close. But it didn't help him on a balmy spring afternoon in September 2020 as he waited in front of his home in Bishop Lavis on the Cape Flats for the motorised gate to open.

It was all over in seconds. CCTV footage showed the slender assassin in a red hooded sweatshirt scrambling across the road towards Kinnear's white Toyota Corolla. As the gunman approached the silhouetted driver, he pulled a pistol from his clothes and fired several closely grouped bullets into Kinnear's upper body. He then swung round and darted away like a phantom. As far as cold-blooded murder goes, it was efficient and deadly. Kinnear had no time to defend himself. His gun was found under his body.

Ten months earlier, one of Kinnear's colleagues, Lt-Col. André Kay, attached to the police's firearm unit, was assassinated in his car in front of his home, also in Bishop Lavis. There was much speculation that Kay's bullet was meant for Kinnear, who lives in the same gang-infested suburb. Both were known as "Colonel K".

Five days after Kay's murder, the AGU placed a 24-hour watch on Kinnear's home, and just four days later, two policemen approached a man loitering in front of his home. A hand grenade fell from his trousers, and he was arrested. He later confessed in a plea agreement that he was a member of the Junky Funky Kids gang and was paid R3 000 to kill Kinnear. He was sentenced to fifteen years' imprisonment. The case against the other members of the gang continues.

A month after the hand-grenade incident, Kinnear's protection was inexplicably withdrawn pending a Crime Intelligence threat assessment, with which Kinnear refused to cooperate. He didn't trust Crime Intelligence because of its links to organised crime. He feared that an assessment would give agents access to his movements and communication. The assessment was abandoned. But Kinnear was left exposed and defenceless – a sitting duck for an assassin's bullet.

🐦 Athi Mtongana @Artii_M, 3 Oct. 2020
The minister of police Bheki Cele arrives at the late anti-gang unit section commander, lieutenant colonel Charl Kinnear's funeral.

🐦 Langelihle Sokhulumi @skinnypants3000, 3 Oct. 2020
Wow, being a minister you live like a rich hip hop star. You have your own driver in the top range SUV.

🐦 Phetogo Monaisa @lesilo_rula, 3 Oct. 2020
Can he not use his own arms to open the door?

The national flag was draped over Kinnear's coffin as it was lowered into his grave. Some of the very generals who had failed him were present, decked out in full regalia with medals shining. They paid tribute – with bowed heads and wet eyes – to a fallen hero. Police minister Bheki Cele spoke some truth for once when he said: "We know he was dealing with our own criminality." Cele spat bile at those who had snuffed out the life of one of South Africa's finest and said: "This is a war. War has dead bodies, as we see [here today]. When you find a war, you don't ask who started it, you fight."

Minutes later, the minister was whisked away by bodyguards and blue lights.

* * *

Daily Maverick @dailymaverick, 4 Mar. 2019
AmaBhungane: SAPS Wars, Part One: The blurry blue line between the cops and the Cape underworld

The genesis of the killing of Charl Kinnear can be traced to the battle for control of Western Cape Crime Intelligence that has created fertile ground for mobsters to infiltrate the unit and subvert its members for their own nefarious endeavours. The internecine warfare has, since its origins in 2013, spread to the office of the Western Cape provincial head, the Anti-Gang Unit, the detective branch and the Hawks. It even slithered up the hierarchical ladder to include deputy national commissioner Lt.-Gen. Sindile Mfazi, Peter Jacobs, police commissioner Khehla Sitole and police minister Bheki Cele.

At the time of Kinnear's murder, Crime Intelligence was riddled by as much infighting and backstabbing as the unit commanded by Mdluli a decade earlier. This all happened against a background of crime spiralling out of control and South Africa sinking into a morass of lawlessness. The police leadership of today is as limp and uninspiring as a decade ago. Ironically, the police commissioner of that time is now the minister of police. He was a failure then, and he remains so today.

The warfare in Crime Intelligence is a long and complicated matter and has been admirably examined by *Daily Maverick* journalist Caryn Dolley in her book *To the Wolves: How Traitor Cops Crafted South Africa's Underworld*. She dissects the rotten carcass that is Western Cape Crime

Intelligence with the skill and finesse of a surgeon. As she describes it, the battle consisted of basically two groups, though others emerged as time went on. On the one side were Peter Jacobs, Jeremy Vearey, Anti-Gang Unit (AGU) commander Maj.-Gen. André Lincoln, Charl Kinnear and several of their underlings.

In the opposite corner were one-time Western Cape police commissioner Khombinkosi Jula and two of his top generals, Mzwandile Tiyo (Crime Intelligence) and Maj.-Gen. Patrick "Porn Cop" Mbotho (head of detectives). This faction also included a top Crime Intelligence officer, Brig. Sanjith Hansraj, and a bunch of their henchmen. Several Crime Intelligence generals and senior officers, especially those from the Mdluli era, supported this faction. The Jacobs group referred to them as running a "rogue unit". There was no trust between the two factions: they undermined each other when they could and accused each other of criminality and of having links to gangsters and criminals.

When police commissioner Khomotso Phahlane suspended Vearey and Jacobs during Operation Impi in 2016, he appointed Mbotho and Tiyo in their positions. It gave the "rogue unit" – at least for a while – the upper hand in the Western Cape. Mbotho inherited Operation Impi from Vearey. He removed the operation's chief investigator, Lt.-Col. Clive Ontong, on the eve of the prosecution of gun-runner Chris Prinsloo's accomplices. It remains a perplexing riddle: why were Phahlane and Mbotho seemingly intent on disrupting the investigation into rogue guns on the Cape Flats when so many people, including children, had died as a result?

The director of public prosecutions in the Western Cape, Advocate Rodney de Kock (now deputy national director of public prosecutions), wrote to Khombinkosi Jula in August 2016 and noted that Ontong had performed all the arrests, done all the searches, traced and interviewed the witnesses and taken most of the statements. He said the conclusion of the investigation would be severely compromised without Ontong. Despite Jula's assurance that the investigation would continue, De Kock wrote to him again a few months later, saying that Mbotho had stopped Operation Impi altogether and refused to allow Ontong to travel to Gauteng to prepare for the prosecution of the accused. It was only after the suspension of Phahlane, the reinstatement of Vearey and the appointment of Mbotho as Hawks head in the North West that Operation Impi was revived.

In 2017, a new underworld thug was making himself known in the fairest Cape: Nafiz Modack. Branded an extortionist and intimidator, he was accused by police of using strongarm tactics to wrest control of the lucrative nightclub security operations in the Western Cape. A former importer of exotic cars whose company went bust, Modack is always insulated by a troop of Ray-Banned man-tanks who guard his every move. He often wears T-shirts with the word "BOSS" on them.

The security industry in Cape Town is central to drug dealing, extortion, prostitution and gun running in the city. Business owners across the city have been bullied and threatened to make them use certain security companies or pay protection fees. The same has happened to clubs and entertainment venues because whoever regulates security and access at the doors also controls the flow of narcotics.

Modack soon gained the fearsome reputation of commanding an army of muscle and firepower. He made a bid to wrest control of the city's security turf occupied by the Lifman group comprising "gentleman gangster" Mark Lifman, Sexy Boys gang leader Jerome "Donkie" Booysen, bouncer boss André Naudé and 27s gang boss William "Red" Stevens. Booysen miraculously survived several attempts on his life that landed him in intensive care, Naudé was shot at, and Stevens was murdered in February 2021. Naudé, Lifman and Booysen are currently standing trial for the murder in 2017 of "steroid king" Brian Wainstein.

As the different Crime Intelligence groupings levelled allegations against one another that they were in cahoots with gangsters, Modack and his cohorts were arrested and charged with extortion and money laundering in December 2017. The investigating officer was Charl Kinnear, who took the stand in Modack's bail application. The unassuming and soft-spoken cop, blessed with a methodical mind, was pitted against the alleged extortionist in the dock, who looked bored and amused as he listened to the evidence against him.

𝕏 James Bond Nkosi @BondNkosi, 3 Oct. 2019
Alleged gangster Nafiz Modack brings 40-strong security force to court.

Kinnear said he had a recording of Modack speaking about his relationship with top-ranking police officers. Said Kinnear: "Nafiz Modack states he was dealing with high-ranking police officials and, should there ever be a problem, Tiyo and Mbotho can sort it out." He was of course referring to generals Mzwandile Tiyo and Patrick Mbotho.

Although Modack was later acquitted on all charges, there is more evidence of his relationship with top policemen. Journalist Caryn Dolley watched in 2017 as Modack met Northern Cape provincial police commissioner Lt.-Gen. Risimati Shivuri at an upmarket hotel, and there is a photograph of Modack meeting one-time Gauteng Hawks head Prince Mokotedi in Cape Town.

In December 2018, Kinnear dispatched a 59-page letter to police commissioner Khehla Sitole in which he alleged the existence of a dirty-tricks or rogue unit within Western Cape Crime Intelligence. He claimed that six policemen, under the command of Sanjith Hansraj, had attempted to frame him and some of the most prominent policemen in the province, among them André Lincoln, Jeremy Vearey and Peter Jacobs, for crimes they had not committed. All the targeted policemen were involved in underworld crime investigations. Kinnear said in his letter that one of the officers he mentioned had a close relationship with Modack. They had also allegedly approached gangsters and drug dealers to make statements against members of the Vearey faction.

𝕏 Daily Maverick @dailymaverick, 28 Jan. 2019
Report: Crime Intelligence head Peter Jacobs recommends WC rogue CI unit be disbanded and members criminally investigated.

Following up on Kinnear's complaint, Jacobs said in a memorandum to Sitole that "the rogue unit was operating like a vigilante group within the SAPS . . . This unit ran parallel investigations, they tampered with evidence and witnesses, and, most concerning, they opened dockets and false criminal investigations into the officers who were complaining about them, including Lt.-Col. Kinnear. The allegations, if true, posed a high national security threat."

In July 2019, Sanjith Hansraj submitted a formal grievance against Jacobs, labelling him a racist for trying to oust "two African managers" in the Western Cape. According to Hansraj: "Lt.-Gen. Jacobs is a threat to national security and must be removed from office with immediate effect. He is a constant proxy to corruption if not a corruptor/corruptee, so he needs to be investigated." According to the grievance, which was sent to Sitole and Cele, Jacobs had stopped Hansraj from investigating the notorious Stansfield gangster family and was a co-conspirator in the corruption being investigated.

News24 @News24, 9 July 2019
Gang Wars Part 3: One month, 883 gunshots – Hanover Park's gunfire in numbers

News24 @News24, 21 July 2019
Gang Wars Part 5: Groote Schuur treats up to 90 gunshot victims a month: "And we're only seeing the survivors"

As Crime Intelligence tore itself apart, gang-related violence on the Cape Flats soared, to the extent that government deployed the army in gang hotspots to assist the police in quelling the violence. It was also a deadly time for policemen investigating the various Modack dockets and cases.

News24 @News24, 9 July 2019
Father of Hawks detective shot dead in car outside his Cape Town home

In July 2019, five hitmen, among them Terrible West Siders gangster Abongile Nqodi, drove to the beach village of Melkbosstrand, near Cape Town. Nqodi had a .38 revolver containing five bullets and was on a mission to assassinate Hawks officer Capt. Nico Heerschap, who was part of a task team investigating Nafiz Modack. He was also due to testify in a firearms case in a few days' time. When the gangsters arrived at the given address, they saw a white male in a Toyota Land Cruiser pulling out of the driveway. Nqodi and an accomplice walked up to the vehicle and shot the driver twice in the head. The victim turned out to be Heerschap's 74-year-old father, also Nico, who was taking his grandchild to school.

With blood flowing in the fairest Cape, police management transferred Western Cape provincial commissioner Khombinkosi Jula to lead police in KwaZulu-Natal. In a letter he wrote upon his departure, Jula said: "I'm grateful for all the lessons I've learned in Western Cape and for surviving all the cut-throat wars which were waged against me."

Deputy national commissioner Sindile Mfazi was appointed as acting provincial commissioner for the Western Cape in a caretaker role until management could find a suitable candidate to fill the post. Jeremy Vearey was regarded as the most suitable candidate by most politicians and commentators, except Democratic Alliance (DA) politicians, who accused him of being too close to the ANC.

🐦 **Sunday Times** @SundayTimesZA, 13 Oct. 2019
Alleged mobster Nafiz Modack says Western Cape's head of detectives Jeremy Vearey is guilty of extorting money.

Vearey's reputation suffered a blow, however, when *Sunday Times* journalist Aron Hyman published what he claimed was an audio recording of a conversation between Vearey and a close associate of Nafiz Modack. When the gang leader was arrested in 2018, police confiscated guns from his bodyguards. Modack said in an affidavit that Vearey had attempted to extort money from him when he asked Modack's associate, Mohamedaly Hanware, to speak to the general to get the guns back. Modack said Vearey wanted R40 000. On the recording, the person identified as Vearey said to Hanware: "Nafiz, I'm doing a lot of work for that guy, for Nafiz." The conversation was spiced with code words; for example, "packets of biltong" referred to R10 000 in cash, and "olive trees" and "roses" to firearms. Hanware spoke of "four packets of biltong" and asked Vearey when Modack could get his "olive trees" back, to which he replied: "Just give me some time."

The timing of Modack's affidavit and the leaking of the recording to the *Sunday Times* were both highly suspicious. They coincided with police management pondering the appointment of a new Western Cape provincial commissioner.

The story fell apart when Hanware said he had never spoken to Vearey about bribes. In his book *Into Dark Water: A Police Memoir*, Vearey tells how he met *Sunday Times* editor Bongani Siqoko three weeks after the publication of Aron Hyman's report. Siqoko showed the policeman the documents Hyman had been fed by a Crime Intelligence "rogue unit" captain. The allegations were made by convicted criminals, known gangsters and a police officer arrested for murder. But the newspaper retracted its story only several months later when it said: "It subsequently appeared that our information was incorrect, in that the voice on the recording is not that of Vearey. We retract any suggestion that the recording features Vearey's voice and apologise to him for any embarrassment that may have resulted."

🐦 **News24** @News24, 12 Dec. 2019
JUST IN: Yolisa Matakata appointed Western Cape police commissioner

It came as no surprise, therefore, that police management and Bheki Cele overlooked Jeremy Vearey for the province's top police post. Their choice, police veteran Lt.-Gen. Yolisa Matakata, had seen it all: a provincial head of Crime Intelligence, a provincial police commissioner and deputy head of the Hawks, where she was Berning Ntlemeza's trusted sidekick.

Matakata inherited a province with a thriving killing industry. On the day of the announcement of her appointment, gang leader Tauriq Solomon was murdered in Mitchells Plain. This spurred retaliation attacks. The next day, legendary gangster Rashied Staggie was shot dead in London Road in Salt River. Security boss and alleged drug dealer Tim Lotter met his maker in the suburb of Goodwood, courtesy of an assassin who riddled his body with bullets. Soon afterwards, another of the Mother City's gunmen fired four bullets into Charl Kinnear.

* * *

At 3.25pm, minutes after Kinnear had gasped his last breath, one of his three cellphones was pinged by Gauteng debt collector Zane Killian. He had tracked Kinnear's phone 38 times that day by means of cellphone software that determined its exact location through latitude and longitude readings. This is referred to as pinging and it is unlawful unless one has the permission of the person being tracked. Killian stopped using the platform after Kinnear's last ping.

🐦 **eNCA** @eNCA, 24 Sept. 2020
Hawks confirm arrest in connection with Kinnear murder

It took police six days to hunt down Killian, a lowly former professional rugby player, and charge him with the murder of Charl Kinnear. He was also charged with the attempted murder of attorney William Booth, who had survived an assassination attempt in April 2020 when five shots were fired at him. Killian pleaded not guilty.

🐦 **Sam Sole** @SamSoleZA, 15 Dec. 2020
MUST READ – Targeting AGU Team C: How Zane Killian tracked anti-gang cop Charl Kinnear and his team. An investigation by News24.

WHEN EVERYBODY DOES NOTHING

🐦 News24 @News24, 24 Oct. 2020
Hawks, Crime Intelligence and senior SAPS officials knew that the phone of murdered Anti-Gang Unit detective Charl Kinnear was being tracked at least two weeks before his murder – and were told who was behind the monitoring.

Over six months, Killian unlawfully stalked and pinged Kinnear's cell-phones 2 442 times. A News24 analysis of the debt collector's phone surveillance showed how he meticulously tracked Kinnear's phone while the gang-buster conducted a massive firearms licensing fraud investigation that disrupted a steady supply of guns and ammunition to the underworld. This made Kinnear the prime target of a host of crime bosses and their pet policemen.

🐦 IOL News @IOL, 29 Apr. 2021
Controversial businessman Nafiz Modack has been arrested, allegedly for the murder of Cape Flats top cop Lieutenant-Colonel Charl Kinnear.

🐦 Richard Spoor @Richard_Spoor, 29 Apr. 2021
Only IOL calls him a businessman.

Following a high-speed car chase, Modack was apprehended and charged with murdering Kinnear and conspiring to murder him five times, illegal telephone tracking, racketeering, kidnapping, intimidation, corruption, gang-related extortion, and contravening the Prevention of Organised Crime Act (POCA). In October 2021, more charges of racketeering, fraud, money laundering, uttering and contravention of the VAT Act were brought against Modack. His mother, brother and a SARS employee joined him in the dock for the latest charges. According to evidence in Modack's bail application, the underworld boss was so livid when Charl Kinnear arrested his wife in a gun licensing investigation in October 2019 that he allegedly began plotting the demise of the detective. If convicted, Modack and his troop face life imprisonment.

Infuriated Modack plotted revenge after Kinnear had his wife arrested, court hears

Nafiz Modack is being deprived of exercise and is staying in solitary confinement conditions as judgment in the bail application remains delayed due to other applications by his counsel.

Several of Modack's henchmen have also been charged, among them lowlife enforcer Jacques Cronje, who, according to the state, formed the intimidation and threat wing of the Modack criminal enterprise. Evidence in their bail applications illuminated the parallel universe in which they lived. Cronje told the court that just before his arrest, he had woken up in a morgue after being shot seven times. Authorities thought he had met his maker and placed his "corpse" in the morgue fridge.

An investigating officer checked Cronje's fanciful claims and found that he hadn't exactly risen from the dead. He had been involved in a brawl outside a bottle store in Koeberg Road in Cape Town in December 2020. It had started with Cronje objecting to someone staring at him. "Wat kyk jy? [Why are you looking at me?]" descended into verbal insults like "Jou poes!" (an untranslatable Afrikaans swearword) and then Cronje was stabbed and shot twice.

Also rubbing shoulders in the dock with Modack and Cronje was AGU sergeant Ashley Tabisher, who is said to have had a corrupt relationship with them. In evidence at Tabisher's bail application, police played telephone recordings between him and a Modack associate in which he was promised that "everything that is skew can be made straight with money", but he had to stick to his part of the deal: keeping Modack up to date about imminent raids at his house. Tabisher allegedly sold his soul for a mere R10 000.

𝕐 Daily Maverick @dailymaverick, 20 Jan. 2021
AGE OF THE ASSASSIN: Charl Kinnear murder case: NPA says more suspects will be arrested and charged

After a bail application lasting eight months, during which five interlocutory applications were heard, a magistrate in the Blue Downs court ruled that Nafiz Modack and his co-accused would stay behind bars. He said they had failed to show the existence of exceptional circumstances warranting their release on bail. The state prosecutor told the court that more arrests were expected, and that the names of the new accused would be added to the charge sheet at their next appearance.

There was further bad news for the accused: the magistrate said there was no available date for a pre-trial conference in the Western Cape High Court in 2022. The matter would only be heard in 2023.

𝕐 Daily Maverick @dailymaverick, 8 Apr. 2022
AGE OF THE ASSASSIN: Hitman implicates Modack directly in murder of father of ex-Hawks officer Nico Heerschap.

Adding to the woes of Modack was the confession of Terrible West Siders gangster Abongile Nqodi to the 2019 murder of the father of a Hawks police officer. Nqodi faced charges of murder, gang activity, conspiracy to commit murder, and possession of an unlicensed firearm and ammunition linked to Heerschap's murder. He reached a plea and sentence agreement with the state: in return for a 55-year term of imprisonment for these crimes, he would testify against those implicated in the murder. He said in his plea agreement that the hit had allegedly been funded by Modack, who undertook to pay them R60 000. He claimed he met the gang boss just after the murder in Kuilsriver. He told him they had done a good job and should not worry about any legal fees in future. However, when it emerged that they had assassinated Heerschap senior, Modack allegedly coughed up only R25 000, which they split between the five of them.

* * *

🐦 **Marianne Thamm** @MarianneThamm, 24 June 2022
IPID FILES ON POLICE: No one had Kinnear's back: Ipid calls for criminal
charges against superiors and members of WC rogue unit

We all know the saying that the only thing necessary for evil to triumph
is for good men to do nothing. An IPID special task force found that
the murder of Charl Kinnear was the result of monumental failure
and neglect at all levels and ranks in the police. At least six generals,
among them the heads of the Hawks and Crime Intelligence, were
briefed that Zane Killian was illegally tracking every move of Kinnear
by pinging his phone. They had received all Killian's details between
ten and fifteen days before Kinnear's killing and could have pounced
on the debt collector within hours.

As the top brass shuffled the information around, everyone did
nothing. As they reclined in their leather chairs and pondered their
good fortune to be at the top of the police's feeding trough, Kinnear was
without protection while working the barren and windswept Cape Flats
where homicidal mudda-fuckers lurked who would sell their mothers
for a quaff of tik (crystal methamphetamine). As he criss-crossed
the area, one or more of these gangsters received minute-by-minute
updates about his whereabouts in his white Toyota Corolla.

Gauteng Hawks head Maj.-Gen. Ebrahim Kadwa received intelligence about Killian pinging Kinnear's phone on 3 September, more
than two weeks before the murder. Even though the surveillance of
Kinnear's phone was illegal and extremely sinister, IPID found that
Kadwa briefed Godfrey Lebeya only four days later.

But it gets worse. On 16 September, two days before Kinnear's
murder, the Hawks received information that the pinging of Kinnear's
phone had significantly increased. The Hawks informed André Lincoln,
who in turn ordered the AGU to patrol in the vicinity of Kinnear's
home, but by the time he was shot, the patrols had been stopped.

IPID said the Hawks "had sufficient and prima facie evidence at hand to have applied for a search-and-seizure warrant to stop the illegal monitoring, seize equipment and ensure that the ongoing crime being committed against the state was neutralised". Hawks members "acted unlawfully and criminally through their failure to act", which resulted in the killing of Kinnear.

🐦 **Marianne Thamm** @MarianneThamm, 24 June 2022
IPID FILES ON POLICE: "Pinging Kinnear": Hawks' head Godfrey Lebeya failed to protect national security and the top detective

The police watchdog had harsh words for Godfrey Lebeya when it said that he "failed to ensure that the DPCI members implicated investigated the threat against the state and therefore failed to protect the national interest or security of the state". Lincoln was responsible for withdrawing his underling's protection and was as much responsible for Kinnear's fate as the Hawks members who did nothing. In contrast, IPID completely exonerated Peter Jacobs, who was on leave and hadn't received any messages about the pinging of Kinnear's phone.

As one reads through the IPID report, one question persists: why did none of these lacklustre fat cats pick up their Apples or Samsungs to warn Kinnear about the imminent threat? Were they too lazy, too lethargic, too busy plotting their next manoeuvre to outwit an adversary? Or did they simply not care?

There were a host of other failures. A sergeant in the AGU's operations room received an anonymous call two days before the murder saying that a large amount of money was being offered for the killing of Kinnear. The sergeant told the operations room commander, but he also failed to warn Kinnear.

The Crime Intelligence risk assessment of Kinnear in the months leading up to his murder was a disaster. Although he initially refused to cooperate with Crime Intelligence, he indicated by March 2020 that he would assist. The two colonels responsible for the assessment told

IPID that when the president declared a national lockdown because of Covid-19, it prevented them from completing their work. They were, however, not bound by the travel restrictions and, when IPID asked to see their initial work, they couldn't produce anything.

The IPID task team also found that a "rogue unit" existed within Western Cape Crime Intelligence and that members of the unit had investigated Kinnear, Vearey and Jacobs. The team had not registered any of their investigations and none led to any prosecution. The animosity between SAPS members and "rogue unit" members created the atmosphere that enabled mobsters like Nafiz Modack to infiltrate the police and monitor the movements of key role players.

In an act of extreme recalcitrance, Khehla Sitole refused to make himself available to IPID to answer questions about the failure of the police response to the imminent threat against Kinnear. He ignored requests to meet them, despite being obliged by the Independent Police Investigative Directorate Act to cooperate with any of their investigations.

CHAPTER 11

Thirteen white elephants

IN JULY 2021, two infernos fused to lay waste to parts of KwaZulu-Natal and Gauteng. The one blaze was ignited and stoked by organised criminal networks and elements of the radical economic transformation (RET) faction within the ruling party, which exploited the incarceration of former president Jacob Zuma.

The other was ignited by ordinary people who had for years been the victims of the ANC's failed economic policies, rising poverty, rampant unemployment, state capture and lack of service delivery.

The insurrectionists tried to force KwaZulu-Natal and Gauteng to a blazing standstill, get rid of Cyril Ramaphosa and seize power.

Had this faction succeeded in taking control of crucial elements of the economy, they would eventually have made the Guptas' state-capture looting seem like a six-year-old nicking a chocolate bar from a candy shop.

Using social media, the gangster networks and their political allies mobilised idle young men and women and turned their anger into devastating tools of political revolt.

🐦 **Sphithiphithi Evaluator** @_AfricanSoil, 9 July 2021
JUST IN: Current situation in KwaZulu Natal Trucks on fire!
#FreeJacobZuma protests; roads blocked; it has escalated to many parts in KZN #KZNshutdown

𝕐 Mandisa @MandiMbuli, 9 July 2021
WE DOING IT. POLICE ARE STUCK IN TRAFFIC Please continue to close all FREEWAYS to KZN and DURBAN CLOSE All Roads to Police Stations All roads to airports harbors.

𝕐 Sphithiphithi Evaluator @_AfricanSoil, 9 July 2021
KwaZulu-Natal is BURNING!
#FreeJacobZuma protests all over the province! #ShutdownKZN
Ramaphosa, Zondo and Thuli Madonsela this is all your evil work!

𝕐 Matshakatshaka @Matshakatshaka1, 9 July 2021
Yes, burn kzn to the ground, destroy all infrastructure and all means of production. Vandalise Durban port. Render KZN under uninhabitable.

𝕐 Busi Senna @busi_senna, 9 July 2021
Yes yes yes Concourt must be next

On the pretext of protesting against Zuma's jailing, mobsters and thugs blended with the truly desperate and dispossessed to loot and burn everything in sight. The police didn't know who were part of these networks and, when confronted by mobs of raiders, they had no idea how to stop them. The rioters realised this. They mocked police with a gleam in their eyes that said: "Come and get us if you can!" No, said our troopers in blue, we can't. Help yourself.

Once upon a time, the police had a riot unit at hand, equipped to the teeth to curb civil unrest and control unruly crowds. For example, the unit possessed trailers that released rolled barbed wire that could cordon off an area within minutes. Wouldn't these rolls of barbed wire have come in handy to protect shopping malls and other property against the marauders? But the trailers and equipment have fallen into disrepair.

The riot police were replaced by the Public Order Policing (POP) unit. In 1995, there were 31 POP units with 11 000 members. By 2014, its numbers had dwindled to less than 5 000. After the Marikana massacre, there were efforts to rebuild the POP. In 2018, police minister Bheki Cele unveiled a resuscitated POP with 41 units, which were capacitated with new-generation Nyala armoured vehicles, water cannons, video cameras and protective gear. In a display to the public, police used water tanks, rubber bullets and stun grenades to bring rowdy protesters under control.

In March 2021, just three months before the unrest, Cele announced that the police had spent R598 million to better equip police officers responding to incidents of public disorder and violence. He boasted that 6 300 policemen had been trained in crowd management. So why, then, did police become onlookers in the subsequent destruction in KwaZulu-Natal and Gauteng that tore R50 billion off the ailing economy, cost 150 000 jobs and resulted in the deaths of more than 340 people? Where were the water cannons and the new Nyalas – the recently trained POP? As shopping centres and warehouses went up in flames and alleged looters were intercepted and killed by vigilantes, everyone wanted to know: where was the intelligence that should have forewarned the government of the looming calamity?

🐦 **Yusuf Abramjee** @Abramjee, 29 July 2021
Police Commissioner Khehla Sitole has admitted that the @SAPoliceService is "powerless and handicapped". He says nine helicopters are grounded for years – also dozens of vehicles and Nyalas. The SAPS is in a mess!! @CyrilRamaphosa must act and fire the useless leadership.

* * *

To find answers to the wretched police performance, one must travel back a few months before the insurrection to study the condition in which Crime Intelligence found itself. Its new boss, Peter Jacobs, had by then managed to get most of the unit members working again, reinstated disciplinary charges against top officers who had looted the secret fund, purchased surveillance equipment and initiated new intelligence projects. There were signs that Crime Intelligence was waking up from its decade-long slumber. But the efforts by Jacobs to root out corruption and instil a culture of accountability made him unpopular not just among the "old guard" at Crime Intelligence, but also with police commissioner Khehla Sitole.

The long knives were out for Jacobs from the moment he set foot in Crime Intelligence. Following Cyril Ramaphosa's declaration of a national state of disaster arising from the Covid-19 pandemic, the Treasury gave state institutions permission to purchase emergency personal protective equipment (PPE) for their workers. Jacobs used the secret account to purchase R1.1 million of protective equipment for Crime Intelligence's spies and agents.

The Crime Intelligence purchase was minuscule compared with the R1.6 billion the SAPS spent on PPE equipment within the first few months of lockdown. The *Daily Maverick* reported that the latter acquisition amounted to R19 500 for every policeman and included items like R3 600 for five-litre containers of liquid soap. Police spin guru Brig. Vish Naidoo didn't deny the police shop-fest but slammed the *Daily Maverick* for publishing a document that bore a classification sign indicating it was a confidential document. He said the acquisition had been investigated and no wrongdoing was found.

Inspector-general of intelligence (IGI) Setlhomamaru Dintwe found in a provisional report in November 2020 that the Crime Intelligence expenditure had been irregular because the secret services account could be used only for actions, projects and services of a clandestine nature. There was no indication that Jacobs had acted with criminal or unlawful intent, and Dintwe had not yet spoken to him to obtain his version of events. But Sitole was onto the matter like a flash and suspended Jacobs.

Jacobs's nemesis, deputy national commissioner for crime detection Lt.-Gen. Sindile Mfazi, appointed head of counter- and security intelligence Maj.-Gen. Feroz Khan as acting head. Referred to as the "millionaire cop", Khan is a controversial figure and is widely regarded as a member of the "old guard". According to the *Daily Maverick*, Khan is a wealthy businessman and the director of eight active businesses, including a motor-parts chain said to be worth R21 million. He claimed to have permission to run his businesses.

Khan's appointment was illegal as Mfazi had no authority to appoint him. Sitole, who should have made the appointment, looked on in silence, while Bheki Cele reacted furiously. The suspension of Peter Jacobs happened as he was about to present the R529 million secret services account budget to Parliament's portfolio committee on intelligence. With Jacobs gone, Khan had to finalise the budget, but, because he was unlawfully appointed, Cele refused to sign it, expressing reservations about expenditures and the secret services account.

Jacobs fought his suspension tooth and nail, arguing that he was punished for rooting out corruption in the division. Sitole told him that he could return to work on 3 March 2021 because the Labour Relations Act required that a disciplinary process against him be completed without delay, which had not happened. When Jacobs reported for work, Sitole handed him a letter that said: "You are hereby instructed to assume duty at Division Inspectorate, immediately. Kindly take note that your placement to the post for the Divisional Commissioner: Inspectorate is being effected in the interest of the service and for service delivery requirements."

🐦 **Pieter du Toit** @PieterDuToit, 4 Mar. 2021
Crime Intelligence: Night of the long knives sees suspended, reinstated CI head Peter Jacobs fall.

This must have been Jacobs's worst nightmare – being secreted by Sitole in the Inspectorate Division, the graveyard of police dissidents. He has ever since been a pen pusher in a unit that is tasked with conducting inspections and evaluations of police stations, as well as fielding internal complaints. It is a dead end in the SAPS, and there is no coming back from there.

🐦 Newzroom Afrika @Newzroom405, 11 Mar. 2021
@XoliMngambi: Is Peter Jacobs still head of Crime Intelligence right now?
Bheki Cele: "I don't know."
Xoli: "How can you not know Minister?"
Cele: "You know what . . . I don't know."

When Deputy Chief Justice Raymond Zondo asked the Constitutional Court to find Jacob Zuma guilty of contempt of court and send him to jail for defying a subpoena to appear before the State Capture Commission, Crime Intelligence was, once again, in flux. Attempting to bring stability to the unit, Sitole appointed police veteran Lt.-Gen. Yolisa Matakata to act as Crime Intelligence head.

By the time Matakata went on leave for three weeks in June 2021, Bheki Cele had still not signed the budget for the secret account. In her absence, Sindile Mfazi made another bizarre decision when he appointed Maj.-Gen. Obed Nemutanzhela as the acting Crime Intelligence divisional commander. The former guardian of the secret services account, Nemutanzhela was deeply implicated in its abuses and was thrice charged departmentally by Peter Jacobs for this reason. His disciplinary hearing stalled with the departure of both Jacobs and Vearey. Nemutanzhela had neither the moral authority nor the know-how to head Crime Intelligence, yet when the Constitutional Court sent Jacob Zuma to prison on 29 June 2021, he was holding the reins.

As KwaZulu-Natal and Gauteng exploded in an orgy of violence and looting in July 2021, the secret account budget was still lying on Cele's desk, thereby starving agents and projects of operational funds. Crime Intelligence had no money to pay its informants. It was also starved of operational funds for petrol, airtime and other expenses. Cele only signed the budget on 2 August 2021 – almost eight months late.

Cele later claimed that the Treasury had approved an advance of R129 million to the Crime Intelligence secret account two months before the violence. Intelligence management said the money was "ring-fenced", meaning that it was already allocated to other projects.

* * *

🐦 Carl Niehaus @niehaus_carl, 30 June 2021
I was yesterday, when that prison sentence was imposed on @PresJGZuma, outraged by the vindictiveness & injustice. This morning I woke up even angrier. Apartheid criminals such as FW de Klerk & Wouter Basson are not jailed, but our ANC government does this to one of our own!

🐦 Sefiri Mamphela @tlouymamphela, 30 June 2021
You didn't sleep neh

🐦 Carl Niehaus @niehaus_carl, 30 June 2021
No, I could not. This hurts deeply, and angers me very much.

The apex court gave Zuma a week to turn himself over. As he retreated to his sanctuary in Nkandla in northern KwaZulu-Natal, angry followers began assembling outside the compound. They fired shots in the air, mocked the police and threatened violence. Using social media platforms, supporters warned that the country would pay the price if Zuma was incarcerated.

🐦 The Witness @WitnessKZN, 3 July 2021
UPDATE: Shots fired, journalists threatened outside Zuma's home in Nkandla

🐦 **The Muzikal Frik Gay DJ** @DjUGIN, 4 July 2021

Shots fired near Nkandla and eShowe Tensions rising on the Police Blockade areas It's safe to say this country is gona BURN !!!!! Khuzani Khuzani Guys! Yelelani uZuma once!

Crime Intelligence's top leadership scrambled to provide South Africa's security cluster with reports about the extent of the instability and the dangers looming in the gathering of pro-Zuma forces at Nkandla. Analysts at Crime Intelligence identified the mobilisation of the trucking industry, taxi bosses and hostel residents as potential hotbeds for violent insurrection. But the reports were vague, lacked detail and were unable to provide scenarios of how the violence might unfold.

A case in point is the Crime Intelligence project on the All Truck Drivers Forum (ATDF), an organisation closely aligned with uMkhonto we Sizwe Military Veterans Association (MKMVA) and, in turn, with Jacob Zuma. Crime Intelligence had some success in its investigation into the ATDF with scores of arrests in 2019 and 2020.

But the intelligence operation ground to a halt in April 2021 when the secret services account ran out of money. The agents had infiltrated both the ATDF and the MKMVA but lost their informants in the build-up to the insurrection. They claimed that they had no money to pay them.

The ATDF and the MKMVA together formed an unholy alliance of those committed to Jacob Zuma's idea of radical economic transformation. The veterans' association was no longer just a league of celebrated former ANC combatants but had mutated into a mercenary outfit of Zuma zombies and Ramaphosa detesters. The ATDF, for its part, had descended into a xenophobic and criminal enterprise that had no qualms about sabotaging the economy and torpedoing job opportunities.

*   *   *

In a warehouse of the police's Technology Support Unit in Silverton, Pretoria, are stored thirteen electronic devices that could have changed the face of the July insurrection. When Jacob Zuma's supporters began vowing to spill blood in defence of uBaba, Crime Intelligence agents, armed with just one of these devices, could have cloned and "grabbed" the cellphone or smartphone of every Zuma defender at Nkandla. They would have been able to pinpoint the phone's exact location (and obviously that of the user), intercept its calls and download or read all its data, including SMSs, WhatsApp messages and Facebook Messenger. Police could have compiled profiles of every Zuma stormtrooper advocating war and violence. They, in turn, would have led police to a host of other potential insurrectionists, who could have become targets of second, third and fourth devices.

Police had ten days to prepare for the insurrection, between the time Constitutional Court Judge Sisi Khampepe sent Zuma to jail for fifteen months on 29 June 2021 and the first visuals of a truck blocking the Tongaat Toll Plaza, north of Durban, on 8 July 2021. However, one would expect Crime Intelligence to have been on high alert even earlier, following the State Capture Commission's request to the Constitutional Court in February 2021 to imprison Zuma for failing to appear before Judge Raymond Zondo. The first rumbles of protest were then already audible.

Once the violence and looting started, the devices, which are mobile, could have been deployed in hotspots in KwaZulu-Natal and Gauteng. They could have tracked the tweets of insurrectionists like Sphithiphithi Evaluator, later exposed as the 36-year-old Zamaswazi Majozi, a leading voice in the radical economic transformation (RET) political faction. Besides cloning her phone, Crime Intelligence could have scrambled or jammed her signal, rendering her phone useless for at least some time.

The devices I am talking about are International Mobile Subscriber Identity (IMSI) catchers, commonly known as grabbers. Intelligence and security agencies around the world use them to combat terrorism, organised crime and civil unrest. On the downside, a grabber can be a devastating tool in the wrong hands, which is why it is classified as military equipment and requires the issuing of an end-user or exemption certificate. This is an official document, issued by the importing state, that certifies that a government agency is the ultimate recipient of what is defined as an international transfer of weapons or military equipment.

Grabbers are eavesdropping devices that deceive cellphones and smartphones by imitating the signal given off by mobile towers and duping them into connecting with the grabber and giving up their data. Once a grabber is activated, it can capture and clone phones within a radius of several kilometres. The phone user will be unaware that a grabber has taken control of his or her device.

When Jacobs arrived at Crime Intelligence in 2018, he found nine grabbers, of which six were broken and beyond repair. The other three were outdated and were limited to 3G technology. None of the grabbers had end-user or exemption certificates and all were being used illegally by Crime Intelligence. This meant that none of the evidence produced by the devices could be used in court.

In its 2016 annual report, Parliament's joint standing committee on intelligence said that South Africa's intelligence agencies were being left behind by rapid technological advances and had difficulty in fighting cybercrime. According to the committee: "Most of the equipment installed at the OIC was done at its establishment in 2002." The OIC is the Office of Interception Centres, situated within the State Security Agency, which provides a centralised interception service to law-enforcement agencies.

Jacobs embarked on a grand R112 million project to equip Crime Intelligence with new grabbers, special vehicles in which to fit them, and other surveillance equipment like drones. As smartphone technology advances, so do grabbers. Earlier devices worked with 3G and have now been upgraded to 4G and 5G. The Crime Intelligence chief and police technical experts identified British manufacturer CellXion as the preferred supplier for thirteen devices. The company also supplies the British armed forces with grabbers.

Both Cele and Sitole were involved in the procurement of the devices and were fully informed from the word go. Sitole's deputy and confidant, Lt.-Gen. Francinah Vuma, joined Jacobs in the United Kingdom to clinch the deal with CellXion. According to police regulations, both Jacobs and Vuma would have had to submit motivations why they needed to travel across borders and their requests had to be approved by both Sitole and Cele. News24 reported that Vuma had approved the procurement in July 2019 and made the payment in three tranches nine months later. The devices arrived in South Africa in March 2020, but instead of being rolled out to the various provinces, they are stuck in a police storeroom in Silverton and can't be used.

🐦 **News24** @News24, 15 June 2021
EXCLUSIVE: Cops splurge R100m on spy technology they cannot use.

Grabbers are so-called listed equipment that cannot be used without an exemption certificate under the Regulation of Interception of Communications and Provision of Communication-Related Information Act (Rica), which regulates the use of mobile signal interception technology. The minister of justice must issue the exemption certificate but can only do so with the sanction of all ministers in the security cluster, which includes defence, state security, correctional services and police as well as the minister of communications and digital technologies. Using a grabber without a certificate is illegal.

Early in 2021, Crime Intelligence sent a memo to police commissioner Khehla Sitole saying: "The equipment has been tested and is waiting to be distributed to the provinces. The provincial technical teams have received theoretical training on its use. The exemption certificate is still outstanding, which is preventing the rollout of the new technology." It is unclear when the police applied to the minister of justice for an exemption certificate, why it was denied or what caused the delay, but I want to fast-forward to the testimony of Bheki Cele at the Human Rights Commission (HRC) hearings about the July 2021 insurrection. He faced a panel of evidence leaders and HRC commissioners five months later.

During his mostly self-congratulatory version of events during those fateful eight days in July, Cele said that KwaZulu-Natal provincial police commissioner Lt.-Gen. Nhlanhla Mkhwanazi had enquired after the equipment Crime Intelligence had bought. Referring to the grabbers, Cele said: "But that equipment, we cannot use it, because there are protocols, there are laws. One of those laws says that if Crime Intelligence of the police buys the equipment, especially the interception equipment, the minister of police must request the minister of justice to grant the permission for those things to be utilized. Which I think is correct because police can be naughty sometimes! But the minister of justice must speak to the minister of state security and the minister of defence. After that the minister of justice will have to speak to the minister of communications. Those equipment is there, it's bought! It is R112 million. I think I have requested the minister of justice twice that we release that equipment."

Neither the evidence leaders at the hearing nor the media picked up this part of Cele's evidence and didn't pursue the matter. The minister of police, who was ultimately responsible for obtaining the end-user or exemption certificate, had failed to do so. The grabbers are two years old and, with advancing smartphone technology, they are probably already outdated. They will be massively expensive to update, and the technicians will need retraining.

How difficult can it be to arrange for such a certificate? And what did Cele do after asking justice minister Ronald Lamola a second time for the certificate? Did he follow up, or did he leave the matter unresolved? As the Cabinet meets every week, Cele could have spoken to Lamola and the ministers of defence, state security, correctional services and communications. Why didn't Cele ask his close ally, Cyril Ramaphosa, to intervene and assist him? I am sure the president would have been eager to get the grabbers working. In his 2019 state of the nation address, Ramaphosa said: "The South Africa we want is a country where all people are safe and feel safe. Let us therefore work together to ensure that violent crime is at least halved over the next decade." With the incidence of serious crime rising, grabbers are vital in the fight against organised crimes like cash-in-transit heists, business robberies, drug trafficking, kidnappings, extortion, protection rackets and bribery.

Crime Intelligence has neither the money nor the time to buy new grabbers. A procurement of this nature is a cumbersome and timely exercise. Moreover, the Crime Intelligence budget for the next financial year has been slashed by R89 million.

I can already see the blame-game playing itself out. Sitole will wash his hands of the matter and blame Jacobs and Cele. The minister will claim he had done everything he could and accuse the former commissioner. He has already pointed a finger at justice minister Ronald Lamola. Jacobs will say that the procurement was carried out according to the book and that he is not responsible for the mess.

Meanwhile, the inspector-general of intelligence (IGI) blames the mess on Peter Jacobs. He found that the grabbers were unlawfully purchased and resulted in wasteful and fruitless expenditure. According to Setlhomamaru Dintwe, Crime Intelligence was initially quoted R63 million for the grabbers. This figure then ballooned to R73 million and the final bill amounted to R102 million. Dintwe said his investigations revealed "gross negligence, ineptitude and lack of diligence on the part of Divisional Management of Crime Intelligence".

Although the criticism of Jacobs may be valid, the purchase was approved by Sitole while Vuma conducted the financial transaction. The IGI doesn't have the authority to investigate the minister of police and his findings are, unlike those of the public protector, not binding; they are mere recommendations. The IGI often detects wrongdoing and reports it to the authorities without anything happening. This may be another of those cases.

In the end, the only winner is serious and violent crime.

* * *

𝕏 News24 @News24, 30 Nov. 2021
National police commissioner Khehla Sitole was clueless during his testimony at the SA Human Rights Commission hearing into the July unrest on Tuesday when he could not recall the number of people who died in Phoenix.

If you think that I am overly harsh in my criticism of Bheki Cele and Khehla Sitole's handling of the July 2021 riots, I invite you to follow their testimony at the Human Rights Commission (HRC) in November and December 2021. It is widely available on the internet. But viewing their performance, especially Sitole's jabber, comes with an extreme warning: it can reduce big men to tears and incline lesser mortals to slash their wrists.

Cele, sporting his customary fedora, was far more engaging than the stumbling Sitole. But like his erstwhile commissioner, Cele showed an inability to reflect honestly on the police's massive failure to protect property, lives and the integrity of the South African state during the violence, unrest and insurrection. Both claimed a job well done.

𝕏 Cape Argus @TheCapeArgus, 30 Nov. 2021
SA's crime intelligence was in the dark during July unrest, looting – SAHRC hears

𝕏 Diana @Letsoalo_Diana, 30 Nov. 2021
Police Commissioner Khehla Sitole, at the SAHRC Hearing:
SAHRC Question: "So the allegation that you were nowhere to be found during the July unrest is wrong?"
Khehla Sitole: "It may not be wrong, but it is not true"

𝕏 Born Brave @DrSelwin, 30 Nov. 2021
Yerrrrr Khehla Sitole is being grilled, this is very embarrassing

During South Africa's eight days of shame, Sitole was nowhere to be seen. The former sheriff-in-chief had ensconced himself somewhere in a "command room" from where he claimed he managed and directed the police's pathetic response to the violence. Sitole and Cele did not speak to each other once during the unrest.

🐦 **EWN Reporter** @ewnreporter, 30 Nov. 2021
Sitole tells the inquiry that there was an early warning report received but there was no need to send it to the Minister at the time, saying it was a just a normal routine intelligence report.

Commission evidence leader Advocate Smanga Sethene: "For the national commissioner to sit in that command room . . . you should be sitting there knowing that you have furnished the minister with an intelligence report, and he has duly given it to the president."

Sitole: "The intelligence report that was received, there wasn't a requirement for me to provide it to the minister."

Sethene: "And I am saying to you that would be a gross dereliction of duty."

Sitole: "And I say no. There is a reason why the report was not generated."

Sethene: "What is the reason?"

Sitole: "Firstly, it is capacity and resources. And secondly, intelligence – and this does not just lie with SAPS – it is all intelligence in the country. They could not rise or pick up on the level of the modus operandi."

Sethene: "You realised all these incapacities when you resumed office on 22 November 2017; it is July 2021. You have done absolutely zilch about it? Isn't that a gross dereliction of duty?"

Sitole: "No?"

Sethene: "What is it?"

Sitole: "It is not me who provide resources."

Sethene: "Where is the intelligence report to warn the president and the minister prior to the July unrest? Do you have it?"

Sitole: "I don't have it."

Sethene: "Then that is a dereliction of duty on your part."

Sitole: "They need resourcing and support in order to generate the products that you refer to, and which are not there."

How ironic that Khehla Sitole lamented this lack of intelligence when he personally handed the division back to the idiots who had messed up for years. And then he wondered why he had zero intelligence.

* * *

🐦 Eyewitness News @ewnupdates, 1 Dec. 2021
Sitole nowhere to be seen during July riots, Cele tells SAHRC in statement

🐦 News24 @News24, 3 Dec. 2021
EXCLUSIVE: Bheki Cele: Blame Khehla Sitole for July unrest, not me

Accusing the national commissioner of incompetence, Cele said in a 26-page affidavit to the HRC: "Since December 2020, the minister has not received any intelligence report/briefing from the SAPS on any matter." In his evidence about Sitole's "disappearance" during the unrest, Cele said: "I hear we were trying to find him in the wrong places. He should have tried to have been in the right places. And the right places were where things were happening. It is where people were dying. It is where looting was taking place."

Cele denied that Crime Intelligence was starved of money because of his tardiness in signing the secret services account. Said Cele: "No, there was money. To such an extent R138 million was granted in May. They had R129 million." Several top Crime Intelligence officers told me this was untrue because the funds in the secret account that had rolled over from the previous financial year were already "ring-fenced" and earmarked for existing projects and other payments. There were no funds for new intelligence ventures.

News24 @News24, 13 July 2021
#UnrestSA: We have a list of 12 instigators, Cele says

Sean @SeanP88ZA, 13 July 2021
There better be AT LEAST 2 Zumas on that list

News24 @News24, 16 July 2021
LIVE: Ramaphosa on #UnrestSA instigators: "We're going after them, we've identified a good number"

CHAPTER 12

The sheriff

THE PARLOUS STATE of the South African Police Service (SAPS) of 2022 is the result of two decades of failed leadership by a string of commissioners and police ministers who were out of their depth, generally useless and often crooked. Yet, as the tentacles of crime reached into every corner and suburb of our land and brought us to the brink of a gangster state, every one of these bureaucrats and office bearers gloated about his or her accomplishments in keeping the devilry at bay.

In 2006, police minister Charles Nqakula (2002–08) referred to opposition MPs concerned about the rising crime rate as "constant moaners" and said: "There are two options. You can complain until you are blue in the face or leave the country so that the rest of us can get on with our work." The ineffectual Nqakula acted as though he was oblivious of the fact that in the three previous years under his watch, 57 162 people had been murdered and 380 173 had been victims of robbery with aggravating circumstances. At the same time, his police commissioner Jackie Selebi (2000–09) was being wined and dined by a notorious drug dealer and showered with gifts and money. At least Selebi went to prison because the Scorpions still existed at the time and were not scared to take on top officials.

Jacob Zuma's choice as police minister, Nathi Mthethwa (2008–14), got the president's state-capture ambitions off to a perfect start. Mthethwa headed a ministerial panel of Zuma acolytes who irregularly appointed Richard Mdluli as Crime Intelligence chief and who sat back and watched the dirty-tricks campaigns unfold against Anwa Dramat, Shadrack Sibiya and Johan Booysen. Mthethwa later received a wall around his house in KwaZulu-Natal, courtesy of the Crime Intelligence secret account.

Zuma's choice as his police commissioner, Bheki Cele (2009–11), was implicated by the public protector and a judge in an unlawful property deal signed off by the Department of Public Works. As a result, Zuma had to fire Cele and in his place appointed Riah Phiyega (2012–15) as the country's first female police commissioner. She ignored a court order to institute a disciplinary hearing against Mdluli and was found by a board of inquiry to be unfit to hold office after police massacred 34 mineworkers at Marikana.

Nathi Nhleko (2014–17) succeeded Mthethwa. He will rot in the dustbin of history for unlawfully appointing Berning Ntlemeza as the head of the Hawks and for being one of Zuma's most committed human shields. Everyone remembers his performance in Parliament justifying the "security upgrades" to Zuma's Nkandla compound where the amphitheatre became a "retention wall", the swimming pool a "fire-pool", and the cattle kraal a "cultural necessity".

While Phiyega was on suspension with full pay, Zuma appointed Khomotso Phahlane as acting police commissioner. He served for two years. He was dismissed for dishonesty while facing fraud and corruption charges relating to irregular procurement worth R84 million.

Fikile "Mr Fearfokkol" Mbalula succeeded Nhleko but mercifully stayed for only a year before Bheki Cele's spectacular comeback from the political wilderness as Cyril Ramaphosa's choice as his minister of police. Phahlane's successor was Khehla Sitole, Zuma's gift from hell to the nation before his removal from office.

Every one of these commissioners and ministers left the SAPS in a worse state than they found it. They ran the police service like a spaza shop and made bad and compromised decisions. The SAPS is no different from a corporation. What does a failing CEO do? Besides making shitty decisions, he surrounds himself with deputies and underlings who will at best be on his intellectual and capability level, but preferably a notch below; otherwise, he feels threatened. If you look at the top echelons of the police, there is an acute lack of excellence, innovation and dynamism. They are a bland, tired and exhausted lot. Why is that?

I turned to former KwaZulu-Natal Hawks head Johan Booysen, who is now investigations head at Fidelity Security and has daily contact with various units in the SAPS. He says: "The rot is systemic. The current police leadership is a result of a compromised system. They don't appoint honest people because it can later bite them in the arse. They appoint lackeys that owe them, and they get consumed in a vortex of inefficiency and corruption. Those not involved in corruption are like ostriches with their heads in the sand. They want to spend their last years in peace and build their pensions. Others, because of their ignorance of Treasury regulations, get drawn into irregular transactions. It is a vicious circle with no end in sight."

In his submission to the State Capture Commission, Crime Intelligence's Brig. Tiyani Hlungwani said: "I have been long enough in the service to know that appointments of individuals are based not on skill and competence but on patronage. These patronage networks have done a great disservice to our country and its people as the SAPS is thus far failing to combat violent crimes that have engulfed the country's citizens. It has also disadvantaged a lot of skilled, ethical and competent cops in favour of corrupt networks who are only there to do someone's bidding."

Under Jacob Zuma, the police declined into a bunch of fractured, bungling and hopeless law enforcers who failed to act against state capture and lost the war against crime. Virtually every appointment Zuma made in the law-enforcement agencies – from Tom Moyane to Richard Mdluli, Shaun Abrahams, Nomgcobo Jiba, Arthur Fraser, Berning Ntlemeza and Khomotso Phahlane – was aimed at parachuting pliable heads and incompetent stooges into top positions. The weakening of law-enforcement institutions was an integral part of the state-capture project.

I do not believe that the appointment of Khehla Sitole in November 2017 was any different. Zuma was facing a state-capture commission and the last thing he wanted was a dynamic police commissioner and a revitalised police force, whether it was his proxy, Nkosazana Dlamini-Zuma, or Cyril Ramaphosa who clinched the ANC presidency.

🐦 **News24** @News24, 26 Nov. 2017
"I have no skeletons" – career cop takes over top job

A former policeman from the apartheid homeland of KwaNdebele, Sitole came out of nowhere to become South Africa's top cop. The national police commissioner manages a government department of more than 180 000 employees and an annual budget of close to R100 billion. He or she is, in that sense, just about the country's top civil servant.

Sitole had scant qualifications for the job. During his evidence before the Human Rights Commission (HRC) in 2021, Sitole conceded that he didn't even have a national diploma in policing, a minimum prerequisite for most of his underlings.

Said Advocate Smanga Sethene for the HRC: "You matriculated in 1984. Is there any further qualification you obtained since you matriculated?"

Sitole: "No, not at tertiary level."

Sethene: "A person charged with responsibility to manage those billions has to have requisite qualifications?"

Sitole: "I agree."

In the days following his appointment, Sitole roped in his cronies. Chief among them were Francinah Vuma and Lebeoana Tsumane, both promoted to deputy national commissioner with the rank of lieutenant-general. Sitole and Vuma have a shared history that goes back to 1987 when they worked as constables in the police station in KwaMhlanga, then capital of the KwaNdebele homeland. Tsumane and

Sitole also have a long history in common, as both served as provincial commissioner in the Free State.

Sitole assured the nation after his appointment that he was clean and had no skeletons. The honeymoon lasted all of two weeks.

* * *

SowetanLIVE @SowetanLIVE, 13 Dec. 2017
Strippers and sex workers ready for ANC conference

Ugliest One @titus_mongwe, 13 Dec. 2017
ANC sex conference

Narike @NarikeLint, 14 Dec. 2017
Happens at every ANC conference. Hos & blessees fly in from around the country; prices are increased 10-fold

A decade after the ANC had elected Jacob Zuma as its leader at Polokwane, more than 5 000 ANC delegates gathered at Nasrec, on the southwestern edge of Johannesburg, to elect a new president. Politically, the country was balanced on a knife-edge. As it prepared to elect its new leader, the ruling party was once again immersed in internal squabbles, intrigue and scheming.

Zuma's proxy and a champion of the radical economic transformation (RET) faction of the ANC, Nkosazana Dlamini-Zuma, was pitted against billionaire businessman and former ANC secretary-general Cyril Ramaphosa. The choice was, on the face of it, between a continuation of the Zuma era of state capture and economic decline, on the one hand, and a change in gear that would return the organisation to constitutionalism and the rule of law, on the other.

As final preparations got under way to host the delegates, police minister Fikile Mbalula phoned Khehla Sitole and told him that there was a security breach at Nasrec that might jeopardise the safety of

Zuma and members of his Cabinet. The minister said he would send his adviser, Bo Mbindwane, to brief him on the threat. Mbalula was a close ally of Dlamini-Zuma and had lauded her a few days previously for her "bravery, courage, foresight and wisdom", while Mbindwane had been described as a Zuma praise singer.

RSA Minister of Police @MbalulaFikile, 14 Dec. 2017
The only thing that can STOP NDZ is fraud and anarchy both will be nipped in the bud

Bo Mbindwane @mbindwane, 10 May 2017
The anti Zuma sausage machine is a red herring against the full emancipation of the black body. Racism & racial empathy gap is at play.

Later the same day, Sitole and three of his most senior generals, Francinah Vuma, Lebeoana Tsumane and Crime Intelligence acting head Bhoyi Ngcobo, met Mbindwane at the Courtyard Hotel in Pretoria. Also present at the meeting was a controversial supplier of surveillance and other equipment to Crime Intelligence and the SAPS. He was Inbanathan Kistiah, director of I-View Integrated Systems.

The hushed conversation around the table was about the security threat. Sitole later said that the Cabinet had been briefed about the threat and that the operation was directed by former Zuma bodyguard Bhoyi Ngcobo. Apparently "electromagnetic blankets" had been detected in Johannesburg hotel rooms while foreign hitmen, disguised as journalists, were said to have entered the country. There were also rumours of foreign spies and assassination plots. The group concluded that Crime Intelligence needed a new grabber to counter the threat. And how convenient that Kistiah was there and, incidentally, had one available. The matter was urgent and, as the deal had to be concluded within a day or two, the generals were going to use the Crime Intelligence secret account to procure the device. The account was out of public sight and could be accessed by the generals in minutes.

The cost of a state-of-the art grabber was around R7 million, but this one was going to be invoiced for an almighty R45 million. The hugely inflated price of the grabber was not a problem. I-View, although in business rescue and not on the SAPS supplier database, had previously supplied Crime Intelligence with surveillance material, albeit at exaggerated prices.

An IPID investigation later concluded that the purchase of the grabber was just subterfuge because at least part of the money was going to be laundered into the coffers of the RET faction to buy votes for Dlamini-Zuma. The dabbling of Crime Intelligence in the ANC's elective conference was not new. In 2012, when Jacob Zuma stood for his second term as ANC president, Crime Intelligence agents descended on Mangaung with R50 million in cash, also taken from the secret services account. The money was never properly accounted for and is the subject of an investigation to this day. This account appears to have been used as a piggy bank for Zuma to ensure his own political survival and that of those he chose as his proxies to continue his legacy.

* * *

🐦 **SowetanLIVE** @SowetanLIVE, 26 Feb. 2018
BREAKING: Mbalula out, Cele in – Ramaphosa announces cabinet changes

By the time that Bheki Hamilton Cele made a comeback to the top echelons of government as Cyril Ramaphosa's minister of police in late February 2018, the national commissioner and his deputies were already deeply compromised and the subjects of an IPID investigation into their quest to fraudulently acquire a grabber at a hugely inflated price. For the next four years, Sitole, Vuma and Tsumane would use every legal trick in the book and hide behind intelligence legislation to avoid accountability for their roles in the saga.

As Sitole and his acolytes spent millions of taxpayers' money to embark on a Stalingrad strategy to conceal their complicity, the truth slowly oozed out from the copious court applications, leaks to the media and evidence at the State Capture Commission. In the first place, there was never a security breach. The State Security Agency (SSA) had swept the ANC venue at Nasrec and did a safety assessment just before and during the ANC conference. It also turned out that the alleged security menace – suspicious foreigners disguised as journalists – were nothing but backpackers.

IPID was at the time also investigating several of I-View's other contracts with the police. In 2016 and 2017, Crime Intelligence paid the company R33 million for software intended to monitor social media sites. The police didn't follow tender procedures and IPID found no evidence that I-View had installed the software on the Crime Intelligence systems. The same happened when Crime Intelligence paid the company R21 million for a system designed to encrypt cellphone conversations and block surveillance. I-View also sold bulletproof vests to the police at R33 000 per item, while they should have cost between R5 000 and R10 000 per vest.

Years after the noxious meeting between the police top brass, Bo Mbindwane and the I-View director, Sitole said in court papers that Fikile Mbalula had played a crucial role in the attempt to acquire the grabber. This explains the role of Mbindwane, his adviser, at the meeting. The blustering Mbalula has miraculously escaped any scrutiny of his role in the debacle and effortlessly moved from the Dlamini-Zuma camp to the Ramaphosa fold as transport minister. Mr Fearfokkol has a history of fixing fokkol. South Africa's railway system, for example, remains in a devastating state of disrepair.

Sitole said that he had involved Vuma in the grabber deal because of her "extensive knowledge and experience in procurement procedures", while Tsumane would have implemented the operation. Said Sitole: "I told them to proceed with the procurement of the device that was apparently needed in order to secure the congress. The said device was apparently necessary to deal with the security breach. I further advised them that whatever they do should be within the prescripts of the law."

Even a junior civil servant would have known that the intended purchase contravened the prescripts of the Public Finance Management Act and amounted to fraud. And a simple Google search would have told the generals that the price of the grabber was inflated six- or eightfold. It also remains a mystery how the national commissioner and his three generals, who had more than a century of policing experience between them, thought they could counter a menace by unlawfully buying a device that nobody at Crime Intelligence knew how to operate. Everyone must have known that this was a grand scamola. Later, the State Capture Commission heard evidence that there was no need for such a device and that the head of the Crime Intelligence cyber unit, who had to perform a needs analysis, was not involved or consulted. Said IPID head Robert McBride: "IPID therefore reasonably suspects that this was an unlawful attempt to steal public money through a rigged procurement process."

It was left to two brigadiers in Crime Intelligence to save the day. In an affidavit to the State Capture Commission, Brig. Tiyani Hlungwani, attached to the unit's finance department, said he was pressured to release the funds but refused because proper processes were not followed and the price was hugely inflated. Crime Intelligence head of operational legal support Brig. Dumisani Chili warned Ngcobo that the unit couldn't conclude any new contracts with I-View as it was being investigated by IPID. He told Ngcobo not to involve himself in "wrong things".

Humbulani Innocent Khuba, a chief director at IPID, said in an affidavit to the commission that he had received a call from a policeman who told him about the purchase of the grabber and said that the money was intended for Nasrec. The whistle-blower submitted an affidavit in which he reiterated that there had been no urgent need to buy the device. Soon afterwards, IPID's national head of investigations,

Matthew Sesoko, spoke to Sitole and told him that his spending spree was illegal and that the SAPS couldn't do business with I-View. Sitole hastily ordered his generals to abandon the procurement.

* * *

Two months after Sitole's abortive plot to acquire a grabber, IPID scheduled interviews with the new commissioner, Francinah Vuma and Lebeoana Tsumane. The two cancelled at the last minute and told IPID to approach Parliament's joint standing committee on intelligence as the matter related to the Intelligence Oversight Act.

This was the start of protracted lawfare between IPID executive director Robert McBride and Khehla Sitole. A few months later, IPID obtained a subpoena to compel Sitole to hand over documents pertaining to the purchase of the grabber. The commissioner, his two deputies and Bo Mbindwane responded by obtaining a High Court order blocking the execution of the order pending an application to set aside the subpoenas.

As the first applicant in the matter, Francinah Vuma provided the founding affidavit in which she said she and Tsumane were tasked to deal with the "treat" (sic). She stated: "While assessing the treat [sic], it became apparent that there was a special equipment [sic] that needed to be procured. All the available services providers who were approached were unable to provide equipments [sic] . . ."

No wonder Pretoria High Court Judge Norman Davis hit police top management for a six. More than three years after IPID caught Sitole and his generals with their pants down, Davis rejected their application and ordered the applicants to declassify the documents that IPID needed. He found that Sitole and the other applicants had placed the interests of the ANC ahead of those of the country, and they were therefore in breach of their duties. In dismissing the application, Davis ordered the police to pay IPID's legal costs.

🐦 **Daily Maverick** @dailymaverick, 16 Feb. 2021
NASREC PLOT: Ramaphosa asks for documents implicating SAPS senior
leadership in alleged R45m bid to defraud Crime Intelligence.

As Sitole and his generals gave notice that they were appealing against
Davis's judgment, Ramaphosa finally entered the fray. Cele wrote to
Sitole a few days later and said there had been a communication from
the president to request all documents relating to the judgment. Said
Cele: "I herewith direct that you provide me with a full report on all
I-View matters and the implications to the SAPS, including your own
involvement and all other senior officers who were cited in the High
Court judgment." Nothing happened.

A month later, Davis dismissed an application by Sitole, Vuma and
Tsumane to appeal against his judgment and slammed the applicants
with another cost order. They took their appeal to the Supreme Court
of Appeal (SCA). SCA justices Malcolm Wallis and Nolwazi Mabindla-
Boqwana ruled: "The application for leave to appeal is dismissed with
costs on the grounds that there is no reasonable prospect of success
in an appeal and there is no other compelling reason why an appeal
should be heard."

🐦 **Daily Maverick** @dailymaverick, 21 July 2021
Appeal court confirms Khehla Sitole's "breach of duty" – his job as head
of SAPS now untenable.

One would have thought that this was the end of the road for Sitole
and his generals. At taxpayers' expense, they once again launched an
SCA application, this time to appeal against the refusal of Wallis and
Mabindla-Boqwana to grant them an appeal. In the process, they threw
more public money at a lost cause. By the time Parliament's portfolio
committee on police assembled for its 29 July 2021 sitting, three
court judgments had delivered a devastating indictment of Sitole and
his two top generals. The grabber saga had by then been reported in

every major news publication. Ramaphosa and Cele had requested the documents and must have been fully briefed on the matter.

Both Sitole and Cele attended the committee meeting. One would expect members to have been on to them like a pack of hungry wolves. But the record of Parliament's police committee is shameless. Its members had acted in breach of their oaths by allowing Hawks head Berning Ntlemeza and his cronies unfettered space to capture the unit and hollow it out. When Anwa Dramat, Johan Booysen and Shadrack Sibiya were driven from their posts and hauled before the courts on trumped-up charges, the police committee was silent. There were a few lone voices of protest from the opposition parties, but they were swamped by the majority ANC members, who sat there like stooges and pretended everything was fine.

Nothing changed when Sitole and his two generals came before the portfolio committee. Throughout the Nasrec grabber saga, ANC members launched scathing attacks on IPID and Robert McBride instead of seeking the truth. ANC MP Leonard Ramatlakane, who led the committee, told his fellow committee members – without having had access to any documents – that IPID's probe was a "red herring" and "devoid of any truth". Only the Democratic Alliance's Andrew Whitfield bothered to ask if there would be disciplinary charges against Sitole, Vuma and Tsumane, and if they would resign. Sitole hid behind the sub judice rule: "No grabber was procured. The matter is still on review. The question on whether we would resign or not, I would say is premature."

🐦 Daily Maverick @dailymaverick, 30 July 2021
SAPS IN CRISIS: Minister of Police Bheki Cele tells Parliament he was unaware of Sitole "grabber" court case finding

Although Cele detested the national commissioner – their fallout following the July 2021 looting and violence had become public – he was forced to back him in the grabber case. Suffering from an acute bout of liarrhea, Cele said to Parliament: "I know nothing about this thing.

Just nothing! I know nothing about the original case. I know nothing about the case when it was decided in the court. I know nothing about the case when it was appealed the first time. I know nothing about the results, I only knew yesterday by chance that this decision was taken on the 30th [of June]. The less I talk about it, the better for me."

It is impossible that Cele did not know about the case as it had been in the news for years, and publications and news sites like the *Daily Maverick*, News24, *TimesLIVE*, amaBhungane and the *Mail & Guardian* had reported extensively on the matter. Doesn't he read a thing? Has no adviser or colleague told him that the High Court ruled that the commissioner and his two deputies were in breach of their duties?

Cele further told the committee: "The only problem I have is that some of these decisions are written with cost. Now, it is not clear for me whose cost is that. Since it involved the national chairperson, a senior person to the national person, we have to sign these legal finances and all that. I have signed nothing, I know nothing. I am told by rumours we are round about 1.8 million but I know nothing about that. So, I will end there."

Cele had to approve the legal costs that Sitole and his cronies incurred in preventing IPID from gaining access to the documents. He said he signed nothing. So, who did? It seems like an irregular expense. Was it investigated? And has Cele taken any steps to recoup the money? True to form, the committee left it just there.

By October 2021, Ramaphosa seemed to have reached the end of his tether with Sitole. Finally, everyone thought, the police commissioner was on the ropes. In that month, Ramaphosa invited Sitole to respond to the president's notice to suspend him. In his representations to the president, Sitole said he was the victim of bad legal advice and a plot by Robert McBride to tarnish his name and oust him. The former IPID head wanted his job, Sitole claimed. Sitole's lawyers said to Ramaphosa: "The national commissioner, who was not party to I-View [contracts] and was subsequently appointed after the procurement process, had no reason to deliberately refuse to provide IPID with the relevant documents but had to make certain that he acts lawfully in providing such documents."

Again, nothing happened, not even when the Supreme Court of Appeal once again handed down a judgment against Sitole, Vuma and Tsumane a month later. According to SCA acting judge president Xola Petse, there existed "no exceptional circumstances" for him to reconsider the original court judgment that there were no grounds to grant an application for leave to appeal. Despite defeat number four, the grabber case had to be kept under wraps at all costs, so Sitole approached the Constitutional Court for yet another challenge. Neither Ramaphosa nor Cele uttered a sound about the expenditure of yet more public funds on a hopeless, doomed and desperate legal challenge.

* * *

No one in police top command seemed to be in a hurry to finalise disciplinary proceedings against Crime Intelligence generals and "rogue unit" policemen considered to be aligned with the Jacob Zuma faction, as cases had been dragging on for years. Yet Sitole moved with great speed against those regarded as being sympathetic to Bheki Cele. The first was Peter Jacobs; the second, South Africa's foremost gang expert, Maj.-Gen. Jeremy Vearey.

It is almost impossible to imagine the cops making a dent in Cape gangland without Vearey's expertise. But after serving for 26 years and having faced some of the most notorious hoodlums in the Western Cape, Vearey's police career was in jeopardy – over a Facebook post. Never one to put a guard in front of his mouth, Vearey fired off a series of Facebook posts between December 2020 and February 2021 in defence of his long-standing ally and former comrade-in-arms, Peter Jacobs. The former Crime Intelligence head was at the time fighting his suspension by Sitole over the procurement of Covid-19 protective equipment for his agents. Vearey also represented Jacobs in his disciplinary process. One of his posts carried the words "MOER HULLE!", along with a link to a News24 article on Jacobs approaching the Labour Court to stop Sitole from continuing with the disciplinary hearing against him.

Police top brass accused Vearey of defaming the image of the national commissioner and bringing the SAPS into disrepute. Sitole charged him with misconduct. The police regarded the alleged offence of such a serious nature that the disciplinary hearing was held as an "expeditious process", which is a shortened procedure that does not make provision for witnesses to be called or for cross-examination. The police had translated Vearey's "Moer hulle!" as "Fuck them!", although he contended that in the Afrikaans variant that is spoken on the Cape Flats, Afrikaaps, it was meant as words of encouragement to Jacobs. It is, for example, frequently heard at rugby matches and other sports events to encourage teams.

🐦 **Dennis Cruywagen** @DennisCruywagen, 31 May 2021
Common expressions that I heard as a child. I also used some of them:
Jou Ma se Moer; Ko os Moer Hulle (often said before a game of footie or
a fight); Ek skop jou in jou Moer; Jou Moer; and many more. Those who
were in charge of Jeremy Vearey's DC hearing need language lessons.

The chairperson of Vearey's disciplinary hearing, Eastern Cape police commissioner Lt.-Gen. Liziwe Ntshinga, found Vearey's Facebook posts to be derogatory, offensive, insulting and disrespectful. She said they had brought the SAPS into disrepute and recommended to Sitole that he fire Vearey. He did so immediately.

Vearey said his dismissal was nothing but part of a strategy to get rid of him, Peter Jacobs and André Lincoln. "I respectfully submit that my dismissal is none other than a method to achieve ulterior motives of senior police management." Vearey challenged his firing and turned to the Safety and Security Sectoral Bargaining Council. Unlike the police disciplinary inquiry, the hearing of the bargaining council admitted evidence, which ultimately descended into a linguistic analysis of the word "moer". Vearey insisted that the word had no sinister meaning and couldn't incite violence. "Moer hulle, when you come into the Cape Flats, means 'Go for them'. In sporting at school, it would mean encouragement, 'Go for it'."

Everyone who grew up speaking Afrikaans – or Afrikaaps – would agree that Vearey's explanation was spot-on. Everyone except Maj.-Gen. Jan Scheepers, deputy provincial commissioner in Limpopo, who was appointed to investigate Vearey's Facebook posts. Scheepers, who is Afrikaans-speaking, told the hearing that he believed the words Vearey used in his posts bordered on treason. "What he's saying as a senior general, that is treason . . . you have a senior general in the police rising up against your national commissioner . . . you're trying to unsettle the peace and stability of the country." Scheepers said that when he as a hunter saw an animal perfectly positioned for shooting, he would say "Moer hulle!" before pulling the trigger. In the hunting environment, it means "to kill" and its use thus shows aggression, he contended.

This is unadulterated bullshit – and Scheepers knows it. It is idiocy to equate "Moer hulle!" with treason and encouraging the destabilisation of the country. Scheepers had probably been stuck in Limpopo for some time, and this was his moment to shine and score some serious brownie points with the national commissioner. In fact, just a few months later, Scheepers was appointed as the acting provincial commissioner in Limpopo.

Liziwe Ntshinga, who had chaired the first disciplinary hearing, testified that, based on Scheepers's evidence, she understood "Moer hulle!" to mean that Vearey encouraged Jacobs to go and hit "them" (presumably her and the police management) in court. Ever heard anything more nonsensical? Ntshinga was, incidentally, promoted to deputy national commissioner three months after recommending Vearey's dismissal. She has in the meantime taken control of Crime Intelligence.

It emerged during the council hearing that Vearey's Facebook posts might have gone unnoticed had it not been for Crime Intelligence officers in the Western Cape who made screengrabs and forwarded them to SAPS spokesperson Vish Naidoo, who sent them up the ladder. Vearey was probably right when he said there was a political motive behind his dismissal. He was the last of the Jacobs group standing.

𝕐 Daily Maverick @dailymaverick, 16 Nov. 2021
SAPS IN CRISIS NEWSFLASH: Axed detective boss Jeremy Vearey's dismissal "is fair", bargaining council rules.

𝕐 Max du Preez @MaxduPreez, 17 Nov. 2021
Moer hulle, Jeremy. This is an outrage.

Vearey has vowed to continue fighting his case in the Labour Court, but even if he wins, he is, for all practical purposes, gone. His position has been advertised and, by the time you read this, someone might well have been appointed in his place. If he ever returns, he will probably join Peter Jacobs at the police Inspectorate, where they will await their pensions.

I have said from the word go that Vearey made a mistake in posting his Facebook comments because he gave Sitole ammunition to take him out. If the national commissioner were a bigger man, he would have summoned Vearey to his office, shat on him from a dizzying height and ordered him to remove his posts and get on with his job, which was to catch gangsters and dangerous criminals.

Within just more than a year, as though in one big swoop, South Africa lost four of its finest lawmen: Peter Jacobs, Jeremy Vearey, Charl Kinnear and André Lincoln. One was murdered, another retired, a third was fired and the last is trapped in a tomb at police headquarters in Pretoria. Among them, these four men had more than a century of police experience and knowledge – institutional memories that are rare and irreplaceable. Cops like Vearey and Jacobs, both approaching retirement age, should have been used by the police long after their years of service to train and guide younger cops in the art of investigating cases and solving serious crime.

How ironic that Sitole shafted Jacobs for using the wrong account to purchase protective equipment and fired Vearey for Facebook posts, yet he and his two deputies have for more than four years evaded giving account for their alleged intention to defraud the state.

* * *

Khehla Sitole's legacy is appalling. He commanded the police in a time of rising crime, managed a divided and depleted service, engaged in debilitating bickering with the police minister, led an apparent conspiracy to defraud the state, and ensconced himself in an "operations room" as his underlings looked on helplessly while people in KwaZulu-Natal and Gauteng went on the rampage and set the country alight. He has also failed to account for his role in the abortive grabber purchase and scoffed at demands by IPID to answer questions about the assassination of Charl Kinnear. This all happened despite President Ramaphosa's promise of renewal, of a new dawn, and his declaration of war on crime. Sitole was implicated in attempted fraud and the ANC's factional politics even before Ramaphosa took office, yet his ruinous command of the service was tolerated for another four years. And when the president eventually acted, Sitole was given the softest landing possible.

🐦 **Daily Maverick** @dailymaverick, 25 Feb. 2022
SAPS IN CRISIS: Police Commissioner Khehla Sitole bows out after mutual agreement and "in the best interests of the country".

Sitole rode into infamy with his full pension intact as though he had completed his five-year contract, which would have expired only in November 2022. His departure sends a message to the many miscreants in the SAPS and, for that matter, in all the law-enforcement agencies: just hang in there for long enough and employ a Stalingrad strategy, and you will leave with a bag full of cash and the sincere appreciation of the country's highest office.

* * *

𝕏 **eNCA** @eNCA, 31 Mar. 2022
Lieutenant-general Fannie Masemola has been appointed as the new police commissioner. The 58-year-old has been serving as the deputy national commissioner for policing.

Is it more of the same or can Fannie Masemola instil new life in the SAPS after the calamitous reign of Khehla Sitole? Any one of the police's 200 or so generals would have been an improvement on the previous commissioner, except for a few loiterers at Crime Intelligence, Prince Mokotedi at the Inspectorate and Alfred Khana at the Hawks. For the first time ever, a panel appointed by Cyril Ramaphosa interviewed shortlisted candidates and recommended Masemola to the president. For a career policeman with a solid (yet unspectacular) track record, the early signs were promising.

Masemola suspended Sitole ally and deputy national commissioner Lt.-Gen. Francinah Vuma, who was implicated in the Nasrec grabber saga and who was found by the High Court to have breached her duties. She retaliated by writing a letter to Ramaphosa accusing Cele of a host of crimes and said that he wanted her killed. She said she was investigating several contracts that implicated Cele and some of his generals. "Because of my investigations and refusals [to approve certain contracts], I am being dealt with to ensure that I know my place. I am both scared for my life and my livelihood as both are being threatened."

One of Masemola's earliest appointments was that of Hawks deputy head Lt.-Gen. Tebello Mosikili, who was, after less than two years at the premier crime-fighting unit, promoted to deputy national commissioner for policing.

In May 2022, Masemola received a visit from former Hawks head Shadrack Sibiya, whose police career had been ended by the thuggery of Hawks wrecker Berning Ntlemeza seven years earlier. A full bench of the Labour Court of Appeal had found that a lower court erred in 2020 when it ruled that although Sibiya's dismissal was "procedurally and substantially unfair", it had no power to order his reinstatement in the SAPS. The three appeal judges ordered that Sibiya must get his job back, either in the position he occupied at the time of his dismissal – as the head of the Hawks in Gauteng – or in another post at the same rank and level.

Sibiya had unearthed a mountain of corruption during his stint as group head of forensic and investigation services at the Johannesburg municipality (which the Hawks and the NPA largely failed to prosecute) but spent his final days at the metro fighting allegations that he had purchased "spying equipment" and even a grabber for his unit. One of the architects of the smear campaign against Sibiya was acting city manager Floyd Brink, a controversial official because of his historical links to Julius Malema. In April 2013, Brink was a manager at the Limpopo department of transport when police arrested him and several other officials and business people for fraud and corruption. Julius and his cousin Tshepo Malema were amongst the suspects. The cases went nowhere and Brink was acquitted.

Brink was appointed as chief operating officer at the Johannesburg metro in 2018 when the Democratic Alliance (DA) governed the metro through a coalition headed by mayor Herman Mashaba. The DA relied on the EFF's support to control Johannesburg, and the appointment of Brink was reportedly a quid pro quo between the DA and the EFF – an allegation denied by Mashaba. Brink became the acting municipal manager in early 2022.

Brink served the former Hawks general with a notice of suspension for having procured "intelligence gathering tools without authorisation from the SSA and in contradiction of applicable legislation" and for not having a top-secret security clearance. When Johannesburg mayor Mpho Phalatse stepped in and ordered the reinstatement of Sibiya, she was accused of subverting evidence against him.

Allegations of illegal spying equipment and "rogue units" were common during the state-capture era to isolate, discredit and get rid of officials who opposed fraud and corruption. The dirty-tricks campaigns seem to have continued into Ramaphosa's era of renewal. The allegation that Sibiya didn't have a security clearance was ludicrous because he was a commander in the Hawks, which required the highest approval. There is often an ulterior motive in attempting to get rid of officials of the calibre and quality of Shadrack Sibiya.

🐦 **News24** @News24, 27 Apr. 2022
Acting Joburg city manager Floyd Brink placed on special leave while investigator probes misconduct claims

Mpho Phalatse placed Floyd Brink on special leave amid an ongoing investigation into allegations of misconduct related to R320 million worth of procurement deals. The alleged irregularities that implicated Brink in possible fraud and corruption are contained in a forensic report compiled by Sibiya's forensic and investigation services at the metro.

Before Sibiya's departure from the Johannesburg metro to rejoin the SAPS, Phalatse invited the SSA to inspect the "spy equipment" that Sibiya had purchased. A team from the intelligence agency descended on the metro in April, and at the end of July 2022, SSA director-general Thembisile Majola said in a report that the equipment had been tested, analysed and inspected and that "it is not intelligence-gathering equipment as alleged". She said: "The SSA would like to conclude that there was no contravention of its governing legislation."

Sibiya didn't want to go back to the Hawks, and he agreed with Masemola to be deployed as the head of organised crime within the detective services of the SAPS. When Godfrey Lebeya was appointed

Hawks head in 2018, it was widely regarded as bad news for organised criminals roaming the land and acting with impunity. Only time will tell if Shadrack Sibiya can make any difference.

CHAPTER 13

The Cat in the Hat

🐦 **Sunday Times Daily** @SunTimesDaily, 21 Feb. 2022
Cele vs Sitole: "Two bulls in the kraal trying to do the same job"

FOR FOUR LONG years, President Cyril Ramaphosa allowed the feud and the bickering between his national police commissioner and his police minister to fester into a debilitating affliction that affected policing on every level. The crime rate spiked, units like Crime Intelligence remained in flux and some of South Africa's very best law enforcers became casualties of the skirmish. As a result, the police proved unable to react to the looting, violence and revolt of July 2021 with ample, decisive and game-changing force.

For four long years, Ramaphosa failed to act against Khehla Sitole, a relic from the Zuma state-capture era. And every three months for four long years, Ramaphosa watched Bheki Cele announce an increase in the incidence of murder, robbery and sexual violence. Today, every South African feels as vulnerable and exposed as during the Zuma years of state capture. The current state of policing and the rise in crime are arguably Ramaphosa's single biggest failure as president.

It didn't need to be that way. By the time Ramaphosa assumed office in February 2018, Sitole and his cronies were already the subject of an IPID investigation and directly implicated in attempting to defraud the state. Ramaphosa should have acted against Sitole then. He didn't. Instead, he and Cele allowed Sitole and his two deputies, Francinah

Vuma and Lebeoana Tsumane, to squander millions of rand in taxpayers' money on delaying and frustrating the investigation against them.

There is only one explanation for Ramaphosa's conduct: protecting the ruling party from the embarrassing revelations of how its top-ranking members have looted the Crime Intelligence secret services account to fight their factional and political battles. In 2022, a recording surfaced at an ANC national executive committee meeting where Ramaphosa can be heard saying that he would rather have his own presidential campaign (against Nkosazana Dlamini-Zuma) investigated than probe "some campaigns" ahead of the 2017 elective national conference, to avoid further embarrassment to the ANC. The president said: "We also know as ANC cadres that, in some cases, state money has been used in some campaigns." It is obvious that this dirty washing must remain in the laundry basket at all costs. Ultimately, Ramaphosa is guilty of putting the interests of the ANC before the welfare of his people.

* * *

Bheki Cele shares a common trait with Sitole: an unfitness to hold office. When Cele first took office as national police commissioner in May 2009, he was initially credited with stabilising the crime rate. He also had a lot of support on the ground for his remarks that police should be able to "shoot to kill" criminals without worrying about "what happens after that". Cele didn't just talk tough; he also looked the part with a fashion style reminiscent of a 1950s gangster. Always donning a fedora, he earned the nickname "Cat in the Hat".

🐦 **TimesLIVE** @TimesLIVE, 1 Aug. 2010
Bheki Cele's R500m police rental deal

In August 2010, the *Sunday Times* reported that billionaire business-man Roux Shabangu had clinched a dodgy R500 million property deal with Bheki Cele and the Department of Public Works for new police headquarters in Pretoria. The deal never went out to tender and it violated Treasury regulations. The police had in fact signed the deal before Shabangu had even bought the building. It then emerged that there was a similar lease deal for the provincial police headquarters in Durban. The deal, also signed off by Public Works, was valued at R1.6 billion, which was, according to estimates, almost three times the going rate for rentals in the area.

After an investigation, Public Protector Thuli Madonsela found that Cele was guilty of improper conduct and maladministration in the police's conclusion of the Pretoria and Durban lease deals with Shabangu. She said that Cele had breached the Constitution and the Public Finance Management Act because the lease had not been discussed in a fair, transparent and cost-effective manner.

Zuma had no choice but to suspend Cele and appoint a board of inquiry into his fitness to hold office. Free State acting judge president Jake Moloi and two top advocates, Anthea Platt and Terry Motau, found Cele dishonest and unfit to hold office. They called for a criminal investigation, saying that there was a questionable relationship between Cele and Shabangu.

The odour of corruption has always permeated the police property lease deal. Why was the commissioner so eager and in such a hurry to conclude the leases when they were about three times the going rate for rentals in the respective areas? What was in it for him? Although Cele slammed Moloi and professed his innocence, Zuma had no choice but to fire him in June 2012. Cele was in the wilderness for two years before Zuma appointed him as deputy minister of agriculture, forestry and fisheries in May 2014, a position he held until Ramaphosa made him police minister once again in February 2018. Cele had by then changed his political loyalties and emerged as one of the most important figures campaigning against Zuma in divided, rebellious and factional KwaZulu-Natal.

🐦 Redi Tlhabi @RediTlhabi, 26 Feb. 2018
Why did Bheki Cele lose his job as Police Commissioner again? So he comes back as Minister? I like him a lot, get along with him but facts and principles matter

🐦 Shadow @couch_guerilla, 26 Feb. 2018
Rock and a hard place. Finding principled ministers within ANC might be a tall order

*　*　*

Throughout the state-capture era and into Cyril Ramaphosa's new dawn, the names of his police minister and that of a convicted drug dealer have been inexplicably linked: Bheki Cele and Timmy Marimuthu. The friendship between the two is, in some ways, reminiscent of the mutually corrupt relationship between Cele's predecessor, Jackie Selebi, and his friend-with-benefits, Glenn Agliotti – also a convicted drug dealer. Agliotti showered Selebi's wife, Anne, with designer handbags, while the commissioner received suits and envelopes stuffed with cash. Selebi famously remarked of Agliotti: "He is my friend, finish en klaar [and that is the end of it]." The bromance landed Selebi with a fifteen-year prison sentence. There is no concrete evidence of Cele being in a similar relationship with Marimuthu, but there is enough circumstantial evidence to require the minister to explain his association with a convicted drug dealer – which he has refused to do.

A former apartheid-era policeman, Marimuthu was convicted in 1992 of dealing in Mandrax tablets and sentenced to four years' imprisonment. According to the Jali commission of inquiry into prison corruption, Marimuthu spent three days in prison before being released on bail. Although his appeal was dismissed in November 1997, he never went back to prison. Judge Thabani Jali said in his commission report that "sinister and extraordinary manoeuvrings had taken place behind the scenes" to assist Marimuthu to escape prison time, and that the suspicion remained that "money changed hands somewhere". After his prison stint, Marimuthu ventured into road construction. This was when he allegedly met Cele, who was then the MEC for transport, community safety and liaison in KwaZulu-Natal.

Marimuthu, also a lay preacher, has no qualms about blessing those that smooth his highway to riches. In 2010, the slick-tongued Marimuthu spoke at a Christian summit on wealth creation in the United States (his lecture is on YouTube). The slender, moustached entrepreneur was talking big: how he had blossomed from an apartheid policeman (he left out the drug conviction) into a billionaire who owned 32 houses. He told his audience that after various failed business ventures, "a very good friend in government" advised him to purchase trucks and get into construction. His first contract was for R18 million and in the same month he obtained another for R32 million. "I drive a Bentley convertible; my wife drives an Aston Martin convertible. My son, who is 23, drives a Lamborghini Spyder convertible. I have a Ferrari in the garage that I don't even use. My daughter has a Q7 and a Cayenne Porsche. Two S-class Mercedes . . . an ML63 to make some noise now and then."

He urged his listeners not to shy away from offering brown envelopes to those who could bless their ventures. But Marimuthu warned: "In a Christian vocabulary we must not use 'bribery' and 'corruption' . . . If you don't bless somebody to get a job, then the heathen will do that and you've lost out."

In his evidence before the State Capture Commission, a former accountant at Crime Intelligence's secret account, Col. Dhanajaya Naidoo, said he had heard over time from several colleagues that Cele had awarded large contracts to Marimuthu that made him "very wealthy or extremely wealthy". This evidence was repeated by Hawks investigator Col. Kobus Roelofse.

The gravity of Marimuthu's alleged felonious activity is contained in a 2011 top-secret Crime Intelligence profile, compiled during the

The Johannesburg book launch of *The President's Keepers* in Hyde Park, attended by more than a thousand people. The lights mysteriously went out and Pauw signed books afterward by the light of a cellphone.

Jacob Zuma at the State Capture Commission. His refusal to testify resulted in a 15-month prison sentence.

Zuma spymaster Arthur Fraser, who tried to remove *The President's Keepers* from the shelves. He now plays a significant role in the ANC's radical economic transformation faction that is trying to unseat President Cyril Ramaphosa.

ABOVE Former president Jacob Zuma with a major benefactor, Roy Moodley, at the Durban July. Moodley was fingered at the State Capture Commission as one of the main capturers of Prasa.

LEFT Hawks head Lt.-Gen. Godfrey Lebeya, appointed to resuscitate the unit – which is still operating at half its capacity.

The five-star AM Lodge in Limpopo, a haven of luxury for the rich and a monument to state capture, acquired with the ill-gotten gains from unlawful Prasa contracts.

ABOVE Former Prasa board chairperson Popo Molefe, who exposed state-capture looting at the rail agency.

RIGHT Former Prasa group chief executive Lucky Montana, under whose watch billions of rand of taxpayers' money were channelled into unlawful and corrupt contracts.

LEFT Former Gauteng Hawks head Shadrack Sibiya, framed for murder to get rid of him because he fought corruption. He was recently reinstated in the SAPS.

BELOW LEFT The day Zuma appointed Berning Ntlemeza as head of the Hawks, all hell broke loose.

BELOW RIGHT Former eThekwini mayor Zandile Gumede in the dock for fraud and corruption.

GALLO IMAGES

GALLO IMAGES

AAI FOTOSTOCK

GALLO IMAGES

Former police crime intelligence head Richard Mdluli, one of the major Zuma keepers, was sentenced to prison for kidnapping and assault. He is standing trial now for fraud and corruption.

Violence and looting in July 2021 followed the imprisonment of Jacob Zuma for contempt of court. It led to the deaths of at least 354 people, damage worth more than R50 billion and 150 000 job losses.

Inspector-general of intelligence
Dr Setlhomamaru Dintwe testifies at the State
Capture Commission.

Cape gangster Nafiz Modack, now on trial
for, among others, the murder of top cop
Charl Kinnear.

Former Western Cape detective head Jeremy Vearey pays tribute to Kinnear at a memorial service.

Police minister Bheki Cele and former commissioner Khehla Sitole. They never got along and inflicted serious damage on the police.

Former prosecutions boss Shaun Abrahams and his henchman Nomgcobo Jiba – both deeply implicated in state capture, and both gone.

Former Hawks boss Johan Booysen (left) and former SARS executive Johann van Loggerenberg: heroes of the war against state capture.

Former SARS commissioner Tom Moyane, the Zuma lackey that wrecked the revenue service.

Crime boss Mark Lifman leaves the court in Cape Town. Tom Moyane's henchmen at SARS "doctored" his R600 million tax bill. He is now up for murder.

EFF leader Julius Malema and former Carnilinx/ Mazzotti chef Bright Kumwembe. The picture was taken in the apartment at the Raphael Penthouse Suites in Sandton.

Former top state security official Thulani Dlomo, who ran a rogue intelligence unit on behalf of Jacob Zuma.

The top management of the defunct VBS Bank in the dock after being implicated in the theft, fraud and embezzlement of R2.2 billion of the bank.

investigation into him. The report stated that Marimuthu had Cele "on his books", and "he is now apparently boasting that he is getting closer to Zuma. The president should resist any advances of Marimuthu as any relationship that is fostered will invariably cause embarrassment."

The report said Marimuthu controlled various companies through his children. These entities allegedly received state contracts worth tens of millions of rand. According to the report, Marimuthu had expanded his business interests to Mozambique, where he was involved in road construction. "Preliminary investigations reveal that Timmy is paying for pilot training for a person who will fly drugs from Mozambique into South Africa."

Col. Dhanajaya Naidoo explained to Judge Raymond Zondo in his evidence at the State Capture Commission that Crime Intelligence, and especially the chief financial officer of its secret account, Maj.-Gen. Solly Lazarus, used Marimuthu and his mob to buy influence over Cele. In return, Marimuthu and his family were appointed as secret agents.

Lazarus once asked Marimuthu to arrange a meeting for him with Cele in Durban. Naidoo, who is related to Lazarus, accompanied the general to Marimuthu's villa in Umhlanga Rocks outside Durban for the meeting. Naidoo had to draw an "advance" of R40 000 from the secret account and bring it with him, which he assumed was for Cele. Naidoo, who was not allowed to attend the meeting, told Judge Zondo: "I had the cash and I subsequently handed him [Lazarus] the money. This was my belief that that money was intended to pay General Bheki Cele."

Judge Zondo: "But this was all – your assumptions? He did not say that himself?"

Naidoo: "No, Chair. He did not. It is an assumption."

Commission advocate: "Then after this meeting did General Lazarus return all or any of the money back to you?"

Naidoo: "Chair, none of that money was returned to me and I – and an assumption again on my part that the money was handed over to General Bheki Cele."

🐦 **SowetanLIVE** @SowetanLIVE, 30 Sept. 2019
Bheki Cele rubbishes "assumptions" he took bribe to protect "corrupt" official.

Cele said after Naidoo's evidence that he would not respond to "assumptions" and asserted that there was "no evidence" against him.

There was also testimony at the commission that implicated Marimuthu in serious sexual assault. One of his female friends was barely eighteen when Solly Lazarus enlisted her in the Crime Intelligence agent programme. Kobus Roelofse and his Hawks team discovered that she frequently travelled with Marimuthu and stayed in safe houses with him. When they confronted her, she told them that Marimuthu, whom she had met at church, had raped her. She was also coerced into having sex with another top Crime Intelligence officer. She repeated her allegations under oath and made an affidavit.

Said Roelofse: "This was brought under the attention of not only police management but also the then Inspector-General of Intelligence (IGI), Ms Faith Radebe. It was decided it should be investigated by Ms Radebe. That event also shocked her, and she indicated that it should be investigated thoroughly."

The IGI did not have the mandate to investigate allegations of rape and referred the matter back to the police. During the State Capture Commission hearing, the evidence leader asked Roelofse: "Did the investigation continue into these allegations?"

Roelofse: "No, Chair. It did not. This investigation was stopped."

Naidoo testified that Lazarus had ordered agents to install cameras in Marimuthu's love nest. The general was concerned that Marimuthu knew too much about the crookery in Crime Intelligence. Naidoo said: "General Lazarus wanted to have some recording of Mr Marimuthu's engagements with his girlfriend so that probably he could have some evidence against Mr Marimuthu should the need arise."

* * *

Timmy Marimuthu and Bheki Cele became central figures in claiming one of the first major scalps of the state-capture project: SARS commissioner Oupa Magashula. In May 2011, Cele was having lunch with Magashula at a fish restaurant in Umhlanga Rocks on Durban's north coast. Both men were flying high, having been selected by Jacob Zuma at the beginning of his term of office to lead two of the country's most vital institutions.

Cele was not just gaining increasing popularity because of his no-nonsense attitude towards crime, but he had also recently tied the knot with a glamorous woman two decades his junior, and he was apparently flush with money. Several newspapers had reported that a few weeks before the lavish wedding and with a lobola bill pending, at least a million rand – but possibly as much as R5 million in cash – was stolen from Cele's Umhlanga mansion. He denied the theft, although it was confirmed by several police sources.

The *Mail & Guardian* reported that prior to meeting his bride, Cele had bought his then girlfriend a house and a Mercedes-Benz and showered her with expensive clothes and gifts during their relationship. In May 2010, Cele reportedly left behind about R40 000 in cash after disembarking from an aeroplane on a flight between Johannesburg and Durban. When the bag was later recovered, the money was gone. Cele said it was "only" R20 000.

During his reign as South African Revenue Service (SARS) commissioner, Pravin Gordhan had groomed a handful of officials to lead the service into the new millennium and enable it to collect enough money to meet South Africa's vast social grants needs and developmental requirements. Among them was the highly skilled Oupa Magashula, a convert of Gordhan's higher-purpose philosophy. In order to effect their state capture, Zuma's keepers had to rid the revenue collector of all these officials, including Magashula. He was the first to go. The fabrication of a SARS "rogue unit" was used to get rid of the rest.

You might well ask what a lunch between Cele and Magashula had to do with the evisceration of the revenue collector. Everything, and it all had to do with Timmy Marimuthu, who joined the two at their lunch table. Magashula had met Marimuthu only briefly beforehand, and there can be little doubt it was Cele who had invited him to join them for lunch. Marimuthu was at the time the subject of a major SARS tax-evasion investigation, which discovered tens of millions of rand from undisclosed proceeds in various bank accounts. How convenient to meet the SARS commissioner when you are embroiled in a major tax probe. Marimuthu would later claim that he had Magashula in his pocket.

Magashula's first mistake was meeting a delinquent taxpayer under investigation. During the lunch, Marimuthu told the revenue commissioner of a young woman with an accountancy degree who wanted a job. The tax boss responded that SARS might be interested in employing her, upon which the businessman phoned her. Marimuthu said to the woman that Magashula was a "mate of mine" and passed the phone to the tax boss. In a conversation spiced with sexual innuendo, Magashula and the woman discussed a job at SARS.

What Magashula and Marimuthu did not know was that Crime Intelligence was at the time bugging the drug dealer's phone as part of its investigation into his alleged criminal activities. The conversation between Magashula and the woman yielded no evidence, and the investigation into Marimuthu was stopped. But two years later, as Zuma's intelligence agencies plotted the capture of SARS, someone remembered the conversation, dug it up, edited the tape and leaked it to *City Press*.

🐦 **City Press** @City_Press, 24 Mar. 2013
Caught on tape – Tax boss and drug dealer: Cosy liaison with head of Sars revealed in jobs-for-pals scandal.

Faced with evidence of possible impropriety by his commissioner, finance minister Pravin Gordhan had no option but to appoint retired Constitutional Court judge Zak Yacoob to investigate the matter. It turned out that Magashula had done little wrong: upon receiving the woman's CV, he forwarded it to his human resources department. SARS never employed her. But Magashula lied to Yacoob about Marimuthu, whom he claimed to have seen for the first time at the restaurant. It turned out that the tax boss and the narcotics peddler had met briefly before. He also said the woman had never sent him her CV, which she had. After the Yacoob inquiry, Magashula resigned with immediate effect.

𝕏 **News24** @News24, 12 July 2013
Sars commissioner Oupa Magashula resigned with immediate effect following the outcome of a fact-finding inquiry.

The demise of Magashula was crucial for the eventual capture of SARS. Had he stayed, he would have fought the seizure of the tax administration tooth and nail, and he would have had the support of virtually his whole executive. Until then, he had had an impeccable record and it would have been impossible for Zuma to get rid of him. Although the president appoints the SARS commissioner, he cannot just fire him. This requires a commission of inquiry into his fitness to hold office.

Just fifteen months after the departure of Magashula, Zuma parachuted Tom Moyane into SARS. Marimuthu and Crime Intelligence had done Zuma's dirty work for him in one brief phone call.

* * *

Following Jacob Zuma's sacking of his police commissioner, Bheki Cele found himself in the financial and political wilderness. Recently married and a father of five, Cele needed a benefactor to sustain his lavish lifestyle. According to an amaBhungane investigation, published by News24 and the *Daily Maverick*, Cele told people in private that, when he was down and out, Marimuthu was the only one who put food on his table. The convicted drug dealer allegedly diverted a portion of his fees that he earned as an informer from Crime Intelligence for Cele's benefit. This lasted until Zuma appointed Cele as a deputy minister in 2014.

As we have seen in an earlier chapter, in 2019 newly appointed Crime Intelligence boss Peter Jacobs descended on Marimuthu and his family, who had been appointed to positions within the unit and ordered them to report for duty. A secret Crime Intelligence report, the authenticity of which is beyond doubt, documented the reaction of the convicted drug dealer. Marimuthu peppered Bheki Cele with phone calls, and on 13 August 2019, he and his wife, Neermala, boarded British Airways flight BA6300 from Durban to Cape Town to see the police minister.

I don't know if Marimuthu managed to have an eyeball-to-eyeball with Cele, but the report noted as well that "various high-ranking SAPS and government officials" frequently met Marimuthu at his villa in the exclusive gated suburb of Ilala Ridge in Umhlanga Rocks. According to the note: "The contact further indicated that meetings took place in the lounge area and Timmy would hand over packages to certain officials as they were exiting. He suspected that the packages contained money."

The note mentioned that "one person that stood out according to the contact was Minister Bheki Cele" and that Marimuthu ordered that he be cooked a "special mutton curry". The note added: "Timmy claims to have Bheki Cele in his back pocket and the minister is always at his beck and call."

🐦 **IOL News** @IOL, 1 July 2021
LISTEN: Bheki Cele's "adviser" caught on tape

🐦 **Yusuf Abramjee** @Abramjee, 3 July 2021
Comment: So a convicted drug dealer advises the Police Minister on issues concerning politics & drug operations. We are in serious trouble.

There have been other curious events concerning Cele and Marimuthu. IOL and Independent Media newspapers said Marimuthu had been caught on tape advising Cele about issues concerning politics and drug operations in the city and in KwaZulu-Natal. In a recording made just before the December 2017 ANC conference at Nasrec, Marimuthu suggested Cele sideline certain top cops and advised him on which tenders to investigate.

There is no doubt that the voices on the recording are those of Cele and Marimuthu. Neither has denied the conversation. All the same, little reliance can be placed on the recording because it might have been edited and parts spliced together to give it a certain meaning. More significant is the reason why it was leaked and by whom – something IOL did not tell us. That it was published by the radical economic transformation (RET) faction's favourite media house says everything.

* * *

Bheki Cele has the dubious achievement of playing an integral role in getting rid of the one anti-state-capture warrior who kept standing throughout the calamitous Zuma era and who fought the scourge tooth and nail. The former uMkhonto we Sizwe operative Robert McBride, once despised by most white South Africans for planting a bomb that killed three white women and injured 69 people in a Durban beach-front bar, spent five years on death row. In February 2014, the Zuma administration appointed him as executive director of the Independent Police Investigative Directorate (IPID), assuming that he would be a loyal Zuma servant.

As the former president and his cronies seized one law-enforcement agency after the other, McBride emerged as a gladiator against state capture. In the process, he had to fight his suspension and bogus criminal charges laid against him by minister of police and Zuma acolyte Nathi Nhleko.

Under McBride's leadership, IPID laid bare the fabricated murder and kidnapping charges against Anwa Dramat and Shadrack Sibiya and exposed Berning Ntlemeza's rogue Hawks unit. IPID investigated fraud and corruption charges against acting police commissioner Khomotso Phahlane, leading to his suspension and prosecution. And then, crucially, on the eve of the ANC's elective conference at Nasrec, IPID blocked the R45 million purchase of the grabber. In doing so, the police watchdog saved the police and the taxpayer many millions. And, who knows, it might have played a decisive role in preventing Nkosazana Dlamini-Zuma from becoming president.

After stopping the procurement of the grabber, McBride could have walked away quietly and remained IPID executive director. Nobody would have known. It was probably what the movement expected from him. But that's not McBride. Tenacious bull terrier that he is, he launched a full-scale probe into the grabber case. In doing so, McBride became a liability for the ANC because his probes into Crime Intelligence threatened to expose the political ramifications of the looting of the secret services account. Heaven knows what IPID would have discovered next; therefore, McBride had to go. Bheki Cele was the executioner who had to throw his comrade under the bus. It was a treacherous act in defence of the ANC that had nothing to do with McBride's performance, credibility or ability.

🐦 **Daily Maverick** @dailymaverick, 27 Feb. 2019
IPID: The curious, agonising, perplexing case of the ANC vs Robert McBride

In September 2018, McBride wrote to Bheki Cele to enquire if the minister intended to renew his five-year contract, which would expire at the end of February the next year. Cele didn't respond. McBride wrote another letter a month later, and again Cele failed to reply. It was only towards the end of January 2019 that Cele informed McBride that his contract would not be renewed. He said there were serious allegations of corruption against McBride – among other things that he had paid himself R1 million for unused leave credits without approval, appointed staff irregularly, forced out staff who refused to implicate Phahlane in maladministration, leaked information to the media and obtained evidence through unlawful interception. Cele's allegations were disingenuously based on nameless and unsubstantiated complaints received by Public Protector Busisiwe Mkhwebane not long before McBride's contract came up for renewal.

Cele's decision not to renew McBride's contract triggered a slew of lawsuits initiated by the IPID head. The litigants agreed that Cele's decision was preliminary and needed to be confirmed or rejected by the parliamentary police committee. Cele said to the committee that the complaint against McBride was serious and "cast significant doubt on his fitness and propriety to hold office as executive director". He claimed the complaint constituted a prima facie case against McBride. This was nonsense. The complaint meant nothing. You or I or, for that matter, Bheki Cele could have laid the complaint before the public protector. His was a tried-and-tested strategy to cast aspersion on and taint adversaries of the state-capture project.

When the parliamentary police committee met to discuss McBride's future, ANC members lynched him, and some of them did their utmost to humiliate him. They suddenly questioned McBride's security clearance and vetting, and his entitlement to access classified documents. Leading the blitzkrieg, ANC MP Leonard Ramatlakane accused McBride of using the grabber case to secure an extension of his contract, saying he was "clutching at straws". Ramatlakane added: "The sense I am getting is that it is just a political issue. As I sit here, I don't know who has been charged for this. It was mentioned the money was going to buy a grabber. How can a grabber go and work at an ANC conference? You don't need the grabber for voting in the ANC conference. It is a red herring. It is for the public, for the media to write about."

The committee voted not to renew Robert McBride's contract. With McBride gone, Cele had twelve months to present his choice of a successor to Parliament for approval. It took him sixteen months, which meant that he had failed to comply with the IPID Act.

As for the host of accusations that Cele had relied on not to renew McBride's reappointment, Busisiwe Mkhwebane eventually substantiated only one allegation. She found in October 2019 that McBride had improperly appointed a deputy director at the police watchdog. The irony was that the Public Service Commission had previously investigated the same complaint and found it unsubstantiated. McBride labelled Mkhwebane's finding "irrational".

McBride had a gentler fall than Anwa Dramat and Ivan Pillay, but the message was clear about what would happen to those who dared lift the lid on the rotten corpse in Luthuli House.

* * *

Ever since Judge Moloi found against Bheki Cele in 2012 for his part in property deals with Roux Shabangu, Cele has vowed to clear his name. At the time he described Moloi's conduct as "judicially unethical" and his firing as "irrational and arbitrary". Cele then submitted a review application against the findings of the Moloi inquiry. Because Cele was the applicant, he had to ensure that his case was court-ready, initiate a pre-trial conference with Zuma's legal team and request a court date. He did nothing of the sort, and for the next six years nothing moved or happened. After Cele's appointment as a deputy minister in 2014, everyone assumed that his review application had gone away. It hadn't.

Fikile Mbalula: Mr Fix @MbalulaFikile, 9 Apr. 2019
Court sets aside 2012 decision to fire Bheki Cele as police commissioner

When the South African political landscape changed in 2018, Cele dusted off his review application. The new president was Cyril Ramaphosa, and although he was then technically the owner of the Moloi report, he was not going to oppose the application of an ally who had helped him come to power. He consequently withdrew as a respondent from the case.

Cele was now, as minister of police, both a respondent and the applicant. The commissioner of police, over whom the minister held sway, was another respondent. Sitole was not going to oppose the application either. Judge Moloi, who was the first respondent, had died in August 2017. There was therefore no one who opposed Cele's application. As an unopposed application, there were no legal arguments in court and a judge simply set the findings and recommendations of the inquiry aside. This meant that Zuma's reasons for firing Cele had also been set aside. It was almost as though the report had never existed.

Although Cele claimed to have cleared his name, he hadn't. He has never taken either of the two public protector reports on review. The findings of Thuli Madonsela thus still stand.

* * *

Unfortunately for Bheki Cele, the saga of the police property lease refused to die. In 2021, a letter from Accountability Now director Advocate Paul Hoffman SC landed on the desk of the head of the NPA's Investigating Directorate (ID), Advocate Hermione Cronje. Hoffman had brought the original complaint against Cele to the public protector after the story broke in the *Sunday Times* in 2010.

The remedial action by the public protector is binding, and in this case she ordered the SAPS to investigate the leases to determine if any crime had been committed. The Moloi inquiry had also recommended a criminal investigation. In his letter of 2021, Hoffman demanded to know what had happened to the police investigation into Cele. Hoffman wrote: "You will appreciate that the remedial action specified by the OPP [Office of the Public Protector] is binding on SAPS and the minister. Our concern is that agreeing to lease premises using public money at about three times the going rate would appear to be prima facie corrupt, but nothing seems to have been done to address any possible criminality in the matter for want of sufficient evidence."

Cronje ordered ID investigators to find out the status of the investigation. The Democratic Alliance had laid criminal charges against Cele at the Claremont police station in Cape Town in August 2011. A docket was opened and transferred to the Hawks in Pretoria. There was no record that such a case existed, and it took investigators several months before they located the docket at the serious economic offences unit of the Hawks. The investigating officer, a Hawks colonel, had in the meantime died.

Much of the docket had been emptied. There were twelve affidavits from the investigating officer to obtain by subpoena the phone records and bank statements of Bheki Cele and Roux Shabangu. The phone records are still in the docket but have never been analysed. The bank records are gone.

The relationship between Cele and Shabangu was vital to the investigation. Cele contended that he hadn't known Shabangu beforehand, while Judge Moloi found that it was clear the two had had a relationship before the lease agreements. The phone records are crucial to determine the truth.

The decade-old investigation against the Cat in the Hat will have to begin afresh. Does the ID have the resolve to investigate the minister of police? Although the NPA is legally shielded from government meddling, many of the directorate's investigators are members of the Hawks who have been seconded to the prosecuting authority.

Fifteen years ago, the Scorpions confirmed their independence and their commitment to upholding law and order when they brought to book Jackie Selebi, a close ally of President Thabo Mbeki, for corruption and bribery. Are we now in 2022 at a crossroads and will the Investigating Directorate stand up not only as an instrument to smash state capturers and their enablers, but also as a future force to guard the nation against grand-scale venality?

CHAPTER 14

Of unsound legal mind

BESIDES THE HAWKS and Crime Intelligence, the major law-enforce-ment agency that was "captured" during the Jacob Zuma era was the National Prosecuting Authority (NPA). Here, a cabal of senior prose-cutors, including heads and acting heads of the agency like Nomgcobo Jiba and Shaun Abrahams, violated their oaths of office and assisted the state-capture project. Their names will go down in South African history in ignominy. Under their watch, the NPA was hollowed out and rendered unfit for the task of bringing the state capturers and looters to book. This also involved hounding those law enforcers who were doing their best to stop the rot in the state.

There is no better example of this than the NPA's maniacal obsession with nailing Johan Booysen, the KwaZulu-Natal Hawks head. This kind of legal blitzkrieg enabled the keepers to extract the corruption busters from their midst and lay waste to the law-enforcement agencies. So desperate were Shaun Abrahams and Nomgcobo Jiba's legal hyenas to claim Booysen's scalp that they perjured themselves, committed fraud and, in the case of senior state prosecutor Sello Maema, superimposed the signature of a potential witness on an "unsigned affidavit" to create the impression that there was evidence implicating the Hawks general and his unit in murder and racketeering.

The extent of the lies of the NPA cabal were laid bare when Cyril Ramaphosa's new-broom appointment, Shamila Batohi, commenced her duties as prosecutions boss in February 2019 and was confronted by Booysen's review application. By then, the prosecution of Booysen and 26 members of the Cato Manor serious and violent crimes unit had spanned almost seven years with more than 20 High Court appearances and millions of rand in legal costs – without any evidence being led. The men were suspended for years; three died during their prosecution and several lost their police careers.

Booysen was charged in 2012 when the NPA mounted a prosecution against him and his men for, among other things, murder and racketeering. This prevented him from concluding his investigation into wealthy Durban businessman Thoshan Panday, who was connected to the president's family and who reportedly boasted Edward Zuma as a "silent partner".

Panday scored R47 million in 2010 FIFA World Cup tenders from the SAPS. Two police officers in supply-chain management gave Panday a monopoly on providing goods and services to the police for the World Cup. For example, he bought generators for R4 000 each and resold them to the SAPS for R94 000 each. When Booysen got a tip-off that Panday had obtained the tenders illegally and corruptly, he was onto the businessman in a flash and froze all further payments to him. Booysen recalled how Edward Zuma came to see him in June 2011 and begged him to release a R15 million payment to Panday. He refused.

Then KwaZulu-Natal police commissioner Lt.-Gen. Mmamonnye Ngobeni ordered Booysen, in the presence of Panday, to stop the investigation. He refused and told her she was acting illegally. It later emerged that Panday had whipped out his credit card to sponsor a lavish birthday party for Ngobeni's husband, Lucas Ngobeni, who was also a general in the police.

To get him off his back, Panday offered Booysen a cash bribe of R2 million – with more to come later. Panday's pet cop in supply-chain management acted as the deal broker. Minutes after he had put the bag of cash, totalling R1.42 million, in Booysen's car, the Hawks pounced on him. Panday was arrested soon afterwards.

Like so many other policemen or public officials, Booysen could have driven off with the cash in his boot and walked away from the Panday case. By refusing to do so, he invited a troop of state-capture gremlins into his life who connived with the likes of Nomgcobo Jiba, Shaun Abrahams and Berning Ntlemeza to destroy his police career and put him in prison.

Following Booysen's refusal to back off from the Panday investigation, a "dossier" that implicated him and the Cato Manor serious and violent crimes unit, which fell ultimately under his command, in 28 extrajudicial killings and a host of other crimes was passed to the *Sunday Times* investigations unit. The newspaper plastered on its front page a photograph of gun-toting, booze-swigging policemen allegedly celebrating the killing of five robbery suspects in January 2009.

🐦 **The Witness** @WitnessKZN, 22 Aug. 2012
BREAKING: KZN Hawks boss Johan Booysen is in police custody, as IPID swoops on Cato Manor cops in Durban.

Jiba, then acting national director of public prosecutions, selected six prosecutors to work on the Cato Manor case, among them Sello Maema, who was appointed as the lead because of his supposed experience in organised crime cases. As Booysen was not the direct commander of the unit and did not participate in any of the alleged killings, Maema and his cohorts had to concoct racketeering charges against him. According to South African law, racketeering is the planned, ongoing, continuous or repeated participation in a criminal enterprise. The NPA alleged that Booysen and the unit had conspired to kill suspects so they could claim financial rewards from the police for manufactured acts of bravery. To substantiate their claim, the prosecutors said Booysen had applied for financial rewards for the men after one such incident. The payout amounted to R10 000 per policeman. Did Jiba and Maema honestly think that Booysen would have sanctioned cold-blooded murder for R10 000 after having walked away from Panday's R2 million bribe?

Maema and his prosecutions team prepared an indictment of 116 charges, ranging from murder and racketeering to house-breaking and theft, perpetrated between 2008 and 2011. It looked set to be the biggest and most complex prosecution of policemen in legal history.

According to the Prevention of Organised Crime Act, the prosecution of a racketeering suspect can only commence once the national director of public prosecutions receives a memorandum from the prosecutor and issues a certificate. After Jiba had done so, she ordered the acting director of public prosecutions in KwaZulu-Natal, Advocate Simphiwe Mlotshwa, to ensure that the case was enrolled urgently. Because the offences happened in his jurisdiction, Mlotshwa had to institute the prosecutions. He told her that he would only sign once he had studied the evidence against the accused.

Mlotshwa came under pressure to prosecute certain controversial cases without following NPA judicial protocol. But he became intent on prosecuting high-flying ANC politicians Mike Mabuyakhulu and Peggy Nkonyeni for corruption and racketeering. The two, who were known to be close to Jacob Zuma, were among 23 people indicted for fraud for the corrupt awarding of KwaZulu-Natal provincial contracts worth R144 million. It became known as the "amigos case". This cost him his job.

𝕏 Sam Sole @SamSoleZA, 16 July 2012
Simphiwe Mlotshwa, acting head of prosecutions in KwaZulu-Natal, has been axed – as we predicted 10 days ago. Bad news.

To replace Mlotshwa, Jiba catapulted the head of the NPA's tax unit in KwaZulu-Natal, Advocate Moipone Dinah Noko, into the position of acting director. Soon afterwards, Zuma appointed her as permanent director of public prosecutions in KwaZulu-Natal. Noko made a mockery of her oath to prosecute without fear or favour by withdrawing the bribery charge against Thoshan Panday and his police accomplice, Col. Navin Madhoe. She gave no reason for doing so. She did the same in the "amigos case" by abandoning the prosecution against Mabuyakhulu,

Nkonyeni and several other accused. With Simphiwe Mlotshwa out of the way, Noko ordered the prosecution of Booysen and his men.

🐦 **Mzilikazi wa Afrika** @IamMzilikazi, 24 Aug. 2012
@Durban magistrate's court for the Cato Manor case with more than 100 angry and bitter eyes trying to kill me.

The NPA and the *Sunday Times* soon produced another witness: "whistle-blower" Aris Danikas, a former police reservist at Durban Organised Crime, who claims he fled South Africa in 2008 for Greece because he lived in fear of the Cato Manor unit after he wanted to expose police brutality.

Landing on safe soil in Europe after his alleged close shave with the Cato Manor unit, Danikas recounted the string of murders and tortures allegedly committed by Booysen and his men. He said he had received death threats, that he had "witnessed too much" and that he was haunted by what he had seen. "Every day when I go to sleep, I wake up kicking doors, kicking the air," he said in an interview with a European news agency.

Booysen rejected Danikas's claims and said he had left South Africa after being suspended for bringing the police into disrepute. Booysen also claimed that Danikas had disappeared with R300 000 from a former business partner, something he has vehemently denied.

This was seemingly the end of Booysen's police career. How do you come back from being accused of mass murder? Not even Eugene de Kock or Dirk Coetzee was accused of so many killings. Booysen spent every inch of his energy over the next few years fighting the assault on two fronts: the NPA and the police. His first victory came when a police disciplinary inquiry, headed by a top senior advocate, found him not guilty on all the charges. But this had no effect. Hawks head Berning Ntlemeza later suspended him and brought other trumped-up charges against him.

Booysen then took Jiba's authorisation to charge him with racketeering and murder on review. In February 2014 Judge Trevor Gorven of the Durban High Court ruled that Jiba's decision to prosecute Booysen was irrational. In finding that she had no evidence to order Booysen's prosecution, Gorven said: "The impugned decisions were arbitrary, offend the principle of legality and, therefore, the rule of law, and were unconstitutional."

🐦 **Daily News** @DailyNewsSA, 26 Feb. 2014
Murder and racketeering charges against KZN Hawks boss, Maj Gen Johan Booysen, set aside in Durban High Court today

Of the 23 dockets in question, only two mentioned Booysen, but they didn't implicate him in any offence. Of the 290 statements in the dockets, only three mentioned him but none implicated him directly. Danikas's "affidavit" formed part of the docket, but Judge Gorven said that not only was his statement neither signed nor dated, but even if it were an affidavit, it had no value in the prosecution because the content did not cover the indictment period. Only one incident in the Danikas "affidavit" fell within the period of the alleged crimes, and Booysen was not even mentioned in that incident.

Following the ruling, Booysen laid charges of fraud against Jiba for "misrepresenting evidence". This should have been the end of Booysen's prosecution – and that of his men – and the beginning of a judicial process to make Jiba account for her irrational and unconstitutional decision-making. She was charged with perjury and fraud, but two months before her trial date, Shaun Abrahams was appointed as national director of public prosecutions. He promptly withdrew the charges against Jiba. (A full bench of the High Court ruled at the end of 2017 that his decision was irrational and ordered the reinstatement of the charges.)

Abrahams's next mission was to get Booysen back in the dock. Before issuing another certificate, Abrahams ordered Sello Maema to travel to Greece to get Aris Danikas to sign the affidavit. Maema had further consultations with Danikas who, by his own telling, provided the prosecutor with further evidence. Upon Maema's return to South Africa, Abrahams issued a new certificate for Booysen's prosecution on racketeering charges in 2016. The general was back in the dock.

City Press @City_Press, 20 Feb. 2016
Suspended KZN Hawks boss Johan Booysen, who successfully forced the state to withdraw the charges, was re-arrested

Glenn @GlennfromZA, 20 Feb. 2016
Another snotklap coming for the NPA. "Independent and without fear or favour" – ag please

* * *

News24 @News24, 13 Aug. 2018
ConCourt finds Abrahams' appointment as NPA boss unconstitutional and invalid

Angelo @Angelo_Jacobs, 13 Aug. 2018
Hahaha. #shaunthesheep has been skinned!

In August 2018, the Constitutional Court found Abrahams's appointment as national director unconstitutional and invalid. Despite describing himself as "nobody's man", Abrahams had to vacate his sheep pen. He mercifully vanished into obscurity – well, almost. Not finding himself on the most wanted list as a defence advocate (would you hire him if your freedom depended on it?), he pursued legal opportunities in countries like Lesotho and Botswana. In Lesotho, Abrahams was appointed to prosecute the murder and treason case against former army chief Lt.-Gen. Kennedy Kamoli and five others. With Abrahams in attendance, the court set the case down for trial in January 2022. He didn't show up for the first day of the trial and offered no explanation. As the prosecution scrambled to find a new lead counsel, the case had to stand over for another day. On that day, Abrahams was back, again offering no explanation. The judge lambasted Abrahams for failing "his legal and ethical obligations", having no regard for the plight of the accused and treating the court in a "cavalier" manner. He was banned from participating further in the trial, but on appeal he was reinstated. Between 2018 and the end of 2021, Lesotho's justice department paid Abrahams almost eight million Lesotho loti, which is the equivalent of eight million rand. They still owe him another two million.

* * *

If newly elected President Cyril Ramaphosa had any hope of restoring the prosecuting authority's credibility, he had to start mopping up the mess left behind by Shaun Abrahams and Nomgcobo Jiba. She and several of her henchmen were still lurking in the top echelons of the NPA like noxious spiders. Ramaphosa appointed retired Constitutional Court Judge Yvonne Mokgoro to head an inquiry to determine if Jiba and her accomplice, special director of prosecutions Lawrence Mrwebi, were fit to hold office, and gave them notice of their suspension. At around the same time, Ramaphosa broke with tradition and announced the setting-up of an advisory panel to identify and conduct interviews with suitable candidates for the position of national director of public prosecutions. It was the first time since the unit's establishment in 1998 that the process would be transparent. Finally, in December 2018, Shamila Batohi was announced as the new director.

🐦 **Karyn Maughan** @karynmaughan, 1 Aug. 2018
BREAKING: President Ramaphosa has given Nomgcobo Jiba, Lawrence Mrwebi notice that he intends to suspend them, and will institute inquiries into their fitness to hold office.

🐦 Daily Maverick @dailymaverick, 5 Feb. 2019
NPA 2.0: Shamila Batohi, the woman with the country on her shoulders

Leaving behind her prestigious job as a senior legal adviser at the International Criminal Court in The Hague in the Netherlands, Batohi returned to her home country and took up the poisoned chalice of the headship of the NPA. In the preceding 14 years, seven permanent and acting national directors had held this office and all had departed long before their terms expired. Batohi was not only burdened with an organisation hollowed out by state capture, but she also had to accomplish what many of her predecessors had failed to do: bring Jacob Zuma and his cronies to book for state capture.

Imagine walking into an organisation where Nomgcobo Jiba is your deputy and where a host of top prosecutors and directors have violated their oaths of office by actively participating in state capture by instituting trumped-up charges against those that opposed the scourge. Unchallenged and unchecked, this band of miscreants might eventually bring the house down on you.

It was unthinkable that Batohi and Jiba could sit under the same roof. The new boss needn't have worried: the findings of former Constitutional Court justice Yvonne Mokgoro, appointed to investigate the fitness of Jiba and Mrwebi, were utterly damning, and they were fired.

🐦 Mandy Wiener @MandyWiener, 25 Apr. 2019
Justice Mokgoro's findings on #Jiba and #Mrwebi are utterly damning. She's made findings on their integrity, transparency, ethics, accountability. They must finally go so the NPA can recover.

🐦 Qaanitah Hunter @QaanitahHunter, 26 Apr. 2019
#NPA Jiba pleaded to Ramaphosa not to fire her saying she is married with three kids and has to take care of her mother. Ramaphosa has rejected her request to be made a public prosecutor instead of firing her. The president rejected this saying she is dishonest.

Days after first occupying the hot seat at the prosecution authority, Shamila Batohi ordered four of her top prosecutors, deputy national director Rodney de Kock, Limpopo director of prosecutions Ivy Thenga, Western Cape deputy director of prosecutions Shareen Riley and senior state advocate Elijah Mamabolo to review the racketeering prosecution certificate and evidence against Johan Booysen. The four prosecutors produced a 96-page report in June 2019. Batohi kept the report under close wraps for more than a year, probably because of the embarrassment it would cause the NPA. When it was eventually leaked, it laid bare a legal scam-fest in the NPA.

* * *

𝕏 Daily Maverick @dailymaverick, 5 Aug. 2020
DECADE OF DECEIT LAID BARE: Confidential NPA report exposes senior officials who lied about Johan Booysen, yet they are still employed.

It turned out that Jiba, Abrahams, Noko and Maema were all part of the web of deceit and lies that was spun to prosecute Booysen and his men. How they ever thought a judge would fall for their trickery once the case got to trial boggles the mind. The De Kock panel also interrogated the new evidence that Maema had brought back from his meeting with Danikas in Greece. This turned out to be another unsigned "affidavit", but in Greek. Despite having no English translation of the "affidavit" and no Greek-speaking prosecutors, Abrahams had said he was satisfied with the "new evidence" and issued a second prosecution certificate. Danikas had signed his Greek affidavit under the mutual legal assistance agreement between Greece and South Africa only eight months after Abrahams issued the certificate. He later refused to sign an English translation because he claimed it contained mistakes.

According to the panel, Danikas had presented no new evidence to the prosecution and, after his refusal to sign the English translation, Maema had superimposed his signature on the translated "affidavit".

When the panel asked Maema for an explanation, he said: "When I represented it to Danikas after it was translated, he pointed out a number of mistakes in the statement and refused to sign it. His signature on the Greek version was just imposed [sic] on the English version." There could have been no lawful reason for Maema to have "imposed" a signature on an affidavit except to create the impression that the English version was signed and commissioned. The De Kock panel found the state's reliance on Danikas's evidence "puzzling" because he didn't "implicate Booysen and the other accused . . . and will not assist the prosecution to prove the racketeering charges".

The prosecution had two other witnesses they said would implicate Booysen and his men in a criminal enterprise, but the De Kock panel found that their version "amounts to double hearsay" and was of "a very low probative value". The panel said it was a mystery why the prosecution charged several policemen who had played no role in the incidents, while others mentioned in the dockets were not charged. The sloppy prosecution team had even charged deceased policemen. Capt. Neville Eva had been charged with "managing a criminal enterprise", though he died in 2012. Capt. Vincent Auerbach was also charged, but he died in January 2013.

The panel said it was "absurd and ludicrous" to suggest that Booysen, the so-called manager of the criminal enterprise, would involve himself in killings for a reward of R10 000. Several policemen who were charged had received no reward, while others who were rewarded were not among the accused. Said the panel: "There was insufficient evidence placed before both Jiba and Abrahams to warrant Booysen's prosecution."

Aris Danikas hasn't given up. He pops up regularly on whistle-blower platforms. He's been described by social activist John Clarke as an "amazing soul" who had to flee South Africa to seek refuge in Greece because of his "evidence of police atrocities". How does a Greek citizen become a refugee in Greece?

* * *

𝕐 Mandy Wiener @MandyWiener, 9 July 2019
BREAKING: Shamila Batohi has announced the racketeering charges against General Johan Booysen are being withdrawn. The reversal of the Jiba era is underway.

𝕐 TimesLIVE @TimesLIVE, 17 July 2019
There was spontaneous applause, cheers and tears in the Durban high court on Wednesday when charges were withdrawn against the remaining 27 accused in the so-called Cato Manor "death squad" case.

Sello Maema believes to this day that there is a prima facie case against Booysen and the Cato Manor unit and that they should stand trial. He declared in his affidavit to the State Capture Commission: "The process that was followed in arriving at the conclusion of the De Kock report was irregular and unlawful, and no weight should be put on it." Moipone Noko made no representation to the commission, but the De Kock panel handed a loaded gun to Shamila Batohi to blast two of her most disreputable prosecutors into oblivion. She didn't. Instead, Batohi sent Noko to the North West province as director of prosecutions with Sello Maema as deputy director. With the notorious Maj.-Gen. Patrick "Porn Cop" Mbotho as the Hawks head in the province, the North West appears to have become a dumping ground for discredited law-enforcement officials.

In October 2020, Noko penned a 57-page open letter to her NPA colleagues in which she said: "I cannot continue to stay silent while I am traumatised and made to feel like I am parading naked in public due to this unfair and unjust treatment for simply doing my job. I need to be shown who I have sabotaged and made them fail to do their duties." Rather than face an inquiry to find out, she quit. Noko said: "I am tired, and this is a decision that is long coming based on how I've been bashed and vilified throughout the years. I can't take this anymore. I am just tired."

* * *

🐦 **Newzroom Afrika** @Newzroom405, 8 Feb. 2021
Durban businessman Thoshan Panday and former KwaZulu-Natal Police Commissioner Mmamonnye Ngobeni are back in court today. This time with seven other co-accused in a multimillion Rand tender corruption case.

How the pendulum has swung for Johan Booysen and Thoshan Panday over the course of a decade!

Panday went from a politically connected beneficiary of crooked police tenders to the accused in a criminal case that can land him fifteen years or longer behind bars. Booysen went from a "death-squad commander" and murder accused to a never-say-die hero who fought an unjust system and emerged victorious.

Today, it is Booysen's time to collect for having been hauled before the courts on trumped-up charges and for enduring two suspensions from the SAPS and, ultimately, a destroyed police career. In February 2021, he filed a R7.6 million damages claim because of his unjust prosecution.

Charged with heading a criminal enterprise, wise-guy Thoshan Panday is now the one facing long-term imprisonment. In May 2021, he appeared in the Durban Magistrate's Court in a corruption case relating to the 2010 FIFA World Cup. The state plans to present evidence that the businessman turned his racket into a family affair. Panday allegedly used entities registered in the name of family members to launder and hide the proceeds of his crimes.

Standing next to Panday's family in the dock were Mmamonnye Ngobeni, Col. Navin Madhoe and Capt. Aswin Narainpershad. Panday and his not-so-happy family face 261 counts, including fraud, corruption, racketeering, forgery, extortion and money laundering. The case has been transferred to the High Court.

🐦 Orrin Singh @orrin417, 7 May 2021

In order from left to right: Arvenda Panday, 69 (Thoshan's mother), Privisha Panday, 45 (Thoshan's wife), Seevesh Ishwarkumar, 44 (Thoshan's brother-in-law), Kaja Ishwarkumar, 37 (Thoshan's sister) and Tasleem Rahimna, 35 (Thoshan's personal assistant).

🐦 Sue Khan @iamsuekhan, 7 May 2021

Yes hang your heads in shame greedy buggers

CHAPTER 15

Ever the bridesmaid, never the bride

🐦 **Andrew Feinstein** @andrewfeinstein, 3 May 2019

State Capture: The prosecutors were the willing executioners too. A cabal of senior prosecutors, including former NPA bosses Shaun Abrahams and Nomgcobo Jiba, violated their oath of office and "enabled" State Capture

DURING THE LATTER days of the State Capture Commission, senior state advocate Sello Maema dumped an affidavit and attachments of more than 2 700 pages on Judge Raymond Zondo. He was followed by fellow state advocates Dr Torie Pretorius (727 pages), George Baloyi (364 pages), Molatlhwa Mashuga (430 pages), Anthony Mosing (1 220 pages), Andrew Chauke (925 pages), Raymond Mathenjwa (1 470 pages) and Marshall Mokgatle (1 490 pages). These eight state prosecutors stand accused of being members of a cabal of lawmen at the National Prosecuting Authority (NPA) who were used by former prosecutions bosses Nomgcobo Jiba and Shaun Abrahams to bring trumped-up charges against those civil servants who opposed state capture and posed a threat to Jacob Zuma and his cronies.

Between them, they mercilessly persecuted Hawks head Anwa Dramat and two of his provincial heads, Johan Booysen and Shadrack Sibiya; SARS commissioner Oupa Magashula, acting SARS commissioner Ivan Pillay and investigations executive Johann van Loggerenberg; finance minister Pravin Gordhan; top NPA prosecutor Advocate Glynnis Breytenbach; and IPID executive head Robert McBride and senior IPID officials Matthew Sesoko and Innocent Khuba. Colluding with Berning Ntlemeza's lapdogs at the Crimes Against the State Unit (CATS) of the Hawks, these prosecutors pummelled their victims into submission.

The eight NPA prosecutors occupy crucial positions at the NPA and pose a massive obstacle for new national director Shamila Batohi in renewing and rejuvenating the organisation. They are, like so many other compromised civil servants, clinging to their positions, probably for the sake of their pensions and status.

🐦 **News24** @News24, 23 July 2021
"Advocate Tebogo Mathibedi SC, for the NPA officials, told acting Chief Justice Raymond Zondo, who chairs the commission, they had performed their statutory duties and obligations without fear, favour or prejudice."

Besides burying Judge Zondo under more than 9 000 pages of "evidence", the eight prosecutors also brought a combined submission of 239 pages to the commission in which they professed their innocence. The senior counsel for the cabal, Advocate Tebogo Mathibedi, told the commission: "The implicated officials are career prosecutors who faithfully and diligently served the NPA and the country for decades. It is highly improbable that these officials will give away their personal and professional integrity and careers for political and corrupt reasons." Perhaps Mathibedi should have explained to the commission why none of these cases resulted in a guilty verdict. In fact, no case, except for that of Glynnis Breytenbach, made it to trial – and she was acquitted. In every other instance, charges were withdrawn.

Mathibedi argued that the accusers had not an "iota of evidence" to implicate his clients in state capture and were themselves "subjects of criminal investigations". He said that some "corruption busters" were "criminals" who sought to protect "certain individuals". The senior counsel, assisted by three junior advocates, was spinning at the speed of a Hoover.

For the state-capture project to succeed, chief enablers and keepers in the law-enforcement agencies like Abrahams, Moyane, Fraser and Ntlemeza required pliant and obedient officials to kill politically sensitive cases and hunt down those who resisted and impeded the project. These officials actively assisted in hollowing out the agencies to ensure that there were no consequences for the capturers and the looters. The state-capture project didn't always require overt action like a malicious prosecution. Sometimes an official or prosecutor was required to do nothing more than not investigate or prosecute a case. Just occupying a post could prevent a more efficient official from doing something.

Evidence at the State Capture Commission implicated the cabal of eight in the malicious prosecution of those posing a threat to the Zuma zombies. These legal eagles all had their own reasons for choosing to be on the wrong side of history – be it survival, monetary gain or blind loyalty.

Why did Torie Pretorius, a senior state advocate with 45 years of service at the NPA and its apartheid equivalent, the Office of the Transvaal Attorney-General, kneel and submit to the authority of Shaun Abrahams, a legal nincompoop who was once his underling? He is a man who rose from court clerk and traffic court prosecutor to senior advocate and, later, acting special director of the priority crimes litigation unit (PCLU). And why would Pretorius, who was a prosecutor in the sensational trials of apartheid chief assassin Eugene de Kock, death-squad slayer Ferdi Barnard, and chemical and biological warfare commander Dr Wouter Basson be willing to be cast under the bus when Abrahams pinned on him the responsibility for deciding to prosecute Pravin Gordhan, whose case ended in legal embarrassment? Perhaps only Jacobus Petrus "Torie" Pretorius knows why he unleashed the PCLU to hound and badger those opposed to state capture instead of going after the corrupt looters who sucked the country dry.

Having known Pretorius relatively well during his heyday when he was prosecuting apartheid's assassins, I will hazard a guess at why he chose this path. After joining the Department of Justice in 1976, Pretorius mentions in his resumé that in the early 1990s he was an evidence leader at the Goldstone Commission and part of the Pierre Steyn inquiry. South Africa was at the time engulfed in township battles between the Inkatha Freedom Party and the ANC while a Third Force of apartheid securocrats stoked the flames of violence to derail negotiations and prevent a free and democratic election.

In October 1991, President F.W. de Klerk appointed Judge Richard Goldstone to probe public violence and intimidation. Goldstone blew the lid off the Third Force and described, among other things, how top army officers had plotted to undermine the ANC and provoke "black on black" violence. Following Goldstone's raid on Military Intelligence, which uncovered evidence of the army's complicity in the mayhem, De Klerk appointed the defence force's Lt.-Gen. Pierre Steyn in November 1992 to conduct further investigations. Steyn found evidence of state complicity in the ongoing assassinations, train and hostel violence, and the training and arming of Inkatha impis. A month later, following a late-night meeting between Steyn and De Klerk, the president got rid of 23 generals and high-ranking army officers. This was known as "the Night of the Generals".

Steyn's and Goldstone's inquiries are seminal moments on our road to democracy and their names look brilliant on Pretorius's CV – that is, until you read the Steyn report, which was declassified in 2006. Steyn said that Torie Pretorius was "clearly torn by political loyalty" and recalled a personal letter that the advocate had penned to De Klerk in June 1993, starting with the words: "Meneer die Staatspresident [Mr State President]". In his letter, which was written outside his brief, Pretorius warned De Klerk about the "great insecurity" that existed in the armed forces about "a Nuremberg-type scenario" that might follow the advent of democracy. He cautioned that those targeted by Steyn and Goldstone had taken out "insurance policies in the form of documentary evidence", which they threatened to release if they were made "scapegoats". He reminded De Klerk of the president's words to him and another advocate: "Kêrels, ons het genoeg probleme soos dit is – julle moet nie vir ons nog probleme gee nie. [Guys, we have enough problems as it is, so please do not give us more.]"

In the prosecution of De Kock, Barnard and Basson, Pretorius was the junior advocate and he lived in the legal shadow of the legendary Anton Ackermann. In 2001, the International Association of Prosecutors (IAP) bestowed on Ackermann its international special achievement award – the first time that an individual prosecutor had received this honour. When the NPA formed the priority crimes litigation unit (PCLU) in 2003, Ackermann became its first special director with Pretorius (yet again) as his sidekick. The PCLU is an elite unit tasked with prosecuting offences like terrorism, treason, sabotage, insurrection, mercenary activities, national security threats and the proliferation of nuclear material.

The PCLU was later strengthened by the addition of University of Natal law graduate Shaun Kevin Abrahams. He had, like Pretorius, started his NPA career as a clerk before being admitted as an advocate in 2002. He was by all accounts a skilled prosecutor and obtained guilty verdicts against, among others, Nigerian guerrilla leader Henry Okah on terrorism charges, right-wing extremists who conspired to attack the ANC leadership at its elective conference in Mangaung in 2012, and Rwandan agents who attempted to assassinate former army general Kayumba Nyamwasa, then in exile in South Africa.

When Ackermann retired, the young Abrahams was promoted over Pretorius's head to become PCLU acting special director, a post he held for seventeen months before Zuma appointed him on 18 June 2015 as national director of public prosecutions. He was elevated to this post just three months after his 38th birthday.

The career of the degree-rich Pretorius (he holds two master's degrees and a doctorate in law from the universities of Pretoria and London) reached its pinnacle when Abrahams promoted him to act as PCLU special director. After years of being forever the bridesmaid, never the bride, it was Pretorius's time to shine. Nearing retirement age, he also knew that an eventual permanent promotion to special director would do wonders for his pension.

In November 2015, Abrahams referred the following cases to the PCLU: the State versus Robert McBride and others, the SARS "rogue unit" investigations, two cases against the NPA's Glynnis Breytenbach, and the State versus Johan Booysen and others. The cases of the State versus Gordhan and others, and the State versus Pillay, Van Loggerenberg and another, were later added to the list. Abrahams had turned the PCLU into a state-capture war room with Torie Pretorius as the battle commander. It is also clear from Pretorius's affidavit and submission to the State Capture Commission that he never questioned any of Abrahams's orders but pliantly followed them to the letter.

The two strengthened the PCLU with three experienced prosecutors: senior deputy directors Khulekani Raymond Mathenjwa and Sello Maema and deputy director Jabulani Mlotshwa. Mathenjwa and Maema hold between them six law degrees and several diplomas. Mathenjwa boasted in his affidavit before the State Capture Commission that he had successfully prosecuted a host of high-profile crime cases and was a member of the NPA team that reinstated corruption charges against Jacob Zuma. Maema claimed to be an organised crime specialist and had been in charge of five racketeering prosecutions. It was because of this that he was appointed as the lead prosecutor in the Johan Booysen–Cato Manor matter.

Jabulani Mlotshwa didn't join the cabal of eight at the State Capture Commission – with good reason. If you and your employer pretend that you are an advocate and you are not, you keep dead quiet. Mlotshwa's great con emerged in the Randburg Magistrate's Court in Johannesburg when he was prosecuting Paul O'Sullivan for fraud. The accused had allegedly told a client, who was a suspect in another case, that he would get her a suspended sentence if she confessed. During proceedings, Mlotshwa's phone rang. It was the boss, he told the magistrate, and so he had to take it. The court adjourned for a few minutes.

🐦 Team News24 @TeamNews24, 27 July 2017
Shaun Abrahams calls prosecutor in court to answer a complaint.

Abrahams wanted to see Mlotshwa right away. He had received a complaint from O'Sullivan about Mlotshwa's fitness to hold office. The case in the Randburg Magistrate's Court was postponed while Mlotshwa scuttled off to see the top dog. When he returned, he told the magistrate: "My competency and credentials as a prosecutor are being questioned." He requested a three-month postponement while dealing with the complaint. The magistrate refused. Mlotshwa's only witness against O'Sullivan crumbled. The case was dismissed, the second he had brought against the forensic investigator. The first had also failed, and so did the rest that followed.

Mlotshwa was an attorney, but in February 2000 the KwaZulu-Natal Law Society had disbarred him on account of dishonesty. After Mlotshwa was readmitted as an attorney in 2005, the NPA hired him despite the finding of dishonesty against him. An NPA spokesperson said that Mlotshwa had made a full disclosure about his removal as an attorney when he joined the NPA. It remains a mystery, however, how he became a deputy director at the NPA and how he ended up in the elite unit. He has never been an advocate and has never practised as such. Yet the NPA officially referred to him as such in documents. Looking at his feats against Paul O'Sullivan, he was as useful to the keepers and capturers as a one-legged man in a Thai kick-boxing bout.

* * *

In the almost 5 000 pages of affidavits and documents that Pretorius, Maema and Mathenjwa dumped on the State Capture Commission, they expressed their outrage and indignation at being linked to state capture. Yet, while they clubbed the likes of McBride, Booysen, Breytenbach and Gordhan, state capture was in full swing. The NPA looked on while the

Guptas siphoned off billions upon billions of rand from state-owned companies. The prosecuting authority didn't lift a finger when Public Protector Thuli Madonsela exposed the looting at Eskom and Prasa, or when a treasure trove of e-mails to and from the Guptas and their cronies, known as the "Gupta leaks", was exposed in the media. Each of these prosecutors could have made a difference by saying no to what they were doing. They chose not to and greatly assisted in the hollowing-out and eventual destruction of the NPA.

If you believe them, Paul O'Sullivan committed a national priority crime for attempting to leave South Africa with his (valid) Irish passport. The Hawks dragged him off a London-bound plane in front of his two young daughters and charged him under section 26B of the South African Citizenship Act. He became the first person ever to be prosecuted for this offence. The magistrate rubbished Jabulani Mlotshwa when he acquitted O'Sullivan.

If Pretorius and his legal cowboys had a grain of integrity, they would admit that O'Sullivan's prosecution was the result of his investigation of acting police commissioner Khomotso Phahlane for fraud and corruption. He had to be extracted from the investigation at all costs, and the weapon to achieve this was the PCLU.

And can Abrahams, Pretorius and the others say with straight faces that Pravin Gordhan's approval of Ivan Pillay's pension payout of just R1.3 million constituted a crime that should have been handled by a unit dedicated to prosecuting terrorism and cases of national security? A first-year law student could have concluded that there was no intent on Gordhan's part to commit a crime. He approved the pension payout only after receiving a legal opinion, and there was no benefit to him. So why would he have committed fraud if there was nothing in it for him?

🐦 **Daily Maverick** @dailymaverick, 27 Oct. 2016
Game Over for Abrahams, Moyane and Co: Documents prove Gordhan prosecution political.

🐦 Pauli van Wyk @PaulivW, 31 Oct. 2016
Here we go – #NPA #ShaunAbrahams and Torie Pretorius will tell us what'll happen with #PravinGordhan's prosecution.

On the last day of October 2016, Torie Pretorius and Shaun Abrahams were ushered into a briefing room to face a horde of journalists and television cameras about the state of Pravin Gordhan's prosecution. Pretorius's underling of yesterday was about to become his legal executioner. As Pretorius gawped into nothingness, Abrahams, impeccably decked out in a black suit with a yellow silk tie, did a hokey-pokey turnaround and told the world that he had had no part in deciding to charge Pravin Gordhan, Ivan Pillay and Oupa Magashula. That decision had been made, he said, by the acting special director of the PCLU, Torie Pretorius, in consultation with the North Gauteng director of prosecutions, Advocate Sibongile Mzinyathi.

🐦 Pauli van Wyk @PaulivW, 31 Oct. 2016
No wonder poor Torie Pretorius looked like someone with stomach ache this morning. Pretorius will be #NPA #ShaunAbrahams' fall guy.

🐦 Pauli van Wyk @PaulivW, 31 Oct. 2016
"The days of disrespecting the #NPA are over." – #ShaunAbrahams 20 days ago. Today: "It wasn't me."

The gaze of the journalists shifted to Pretorius while the screeching motor drives of their cameras immortalised a defining moment of the Zuma presidency and one of the biggest legal blunders in South African history. It was only after he had perused the docket, said Abrahams, that he realised there was no case against Gordhan, Pillay and Magashula. Abrahams, who must have been fully briefed by Pretorius on the eve of his announcement on 11 October of his intention to prosecute Gordhan and the others, was attempting to portray himself as the saviour; the one who had to mop up the mess left behind by Pretorius.

𝕏 Pauli van Wyk @PaulivW, 31 Oct. 2016
#NPA #ShaunAbrahams: I am satisfied that #PravinGordhan, Pillay
and Magashula didn't have prerequisite intention. Charges withdrawn.

Just when Pretorius must have thought it couldn't get any worse, it
did. While Abrahams attempted to execute him by lethal injection,
journalists turned his demise into a public firing squad. They wanted
to know how the prosecution could have overlooked the legal opinion
Gordhan had obtained beforehand that Pillay's pension payout was
legal. It had been in the public domain for two years.

Abrahams shrugged his shoulders. We didn't know about the opinion
until Gordhan brought it to our attention, he said. This was a normal
process, he fibbed. It happens all the time. A journalist asked him if he
would resign. Not at all, not at all!

𝕏 Mandy Wiener @MandyWiener, 31 Oct. 2016
Let Torie Pretorius speak!

𝕏 Karyn Maughan @karynmaughan, 31 Oct. 2016
He looks traumatized.

𝕏 Annie C @Love_RSA, 31 Oct. 2016
He was shaking when he drank water.

There was no coming back from this: no promotion, no bigger pension
payout, no beach cottage in Hartenbos in the southern Cape. The man
whom the multi-degreed Pretorius had nurtured for years had just
branded him the shittiest lawyer in the land. It is an honour for which
there is stiff competition. The names of Sello Maema and Jabulani
Mlotshwa immediately spring to mind, as does that of public protector
Busisiwe Mkhwebane. I suppose it is a question of who is the shittiest
of the shittiest.

🐦 **Mandy Wiener** @MandyWiener, 2 Nov. 2016
#ShaunAbrahams: I would never throw Torie Pretorius under the bus.
He is a gentleman, a brilliant legal mind, he was my mentor.

🐦 **Max du Preez** @MaxduPreez, 4 Nov. 2016
Why do we never hear from advocate dr Torie Pretorius SC who
apparently made the Gordhan decision? Why is he hidden from us?

🐦 **Sari Botha** @realSariBotha, 4 Nov. 2016
Dr Torie Pretorius is lying under the bus.

From here on, it was downhill at the speed of Max Verstappen's Red
Bull racing car. Fraud charges against Robert McBride were dropped.
Glynnis Breytenbach was acquitted of all charges. Charges against
Johan Booysen and his co-accused were withdrawn, as were those
against the so-called SARS rogue-unit trio.

🐦 **Abram Mashego** @Abrammashego, 1 Nov. 2016
It is not only raining for Torie Pistorius, Shaun Abrahams and the Hawks
but pouring. Now charges agst Robert McBride might be withdrawn

🐦 **TimesLIVE** @TimesLIVE, 1 Nov. 2016
NPA drops fraud charges against Robert McBride

🐦 **The Citizen News** @TheCitizen_News, 21 June 2017
Glynnis Breytenbach partially acquitted, still faces four charges

🐦 **News24** @News24, 28 Feb. 2018
Glynnis Breytenbach acquitted of all charges in NPA case

🐦 Pauli van Wyk @PaulivW, 11 Apr. 2018
#SARS wars: Discussing the #NPA's problematic case against #IvanPillay, Johann van Loggerenberg & Andries J v Rensburg: The case put forward by Torie Pretorius & Sello Maema may be impossible to win because it is riddled with factual errors & logical jumps.

🐦 News24 @News24, 17 July 2019
Charges officially withdrawn against Johan Booysen and co-accused

🐦 News24 @News24, 7 Feb. 2020
JUST IN: NPA withdraws charges against so-called SARS "rogue unit" trio

Following the testimony of Booysen, McBride and others before the State Capture Commission, Torie Pretorius sat down in August 2020 to reply in an affidavit to the allegations of state capture against him. He had by then almost reached the end of his career at the NPA and was fighting cancer. He was never promoted to the position of permanent special director of the PCLU. Following the election of Ramaphosa as president, Pretorius was sent back to his earlier position as deputy director of prosecutions.

Pretorius's chances to shine were long gone, but here was an opportunity to come clean; to enlighten his compatriots about a dark age in the prosecuting authority that rendered the organisation incapable of effectively pursuing the looters and capturers. I wanted Pretorius to again be that man I got to know in the 1990s who mercilessly went for the jugulars of miscreants like De Kock, Barnard and Basson. When I published a book in 1997 about apartheid's death squads, I acknowledged Torie Pretorius and Anton Ackermann as "criminal prosecutors I have come to respect and admire for their contribution in bringing justice to my country". This was an opportunity for Pretorius to do the same again.

He didn't. Instead, his 150-page affidavit is a long-winded justification of why the PCLU, under his leadership, embarked on prosecuting Gordhan and the others. In every case, he insisted there was prima facie evidence to prosecute. "No evidence at all was tendered before the Commission in support of the allegations that I am captured for corrupt or political reasons."

His explanation as to why these cases fell within the ambit of the PCLU borders on the incredulous. He said the unit was ordered to pursue several cases against O'Sullivan because he was a "difficult person" who intimidated witnesses and prosecutors. To prove his point, Pretorius attached e-mails that he, Abrahams and some members of the cabal of eight had received from O'Sullivan in 2018. Referring to them as "criminal skunks", the forensic investigator let rip: "You crooked criminals have been protecting criminals whilst using my taxes to prosecute me. Not one of you will escape justice, no matter what you do to me. You, Abrahams, are top of my clean-up list. Torie, you yellow criminal, you are next . . ."

Glynnis Breytenbach was hounded by the NPA for years for insisting on charging Richard Mdluli for fraud and corruption. Despite being found not guilty in a disciplinary inquiry in 2013, she and her attorney were charged by the NPA in 2016 with defeating the ends of justice, fraud, perjury and contravening the NPA Act. She and her attorney allegedly destroyed official and private data on her official laptop. In acquitting Breytenbach and her lawyer on all charges, Pretoria North magistrate Brian Nemavhidi said neither of the accused had broken any laws because the deletions were made with the knowledge of senior NPA officials, and she did not wipe the files to conceal evidence. "There was no internal investigation or criminal investigation," said Nemavhidi. "That file did not contain anything that would cause accused one to stand trial." So why then did the PCLU charge Breytenbach if senior NPA officials were all along aware of the deletions – and if it wasn't illegal?

Pretorius admitted in his affidavit that he had taken the final decision to prosecute Gordhan, Pillay and Magashula. He added: "As required by protocol, a memorandum was sent to the president, advising the president of the prosecutorial decision." I assume that Pretorius wrote the letter to Jacob Zuma and that Abrahams signed it. "Meneer die President" (Mr President) must have been delighted with Pretorius's decision, as he was desperate to get rid of Gordhan. (After Pretorius's blooper, Zuma had to use a false intelligence report to fire Gordhan five months later.)

When Pretorius had written to "Meneer die Staatspresident" 23 years earlier, he was politically conflicted, perhaps because he thought he was selling out his people. This time, there was no such emotion.

CHAPTER 16

Towers that never lie

WHEN NATIONAL PROSECUTING Authority (NPA) deputy director Sello Maema conspired with notorious police "enforcer" Maj.-Gen. Jan Mabula to put the forensic investigator Paul O'Sullivan and his assistant in prison and destroy the Independent Police Investigative Directorate (IPID) probe of acting police commissioner Khomotso Phahlane, he never imagined that the array of cellphone towers dotted across the country would expose his lies.

Enter cellphone sleuth Thereza Kunneke, a professional intelligence analyst with 22 years' experience in the SAPS, including the Hawks, and at IPID, where she was an acting deputy director. She is currently in private practice. In September 2021, Kunneke signed a 108-page affidavit for the State Capture Commission in which she detailed how she used cellphone technology to triangulate every move of Phahlane, Mabula and several other top policemen for four months from 1 November 2016 to the last day of February 2017. This was at the height of IPID's investigation into Phahlane and at a time when a police task team had been assembled to derail the investigation.

Mobile network companies like MTN and Vodacom record and store vital data of every cellphone call. This includes the numbers of the caller and the receiver, the time and duration, and the location from where the call is made. Cellphone data can thus be used to identify where the phone was present at various times and with which other cellphones it interacted.

Kunneke subpoenaed the cellphone details of Phahlane and the police task team, headed by North West deputy police commissioner Maj.-Gen. Jan Mabula, which had been assembled to save Phahlane from prosecution and get O'Sullivan and IPID off his back. Kunneke then compared the cellphone data with several affidavits submitted to the Zondo Commission, the testimony of Mabula and his henchmen before the commission, and the various dockets opened during the Phahlane investigation.

Her analysis exposed the role of Maema in attempting to derail IPID's investigation into Phahlane, who was fired for dishonesty on 30 July 2020 after sitting at home on suspension for three years while earning his full police salary. He is currently on trial on fraud and corruption charges relating to tenders worth R191 million. There are eleven other accused in the matter, including deputy national commissioner Lt.-Gen. Bonang Mgwenya.

The demise of Phahlane is the story of the courage of Robert McBride and some of his investigators who faced threats, arrest and trumped-up charges during the investigation. Their ranks were infiltrated by elements in Crime Intelligence that attempted to subvert the probe by bribing them. The fall of Phahlane also speaks to the tenacity of Paul O'Sullivan and his assistant, attorney Sarah-Jane Trent. They obtained the initial information about Phahlane's alleged corruption, which later blossomed into the IPID investigation. In the process, they were incarcerated on trumped-up charges, hauled before a court of law and raided.

Love him or hate him, O'Sullivan has a penchant for bringing down corrupt police commissioners. He played a significant role in the downfall of Jackie Selebi, who was convicted of corruption in 2010 and sent to jail for fifteen years. In pursuing corrupt officials, O'Sullivan has been charged at least eight times, but nothing has ever stuck.

* * *

On 9 November 2016, a Ford Kuga entered the exclusive Sable Hills Waterfront Estate on the banks of the Roodeplaat Dam on Pretoria's northern edge. The estate, home to Khomotso Phahlane, describes itself as being "tucked away within the thriving Bushveld landscapes" and as "one of the most luxurious and truly breathtaking estates this country has to offer". In the car were O'Sullivan, Trent and IPID investigators Mandla Mahlangu and Temane Binang. The police watchdog investigators had just commenced their probe into Phahlane and had requested information from O'Sullivan and Trent, the complainants in the case against Phahlane.

O'Sullivan had received information in early 2016 that when Phahlane was the divisional commissioner of forensic services, he was implicated in unlawful tenders that resulted in the procurement of equipment and chemicals that rendered forensic examinations unreliable. O'Sullivan and Trent conducted a lifestyle audit on Phahlane and discovered that he lived way above his means. Much of his six-bedroomed mansion in Sable Hills was paid for in cash, sometimes from the boot of his car. Convinced that the questionable forensic tenders had financed the acting commissioner's elegant lifestyle, O'Sullivan and Trent laid a complaint of fraud and corruption against Phahlane at IPID.

Robert McBride was on suspension at the time for clearing Hawks head Anwa Dramat and Gauteng Hawks head Shadrack Sibiya of kidnapping and murder. Then police minister Nathi Nhleko – a Zuma-ite of prodigious proportions – appointed Israel Kgamanyane as acting IPID director. In doing so, he set up IPID for state capture. Not only did Kgamanyane shelve O'Sullivan's complaint against Phahlane, but, according to evidence at the State Capture Commission, he wreaked havoc by suspending eight senior managers for no reason other than that they had worked with McBride. He went around the country collecting dockets on implicated policemen, among them Ntlemeza, Mabula and the cops implicated in the Thoshan Panday corruption investigation. Thereafter the investigations disappeared – until McBride dug them up again.

Kgamanyane subscribed to the tried-and-tested state-capture philosophy of "if it works, break it" and embarked on an irrational restructuring of the directorate. This saw people being transferred to positions for which they had no competence or experience. Kgamanyane also allowed Crime Intelligence to infiltrate IPID by appointing two of its officers in top positions at the police watchdog: Brig. Tlou Kgomo as head of investigations and Emily Motsogi as a deputy director.

Marianne Thamm @MarianneThamm, 6 Sept. 2016
Concourt finds Robert McBride suspension unlawful and unconstitutional

EWN Reporter @ewnreporter, 1 Nov. 2016
#McBride court in session. Prosecutor Sello Maema to address the court.

McIntosh Polela @toshpolela, 1 Nov. 2016
Fraud charges against IPID boss Robert McBride & two colleagues have been dropped. The NPA keeps losing

Dr @malungelob, 1 Nov. 2016
These Ntlemeza puppet charges not sticking

When McBride assumed office again after fraud charges against him were dropped, Kgamanyane wrote to police minister Nathi Nhleko and asked him to transfer McBride out of IPID to the Hawks. A few days later, he was appointed as a major-general at the Hawks, despite facing disciplinary charges for the havoc he caused at IPID. He stood accused of cooking IPID's books to create the impression in Parliament that the watchdog had performed better under him. Despite this, Nhleko paid him a bonus for his sterling performance.

McBride resurrected the Phahlane investigation and assembled a task team, including Mahlangu and Binang. IPID requested that O'Sullivan and Trent assist with the initial investigation, as they had assembled considerable evidence and had a whistle-blower talking to them. The IPID detectives reported directly to investigations head Tlou Kgomo, who was nothing but a Crime Intelligence mole at the police watchdog. The State Capture Commission heard that Kgomo offered IPID investigators Mandla Mahlangu and Cedrick Nkabinde brigadier positions at Crime Intelligence if they would make false statements to implicate McBride and some of his managers in wrongdoing. Mahlangu made a recording of one of the meetings with Kgomo in which he confirmed that he was working with Jan Mabula to "bring McBride down" and torpedo the investigation against Phahlane.

Mahlangu subsequently opened a criminal case against Kgomo for attempting to defeat the ends of justice by promising him a brigadier's post in exchange for a false statement to impugn the evidence against Phahlane. Soon afterwards, Mahlangu reported that he had received a death threat on his phone. It said: "His [O'Sullivan's] days are numbered. we r on his heels. u must either die with him. we r watching u boy. we r about to finish paul." A few months later, as the net closed around the acting police commissioner, Mahlangu received another message, which said: "If you want to leave [sic] long in peace take my advice and stay away you're being used by high authorities and you will suffer as alone stay the hell away from my relative or I will come after you." An IPID investigation showed that the cellphone messages with the death threats went via a tower situated at the Crime Intelligence head office in Erasmuskloof, Pretoria.

Mahlangu would never see the result of his investigation into Phahlane. Just days before he was supposed to testify against Kgomo in a disciplinary inquiry, gunmen entered the former's smallholding in Jakkalsdraai, north-east of Pretoria, at 3h30 and shot him dead before making off in his Nissan bakkie. His killing had all the hallmarks of a botched robbery – but also of an assassination.

A month later, *City Press* reported that the Hawks had made a break-through when they arrested an alleged hitman, Khumbulani Sithole, who was implicated in taxi violence. Investigators discovered during his interrogation that he was also linked to the killing of Mahlangu. He alleged that police had paid him and three other suspects R50 000 to carry out the hit. In May 2022, Sithole appeared briefly in the Johannesburg High Court on charges of murder, robbery and illegal possession of a firearm. In postposing the case, the judge assured the family that the trial would get under way as soon as possible to bring them answers about how and why another South African hero fell.

Both Tlou Kgomo and Emily Motsogi left IPID in May 2017 after their role in the capture of the directorate was exposed.

*　*　*

During IPID's on-site investigation at Sable Hills, the team interviewed the estate manager and later the building contractor, and obtained copies of the plans of Phahlane's house. The police watchdog established that the acting police commissioner had paid for much of the building of his mansion in cash. The builder received three payments of altogether R710 000 in notes in plastic bags that were hauled from the boot of his car. There were several more cash payments of R129 000 that he also made from his car. Phahlane possessed a range of luxury cars, some of which had been bought with cash. The acting national commissioner clearly had a case to answer about where the money came from.

Phahlane was incensed about the visit to Sable Hills and lashed out at O'Sullivan, who has dual South African and Irish nationality. He maintained that O'Sullivan and Trent had headed and controlled the investigation. Their visit to Sable Hills prompted Crime Intelligence to carry out a security assessment of Phahlane's house. Two Crime Intelligence officers, tasked with the assessment, failed to detect any threat. But the acting head of counterintelligence, Brig. Tim Moyane, changed the assessment on the same day to read: "This is a serious breach of the security of the acting national commissioner and need a criminal case to be investigated on the matter."

🐦 **eNCA** @eNCA, 24 Nov. 2016

Acting National Police Commissioner, Khomotso Phahlane says Paul O'Sullivan's case against him is based on lies.

🐦 **Karyn Maughan** @karynmaughan, 1 Dec. 2016

#Phahlane on Paul O'Sullivan: "some foreigner looks at your house and say this African person does not deserve to be here."

The security assessment was just a smokescreen to justify the appointment of Mabula and his task team to target O'Sullivan, Trent and IPID. Three days before the conclusion of the threat assessment, Mabula had already met Phahlane at Sable Hills and appointed the rest of the team. Among them were Brig. Daniel Ncube, Brig. Clifford Kgorane and Lt.-Col. Ismail Dawood. They all hailed from the North West.

According to evidence at the State Capture Commission, the choice of the members of the Mabula team was deliberate: they were all themselves the subject of multiple investigations conducted by IPID into allegations of torture, murder, attempted murder and assault prior to 2016. Their services must have been engaged by Phahlane because it was likely they had an axe to grind with IPID.

Jan Ntebo Mabula is among the stand-out figures of the state-capture era. He was a close associate of Richard Mdluli and Berning Ntlemeza when he headed the Hawks in the North West. Mabula was instrumental in hunting down officials opposed to state capture, among them Johan Booysen and Robert McBride. He has also been implicated in allegations of extortion, kidnapping and assault with intent to do grievous bodily harm.

* * *

Thereza Kunneke obtained the cellphone records of Phahlane, Mabula, all the members of his team, and Crime Intelligence's Tim Moyane. Her analysis showed that early in the investigation, Brig. Tlou Kgomo, then still head of investigations at IPID, was in regular contact with Phahlane, probably updating him about the investigation. On Tuesday, 22 November 2016, for example, Kgomo phoned Phahlane four times. Mandla Mahlangu and Temane Binang were then still reporting to Kgomo, who had access to the full Phahlane docket.

Phahlane and Motsogi, also a Crime Intelligence plant at IPID, met on 26 November, and three days later Phahlane, Kgomo and Motsogi met again. It is likely that the two IPID officials were updating Phahlane on the state of the investigation. The meetings took place not at his home in Sable Hills but at Zambezi Estate, another exclusive gated development in Pretoria's north-eastern suburbs. It appears that Phahlane was using the residence of a close associate, Maj.-Gen. Sandra Malebe-Thema, to conduct most of his "secret" meetings.

Malebe-Thema, then a brigadier, resigned in 2011 after she was charged with fraud for using police funds to host a birthday party for Phahlane. She was later acquitted. After he was appointed as acting national police commissioner in 2015, he re-employed Malebe-Thema as a general. She was, at the time the meetings took place at her house, the head of basic police development. After making racist comments, she was hauled before a police disciplinary hearing and dismissed.

🐦 **eNCA** @eNCA, 10 Jan. 2019
The South African Police Service has dismissed its Head of Basic Police Development, Major-General Sandra Malebe-Thema

Kunneke also obtained the gate access records of the Zambezi Estate to determine who had entered and left during the four-month period covering her investigation. She discovered that as the Mabula team made its way from the North West to Gauteng on 24 November 2016, Phahlane had three meetings at Malebe-Thema's residence at Zambezi Estate: with Crime Intelligence's Maj.-Gen. Obed Nemutanzhela in the morning, Mabula in the early evening, and divisional commissioner for human resources development Lt.-Gen. Nhlanhla Mkhwanazi in the evening.

The chief director of IPID, Innocent Khuba, said in an affidavit that Nemutanzhela and Mkhwanazi had approached him for information about McBride's relationship with O'Sullivan. They thought McBride and O'Sullivan had committed a crime and wanted information to assist them in proving this. Mkhwanazi promised Khuba a lieutenant-general's post in the SAPS if he cooperated.

*   *   *

By early December 2016, the Mabula team was preparing to pounce on Paul O'Sullivan and Sarah-Jane Trent. Ismail Dawood was tasked with obtaining a subpoena to get their cellphone records dating back to 1 March 2016. But NPA head control prosecutor Gustav Niehaus refused to sign the subpoena. Dawood then phoned a deputy director of public prosecutions, Advocate Helen van Jaarsveld, who said in an affidavit to the State Capture Commission that he had complained to her of being sent from pillar to post as nobody wanted to sign the subpoena. Van Jaarsveld said: "I asked him who had been involved in the matter and was sending him around. He said that he was speaking to Maema . . . and that he [Maema] was giving them guidance. I asked him why he did not request Maema to assist him in obtaining a section 205 subpoena. He said that Maema did not want the section 205 subpoena to be closely connected to him."

Enter Sello Maema, who phoned Advocate Karen van Rensburg, also a deputy director of public prosecutions. Van Rensburg said in an affidavit that Maema had urged her to sign the subpoena. "Maema sought to use his charm to cajole me into agreeing to obtain a subpoena, but I was unpersuaded. I asked him why he did not obtain the subpoena himself, but he laughed it off and explained something along the lines of it would appear suspicious if he were to apply for the subpoena."

Van Rensburg found it strange that Dawood was seeking a subpoena for the period from March to December 2016. In fact, this had nothing to do with the security breach being investigated by the Mabula team, but everything to do with a deep throat spilling the beans about Phahlane to O'Sullivan in March 2016. Once the Mabula team obtained their cellphone records, an intelligence analyst would probably have been able to determine the identity of the whistle-blower by analysing whom they were in contact with.

Maema said in his affidavit to the Zondo Commission: "I deny that I had anything to do with the investigation of the Kameeldrift [Sable Hills Estate] matter involving Phahlane. I deny that I was guiding the Kameeldrift matter behind the scenes. The Phahlane matter is being dealt with in the Pretoria office, and at that time I was seconded to the PCLU."

Why is the role of Maema in the IPID investigation so important? Gladstone Sello Maema was Jan Mabula's counterpart at the prosecuting authority. He also hails from the North West but was transferred to the NPA's priority crimes litigation unit (PCLU) in Gauteng during the reign of Shaun Abrahams. As we have seen, this unit became a key structure in the targeting and prosecution of enemies of Jacob Zuma and the state-capture project. Maema featured in many politically driven and malicious prosecutions that were aimed at public officials fighting corruption. In some cases, like the prosecution of Johan Booysen and his men, Mabula was the investigating officer and Maema the prosecutor.

There were no legal executioners at the NPA more depraved than Sello Maema and the head of the PLU, acting special director Dr Torie Pretorius. They and several others abused their positions and their oaths of office to hunt down state-capture busters. There have been no consequences for them. After the state-capture era, they remain in their positions at the NPA.

But there is another reason. This case illustrates the deceit of a prosecutor who ought to be, according to the NPA's code of conduct, a person "of integrity whose conduct is objective, honest and sincere". A prosecutor should "respect, protect and uphold justice, human dignity and fundamental rights as entrenched in the Constitution". Maema said in his affidavit: "At the time of the Kameeldrift investigation, I was burdened with the heavy load of dealing with the SARS rogue-unit matter and had no time to devote to matters that were not assigned to me." As Kunneke would soon show, cellphone towers never lie.

* * *

In the days preceding the assembly of the Mabula task team in Pretoria, Sello Maema received five cellphone calls from its members. Three were made by Mabula. From 27 November 2016 onwards, the communications increased dramatically. Before meeting Phahlane on this day, Mabula phoned Maema. He also phoned Maema again the following day. On 1 December 2016, Mabula had five telephone conversations with Maema, while Dawood sent Maema two messages. Mabula, Dawood and Maema stayed in contact throughout the next few days. On 7 December, the day that Dawood attempted to get a subpoena to access O'Sullivan's and Trent's cellphone data, he phoned Maema another five times.

The next communication between team members and Maema was made on 21 December 2016, when Mabula called him four times. On 4 January 2017, the Mabula team registered a criminal case against O'Sullivan and Trent at the Kameeldrift police station for fraud, defeating the ends of justice and impersonating IPID officials. On this day, Dawood phoned Maema three times. Thereza Kunneke's analysis showed that in January and February 2017, Mabula had no fewer than 54 communications with Maema. There were also numerous calls and messages between Maema and other members of the team.

In contrast, the Mabula team had far less contact with NPA senior prosecutor Vernon Nemoarane, who was officially assigned to guide them through the investigation. They only contacted him for the first time on 7 December 2016. Thereafter, there was no contact with him until 21 December 2016. They did get in touch with him several times when they opened the docket on 4 January 2017.

Kunneke said in her affidavit: "Maema was assisting the Mabula team behind the scenes and made contact with the team at crucial times during the investigation into the alleged security breach. If he does deny any contact, this would clearly be untrue."

* * *

On Wednesday, 8 February 2017, Jan Mabula and his team obtained warrants for the arrest of Paul O'Sullivan and Sarah-Jane Trent. The two had allegedly impersonated IPID officials, defeated the ends of justice and committed fraud. On the same day, at 19h09, Mabula phoned Maema and spoke to him for about four minutes. The next day, Mabula phoned Maema four times.

𝕏 Mandy Wiener @MandyWiener, 10 Feb. 2017
Paul O'Sullivan's house reportedly being raided by police. He is going to be spitting spiders.

Late on Friday afternoon, a police special task team, including heavily armed cops from the SAPS's Tactical Response Team, pounced on O'Sullivan's business premises in Sandton, Johannesburg. He was not there, but Sarah-Jane Trent was. She was hauled into the back of a police vehicle and taken to a petrol station where she was confronted by more plainclothes and uniformed policemen. Some flaunted semi-automatic assault rifles. One of Mabula's men ordered that Trent's hands be cuffed. After a cop tightened a cable tie around her wrists, she was driven across Gauteng to the Kameeldrift police station on the northern edge of Pretoria. By then, the courts had already closed and she was destined to spend the weekend behind bars.

Police seized Trent's phone, which she had switched off just before she was arrested. She refused to provide them with her password. She never got the phone back. It was later sent to Israel to be unlocked, after which the contents were leaked to the *Sunday Times*. Kunneke's analysis of Phahlane's cellphone shows that he was in regular contact with disgraced former *Sunday Times* journalist Mzilikazi wa Afrika.

As Trent's legal team headed to court on Sunday to bring an urgent application to effect her release, Mabula phoned Maema at 15h48, 18h03, 18h43 and 18h47. The last call between the two was at 20h51 that night. Trent was released on R5 000 bail. She said in an affidavit to the State Capture Commission that she had been booked into a cell with "a blanket stuffed in the toilet and rotting food in the basin with maggots moving from the rotting food, down the sink and wall and all over the floor".

🐦 Team News24 @News24, 12 Feb. 2017
O'Sullivan's assistant released after Sunday evening court bid

The next day, as the task team prepared to execute the warrant for O'Sullivan's arrest, Mabula phoned Maema at 14h25 and spoke to him for six minutes. The team that Mabula assembled to collar O'Sullivan was fit for an assault on an ISIS suicide cell, never mind a middle-aged guy with no bodyguards. It was nothing but another bout of Sullivanophobia, this time because he was assisting IPID in its investigation into Phahlane.

🐦 SAfm News @SAfmnews, 13 Feb. 2017
Police have refused to confirm reports that private investigator Paul O'Sullivan has been arrested.

🐦 Sam Sole @SamSoleZA, 13 Feb. 2017
Acting like thugs. There's no good reason not to confirm arrest.

The Mabula team ignored a High Court order that O'Sullivan had to be given 48 hours' notice of an impending arrest. He had obtained the order because of the many trumped-up and frivolous charges the state brought against him. At that moment, there were four other cases against O'Sullivan before the courts. None of them eventually stuck, and neither would the latest one.

Later that afternoon, as O'Sullivan left the offices of his lawyer in Centurion, eight police vehicles blocked his way. Seventeen heavily armed cops from the SAPS's Tactical Response Team pounced. As O'Sullivan was bundled into a police vehicle and driven across Pretoria to the Kameeldrift police station, his phone was seized. While his lawyers headed to court for an urgent application for his release, Mabula phoned Maema incessantly – at 18h23, at 19h26, at 19h58, at 20h01 and at 21h06.

The court ordered the release of O'Sullivan more than six hours after his arrest. The communication between Mabula and Maema continued the next day with two more calls. The calls over the two days lasted altogether 25 minutes. Trent and O'Sullivan were charged with impersonating IPID officials. O'Sullivan was also charged with fraud, extortion, attempted extortion and intimidation.

𝕐 Daily Maverick @dailymaverick, 19 Feb. 2017
House of Cards: O'Sullivan vs Phahlane – who will outwit, outlast, outplay?

𝕐 Jessica B @JessBezJourn, 7 Apr. 2017
BREAKING! Police, armed with a warrant, at the office of Paul O'Sullivan in bid to seize all computers.

In May 2017, Khomotso Phahlane came to Parliament with a 61-page written submission and with eleven subordinates in tow for support. Phahlane accused IPID of being "captured" and said it should be called OPID – the O'Sullivan Police Investigative Directorate. He declared: "I would like to congratulate IPID and O'Sullivan for a well-orchestrated propaganda machine. They have been excellent. Nothing that is being investigated by IPID hasn't ended up in the media." McBride responded by saying that the police were abusing state resources to target IPID investigators by bringing in a team of "torturers" and "murderers" from the North West.

🐦 **Cathy Mohlahlana** @CathyMohlahlana, 1 June 2017
BREAKING: Lieutenant-General Lesetja Mothiba appointed as acting head of SAPS as Phahlane is suspended.

🐦 **Motaung oa Ramokhele** @LebonaMoleli, 1 June 2017
One acting head replaces another acting head which replaced a head! SATAFRICA MY BELOVED country

Following their arrest, Trent and O'Sullivan laid charges of kidnapping against the Mabula team. Trent also instituted a complaint about the theft of her cellphone. On 31 May 2017, two senior deputy directors at the NPA signed a legal memorandum in which they recommended that the Mabula raiders be prosecuted. The memorandum concluded that "a failure to prosecute will be an injustice to the complainants and the public at large". The final decision to prosecute the Mabula team rested with the acting director of public prosecutions in Gauteng (Pretoria division), Advocate George Baloyi. He has also been implicated in advancing state capture and described as being part of the prosecutions cabal at the NPA that targeted state-capture opponents. In August 2017, Baloyi refused to prosecute any members of the Mabula team, saying there was not enough evidence.

🐦 **News24 – South Africa** @News24_SA, 8 Nov. 2017
IPID officers, O'Sullivan and Trent charged with "racketeering"

When O'Sullivan and Trent appeared in court in November 2017 to face previous charges of impersonating a police officer, fraud, extortion and contravention of the IPID Act, the prosecution slammed an additional

34 charges on them. The new indictment related to the Prevention of Organised Crime Act and alleged that O'Sullivan, Trent and IPID investigators Mandla Mahlangu and Temane Binang had managed a criminal enterprise. The two IPID officials were charged alongside them.

This was the tried-and-tested modus operandi by the NPA state-capture cabal against those they sought to silence, muzzle or suppress. There never was a case against O'Sullivan, Trent or the IPID investigators. Once the case was in court, the cabal could sit by and watch as a lengthy and expensive court process unfolded. The only legal acumen they usually showed was their ability to ensure postponement after postponement. But in this case, the strategy didn't work. The state requested a postponement because it said it was not ready to go to trial and needed more time to investigate. Counsel for the accused objected, the magistrate agreed, and the case was struck off the court roll. The NPA never reinstated charges. The case was clearly another trumped-up effort to silence O'Sullivan and Trent and derail the IPID investigation.

Eyewitness News @ewnupdates, 8 Nov. 2017
Case against O'Sullivan & co-accused struck off roll

Matome Rabothata@mat @khesaseedi, 8 Nov. 2017
It was a shitty case in every way

* * *

News24 @News24, 10 May 2022
"I screamed and screamed" – cop tells court of his kidnapping, torture and assault ordeal.

In May 2022, Jan Mabula and his North West team of rogue detectives sat for hours in the Johannesburg High Court listening as a police warrant officer recounted how they had kidnapped and tortured him sixteen years previously. They afterwards extorted money from his family. Sixteen years: that is how long it took the state to get Mabula and seven of his colleagues in the dock. They were charged with kidnapping, assault with intent to do grievous bodily harm, and extortion. They pleaded not guilty.

The case revolves around a theft from the Benoni police station on the East Rand in 2006. The police had recovered the equivalent of R16 million in US dollars after a heist at Oliver Tambo International Airport. The money was stored in a safe at the serious and violent crimes unit on the ground floor of the police station before it was stolen.

Former Crime Intelligence head Richard Mdluli was at the time the deputy provincial commissioner in Gauteng, and he tasked Mabula and his team with investigating the robbery. Mabula and his men arrested warrant officer Paul Kgoedi and several of his colleagues for their alleged involvement in the theft. This is where the story gets murky as people started dying and disappearing. A policeman who was arrested in connection with the theft and who turned state witness was gunned down. Another was also shot dead in an apparent hit, while a third witness disappeared and was never seen again. Another potential witness, Solomon Nengwane, was reportedly taken into custody on 5 June 2006. Two days later, his family learned that he had died of suffocation in police detention.

Five men, including Kgoedi, were charged with theft. They complained in court that they had been tortured. This was confirmed by a district surgeon who examined them. They laid a complaint with IPID, but the police watchdog said it could not investigate the matter because Kgoedi and his co-accused refused to cooperate with them. In 2008, the NPA withdrew charges against Kgoedi and the others for lack of evidence.

In 2016, Robert McBride revived the torture case against Mabula and his squad. As they were about to appear in court in October 2020 on charges of kidnapping and assault, the South Gauteng director of public prosecutions, Advocate Andrew Chauke, provisionally withdrew the charges. Chauke has been implicated in evidence before the Zondo Commission as a member of the NPA cabal that hounded opponents of the state-capture project. The case was later reinstated.

When Paul Kgoedi finally took the witness stand in May 2022, his evidence could have been plucked from the records of the Truth and Reconciliation Commission. His description of his torment at the hands of Mabula and his cohorts was reminiscent of the worst that the apartheid police had inflicted. Mabula is, incidentally, an apartheid cop who joined the police service in 1984. His men employed every torture tactic that their commander learned from his former masters.

Kgoedi and the others were allegedly shocked while they were tied to chairs. With their faces hooded, they were kicked and assaulted while lying on the floor. They were suffocated with a rubber tube pulled over their faces and choked by water being poured into their mouths and noses. The warrant officer testified that he screamed and cried and felt as though his body was being torn apart after he was stripped naked, tied to a chair, and electric wires were attached to his toes, inside lower lip, inner thighs and genital area. He said he was tortured to force him to make two confessions implicating himself and the other suspects in the theft from the police station.

The case continued at the time of the writing of this book, but it might not be the end of the woes for Jan Mabula and his rogue squad. When Robert McBride dusted off the torture case of Kgoedi and the others, he also revived the investigation into what happened to police informant Solomon Nengwane, who died in police detention in June 2006. IPID's investigation concluded that Mabula and his men beat Nengwane to death and then embarked on a wild cover-up. They claimed that the detainee had died from an asthma attack while in their custody. They dumped his body at the local hospital. The NPA's North Gauteng director of prosecutions, Advocate Sibongile Mzinyathi, allegedly another member of the state-capture cabal at the prosecuting authority, refused to prosecute because of a lack of evidence. Instead, he ordered an inquest into Nengwane's death.

That inquest got under way in Brits in the North West province towards the end of 2021. Mabula and his men were named as "persons of interest" in the inquest and subpoenaed. Mabula and his accomplice, Col. Ismail Dawood, failed to appear. According to evidence in a 2017 High Court application, IPID was at the time investigating at least eleven criminal cases against Dawood.

The inquest into Nengwane's death will get under way only in October 2022 because a new magistrate has been appointed to hear the inquest.

CHAPTER 17

The shadow state

I HAVE AN image of the State Security Agency (SSA), ostensibly the guardian of the constitutional integrity of our Republic. It is of an elephant seal that I saw about a year after publishing *The President's Keepers* when I embarked on a trip to South America. In the southern Chilean town of Puerto Montt is a fish market displaying the finest seafood of the frigid Atlantic: king crabs, metre-long salmons, spiny lobsters and heaps of congrio, similar to our kingklip. Outside the market was a place where mongers and pop-up restaurants cleaned their produce. Behind them was a tiny beach, no wider than a few metres, where this elephant seal was marooned. These unsightly mammals, who take their name from their trunk-like snouts, grow up to six metres long and can weigh more than 3 000 kilograms. Our *boytjie* on the beach was right up there with the biggies. He hardly moved as he awaited the next consignment of fishy leftovers and intestines cast in his direction. When I went back a day or two later, *boytjie* was still on the beach in virtually the same spot. He may still be there, a breathing, heaving and lumbering blob of fat.

And that, dear readers, is my image of South African state security: a tub of lard; a gluttonous splodge of uselessness that has over the past decade gobbled up billions of rand of public money for absolutely fuck-all in return. If I were a jihadi who was plotting to plant a bomb at Cape Town's Waterfront, I would be more concerned about a seagull shitting on my head than about state security detecting my nefarious plans.

The SSA is purely the making of Jacob Zuma, who upon his accession to the highest office in 2009 signed a proclamation that bypassed

Parliament and collapsed South Africa's intelligence agencies into one. South Africa's two major crime-fighting agencies, the Scorpions and the National Intelligence Agency (NIA), were dismantled in the process, thereby setting up these law-enforcement agencies for their eventual capture. In this way, Zuma opened the door for the creation of his secret shadow state, financed by public money – of which much remains missing – and structured and staffed to serve his personal and political interests during his reign of almost a decade.

As Judge Raymond Zondo found in his final report on state capture, Zuma's new intelligence regime shifted the focus from "national intelligence" to "state intelligence" and paved the way for the use of the SSA to serve the interests and power of Zuma and his cronies. Whereas members previously took an oath of allegiance to the Constitution, from then on they swore allegiance to the president.

As a result the SSA, alongside the Hawks and police Crime Intelligence, failed to uncover or investigate any form of state capture. How could they have missed it when journalists, civic organisations and opposition politicians knew exactly what was going on? Despite having an economic intelligence unit, SSA agents also turned a blind eye to the Guptas and their cronies while they laundered billions of rand out of South Africa to their accounts in Dubai. The same happened with the disembowelment of state-owned enterprises like Transnet, Prasa, Denel, South African Airways and Eskom.

Today, we know why. On the one hand, the SSA, and especially the special operations unit (SOU), was nothing but Jacob Zuma's personal Gestapo. It performed dirty tricks on behalf of the president, stuffed his purse and those of his cronies, and shielded him from his political adversaries. On the other hand, the eavesdroppers at the agency were so busy pilfering the secret fund that there wasn't time to read the newspapers and listen to whistleblowers to find out what was happening in the land. Neither did they pay attention to Reserve Bank and Financial Intelligence Centre reports about vast sums of ill-gotten Gupta money leaving South Africa's shores for Dubai.

Judge Zondo said that his commission might have been unnecessary had the SSA detected, investigated and countered state capture when the first symptoms appeared. Instead, Zuma ordered his then minister of state security, Siyabonga Cwele, in 2011 to stop the director-general of the agency, Jeff Maqetuka, and the heads of the domestic and foreign services, Moe Shaik and Gibson Njenje, from investigating the influence of the Guptas over the president and their exploitation of the relationship for personal gain. According to the evidence, Zuma said there was no need for an investigation because the Guptas were good people with whom he had a good relationship. Having lost the confidence of the president, the three spy chiefs resigned, cracking the agency open for Zuma to capture.

Zuma's blocking of this probe was, "if not the fundamental cause of state capture, certainly one of them", Judge Zondo concluded. The SSA was destabilised by a "parallel structure that served the interests of President Zuma rather than the national interest", he added. It enabled Zuma to open the doors to the trio of Indian brothers to "help themselves to the money and assets of the people of South Africa" and enrich their mining-to-media empire. Zuma even replaced his finance minister at their behest.

As the shysters-in-chief, Judge Zondo fingered former state security minister David Mahlobo, former director-general Arthur Fraser and former SOU head Thulani Dlomo. The trio's complicity in state capture illustrates how Zuma as head of state appointed selected ANC cadres in crucial positions to drive the state-capture project. Key among them were the ministers of public enterprises, transport and energy, who saw to it that capture-friendly boards were appointed at Transnet, Prasa, South African Airways, Denel and Eskom. The boards ensured that the group chief executives, chief financial officers and chief operating officers of the various state-owned entities were willing and able to manipulate tender processes to advance the interests of the president's cronies.

Zuma then used and abused the vast powers the Constitution vested in the president to place an army of ANC deployees at the top of the law-enforcement agencies, among them the commissioner of police, the commissioner of the revenue service, the national director of public prosecutions, and the director-general of state intelligence. These appointees did not just turn a blind eye to state capture but also eviscerated their agencies to make sure that there were no consequences for the looters and the capturers. Under their reign, crime spiralled, thugs walked free, prosecutions and convictions of organised criminals disintegrated, tax collection dropped, and state revenue decreased.

The ANC in turn made sure that in the name of the National Democratic Revolution the parliamentary select committees on the police, state intelligence, justice, transport, public enterprises, energy and transport were jam-packed with devoted and loyal cadres who saw no evil, heard no evil and spoke no evil. The behaviour of ANC MPs during the state-capture project provoked the remark from Judge Zondo that given its past record, Parliament might not be able to prevent the scourge from happening in future.

Neither Mahlobo nor Fraser or Dlomo had the acumen, expertise or moral authority that befitted their positions. As political challenges against Zuma intensified towards the end of his first term, the president felt the need for new blood and shifted Siyabonga Cwele to the telecommunications portfolio. He had served Zuma well not just by stopping the Gupta probe and getting rid of three top civil servants who showed far too much independence, but also in the name of national security by halting an investigation by the Hawks, the South African Revenue Service (SARS) and the Special Investigating Unit (SIU) into a parallel intelligence unit that Arthur Fraser and his cronies had set up at the intelligence agency.

Judge Zondo recorded in his final report how SSA domestic head Gibson Njenje met Siyabonga Cwele at OR Tambo International Airport. "When they met, Cwele said the prosecution of Fraser must stop. Despite Njenje's protest that a lot of time and money had been spent on investigations, the minister insisted and said it was President

Zuma's decision. Cwele said the president said the prosecution would compromise national security, despite Njenje's protest to the contrary, and that what was in issue was pure crime."

In Cwele's place, Zuma appointed a 40-something-year-old Mpumalanga departmental head with no intelligence experience. It later turned out that David Mahlobo loved "regime change" conspiracies and Thai pedicures. The advantage of elevating a political nobody to a big somebody is that he or she then owes you big time and will be at your beck and call.

Weeks after Mahlobo became state security minister, the inspector-general of intelligence (IGI) Faith Radebe handed him the report on an investigation into the parallel intelligence network that Fraser had established when he was the agency's deputy director-general in the 2000s. It was called the Principal Agent Network (PAN). Under Fraser's watch, millions of rand in cash were transported in suitcases from a state money depot in Pretoria to "The Farm" – the nickname for the agency's headquarters on the shores of the Rietvlei Dam, south of Pretoria. Much of the money in the PAN slush fund was squandered on appointing agents who were never vetted or on projects that had no value. Hundreds of millions of rand was spent on buying 293 cars for PAN's 72 agents, while officials registered houses and farms bought by the SSA in their own names (and those of their children) and employed family members in senior positions. Millions were channelled to "private individuals". In his final report Judge Zondo recorded evidence presented before him that "there was no reporting line to head office [of the SSA], something which gave Fraser a dangerous amount of unbridled power; there was no oversight or accountability for the projects pursued or expenditure incurred". It was a "free for all and Mr Fraser was a law unto himself".

Besides the IGI's report on the PAN, there was an internal investigation, headed by an advocate. He told in his report how Fraser, in direct violation of SSA security protocols, installed computer servers in his home to make him the lone recipient of all the raw intelligence generated by the PAN agents. Fraser had in fact built a parallel intelligence structure with himself as the chief architect and administrator. In doing so, the investigations found, he may have been guilty of treason.

David Mahlobo had the findings of both investigations at his fingertips when he and Zuma appointed Fraser as SSA director-general in September 2016. Fraser wasn't even vetted properly prior to his appointment. According to Judge Zondo in his final report, Fraser's vetting "circumvented prescribed channels and followed a flawed process". It was completed in "less than three days with non-compliance and poor vetting practices being condoned on the purported urgency of Mr Fraser's vetting". This probably explains why the SSA (and later the Department of Correctional Services) lied about Fraser's academic qualifications on its website when it claimed that he had obtained an honours degree from the University of London. He had in fact never set foot in this prestigious institution, which counts among its graduates (honorary and otherwise) Winston Churchill, Queen Elizabeth II, Mahatma Gandhi, Albert Einstein and, of course, our own Arthur Joseph Peter Fraser.

When I confronted him with the deceit in 2020, Fraser didn't respond, despite promises by his spokesperson that he would do so. Overnight, he changed "London University" to "London Institute", a now defunct learning institution in the United Kingdom. He later released a letter from the secretary and registrar of the University of the Arts London (UAL), previously known as the London Institute, stating that Fraser was a student at the London College of Communication (formerly the London College of Printing), which is one of six colleges that make up the UAL.

Fraser said any member of the public, "including Mr Pauw", was free to contact the registrar to verify his qualification. I did so and was told by the registrar's office that I needed Fraser's consent for the verification. He refused to grant it and said he was fully aware of my "stratagem" and promised to make me account "in the forthcoming trial in the High Court" for my lies and fabrications.

Fraser's rise to the top of the intelligence hierarchy must be seen against the backdrop of the primary objective of Zuma's presidency: to stay out of prison. To avoid spending his last days behind bars, he had to prepare an exit strategy that would guarantee his freedom. That strategy involved getting Nkosazana Dlamini-Zuma elected as president, so that she could keep his keepers, key among them Arthur Fraser, in place.

The politicisation and abuse of the SSA under Fraser and a string of directors-general and top spooks were laid bare at the State Capture Commission. Judge Zondo found that Fraser and Zuma had a mutually beneficial relationship to keep each other out of prison. Zuma's intervention to halt the criminal investigation into the PAN may well have saved Fraser from serving long-term prison time. According to Judge Zondo: "The picture emerges that Mr Zuma put a stop to an investigation that could well have led to Mr Fraser's arrest, prosecution and maybe imprisonment, and Mr Fraser put a stop to Mr Zuma's continued incarceration despite the fact that Mr Zuma's incarceration was in terms of an order of the Constitutional Court."

𝕐 **News24** @News24, 23 June 2022
Former director-general Arthur Fraser is heavily implicated in alleged criminal activity, with Chief Justice Raymond Zondo recommending a fresh investigation.

When Fraser was later appointed as prisons boss, it was payback time. In exchange, Judge Zondo argued, Fraser released Zuma on medical parole "under questionable circumstances and against the recommendations of the Parole Board".

* * *

Hidden in the thousands of pages of evidence and documents interred in the State Capture Commission's archives are two affidavits from one of South Africa's most experienced intelligence bosses. Lloyd "Bob" Mhlanga joined the agency after the advent of democracy in 1994 as the head of counter-espionage before becoming a major-general in the police's Crime Intelligence division. A few years later, he was appointed as the acting head of operations at the SSA, where he participated in both the PAN and Gupta investigations. When Cwele stopped the Gupta probe, he transferred Mhlanga to the ministry of intelligence. He was later employed in the Department of International Relations and Cooperation (DIRCO).

In November 2018, Mhlanga received a phone call from the agency's former domestic head, Gibson Njenje, who was then an adviser to state security minister Dipuo Letsatsi-Duba. President Cyril Ramaphosa had just received the report of the High-Level Panel Review on the SSA chaired by ANC veteran Dr Sydney Mufamadi. He was assisted by nine eminent panellists with expertise in law, security studies, civil society, academia, intelligence and security. The panel had implicated Arthur Fraser, Thulani Dlomo and a host of rogue agents in a series of irregularities and alleged criminality.

Letsatsi-Duba, appointed by Ramaphosa as his state security minister in February 2018, had hardly distinguished herself during the Zuma years when she served at the height of state capture as the chairperson of Parliament's public enterprises committee. Despite being aware of the rampant corruption at state-owned companies, Letsatsi-Duba and her subservient ANC cadres rejected a call from the Democratic Alliance to launch an inquiry into the Guptas' capture of several SOEs. She at least had the honesty, unlike most of her colleagues, to admit later to Raymond Zondo that her committee had "failed to exercise our oversight".

Njenje told Mhlanga that Ramaphosa himself wanted him to head an investigation into further irregularities that had been uncovered at the agency. Mhlanga said in one of his affidavits before the State Capture Commission that he was happy at DIRCO, but he nonetheless agreed to carry out the investigation because the president required his services. He was transferred to the SSA, where Letsatsi-Duba appointed him as the acting head of the domestic branch. Ramaphosa made his appointment permanent in March 2019. Mhlanga's main function was to assist in investigations of corruption at the agency, which became known as Project Veza.

In the weeks and months to come, Mhlanga, together with several top intelligence officials who participated in Project Veza, SSA acting director-general Loyiso Jafta, and IGI Dr Setlhomamaru Dintwe blew the lid off Fraser's parallel intelligence network and a network of secret projects conducted by Dlomo's Special Operations Unit.

Mhlanga said in his affidavit that there were "entrenched corrupt networks" of public officials in the SSA that committed theft, fraud, forgery, and treason to generate "illegal financial flows" to a host of beneficiaries, among them political and executive heads and senior government officials. They did so through manipulating procurement processes, signing fraudulent contracts, and making payments without contracts having been signed. Illegal operations were created as tools for siphoning off funds and for parallel intelligence capacities that posed a risk to national security. According to Mhlanga: "Sustained patterns of financial irregularities resulted in an approximate amount of R1.5 billion being fleeced from state coffers. The funds, taken under the guise of covert operations, emanated from the Treasury-allocated budget as well as retained funds as regulated in terms of the Secret Services Act. These funds were expended both domestically and abroad."

Mhlanga said that Arthur Fraser colluded with David Mahlobo, and later with Bongani Bongo, who succeeded him as state intelligence minister, to establish a "parallel intelligence network relating to influencing civil society". By doing so, Fraser resuscitated the PAN network that he had previously established when he was the deputy director-general. He also asserted his control over the new networks that had been established while he was away, said Mhlanga, and added: "This continued even after his departure from the SSA in early 2018, indicating the entrenchment of his network. He procured state of the art intelligence equipment worth millions, some of which remains unaccounted for."

According to Mhlanga, Fraser centralised a host of projects in the office of the director-general. "While claims were made that certain projects were terminated, investigations indicate that funds continued to be withdrawn for the same projects." Evidence presented to Judge Zondo revealed that the manager in the office of Fraser and his predecessor, Gladys Kudjoe, withdrew temporary advances and cash of more than R505 million, more than €6 million and almost US$10 million between 2013 and 2018. Mhlanga commented: "The settlement of the advances taken do not comply with necessary financial and accounting prescripts. These projects indicate collusion with former ministers Mahlobo and Bongo in running operations to pursue political agendas and interfere with the independence of the judiciary and influence civil society." Kudjoe was caught in a sting operation stealing classified documents and was under suspension at the time of making the affidavit.

Thulani Dlomo, described as a "law unto himself" and enabled by the likes of Arthur Fraser, was the kingpin of the criminal network that plundered the agency. Dlomo was an obscure security head at a KwaZulu-Natal provincial department and the subject of a corruption investigation when he resigned to become the head of the Chief Directorate of Special Operations (CDSO) at the SSA. Known by his intelligence moniker of Silence, he told SSA employees upon his arrival at the agency that he reported directly to Zuma. He became untouchable and all-powerful.

When Sydney Mufamadi, also a former safety and security minister, took the stand at the State Capture Commission to testify about the evidence that his panel had unearthed, he said: "It was clear that the SSA's special operations unit, especially under Mr Dlomo's watch, was a law unto itself and directly served the political interests of the executive . . . The SOU also undertook intelligence operations which were clearly unconstitutional and illegal." Mufamadi concurred with the findings of other investigations that Fraser's PAN programme was riddled with instances of "serious criminal behaviour which had taken place under the guise of conducting covert work and that this behaviour may have involved theft, forgery and uttering, fraud, corruption, and even bordered on organised crime and transgressions of the Prevention of Organised Crime Act".

When acting SSA director-general Loyiso Jafta had to take the stand at the State Capture Commission, the minister objected to his testimony "to protect the interests of national security", but Judge Zondo shot her down. It was soon clear why the minister objected. Jafta told how startling amounts of cash had been carted out of SSA headquarters just before the ANC's elective conference started at Nasrec in Johannesburg on 15 December 2017. The money was for "operations".

Daily Maverick @dailymaverick, 27 Jan. 2021
DAYS OF ZONDO: Secret billions poured into State Security Agency to sustain and protect "Zuma regime", claims Acting DG Loyiso Jafta

Judge Zondo: "The date is given, it is 15 December 2017, 'Collected R19 million'. And then there is R5 million and there is R1.9 million, there is 900 000 and there is 360 000 . . . and there is R2.5 million received, there is R2 million received, there is R2.4 million. I think the next one is R1 million, R30 000, R1.3 million. Ja, it is like money – cash just gets dished out to different people."

Evidence leader Paul Pretorius: "That is an illustrative example but there will be more detailed evidence."

Judge Zondo: "Yes, it is like you can have R19 million, you can have R5 million, you can have R3 million and people take the cash and go . . ."

Judge Zondo was in for an even greater shock when he was presented with evidence by Loyiso Jafta that R9 billion of SSA assets were missing or lost and that R125 million could not be accounted for in the 2017/18 financial year.

Judge Zondo: "R9 billion. I mean, that is a lot of money. How could you have – or could government department not be able to account for R9 billion and I have a suspicion no heads rolled. That money could have gone into a number of people's pockets who were not entitled to it and with R9 billion, imagine what you can do for people?"

* * *

Lloyd Mhlanga together with witnesses known as Mr Y, Ms K, and Dorothy lifted the veil from the secret operations conducted by the SSA during the reign of Jacob Zuma. Judge Zondo allowed Ms K to testify from an undisclosed location without her identity being released. Fraser tried to stop her evidence and, having failed to do so, laid criminal charges a few days later against Mufamadi, Jafta, Ms K, Mr K, evidence leader Paul Pretorius and one of the commission's advocates. He accused them of peddling falsehoods and said through his attorney: "Our client has long indicated that these testimonies were undesirable as they had the potential to compromise the security of the country forever."

The witnesses told how Dlomo recruited non-SSA members into special operations and deployed them as agents to sensitive areas around Jacob Zuma. The Chief Directorate of Special Operations' covert programmes and projects withdrew as much as R1.5 billion from the SSA's secret fund for a variety of projects and programmes, many of which were designed to boost Zuma's faction in the ANC.

The CDSO gave birth to Operation Mayibuye, set up for the benefit of Jacob Zuma and his cronies. Mayibuye consisted of a series of counter-intelligence projects which, according to evidence at the State Capture Commission, "undermined the very core of the constitution" and were "manifestly unlawful and involved criminality". Witnesses alleged that R84 million was siphoned from the SSA to Mayibuye and distributed to the projects. One of these was Project Commitment, intended to keep the president flush with cash. An amount of R2.5 million was allocated monthly to Zuma for the 2015/16 financial year. This was raised to R4.5 million in 2016/17.

Under Project Construção, Dlomo established a presidential security support unit that offered VIP protection services to Zuma, his deputy

Cyril Ramaphosa, and cronies like SAA chair Dudu Myeni and national director of public prosecutions Shaun Abrahams. The operatives of Construção were trained in a foreign country and acted in direct opposition to the police's VIP protection unit. It had an initial budget of R30 million, but that was spent within four months. Nobody is sure where the money went.

Dlomo was also in charge of the SSA's armoury, and his elite gang of rogue spies were handed eleven R4 assault rifles, five submachine guns, a twelve-gauge shotgun, a host of pistols, and bags of bullets. These agents were never trained or vetted; moreover, Dlomo's cousin, who was never in the SSA's employ, also got a gun. The significance of the presidential security support unit is far-reaching because it meant that during the second term of his presidency, Zuma had at his disposal an SSA-funded and -trained private army of heavily armed operatives.

David Mahlobo, who was implicated in initiating and participating in intelligence operations, was Zuma's bagman and had to deliver the money to him. According to evidence presented by Sydney Mufamadi, Mahlobo signed receipts for around R80 million in cash, doled out between 2015 and 2017, collected from the SSA, and allegedly destined for Zuma's use, either personally or politically. There was no concrete evidence, however, that the president received the money.

Dorothy, who was the head of the presidential security support unit within Special Operations, testified that she had to deliver R1.5 million in cash to Mahlobo's official residence in Cape Town. On two other occasions she took R4.5 million in cash to his residence in Pretoria and handed it to him in his study. She withdrew altogether R38.5 million in cash between March 2015 and September 2016.

Project Hollywood set out to surveil and illegally intercept communications of high-profile, politically connected individuals and government officials. A private company was tasked with doing the work and was paid R800 000 a month. It later emerged that the company did not exist. Another entity was paid R500 000 per month in cash to provide "economic services" and data collection and analysis. It was also fictitious.

Project Justice was aimed at "handling sources within the judiciary to influence the outcome of cases against President Zuma". The State Capture Commission was not presented with any evidence that money was paid to judges, and this project may have been nothing but a money-making scheme.

Operation Tin Roof was designed after allegations that one of the first ladies had poisoned the president. Poisoning is a sinister fable in Zuma's paranoid world of endless conspiracies, evil agents and strat-coms (the term refers to a unit in the apartheid police that specialised in dirty-tricks campaigns and misinformation against opponents of the regime). It is therefore not strange that Zuma frequently uses claims of poisoning to demonstrate a dastardly and wicked enemy plot to get rid of him.

In 2015 the president's fourth wife, Nompumelelo Ntuli Zuma, known as MaNtuli, and her three children were banished from Nkandla as the result of a poisoning allegation. While Zuma allegedly received treatment in Russia, SSA operatives kept MaNtuli in a safe house against her will, which Judge Zondo remarked was "a very serious matter". Mahlobo and the SSA also siphoned off millions to set up a fully kitted toxicology unit for Zuma. A toxicology team, consisting of two toxicologists and two assistants, were paid R500 000 per month to check Zuma's food and bedsheets. This amount later ballooned to a monthly R1.8 million. MaNtuli had to undergo lie-detector tests and was interrogated for attempting to poison the president and for allegedly having had an affair with a bodyguard.

The tentacles of Fraser's and Dlomo's militia and Zuma's shadow state reached all levels of society. It targeted the Fees Must Fall movement and civic organisations such as Right2Know, the Zuma Must Fall movement, the Council for the Advancement of the South African Constitution, and even the environmental campaigning organisation Greenpeace.

After being accused of possible treason at the State Capture Commission, Fraser hit back and said through his lawyer that he would respond with his own evidence that would divulge secrets related to presidents, judges and parliamentarians. The commission later said the former spy boss never approached it to give evidence, although he applied to cross-examine certain witnesses. Judge Zondo had rejected that application because the commission rules required that an applicant asking for leave to cross-examine a witness should furnish the commission with a full version of the events in which he had been implicated. Fraser failed to do so.

Following in the footsteps of Zuma and state-capture enablers like Lucky Montana and Brian Molefe, Fraser launched blistering attacks on Judge Zondo and said he lacked objectivity and integrity. He was also "no longer fit to be a judge, let alone chief justice of the Republic of South Africa".

𝕏 City Press @City_Press, 24 June 2022
State Capture report: Arthur Fraser features under the subheading: cash withdrawals, movement of cash, and accountability for cash. The inquiry found that millions of rands were withdrawn for covert projects in the SSA and are unaccounted for.

Raymond Zondo's final report on the SSA is almost 400 pages long, while thousands of pages of oral and documentary evidence are displayed on the commission's website. The judge found that David Mahlobo, Arthur Fraser and Thulani Dlomo were instrumental in the many illegal activities at the SSA, which were committed at the expense of national security and in the service of Zuma's narrow personal and political interests.

Although Mahlobo denied any wrongdoing, Judge Zondo said evidence regarding his involvement was overwhelming and "detailed, given project by project". He said it was "unimaginable that all these people could be lying". The judge also recommended that the Hawks revive their investigation into Fraser's complicity in the alleged abuses of the PAN. Fraser must also be investigated, Judge Zondo found, for his handling of large sums of SSA cash.

Judge Zondo's final report is ultimately a chronicle of how a few crooked individuals – Jacob Zuma, David Mahlobo, Siyabonga Cwele, Arthur Fraser and Thulani Dlomo – trampled on national security and attempted to dismantle our democracy. Their efforts were ultimately undermined not by Cyril Ramaphosa or Raymond Zondo or some law-enforcement agency, but by greed.

The golden thread running through the SSA for the past decade is one of thieving and waste. Like that elephant seal on the beach in Chile, the rogue operatives devoured every morsel and crumb that came their way. And when they were caught out, they skulked back into the shadows.

As for the Guptas, well, who were they? Their names were last mentioned in the SSA in 2011 when Jacob Zuma and Siyabonga Cwele stopped an investigation into their influence over the president.

* * *

Top spy Lloyd Mhlanga regrets the day he received a phone call from SSA special adviser Gibson Njenje, who called him to report for duty in 2018 to investigate allegations of corruption at the spy agency as part of a team working on what was called Project Veza. His stint lasted just more than a year before his contract suddenly expired – according to him, because he discovered alleged malfeasance by the minister of state security.

The story of Mhlanga illustrates that Jacob Zuma's state-capture project did not cease to exist when Ramaphosa took office in February 2018. As I have illustrated in this book, many officials and politicians that embraced and advanced the project continued to cling to their positions after Zuma's exit from office.

During Project Veza's investigation, the team discovered that Dipuo Letsatsi-Duba had been involved in secret SSA operations prior to her appointment by Cyril Ramaphosa as state security minister in February 2018. Mhlanga told the State Capture Commission that she had set up a front company with her husband through which the SSA channelled funds for Zuma's 2012 ANC presidential campaign against Kgalema Motlanthe. Mhlanga said he had confronted Letsatsi-Duba with the team's findings. She explained that the company belonged to her husband and that she had not been involved in its running. Mhlanga said that he did not think that this exonerated her from culpability. Both Letsatsi-Duba and the SSA have denied reports that she was complicit in the agency's special operations.

In April 2019, Mhlanga produced two investigation reports, one detailing the findings of Project Veza and the other explaining the transgressions that occurred at Arthur Fraser's first PAN project when he was SSA deputy director-general. Mhlanga handed the reports to acting SSA director-general Loyiso Jafta and, with the support of his superior, passed them on to the anti-corruption unit of the Hawks.

In the meantime, Njenje, who had recruited Mhlanga in the name of the president, had resigned as Letsatsi-Duba's adviser and was replaced by Advocate Mahlodi Muofhe. After studying the investigative reports, Muofhe called a meeting with Mhlanga and his team and demanded that they hand over their evidence, as the ministry was going to conduct its own investigation. Mhlanga refused as he believed the minister had no right to interfere in operational matters. According to him, Muofhe threatened to deal with the team.

🐦 **News24** @news24, 21 Feb. 2022
SSA DECLASSIFIED I Networks which looted R1.5bn from spy agency still in place as investigations collapse

Six days after the meeting with Muofhe, Letsatsi-Duba told Mhlanga that there was a charge against him that he had received a double salary from both the Department of International Relations and the SSA during the time he had been transferred from the former (where he was a special adviser to the minister) to the latter (where he secured an appointment as head of the domestic branch). Mhlanga was then suspended, despite having repaid the money. Mhlanga told the State Capture Commission that he discovered it was Muofhe who had laid the complaint. The manager of human resources at the SSA explained that double payment was normal and that it would ordinarily be recovered once the transfer was finalised. "I reported [the incident] to President Ramaphosa on 15 May 2019, appealing to him to intervene, on the basis that the charge against me was part of a stratagem to stop the investigation that I had been mandated by him to conduct. To date, I have not had response," stated Mhlanga.

"I, who was brought back to the SSA to assist with the investigation and have done nothing other but performing the job I was appointed to do, have been left unemployed. It is with untold regret that I believe that my removal from the SSA was to stifle the investigation and that the capture of the SSA remains an issue today," Mhlanga told Judge Zondo.

Shortly after Mhlanga's departure, Mahlodi Muofhe was appointed in Mhlanga's post as domestic head of the spy agency. He was supposed to have continued the investigation but, according to top intelligence agent Ms K, testifying to the State Capture Commission from her undisclosed location and with her identity hidden, their investigation was "hampered and sabotaged". Ms K said that Muofhe not only interfered with Project Veza, but also "actively obstructed" their work. "I will also deal with the circumstances under which the Project Veza investigation was effectively shut down by Advocate Muofhe, the director of the domestic branch of SSA. To this effect, the other members of the investigation team and I were redeployed."

🐦 **News24** @News24, 1 Mar. 2022
SSA DECLASSIFIED: Dlodlo, former DG Muofhe "shut down" probe aimed at exposing criminal networks at SSA

In August 2020, the Project Veza team reported Advocate Muofhe's interference to Parliament's joint standing committee on intelligence (JSCI). In addressing the State Capture Commission, evidence leader

Paul Pretorius said: "Ms K was there ready to give the evidence to the JSCI, they did not call on her. It seems that even at the level of the JSCI there was an attempt to bury or push aside evidence that is truly embarrassing and concerning to the South African state." Judge Zondo said in his final report that the committee had failed the country numerous times and that its inaction on several levels had contributed to state capture.

On 11 March 2021, the Project Veza team were locked out of their offices. Muofhe admitted to News24 that he had given the instruction after realising that some of Project Veza's investigators were tampering with evidence implicating people who should have been targets of the Veza investigation but were not. He dismissed any notion that he sought to tamper with or torpedo the Project Veza investigation.

A day after the team were locked out of their offices, investigators from the Investigating Directorate (ID) of the National Prosecuting Authority arrived at the spy agency, accompanied by officials from the office of the inspector-general of intelligence (IGI), to serve a summons on the SSA to release the Project Veza documents. Although Loyiso Jafta complied with the summons and allowed the investigators access to the SSA's premises, Muofhe blocked them. He explained to News24 that the summons was flawed because it was not signed by a judge or a magistrate. Days after the ID and the IGI came knocking on the SSA's door, Jafta was told that his contract would not be renewed. He was replaced by another acting director-general.

When Cyril Ramaphosa took the stand at the State Capture Commission in August 2021, evidence leader Advocate Paul Pretorius put it to the president: "Operation Veza was stopped. Ms K and Mr Y, who were responsible for the collation of this evidence, were taken off their jobs. Advocate Muofhe was tasked with continuing the investigation . . . [but] Muofhe put all the evidence and documentation under lock and key."

Ramaphosa: "It might seem like the process has been stopped or scuttled, but all these things will come to light."

Pretorius: "An efficient, lawful and capable SSA doing its allotted tasks during the state capture years may have made a big difference to what happened."

Ramaphosa: "It happened as [did] many other wrong things, inexplicable things. Our task now as we move forward is to deal with all the things that went wrong. We must admit it was an agency compromised and operating under the milieu of state capture."

Pretorius: "The investigating directorate under the NPA has issued a subpoena for documents. Mr Jafta, whilst he was still there and days before he was removed, authorised and instructed those documents to be released. What the establishment in SSA did, the minister and Mr Muofhe must have been instrumental in this. They said no to the law enforcement, you cannot have the documents."

Ramaphosa: "I am however pleased that the documents are still there, they are under lock and key and the various processes that need to unfold will unfold. Those who have been taken off the job, who know these matters intimately . . . will be able to be brought back to be able to carry on with the work because the reasons . . . for their removal is something that has got to be cogent, and it appears now it is not."

The Project Veza evidence has subsequently been transferred to the Investigating Directorate which, in conjunction with the office of the IGI, has embarked on a massive fraud and corruption probe that spans more than a decade of malfeasance at the intelligence agency. The cases are intricate and convoluted, and a top NPA prosecutor has been appointed to assist the investigators.

So far, not a single state intelligence agent has been charged with any crime committed in the name of state capture. Will we ever see the likes of Arthur Fraser and Thulani Dlomo in the dock? Your guess is as good as mine.

* * *

If you deem the fate of Lloyd Mhlanga and Loyiso Jafta unusual, think again, because it is not. Paul Engelke, the SSA advocate who headed the investigation into the first PAN programme and broke open Arthur Fraser's putrid brainchild was targeted and victimised during and after the investigation and eventually left the country, settling in Russia, where I spoke to him for *The President's Keepers*. He has since returned to South Africa.

South African diplomatic missions around the world are stuffed with former top spooks and their political heads who were either rewarded for their sterling service in keeping the agency's iniquities ensconced in a vault at "The Farm" or had to be whisked away from prying eyes to be veiled in the safety of an embassy. When SSA domestic head Mahlodi Muofhe retired in December 2021, Ramaphosa appointed him as ambassador to South Sudan. While a diplomatic posting to the world's newest country can hardly be described as a plum assignment, Ramaphosa named two former state security ministers, Siyabonga Cwele and Dipuo Letsatsi-Duba, as South Africa's ambassadors to China and Turkey, respectively. This is a rich reward for the man who scuttled both the Gupta investigation and the probe into the first PAN project.

Several other spymasters who served Zuma were also rewarded with ambassadorial posts. Former domestic intelligence head Simon Ntombela became our ambassador in Poland and erstwhile acting director-general and co-ordinator for intelligence Dennis Dlomo heads South Africa's mission in Algeria.

🐦 **Daily Maverick** @dailymaverick, 16 July 2021
CLOSE ENCOUNTERS OF THE MESSIANIC KIND: Confessions of a dangerous mind, a "divinely inspired" Zuma spy Thulani Dlomo

The most bizarre diplomatic appointment must surely be that of SSA special operations head Thulani Dlomo, who was deeply implicated in criminality and dirty-tricks operations at the spy agency. In July 2017 Jacob Zuma appointed him as South Africa's ambassador to Japan. The president obviously knew that Dlomo held the key to cracking open the country's illicit intelligence operations during his reign and thought that he could entomb those secrets by sending him 13 000 kilometres away to the land of the rising sun.

But then Ramaphosa's high-level review panel exhumed some of his skeletons, and Dlomo was recalled to South Africa in January 2019. He was then on secondment from the SSA but went AWOL and was fired nine months later. When Dlomo resurfaced, it was as an ambassador of God on earth (he says he hears God's voice all the time) and a divinely inspired peacemaker in Africa. He promoted his new mission on earth in a book titled *The Encounter*, which he claimed contains truths that can change the destiny of Africa. It was apparently on a visit to Hiroshima and Nagasaki in Japan, the two cities nuked by the Americans during the dying days of the Second World War, that he had a "life-changing encounter with man, history and ultimately, God". Iqbal Survé's *The Star* said *The Encounter* "weaves his personal journey into the book with captivating skill" and highlights a "love for humanity and a desire to make a difference". I'm afraid you won't find it in your friendly neighbourhood bookshop, as it was only published online. I must confess that I haven't read it. I simply cannot, despite the promise that Dlomo has "fire in his voice and a sparkle in his eyes that are contagious".

Others have also been rewarded with top government positions. Former SSA director-general Gladys Kudjoe, who headed the agency from August 2013 until Arthur Fraser's appointment in 2016, is currently the secretary of defence, despite being implicated in wrongdoing at the State Capture Commission.

Affidavits by Project Veza team members have also implicated a top Prasa executive, Mandisa Mokwena, in several of Thulani Dlomo's illicit operations. One was the toxicology project that was set up after Jacob Zuma's "poisoning". A company registered by Mokwena was used for "large amounts of cash" that needed to be pumped into the project, and Mhlanga averred in his affidavit that she received R1.8 million per month "over years". Mokwena, who has been fingered as a key architect of the SARS rogue-unit narrative while on the payroll of the SSA, denied all allegations against her in an affidavit to the State Capture Commission. She said: "The claim that my company . . . [had] been used to transfer large amounts of money needed for the project is inconceivable and false."

Mokwena was at one time a group executive at SARS who left after being investigated for fraud and corruption. In 2010, she and eight other accused stood trial in the High Court on more than forty counts of racketeering, corruption, money laundering and fraud, amounting to R11 million. During the trial, she explained that the large amounts of money paid into her bank account were SSA payments and not kickbacks from the alleged fraudulent schemes. As a result, she was acquitted while most of the other accused were found guilty. Documents show that the SSA spent R15.5 million on Mokwena's defence.

Prasa appointed Mokwena in September 2018 as its head of security at double the salary of the person who had previously performed the job. According to the *Daily Maverick*, she spearheaded a R5 billion investment programme that did not follow any procurement processes. If one looks at the subsequent destruction of Prasa's stations and infrastructure, one can only conclude that Mokwena did a dismal job.

It has been a long-standing practice in the ANC to shuffle compromised officials to positions where they can cause less mischief and escape the public eye – especially if they harbour dirty or embarrassing secrets. This is the only way to justify Cyril Ramaphosa's treatment of Arthur Fraser and David Mahlobo. After dumping Mahlobo as state security minister in February 2018 when he took office, Ramaphosa brought him back in 2019 as the deputy minister of human settlements, water and sanitation. The appointment took place shortly after the president had received the high-level review panel report that implicated Mahlobo in serious wrongdoing.

🐦 **News24** @News24, 17 Apr. 2018
Breaking: State Security Agency DG Arthur Fraser moved to Correctional Services

🐦 **Maggs_ naidu** @maggsnaidu, 17 Apr. 2018
– as a DG or . . . resident???

Ramaphosa moved Fraser sideways to become commissioner of correctional services. If the president had thought it was better to have Fraser inside pissing out rather than outside pissing in, the move backfired when the commissioner ordered Jacob Zuma's release from prison in September 2021 – less than two months after he was jailed for contempt of court for defying a court order that he appear before the State Capture Commission. In granting Zuma medical parole, Fraser went against a recommendation from the Medical Parole Advisory Board, which concluded that the former president did not suffer from a terminal illness. The High Court ruled in December 2021 that Fraser had acted unlawfully in granting medical parole to Zuma. The case is on appeal.

🐦 **eNCA** @eNCA, 1 June 2022
Former State Security Agency Head Arthur Fraser has laid a criminal complaint against President Cyril Ramaphosa. The complaint relates to the alleged theft of money, which he says was hidden on Ramaphosa's Phala Phala farm in Limpopo.

The burly former superspy showed another middle finger to the president when he arrived at a police station in June 2022 and opened a kidnapping and money-laundering case against him, as well as against presidential protection unit head Major-General Wally Rhoode and several Crime Intelligence members, for allegedly concealing a burglary at Ramaphosa's Phala Phala game farm near Bela-Bela in Limpopo. According to Fraser's affidavit, Ramaphosa had at least US$4 million (around R60 million) in cash stashed in a couch at his farm – and then played a part in a cover-up following an allegedly illegal investigation into the matter.

The Witness @WitnessKZN, 20 June 2022
In the Witness today: "Arrest Ramaphosa . . . or else we will," says ANC's RET faction

Daily Maverick @dailymaverick, 30 Sept. 2022
PARLIAMENT: Phala Phala dollars came from animal sales, not money laundering, Ramaphosa tells MPs

Nobody is sure how the Phala Phala saga will play out and how it will impact on Cyril Ramaphosa's prospects for re-election at the ANC's elective conference in December 2022. What Phala Phala has done, however, is to elevate Fraser to hero status among those who despise Cyril Ramaphosa and support the radical economic transformation (RET) cabal of the ANC.

SMK @SMK33138377, 1 June 2022
Arthur Fraser doing the lords work . . . fully behind you comrade.

The Zuma Taliban @Sasa_nkala, 23 June 2022
Thank you for ending COVID Thank you for showing us the real state capture Thank you for everything Mr Fraser Mzansi owes you

* * *

How could I have possibly damaged Arthur Fraser's reputation and professional integrity in the eyes of any reasonable man or woman after four investigations – one conducted by the chief justice of the Republic – found prima facie evidence of his possible complicity in serious crime and being in breach of a host of laws? Well, he clearly thinks I did.

From the outset of the publication of *The President's Keepers*, the former spymaster was in full battle mode and released a statement that there were 65 "misrepresentations and/or inaccuracies" in the chapters of the book that dealt with the PAN. I challenged him to name them. He never did.

In a statement published at the time, the Fraser family accused me of "committing the classic journalistic deception of not allowing facts to get in the way of a good story". They claimed that "in his enthusiasm to influence ruling party politics and the 2019 general election, Pauw has allowed himself to be manipulated by an apartheid spy/double agent who has scores to settle – and is now hiding out in Russia". This statement shows the mentality of Fraser and his ilk. The "apartheid spy/double agent" whom the family referred to was former SSA advocate Paul Engelke, who carried out the PAN investigation and then left the agency to lecture in Russia. In their eyes, this made him a spy, perhaps even for the apartheid government.

Every stratagem that Fraser used against me has failed. He failed to remove *The President's Keepers* from the bookshelves, he failed to get me in the dock, and his raid on my office failed to find classified documents. In the end, Fraser became the best publicist I have ever had.

🐦 **702** @Radio702, 8 June 2018
"If Arthur Fraser hadn't tried to stop the book, I certainly wouldn't have sold so many." – Jacques Pauw

Fraser had only one option left: to sue me for defamation, which he did in June 2019. One would have thought that the former spymaster was by then down and out for the count and that his chances of mustering a successful libel case were as good as those of someone suffering from acute acrophobia to reach the summit of Mount Everest.

Fraser said in his summons that he wanted R5 million from me and NB Publishers for besmirching his good name, and a further R30 million for an "economic loss" he suffered because of the bad publicity. He also said that he was "at all material times a director and shareholder" of Resurgent Risk Managers, a company providing "enterprise-wide risk management services", in which he held a 37.5 per cent stake, and that after the publication of *The President's Keepers* his "business partners and clients are reluctant to do business with him resulting in his business ceasing to trade".

After Fraser's first stint at state intelligence ended in 2010, when he resigned during the SSA investigation into the PAN project, he went into business with his former director-general, Manala Manzini, who has also been fingered in the wrongdoing of the PAN. In 2011, they set up Resurgent Risk Managers and scored several lucrative state contracts, among them one of R87.8 million to provide a "risk threat and vulnerability assessment" for Prasa. The contract was awarded by the rail agency's CEO, Lucky Montana, "on confinement", which refers to deals that are awarded without a tender, but only if they can be justified by urgency or a lack of competitors in the market.

The Resurgent contract was among a host of deals investigated in the wake of public protector Thuli Madonsela's damning report on corruption at Prasa. The forensic investigators found that the contract had been irregularly awarded and a proper budget had not been secured, and recommended that criminal action be taken as a result.

Fraser said in his summons that he was a director of Resurgent "at all material times". But according to company records, he was appointed as a director in August 2011 and resigned on 25 September 2016 – one day before Zuma and his intelligence minister David Mahlobo appointed him as director-general of the SSA.

Fraser will not be the first nor the last to use an accusation of racism to escape his predicament. In his summons, he said *The President's Keepers* equates certain individuals, like himself, with "corruption and malfeasance", while my (Jacques's) friends "and those of his preferred race are profiled as paragons of virtue and morality".

Despite Fraser's pledge to make me pay in the "forthcoming trial", he has not exactly been quick off the mark to get to the High Court. We haven't progressed much further than some documentary discovery and a court date, and a trial is a long way off.

CHAPTER 18

Zuma's executioner

"HISTORY NARRATES THAT in human tragedies, war and skirmishes, women are always burdened with sufferings and hardships. The burden of womanhood is a daily struggle encountered by women in all walks of life. Courts should not be meek and gentle when confronted with instances that have all the traits of any attempt to keep women subjugated in any form at workplaces."

You may well ask what this has to do with the tragic events that occurred at the South African Revenue Service (SARS) during the Jacob Zuma era when Tom Moyane annihilated the tax collector and left it to die next to the Hawks, SAPS Crime Intelligence, the National Prosecuting Authority, the State Security Agency, Eskom, Denel, Prasa and Transnet.

When Labour Court Judge Smanga Sethene delivered his judgment in August 2022 in the case of Hope Gloria Mashilo and Tshebeletso Seremane versus SARS, he referred to another ruling that reminded him of the need for the courts to "weave the elements of humanity and compassion within the fabric of formal structures of the law". In this case, Moyane's restructuring of SARS had left two single mothers penniless, impoverished and almost destitute. Sethene thus started his almost lyrical judgment with a quotation from the Qur'an and a reference to the hardship that women in general face.

Mashilo and Seremane are just two of hundreds of diligent SARS officials who became victims of Moyane's organisational revolution at the service when he abandoned its programmes of good governance and modernisation and replaced them with a despotic and ineffectual structure that relied on a culture of fear and intimidation. Judge Raymond Zondo found in his final State Capture Commission report that SARS "offers one of the clearest demonstrations of the patterns of state capture", for the revenue collector "was systemically and deliberately weakened, chiefly through the restructuring of its institutional capacity, strategic appointments and dismissals of key individuals, and a pervasive culture of fear and bullying". SARS, he said, was a "clear example" of state capture.

When Tom Moyane and his lapdogs, chief among them his second-in-command, Jonas Makwakwa, descended on SARS towards the end of 2014, Mashilo was the executive of workplace wellness, who dealt with employee assistance programmes, occupational health, extended sick leave and chronic diseases. She has an MBA degree and earned an annual salary of R1.5 million. Seremane was the executive of integrity, who earned the same salary as Mashilo and was busy completing her MBA degree.

Soon after taking office, Moyane announced to top management that he was going to review the operating model of the service and declared that he had a "script to transform SARS". This was nothing but a subtext for Moyane and his newly formed syndicate within SARS to get rid of officials who stood in their way and replace them with pliant sycophants. There are literally hundreds of tales of officials who fell victim to Moyane, Makwakwa and their henchmen.

Mashilo and Seremane were, like many other executives, surprised by the announcement of a new operating model because SARS was a leading performer among government agencies and did not just meet its targets for revenue collection every year but also frequently surpassed them. But what Mashilo and Seremane didn't yet know was that the script that Moyane alluded to came from the American consulting management firm Bain & Co. and had been devised long before his arrival by himself, Makwakwa, President Jacob Zuma and Bain's top executives in South Africa.

Moyane appointed Makwakwa to head the review process, and both Mashilo and Seremane served on a steering committee. By August 2015, Bain executives had unveiled the new "Moyane structure" to staff; two months later, Makwakwa announced the new structures and posts. The two executives realised that their positions were severely downgraded. Seremane applied for two positions but was unsuccessful. She was ordered to accept a position as a "domain specialist" though nobody knew what the job entailed. It was a position with no functions and no description, and it didn't form part of the organisational structure. The same happened to Mashilo, who couldn't ask her superior for clarity as he had also been demoted. She wrote a letter to Moyane, asking him why her position had been downgraded. He instructed her to report to the chief officer for human resources, who took six months to see her. He eventually told her she had also been appointed as a domain specialist. Thereafter, Seremane, Mashilo and a host of other senior SARS employees spent their time doing nothing while receiving their full salaries every month. They even got performance bonuses.

According to Seremane, this was nothing but a purge of managers and executives associated with the previous leadership of SARS. They were treated like lepers by their colleagues. "So, you wake up in the morning, you come to the office, you get in and there is absolutely nothing to do – when there is so much work actually to be done. And by the way, it wasn't only me, it was a whole bunch of us, probably around 40-plus employees. I'm talking about employees who were not earning anything less [than] 1.5 million not doing anything, is that not wasteful expenditure?"

Both Mashilo and Seremane lodged grievances, but Moyane refused to entertain them. Mashilo compiled a document titled "Breaking the Silence" in which she questioned the legality of the Bain restructuring and argued that many executives were in posts that didn't exist and were consequently wasting public money; the exercise was therefore inconsistent with the Public Finance Management Act (PFMA). She sent the document to finance minister Malusi Gigaba and the chairperson of the parliamentary standing committee on finance, Yunus Carrim. Neither responded. In his judgment, Smanga Sethene said: "By reporting Bain, Ms Mashilo was performing one of the most underrated and thankless constitutional duties: whistleblowing . . . [She] stood firmly for justice for the benefit of SARS and this land."

Mashilo copied her document "Breaking the Silence" to Moyane, who fired her two days later and ordered security to escort her out of Lehae la SARS (Sesotho for 'The Home of SARS'), the headquarters of the revenue collector in Brooklyn, Pretoria. The same fate befell Seremane. "I was never given a hearing, never asked what are the issues. My grievance was dismissed and in the very letter I was told that you are dismissed with immediate effect."

Both Mashilo and Seremane lost everything. Seremane had just got divorced when she was fired. She was a single mother and had no money to pay her children's school fees. Her insurance policies and retirement annuity lapsed. Family and friends had to buy her airtime and bring her food. Once her sisters and mother had relied on her for their upkeep, but after her dismissal she was forced to borrow money from her mother, the recipient of a social grant. The elderly woman slipped into depression and drank drain cleaner. Her daughter also attempted suicide. It was almost impossible to find alternative employment because she had been fired by SARS. How do you explain that to a potential employer?

Mashilo was asked to testify at the Commission of Inquiry into Tax Administration and Governance at SARS, headed by retired Supreme Court of Appeal Judge Robert Nugent. She was then living in Kimberley and couldn't afford to travel to Gauteng to attend the hearings. Nevertheless, she found strength in the proceedings, especially in Nugent's interim report that advised Cyril Ramaphosa to fire Moyane, which he did. In his final report, Nugent outlined how Moyane and Bain had colluded to seize SARS, "each in pursuit of their own interests". The judge's findings exonerated Mashilo and Seremane, the latter of whom did testify before the commission.

In 2018, the two joined forces and approached the Labour Court to set aside their dismissals. They had a meeting with SARS the next year and offered to drop their legal action if the revenue collector reinstated them, paid their salaries from the date of their dismissals, and refunded their legal costs. But SARS refused.

By the time the case came to court, Edward Kieswetter had been appointed as SARS commissioner in the place of the disgraced Moyane. A credible official with a wealth of tax experience, he had to mop up the mess left behind by his predecessor. Yet SARS approached the case as though Bain's restructuring had never happened. Its witnesses claimed that Seremane and Mashilo had been fairly dismissed and that the post of "domain specialist" to which each had been reallocated was meaningful.

Judge Smanga Sethene would have none of it. He said that SARS had negotiated in bad faith and that its conduct in these proceedings merited the utmost censure and displeasure of the court. "To underplay Bain's role at SARS is akin to concealing material evidence and consorting with Bain in corruption." According to Sethene, Mashilo and Seremane deserved the "unwavering protection of this court"; as judge, he couldn't "consort with anyone who tramples upon women to exploit their vulnerability at workplaces". He added that SARS had attempted to defend the indefensible, and slammed a punitive cost order on the tax collector. He ordered that Mashilo and Seremane be retrospectively reinstated as SARS employees as of the date of their dismissals with full benefits and that they report for duty on 1 September 2022.

* * *

Saturday, 11 August 2012, was an inconspicuous day in South African history, although less than week later the Marikana massacre took place. Yet it was on this day that President Jacob Zuma met an Italian business executive – on the face of it, an unremarkable man who should have had no business in meeting the head of state. This meeting set in

312

motion the most devastating episode of state capture during Zuma's reign. Italian-born Vittorio Massone was the head of Bain & Co. in South Africa. The Boston-based company is one of the so-called big three consultancy firms in the United States. It has been branded the "KGB of consulting" because of the veil of secrecy covering its operations. It employs 12 000 consultants in 59 offices across 37 countries.

Massone was appointed as managing partner of Bain in South Africa in 2007 and soon realised the massive business opportunities embedded in the country's weak and vulnerable state institutions. He developed a "final solution" to repurpose and restructure organisations like SARS and Telkom.

Bain bought access to Zuma by paying politically connected businessmen almost R5 million. At his first meeting with Zuma, Massone presented the head of state with Project Phoenix, which involved the restructuring of Telkom. This was going to be a pilot project for Bain's reorganisation of South Africa's state economy that could potentially rake in billions for the consultancy firm. In hindsight, the pilot project at Telkom ended up becoming a blueprint of sorts for state capture.

Even though Bain did not have any public sector experience in South Africa, it soon secured a dubious R91 million contract with Telkom subsidiary BCX, which offers digital telecommunications and IT support services. It hired Bain without any formal proposals being made, and there is no record of the consultancy bidding for the work. BCX ultimately abandoned Bain's turnaround strategies because of a host of shortcomings in the plans. Despite a loss to BCX of R200 million, Massone claims on his personal website that it was "one of his greatest successes". His involvement with SARS never made it onto his website – and for good reason.

While Massone and Bain were driven by profit, Zuma's motivation was more complex. By the time he met Massone, state capture was in full swing, and key allies like Richard Mdluli and Nomgcobo Jiba had taken control of Crime Intelligence and the National Prosecuting Authority. The groundwork had been laid for the removal of Hawks head Anwa Dramat while Zuma had succeeded in stopping a State Security Agency investigation into the influence of the Gupta family. This led to the resignation of the top leadership of the agency.

Zuma and Vittorio Massone met at least 17 times between 2012 and 2014, on each occasion behind closed doors and often at the president's official residence. It was during one of the earlier meetings in 2013 that Massone delivered a briefing to the president that comprised 26 slides under the heading "SARS 2.0". The slides identified what Bain considered to be shortcomings at the revenue collector. It declared at the outset: "In order to transform SARS into an innovative revenue & custom agency, SA government will have to run a profound strategy refresh and focus on execution to reach SARS full potential." Ironically, earlier that same year, Zuma's Cabinet and Parliament itself had approved a strategic plan for SARS for the years 2013/14 to 2017/18. It was a sham: Zuma had other plans for SARS, and the government and Parliament knew nothing about them.

Retired Judge Robert Nugent, appointed in 2018 by President Ramaphosa to investigate governance at SARS, found that Bain "knew nothing of the road SARS had travelled, nor of the vision upon which its organisation had been built, nor of the plans SARS had in place for its development. All it had were figures drawn from public sources. Quite clearly Bain was in search of business, and a 'profound transformation' of SARS would do, whatever the existing situation at SARS."

* * *

If this had been a boxing bout for the crown jewel in the South African civil service, in the opposite corner facing Massone would be former SARS enforcement executive Johann van Loggerenberg. A relentless combatant who fought the seizure of the tax collector tooth and nail and who has ever since been at the forefront of exposing what happened in the state-capture trenches, the 50-something-year-old Van Loggerenberg has emerged with heavy scars from these brawls.

He has, like many who opposed state capture, been fallaciously painted with a criminal brush by Zuma's keepers and kleptocrats. He has been branded a killer, a fraudster, a thief, an apartheid spy, a threat to state security, and a madman. He has even been likened to a paedophile and linked to the apartheid regime's notorious police death squad at Vlakplaas and its chemical and biological warfare programme.

🐦 **Max du Preez** @MaxduPreez, 13 Nov. 2018
Roll of honour of public servants who resisted state capture & were neutralised:
Barbara Hogan
Themba Maseko
Anwa Dramat
Shadrack Sibiya
Johan Booysen
Moe Shaik
Gibson Njenje
Ivan Pillay
Peter Richer
Johann van Loggerenberg
Adrian Lackay
Glynnis Breytenbach and more . . .

🐦 **Snodgrass** @NotMrTwain, 13 Nov. 2018
Any roll of dishonour??

🐦 **Max du Preez** @MaxduPreez, 13 Nov. 2018
List is too long for Twitter . . .

Lean-figured and olive-skinned with piercing eyes, Van Loggerenberg is soft-spoken and reserved and comes across as pedantic. He has meticulously filed years and years of official records and reports, transcripts, newspaper reports, eyewitness accounts, voice recordings, court records and affidavits. And they do not just exist somewhere on a computer hard drive but are also catalogued in his head. Ask him, for example, about Pillay's interlocutory affidavit in the review application against the public protector, and he will quote from it.

To get behind his earnest persona, one must delve into his autobiography, *Cop under Cover*. Van Loggerenberg matriculated in the dying days of apartheid but was still eligible for compulsory national service. He chose to do his service in the police, where he was recruited as deep-cover police agent RS5536 into a new organised Crime Intelligence unit. He adopted the nom de guerre of Jay and for several years infiltrated Durban and Johannesburg drug syndicates. He broke all ties with family and friends and vamoosed into the netherworld of gangland. He said: "During the time I was Jay, I – Johann – had missed the entire decade of my twenties. Reuniting and reconnecting with my family and developing a social circle took some time and effort from all sides. My younger brother had grown up without ever really getting to know me as his big brother, as had my two sisters."

After joining SARS, Van Loggerenberg became as devoted to the revenue collector as he was to the police. His work consumed his whole being and took possession of him. He was a workaholic, had few friends, seldom socialised, often worked over weekends, sometimes slept at the office and showered at the gym. It was officials like him who turned SARS into a world-class institution whose business models were studied by international business schools. According to *The New York Times*: "In a barometer of support for the fledgling new government, tax collections rose year after year, eventually surpassing some benchmarks in much richer, more established democracies, including the United States. SARS won plaudits from the World Bank, Princeton University and other rarefied corners of the world."

Extracting taxes from the so-called illicit economy became an integral part of SARS's success. Five investigation units were formed that ultimately fell under Van Loggerenberg; they targeted big-scale tax dodgers, drug and tobacco smugglers, organised criminals, and gangsters and fraudsters. After the disbanding of the Scorpions, SARS stood out as the most efficient law-enforcement agency in the country. Its tax sleuths hunted down organised crime boss Radovan Krejčíř (bill: R114 million); Capeland gangster Mark Lifman (bill: R388 million); convicted drug dealer Glenn Agliotti (bill: R77 million); Ponzi supremo Barry Tannenbaum (bill: R748 million); strip club owner Lolly Jackson (bill: R100 million); money launderer and ANC benefactor Robert Huang (bill: R1 billion); gold smuggler Juan Meyer (bill: R81 million); businessman Dave King (bill: R3.5 billion); controversial arms dealer John Bredenkamp (bill: R75 million); cigarette manufacturer Hennie Delport (bill: R264 million); and businessman Billy Rautenbach (bill: R60 million).

Targeting illicit money is a perilous occupation. Not only were Van Loggerenberg and his investigators stepping on the toes of organised criminals, but they were also infringing on the patronage network around Jacob Zuma and his cronies. State intelligence structures had become politicised and were used to target Zuma's enemies and settle political scores.

One of the most remarkable documents to emerge from the era of state capture is a 118-page affidavit that Van Loggerenberg filed in this matter. Including a supplementary affidavit and attached documents, the application consists of more than 700 pages. It reveals, in the finest detail and with evidentiary documents, the full extent of the state-capture blitz on SARS. And yet, despite being a public document, it has disappeared in the morass of founding affidavits, supplementary affidavits, answering affidavits and interlocutory affidavits that flooded the courts and media space in the aftermath of state capture. Despite its explosive content, it has never been reported on, probably because it concerns the SARS rogue unit, which is a convoluted story – the cast is vast and the agendas numerous.

The affidavit explains that the destruction of the revenue service was a great team effort that included rogue elements in state security, Crime Intelligence, the Hawks, the tobacco industry and disgruntled former SARS employees who manufactured "dossiers" that were leaked to the media. SARS's probes had created formidable enemies, and there was ultimately not enough political protection for Van Loggerenberg, Ivan Pillay and their brave investigators. Their work was fatally compromised by Zuma's complicity in parachuting into the top position at the revenue service a crony and friend with a master plan to eradicate the investigation units. Their fates were sealed before it dawned on them that they were victims of the seizure of the state's most valuable monetary asset.

At the time, SARS was probing individuals and syndicates implicated in the large-scale looting of the state and its enterprises. The Hawks had asked SARS to investigate the Crime Intelligence top brass who had pilfered the unit's secret services account. A similar investigation was conducted at the State Security Agency, where top officials treated the agency's secret fund like a piggy bank. Van Loggerenberg and his sleuths were not just probing tax evader and alleged money launderer Robert Huang's relationship with the Zuma clan but were also investigating several members of the first family for similar transgressions. SARS posed a far bigger threat to Zuma and his cronies than any other law-enforcement agency in South Africa. His own tax affairs were a mess and his sons Edward and Duduzane were being investigated for tax evasion, as was his nephew Khulubuse Zuma.

SARS had also initiated a project that looked at government tenders across the country. Ivan Pillay mentioned in an affidavit that it concerned "multiple audits and investigations relating to state tender fraud at state-owned enterprises, national government departments and in provinces". SARS had also embarked on a massive investigation into the Guptas' criminal empire and their alleged laundering of billions of rand across the country's borders. It is more than probable that one of the brothers would have mentioned their irritation with the tax collector to Zuma over a plate of Mrs Gupta's excellent chicken tikka masala. It wouldn't have been the first time that a tax delinquent turned to the president for help.

In May 2011, just more than two weeks before local government elections, Zuma met a group of Capeland gangsters at his official Cape Town residence to discuss their and their supporters' votes for the ANC. Among the gangsters were two of the Cape's biggest criminal bosses, Quinton "Mr Big" Marinus and Americans gang leader Igshaan Davids. SARS was at the time concluding a tax evasion case against Marinus. The revenue service had seized his belongings, including his home in the upmarket suburb of Plattekloof, to recover millions in tax debts. Marinus said to the president: "We have our troops inside each community. We will mobilise them and we will swing the vote." He then added: "Sir, we're having big problems with SARS." Zuma reportedly responded: "We will look into that." Pillay brought up this encounter in a subsequent meeting with Zuma.

* * *

During his reign as tax commissioner from 1999 to 2009, Pravin Gordhan had groomed five men to become part of the SARS leadership and enable the organisation to collect enough money to meet South Africa's vast social grants needs and developmental requirements. They were his successor as SARS commissioner Oupa Magashula, Ivan Pillay, Johann van Loggerenberg, strategic planning risk group executive Peter Richer, and tax and customs investigations head Humbulani Gene Ravele. Each was as straight as an arrow, highly skilled and a convert to Gordhan's higher purpose philosophy. To perform state capture, its architects had to rid the revenue collector of all five men.

One of the first opportunities to present itself came in March 2013 when someone in police Crime Intelligence remembered that its agents had recorded a telephone conversation, spiced with sexual innuendo, between Magashula and a young woman in which the two discussed a job at the revenue collector. Crime Intelligence edited the tape so that it contained only the juiciest bits and leaked it to *City Press*. I have referred to this incident in an earlier chapter. The first stumbling block on the road to state capture had been overcome.

Ivan Pillay was appointed in an acting capacity when the commissioner's post was advertised. This attracted around 120 applicants. Several of the candidates occupied top positions in the private sector and had vast experience and expertise in the field of taxation. One of the hopefuls was former prisons boss Tom Moyane. He had had an undistinguished career in government and had served as commissioner of the Department of Correctional Services. In September 2013, he left the department under a cloud and before his contract had expired. He was implicated in a tender scandal of R378 million while commissioner.

On the face of it, Moyane's application should have been chucked in the rubbish bin because he had no tax collection experience. But Moyane had other qualities that made him the president's preferred candidate. An old Zuma family friend and comrade, Moyane proved himself to be a trusted hatchet man for Number One when he participated in the panel that investigated the landing of the Gupta passenger jet at Waterkloof air force base in 2013. The investigation was a complete and successful cover-up and therefore Moyane was, according to the zany universe of the Zumatocracy, ready for higher office.

Days after Moyane's resignation from Correctional Services in September 2013, he met Vittorio Massone of Bain & Co. for the first time. This was a year before his appointment as SARS commissioner. Many more meetings followed during which Bain provided "CEO coaching" for Moyane – at no cost. Bain presented Moyane with a document titled "TM First 100 Days", which outlined the changes he had to effect in his first hundred days as SARS head.

Among these changes was getting rid of one of South Africa's most accomplished civil servants, SARS chief officer of operations Barry Hore. Recruited by Pravin Gordhan in 2005 from Nedbank, where he was a member of the board of directors and head of operations, he was put at the helm of the modernisation of SARS. According to Judge Nugent, he possessed "exceptional skills in that field" and was selected in 1999 as one of the World Economic Forum's "100 Global Leaders for Tomorrow".

Hore's position was earmarked for SARS executive Jonas Makwakwa, who had become Bain's and Moyane's deep throat at the revenue collector and who attended several of the meetings. He stole confidential information about SARS staff and operations and handed it to Bain and Moyane.

* * *

As Tom Moyane was being coached by Bain, SARS executive Gene Ravele got a call from Jacob Zuma's chief legal adviser, Advocate Bonisiwe Makhene, who wanted to see him. When they met, she was accompanied by her husband, Yekani Monde Gadini, a secret agent in the special operations directorate of the SSA. I described Gadini in *The President's Keepers* as part of a "shadowy network of intelligence agents and contracted operatives closely linked to President Jacob Zuma". He popped up like a spectre during some of the most important events I chronicled in that book and as a key player in the protection of Zuma.

Gadini said to Ravele: "We are busy preparing for the appointment of a new SARS commissioner." He said the SSA wanted Ravele to provide them with information that would "lead to the removal of Pillay". He was also asked to meet and brief the commissioner-in-waiting and identify people who would assist and support him. Ravele declined the invitation and, instead, reported details of the meeting to SARS, which are contained in an affidavit of Ivan Pillay.

The assault on SARS intensified on all levels. Tax investigators received death threats and were followed around, laptops with key evidence were stolen, and a tax sleuth probing the tobacco industry was seriously wounded in his driveway. According to affidavits from Pillay and Van Loggerenberg, SSA agents told SARS investigators that "we are coming for you"; a senior police Crime Intelligence officer was recorded as saying that "big heads are going to roll at SARS"; and a serving Cabinet minister warned Van Loggerenberg that he and his associates were about to be "hounded out of SARS, humiliated and must never be able to work again".

The targets of the taxman's probes knew they were being investigated. On 15 November 2013, a Gupta spokesperson and managing editor of the Gupta-owned *New Age* newspaper, Gary Naidoo, wrote an e-mail to Atul Gupta in which he said: "I was given some info by my investigative contact that SARS was investigating the President." Naidoo warned in his e-mail that the Gupta empire was also being investigated and named Van Loggerenberg as at the top of the list of officials scrutinising their financial affairs and accounts.

This e-mail was among a treasure trove of about 200 000 messages sent between the Guptas, their business associates and government officials that were leaked to the media in 2017. They became known as the "Gupta e-mails" and laid bare the skulduggery of the family, showing the extent of Gupta control over Cabinet ministers and parastatal CEOs and board members. Their authenticity has never been questioned and they have also been submitted to the State Capture Commission.

In February 2014, Pillay met Hawks head Lt.-Gen. Anwa Dramat and warned him about criminal attacks on both SARS and the Hawks. In the months to follow, Pillay furnished Dramat with a host of evidence of attacks against SARS, but soon Dramat was gone too. He was suspended for his alleged role in the kidnapping and murder of Zimbabweans in 2010. His successor, Berning Ntlemeza, was known as Zuma's bulldozer, and ate, lived and breathed state capture while destroying the Hawks.

In the same month, Pillay met Jacob Zuma at his office in the Union Buildings in Pretoria to brief him about sensitive SARS projects and the assault on the revenue collector. He also informed his erstwhile ANC comrade that SARS had stumbled upon what seemed to be illicit cash payments for both his son and his Nkandla homestead. He urged the president to submit his tax returns, which were outstanding since Zuma's election as president in May 2009.

Pillay referred to this meeting with Zuma in a 2015 affidavit to the Labour Court when he applied to be reinstated after Tom Moyane had suspended him. Pillay said he had presented Zuma with a document titled "Common Interests between SARS and SSA", an account of "attempts to malign and discredit SARS and concerns about the role of SSA agents in the attack". Outside forces, which included SSA agents, law-enforcement officials and disgruntled current and former SARS officials, were waging a campaign to rid SARS of its top executives.

At their meeting, Zuma listened to Pillay and said he would attend to the matter. He did nothing. Less than a year after speaking to the president, Pillay and several other SARS executives were history. Many more followed soon afterwards.

Days after this meeting, Zuma, Massone and Moyane met and discussed the appointment of a new SARS commissioner. On 26 February 2014, Massone sent a message to his partners at Bain and said: "Guys, met president yesterday night in CT. All good. There was also a Tom . . . and it really seems he is getting that job after election. He was very friendly with me and seems a smart guy to work with."

In April 2014, just a day after Massone had met Zuma yet again, he and senior Bain partner Fabrice Franzen exchanged WhatsApp messages that were revealed at the Nugent Commission.

Franzen: "Ciao – just wanted to check how your 'big meeting' went yesterday. Take care."

Massone: "Thank you, Fabrice, it went very well. Sars is a go, right after the elections. central procurement agency: he loves it, wants an implementation plan. wants to accelerate Phoenix. asked us to organise a workshop with the new Cabinet of ministries after the elections. So I'd say very well."

Franzen: "Congrats!"

Massone: "Be ready for SARS!!!! Tom passes by for coffee next Friday morning, if you want to say hi to him."

* * *

Zuma allowed the capture of SARS to happen, Bain plotted its seizure, and Moyane and his cronies executed the final solution. The groundwork for the capture of SARS was carried out by rogue elements in the law-enforcement agencies, and here nobody played a more prominent role than tobacco vixen Belinda Walter, SSA agent number 5332. She had to befriend Van Loggerenberg, which she did. She had to snare him, which she did. She then had to find dirt on him – but there wasn't any, so she had to manufacture enough excrement to get him out of SARS, which she did. His reputation had to be sullied to the extent that he would be unemployable and could never return to the revenue collector: she almost achieved that, too.

By the time Zuma announced the appointment of Tom Moyane as the new commissioner of SARS in September 2014, the table had been set for the capture of SARS. Johann van Loggerenberg was under siege after Walter made a series of accusations against him, among others that he had shared confidential taxpayer information with her. Although a panel found that there was no substance in her allegations, Van Loggerenberg would be the next of Gordhan's chosen five to perish, cruelly floored and felled by Zuma's headsman.

CHAPTER 19

In the aftermath of carnage

IF THE CAPTURE of SARS were a battle, it would have gone down in history alongside Vegkop, Blood River, Isandlwana and Magersfontein as one of the bloodiest conflicts in South African history. While the gore of fallen Zulu warriors reddened the water of the Ncome River and the remains of almost 900 British soldiers littered the rugged slopes of Isandlwana in KwaZulu-Natal, state-capture skeletons scattered around Lehae la SARS are a reminder of how Jacob Zuma's executioner Tom Moyane wielded his honed machete to slash open and dismember the tax collector before ripping its heart out.

Days after Moyane had taken office as the new commissioner of SARS, the rogue-unit narrative was born when an old, discredited "intelligence" dossier, compiled by a self-confessed rhino smuggler who once worked for one of Van Loggerenberg's units, was dusted off and fed to the investigations unit of the *Sunday Times*. Week after week, the newspaper revealed how Van Loggerenberg and his team of reprobates had bugged Jacob Zuma, run a brothel, spied on taxpayers and intercepted communications. When the newspaper retracted its stories two years later and admitted that they were wrong, it was too late. SARS was by then a shell of its former self.

As executive of enforcement investigations, Van Loggerenberg was the first to go. Moyane suspended him on 12 November 2014, pending a disciplinary hearing to commence in January 2015. Van Loggerenberg chose to resign. He received six months' remuneration in return for signing a restraint agreement. Moyane cynically insisted on a photograph of the two smiling and shaking hands. SARS announced his departure on "amicable" grounds.

On 1 December 2014, SARS *wunderkind* Barry Hore also threw in the towel. Moyane humiliated him by kicking him off the executive committee and then announced through an internal communication to all employees that the modernisation process was suspended. He did not bother to consult the man primarily responsible for elevating SARS into the modern era of tax collecting.

Two days later, Bain's Fabrice Franzen despatched an e-mail to Vittorio Massone with the subject "Goodbye Barry Hore". Massone replied: "Now I'm scared by Tom . . . This guy [Hore] was supposed to be untouchable and it took Tom just a few weeks to make him resign . . . Scary."

Moyane's acting predecessor, Ivan Pillay, was suspended four days after Hore for his alleged complicity in setting up the rogue unit. The Labour Court overturned his suspension, but a few months later, faced with a disciplinary hearing, he also resigned. Head of strategic planning Pete Richer followed suit.

Gene Ravele fell out with Moyane when the commissioner ordered him to investigate the activities of the rogue unit. Ravele reported that there was no such unit and no rogue actions. He had to go. A prince from the Ramabulana royal family of Venda and a law graduate from the University of Limpopo, Ravele had impeccable credentials. He was an anti-apartheid activist who had been detained without trial. He had almost twenty years' experience at SARS and was groomed as a possible future commissioner. Moyane charged Ravele with approving unlawful covert intelligence gathering at SARS and the procurement of tracking devices for the rogue unit. When the revenue service failed to prove its claims, Moyane laid trumped-up charges of fraud against him. The Hawks investigated Ravele for two years before relenting and then dropping the charge. But, by then, Ravele had long since departed.

With the departure of Pillay, Van Loggerenberg, Hore and Ravele, the exodus at SARS resembled the evacuation of the Tunisian city of

Carthage in 146 BC as the Romans set it on fire and reduced it to ashes. By the first half of 2015, the chief officer for legal and policy, the chief officer for human relations, the chief officer for finance, and the chief officer for strategy, enablement and communications had all quit. More than fifty top officials left in the eighteen months after Moyane's appointment.

By the end of 2017, SARS had lost over 200 specialists and most of the revenue service's top investigators had departed. After Moyane took power, SARS did not meet any of its revenue collection targets. During his reign of three and a half years, SARS recorded revenue shortfalls of almost R150 billion. Although Moyane is long gone, the revenue collector still suffers from a debilitating hangover and will for years to come struggle to fill the fiscus. What happened at SARS was nothing but economic treason, perpetrated against ordinary South Africans who are struggling to feed their families and keep their children at school and are forced to access a crumbling public health system.

When Moyane arrived at SARS, there was a full tax investigation against the Guptas under way. It vanished. Instead, SARS assisted the Guptas in obtaining VAT refunds while the rest of the country's citizens were starved of their reimbursements because Moyane was trying to boost his tax collection. In contravention of tax laws which prohibit SARS from paying VAT refunds into a third party's account, Moyane did exactly that. The revenue service paid R420 million in refunds unlawfully into the account of an attorney, a shelf company and a shady businessman. The last-mentioned happened to be involved in business with Moyane's nephew.

*　*　*

Tax sleuth Keith Hendrickse is a stocky and bespectacled man with a hushed voice that belies his ability to unearth and detect malfeasance. He was the head of the Cape Town office of SARS's national projects unit, one of the five investigation units that fell under Van

Loggerenberg. Hendrickse helped set up the unit in 2009 and oversaw some of the most sensitive tax investigations into the most notorious Capeland gangsters.

One of them was "gentleman gangster" Mark Roy Lifman, whom I referred to in an earlier chapter. Hendrickse registered Project All Out in October 2013 to probe Lifman's business and criminal empire. The clean-shaven and square-jawed Lifman is a far cry from his business associate Jerome "Donkie" Booysen, head of the Sexy Boys gang on the Cape Flats. Lifman has been accused of corruption, fraud, money laundering, drug trafficking, cigarette smuggling, paedophilia and transnational organised crime, and has over the years miraculously escaped prosecution and prison time. As so often in the past, it was left to SARS to bring down an organised criminal.

After a full-scale tax inquiry that lasted almost a year, during which 90 witnesses testified, SARS presented Lifman with a tax bill of R388 million. This was followed by lengthy litigation between SARS and Lifman, which he lost. The revenue service was ready to sequestrate Lifman, and commenced by auctioning four of his luxury cars, including two Porsches. Lifman's property portfolio was valued at R92 million, and legal counsel advised SARS that there were "good prospects of collecting substantial taxes".

As Hendrickse and the national projects unit were about to start collecting Lifman's unpaid taxes, the unit members were summoned to a "town hall" meeting for a presentation of Moyane's and Bain's new operating model. It made no provision for national projects nor for a replacement unit. Bain's consultants never spoke to Hendrickse or any of his staff, which meant that the new regime could not have known what the national projects unit did or what cases they were working on.

During the presentation, Hendrickse wanted to know why national projects was not part of the new structure. He was told: "Well, that's because it no longer exists."

The same fate befell one of the tax collector's brightest stars in its crusade against the illicit economy, central projects unit head Pieter

Engelbrecht, who had probed, among others, Dave King and Robert Huang, two of the biggest tax evaders in SARS's history. Moyane also shut down the central projects unit and dumped Engelbrecht somewhere in the innards of SARS without a proper job. He was ordered to leave behind his cases, including the R1 billion tax bill for Robert Huang. In *The President's Keepers* I allocated much space to Huang, a convicted killer and major ANC benefactor who accompanied Jacob Zuma on a business trip to China and imported for the ruling party almost 200 000 ANC T-shirts for the 2014 general election. With Engelbrecht gone, Huang's tax bill went nowhere. Four cases were opened against Engelbrecht, all spurious and with no merit. At least one was proven to be based on fabricated documents.

Bain's new restructuring model didn't provide for any investigation units to target money launderers, large-scale tax evaders, and organised criminals. The units that fell under Van Loggerenberg disbanded one by one. When Hendrickse later testified before Judge Robert Nugent, he said: "From one day to the next, there was suddenly nothing. No structure, no authority, not a care about what would happen to the people or the work. Cases that were in their infant stage had to be abandoned. Some high-profile cases could not be properly completed." The unit was broken up and members were scattered across the revenue collector. Hendrickse was allocated an office where for months "I, as a senior manager, had absolutely no work to do, and was being paid to come to work and do nothing. The situation was soul destroying."

He was eventually demoted to the position of senior specialist. "As we came closer and closer to the 'ring leaders', we discovered that we were trampling on the toes of certain people very close to the ex-president. It became very clear that these individuals were given political protection. It is clear and obvious that Tom Moyane had been put in place to stop all these investigations."

As Hendrickse sat idle in a nondescript office, one of Moyane's henchmen demanded the Lifman docket. "When I asked on whose instructions he was acting, I was told . . . that the instruction came from the commissioner. I said you can't have it. The papers are a whole room full. I can't just give it to you."

Smelling blood, Lifman lodged an application in the High Court in November 2016 to have his tax audit of R388 million reviewed. He advanced the "rogue-unit defence" and claimed that he was being unfairly targeted and victimised. Lifman threatened to interdict SARS from continuing with its efforts to liquidate his companies.

Hendrickse said that, to his horror, he discovered that a SARS specialist forensic auditor had, in writing, promised Lifman an audit review of the tax case against him because of his allegations of "unfair treatment during the investigation/audit". The auditor must have known that it was a sham, as the Tax Administration Act does not make provision for a re-audit, as a later court judgment would prove. There exists in law no such procedure.

* * *

Enter one of the most discerning officials at SARS, who was not even 40 years old when she was appointed as the national manager of criminal investigations and managed a team of 8 regional managers, 42 team leaders and 371 investigators. Ronel van Wyk became a police colonel at the age of 28 before joining SARS, where she climbed up the ranks and obtained an MBA degree.

Van Wyk made a submission to the commission investigating SARS and appeared in camera before Bob Nugent and his panel of experts. Her evidence included confidential taxpayers' information, the details of which have never been released. Among the tax evaders and money launderers with whom Van Wyk crossed swords were mega-evader Dave King, convicted drug dealer Glenn Agliotti, drug lord and international fugitive Nelson Pablo Yester-Garrido, notorious security boss Clinton Nassif, cigarette baron Adriano Mazzotti, mafia boss Vito Palazzolo, apartheid hit squad killer Calla Botha, and EFF leader Julius Malema. Van Wyk said she felt purpose and immense pride in being associated with SARS because she was making a difference in the lives of ordinary people, as effective tax collection ensured there were funds available for social upliftment programmes.

Even though she had managed the criminal investigations unit since 2009, Bain never spoke to Van Wyk except to demand sensitive information about when arrests would take place, for purposes of a media campaign. The consultants had no strategic information of criminal investigations and didn't understand the business unit, the legislative framework, or the roles and responsibilities of Van Wyk and her regional managers. Van Wyk was downgraded to the post of regional manager. All the regional managers became specialists. Van Wyk was forced into accepting the lower position, as otherwise she might have become "disposable". She applied for seven or eight other positions in SARS, without success.

She told the Nugent Commission of staff each receiving in turn a dreaded e-mail from Jonas Makwakwa in October 2015, summoning them to a meeting. Every SARS official who received this e-mail knew they were going to be downgraded or else become redundant. She said this left people "disillusioned, traumatised, worried, negative and more confused than ever before". Despite her own downgrading, Van Wyk was still required to manage criminal investigations on a national level but without managers, a strategic or operational plan, or direction.

When allegations emerged that the Guptas had attempted to bribe deputy finance minister Mcebisi Jonas to become the minister, to "grease" the wheels at Treasury and ensure lucrative state tenders for them, Van Wyk attempted to revive the initial probe that had perished after Moyane's arrival. She suggested that Gupta-linked entities should be investigated to determine if they were tax compliant. Her line manager refused. Van Wyk told the SARS commission that the new operating model did not allow SARS the agility to address threats such as those posed by state capture and the illicit flow of funds. "I am not aware of any SARS investigations into state capture, the Gupta family or related entities," she testified.

In September 2016, the Reserve Bank reported 72 suspicious international transactions of the Gupta company Oakbay to the Financial Intelligence Centre (FIC). The report was shared with law-enforcement agencies, including SARS. Van Wyk said the reports "ended up in a safe of an executive at case selection without any further investigations being pursued".

In the meantime, Moyane had formed his own "investigative unit", which was ostensibly intended to investigate the tobacco industry. In fact, it was nothing but his personal "hit squad" to target his enemies within SARS. One of its members had alleged links with the criminal underworld. He arranged to remove the "stoppers" that prevented a big company from receiving a R45 million VAT refund. SARS was investigating the company at the time for tax evasion and, until the investigation was completed, the company didn't qualify for a refund. The official was allegedly bribed with R9 million. Van Wyk recommended that SARS's anti-corruption unit investigate him but the group executive for criminal investigations changed her report to argue that the official had done nothing wrong.

The head of Moyane's new investigative unit, Gobi Makhanya, called a meeting with Van Wyk and showed her an affidavit. It suggested that her husband was connected to notorious gangsters, among them Mark Lifman and Jerome Booysen. The affidavit contained photos of her children and their cars at their house. Makhanya refused to tell her where he got the information from. Van Wyk told the Nugent Commission that there was not a speck of truth in the allegations against her husband. Her interaction with Makhanya left her traumatised, and she regarded it as nothing but a threat against her and her family. Makhanya used the same tactic of manufacturing spurious charges to target other top SARS investigators and managers whom Moyane wanted to get rid of.

Makhanya and Yegan Mundie then investigated Van Wyk for money that her husband had paid into their bank account. "There was a relentless drive to find something against me in order to charge me. I had no protection from my line management." Van Wyk resigned, partly because of Makhanya's and Mundie's threats, but also because she discovered that her line manager had covered up fraud of R93 million. She said it was clear that management wanted her out of SARS. Once she had handed in her resignation letter, security escorted her off the premises and she was told to serve her notice period from home.

Van Wyk sent this message to her manager: "Not so much as a thank you after 16 years serving faithfully, just being escorted from the premises without the opportunity to engage my people. I will never do anything to harm SARS and it is heart-breaking to think that my leadership treats people in this way."

* * *

✈ Nation Breaking News @NationBreaking, 15 Feb. 2018
SOUTH AFRICAN parliament elects Cyril Ramaphosa as new president following resignation of Jacob Zuma yesterday.

✈ Moneyweb News @Moneyweb, 13 Mar. 2018
Jonas #Makwakwa resigns under cloud of controversy.

✈ Sowetan LIVE @SowetanLIVE, 20 Mar. 2018
SARS boss Tom Moyane suspended.

Tom Moyane and Jonas Makwakwa departed from SARS within a week of each other in March 2018. In the case of Moyane, Cyril Ramaphosa suspended him just more than a month after his election as president. He said he had lost all confidence in his revenue commissioner. As for Makwakwa, he became embroiled in yet another controversy when the *Daily Maverick* reported that New Integrated Credit Solutions (NICS), which had entered a deal with SARS to assist in bolstering the tax body's debt collections, paid R600 000 into his bank account.

When Moyane and Makwakwa packed their bags, SARS resembled a war zone. It was an institution wrecked by division, suspicion, and large pockets of incompetence. The top officials had left, SARS had for years been unable to meet its revenue collection targets, and modernisation had ground to a standstill.

Ramaphosa's means of getting SARS on the road to recovery was the appointment of Robert Nugent, assisted by a panel of tax experts, to chair a commission of inquiry into tax administration and governance at the tax collector. Over the next few months, Moyane's ineptitude was laid bare like the skeletal remains of an animal in the bleak Karoo veld. All those who had been shafted and publicly shamed by Moyane and Makwakwa finally had their say in a public forum and under oath.

Barry Hore, who became the CEO of a bank after leaving SARS, was the bearer of debilitating news when he testified that the Moyane years cost SARS at least R142 billion in uncollected taxes. This was a figure that could be directly quantified and did not include the knock-on or "hangover" effect of Moyane's lamentable decisions. To make up for the shortfall, the government was forced to increase VAT.

🐦 EWN Reporter @ewnreporter, 18 Oct. 2021
#SARSinquiry Hore: after Moyane halted the modernisation process I called him, told him there are huge implications. He said we'd discuss it at a meeting the following week. That never happened.

The SARS commission exposed many of the inane appointments Moyane made after he got rid of some of South Africa's most dedicated civil servants. None was more inexplicable than that of IT chief officer Mmamathe Makhekhe-Mokhuane. The remuneration guideline for her post was R183 000 per month, but she was appointed at a salary of R261 000 per month. She first made headlines after an interview on the SABC's *Morning Live* programme when she was asked about the restructuring of IT at SARS. Instead, she rambled on about bursary programmes and then asked: "Ma'am, can you give me protection from yourself?"

When Makhekhe-Mokhuane testified at the Nugent Commission and was asked about her attendance at certain meetings, she said: "I think this is beyond a waste of your time. Your time, in my understanding of your terms of reference, is to look at the governance, but not what I do as a chief officer, including when I go to the bathroom. With due respect, sir. Please protect me. Please." Rebuked by Nugent, she was offered the opportunity to inspect minutes showing she had attended only one strategy meeting in 15 months. She responded: "I have a very rare eye disease, but let's try." And when asked to give clarity about what she had stated in her affidavit, Makhekhe-Mokhuane cited the date on which the Drakensberg Boys' Choir was established before mercifully dropping her attempted analogy. Nugent described her evidence as "disturbing".

Chief officer of enforcement Hlengani Mathebula, appointed at a salary of R300 000 per month, told Nugent that Moyane called him to his office and gave him a list of names of people he was to "dismiss or suspend". He said Moyane also gave him an additional list of names of people to be appointed in senior and executive positions – also without following due process.

Unlike his predecessors, Moyane ruled by fear and dread. There was no debate and no deliberation. He made irrational and nonsensical decisions. He installed spy cameras all over SARS offices, "even on top of copying machines". When various trees were uprooted around SARS headquarters in Pretoria, leadership explained this was for "security reasons".

Although Moyane refused to testify or make a written submission to Nugent, his Number Three, employee relations chief Luther Lebelo, did take the stand. Lebelo had a reputation for wielding Moyane's axe and dishing out suspension notices left, right and centre. Lebelo, who earned a salary of R350 000 per month, arrived at the commission with five lever-arch files of "evidence" pertaining to the rogue unit.

Much of Lebelo's "evidence" that he wanted to present to Nugent concerned the existence of the rogue unit. Nugent said it was disturbing that Lebelo was intent on keeping the rogue-unit narrative alive and ruled that he was going to "spare Mr Lebelo the pain of hurting those people once again, and of hurting their families. It is time that dignity and decency return to SARS."

Throughout the evidence of 64 witnesses at the commission, the name of Bain & Co. ran like a golden thread through the story of destruction at SARS. Bain's Vittorio Massone made one appearance before the commission before hastily departing South Africa for his native Italy, allegedly to receive medical treatment. He offered an affidavit to Nugent, but the commission later concluded that he did not tell the whole truth and that his version of events was "littered with perjury, both in what he said and in what he didn't".

Towards the end of 2018, Bain offered to repay – with interest – the R217 million it had earned for consulting at SARS. Bain said in a statement: "There is a growing frustration within our firm that we did not recognise the possibility that we may have been used to further a political or personal agenda. We are dismayed by the way our work has been used to further a different agenda than was intended."

🐦 **Qaanitah|Mzekezeke|Hunter** @QaanitahHunter, 16 Oct. 2018
My story today: Judge Robert #Nugent has told President Cyril #Ramaphosa to fire Tom #Moyane now and not wait for the outcomes of his disciplinary hearing.

In an interim report, Nugent said he had heard enough and urged Ramaphosa to fire Moyane. "The day Mr Moyane took office was a calamity for SARS . . . a massive failure of governance and integrity. He turned a world-class organisation upside down, leaving SARS as it is today: racked with intrigue, suspicion and distrust and fear of senior management; information technology that is in decay . . . space for the illicit trade to flourish; loss of long-serving skills; experienced personnel [finding themselves] in supernumerary positions doing little if anything at all; and revenue collection compromised."

🐦 **City Press** @City_Press, 3 Nov. 2018
Ramaphosa fires Moyane over tenure characterised by "reckless" mismanagement.

In an act of desperation, Moyane turned to the highest court in the land to set aside the Nugent inquiry into SARS. He said in his court application that "by any lawful measure or standard, my tenure at SARS was the most successful in the democratic era". The Constitutional Court rejected his application.

A month later, the High Court also rejected Moyane's application to overturn his dismissal, interdict the appointment of a new SARS commissioner, and prevent the commission of inquiry from submitting its final report. The court slammed a punitive cost order on him.

Moyane did take the stand at the State Capture Commission headed by Judge Raymond Zondo and denied any involvement in state capture. He told Zondo "without any fear of contradiction, that the Bain–SARS relationship yielded the best results ever recorded in the entire history of SARS". Zondo didn't believe him and said that both Zuma and Moyane had played "critical roles" in the capture of SARS and its dismantlement. "The SARS evidence is a clear example of how the private sector colluded with the Executive, including president Zuma, to capture an institution that was highly regarded internationally and render it ineffective."

A constant theme in *The President's Keepers* was how Zuma's keepers had eviscerated the law-enforcement agencies, and in particular the revenue service, to protect the president, his family and his cronies from prosecution. This was confirmed by Zondo when he said: "SARS's investigatory and enforcement capacity presented a hurdle to those involved in organised crime, and was, therefore, a target for those engaged in state capture." Despite Zondo recommending criminal charges against Moyane and an investigation into the procurement of Bain's contract with SARS, nothing has happened.

* * *

The SARS rogue unit should have perished with Tom Moyane's demise and Bob Nugent's determination that he had found no evidence that the unit was unlawfully established. But the proponents of the narrative, chief among them the EFF, were determined to keep it alive.

🐦 **Economic Freedom Fighters** @EFFSouthAfrica, 16 Oct. 2018
Malema: We are aware Pravin is working with the rogue unit to continue to fight anyone else who doesn't agree with him. He fights very dirty. We know that the rogue unit is still in operation.

Julius Malema, Floyd Shivambu and the EFF must know that their utterings are convoluted and rubbish. How can they profess to champion the poor when they promote and repeat the bile that Moyane disgorged to enable him to break the tax collector? It resulted in a huge loss to the fiscus and, in effect, less money available to spend on socio-economic upliftment. Once a mean, tax-collecting machine, SARS was reduced by Moyane to a stuttering, oil-spattering wreck.

The EFF have not produced a shred of evidence to support their claims, but they continue to discharge their nonsense on social media. In turn, their trolls and bots and garbologists clog the Twitter waves with piles of rubbish about the rogue unit. The proponents of this narrative have long learned that if you sell bullshit as gospel truth for long enough, the gullible masses may eventually believe it, and you can use it to beat your adversaries.

But along came the most odious of the odious, Public Protector Busisiwe Mkhwebane, who gave new life to the lie when she found in a report of July 2019 that not only had the rogue unit existed and engaged in illegal spying activities, but also that Pravin Gordhan had approved its formation in violation of section 209 of the Constitution. Proponents of the narrative went into overdrive.

T S Moyane @t_moyane, 20 July 2019
In May 2015, I opened a criminal case on "rogue unit", after 2 members of the unit confessed 2 me about being given R1125 million in cash to illegally install secret covert cameras into 15 offices of NPA & Hawks. Media twisted facts, so I thot I must give you real facts.

Maggs Naidu @maggsnaidu, 21 July 2019
R1,125 billion in cash eh? How did they count it??? That's 5,625,000 R200 notes . . . each counted 2,812,500 notes???

Floyd Shivambu @FloydShivambu, 12 Aug. 2020
Jamnandas has no respect for anyone except himself. He must go and answer why he established an illegal intelligence unit to harass and fight against political opponents. People were killed by the rogue unit and we need answers. He must be summoned to appear or face imprisonment.

JvL @JvanLogg, 30 Aug. 2020
I'm still waiting for @FloydShivambu to give details of the unknown murders he published as fact.

Floyd Shivambu @FloydShivambu, 30 Aug. 2020
Am advised not to wrestle with *** in the mud because I will not win. The rogue unit killed a lot of people and were engaged in so many unlawful activities which you are arrested for.

Pravin Gordhan took Mkhwebane's report on review. In December 2020, three High Court judges legally massacred the public protector. A full bench found that Mkhwebane's conclusions were based on "discredited reports and unsubstantiated facts". In setting aside her report, the court said her handiwork "fails at every point", and the judges were satisfied "that the report is the product of a wholly irrational process, bereft of any sound legal or factual basis". In view of her "egregious" conduct during the case, the court ordered Mkhwebane to personally pay part of Gordhan's legal costs. The High Court and the Supreme Court of Appeal rejected her application to appeal in the matter.

🐦 **News24** @News24, 7 Dec. 2020
BREAKING: High Court sets aside Busisiwe Mkhwebane's report on Pravin Gordhan, SARS "rogue unit"

* * *

🐦 **EWN Reporter** @ewnreporter, 27 Mar. 2019
BREAKING #SARS Edward Kieswetter has been appointed as the new SARS commissioner, effective 1 May.

Unlike his predecessor who unilaterally appointed an ineffective home-boy as SARS commissioner, Cyril Ramaphosa named a panel of experts to find a saviour for the revenue service. It recommended Edward Christian Kieswetter, who had impeccable credentials for the job. A former chief executive of Alexander Forbes with a string of academic qualifications, including an MBA degree from a prestigious British university, he had been between 2004 and 2009 a deputy commissioner and chief operating officer at SARS, where he set up the Large Business Centre.

A herculean task awaited the newly appointed Kieswetter. His first mission was to meet staff and allow them to talk to him honestly about the problems and difficulties in the organisation. He found people's spirits broken and their morale at an all-time low. He also spoke to Moyane loyalists and told them: "You must decide where you stand, whether it is on the good or bad side."

He said to *Business Day* a few weeks after taking the reins: "How do I rebuild the trust and improve the morale? My answer is: one person at a time. You have to connect with each of the 12 500 people and demonstrate to that individual that you truly care. Trust isn't built by making big promises, it's by doing many small things."

It is notoriously difficult to get rid of incompetent senior civil servants, but the final report and recommendations of the Nugent Commission produced a wealth of low-hanging fruit for the new commissioner to harvest. In what can be described as Kieswetter's night of the long knives, he suspended four executives three months after assuming office. With Moyane and Makwakwa both gone but their destructive legacy still in place, it was time for Number Three to go. Moyane hitman Luther Lebelo, also a staunch defender of the rogue-unit narrative, was suspended alongside chief officers Hlengani Mathebula and Teboho Mokoena.

IT boss Mmamathe "Protect-me-from-yourself" Makhekhe-Mokhuane followed shortly afterwards. SARS chief legal officer Refiloe Mokoena, who was fingered by Nugent for granting the controversial Gupta family a reported R420 million VAT refund, had already been suspended in October 2018. Nugent heard evidence that Mathebula had unlawfully suspended officials on the commissioner's "hit list" while Mokoena illegally appointed Moyane loyalists at inflated salaries.

Mathebula, Lebelo, Teboho Mokoena and Makhekhe-Mokhuane resigned before facing disciplinary hearings. Refiloe Mokoena chose to fight her suspension, but in November 2019 a disciplinary hearing found her guilty of gross misconduct for facilitating VAT refunds to the Guptas, and fired her.

🐦 **OUTA** @OUTASA, 22 Feb. 2019
Looks like #SARS newly established Illicit Economy Unit means business. Certainly a very welcome move in the fight against #corruption. Hopefully #prosecutions will follow shortly.

Keith Hendrickse and Pieter Engelbrecht were hauled from the crypts to which they were consigned during the Moyane regime and put in charge of the newly established Illicit Economy Unit (IEU). Other tax sleuths not driven out by Moyane joined them.

At the IEU's Cape Town office, Keith Hendrickse revived Mark Lifman's R388 million tax bill, which he had been holding on to throughout the Moyane years. At head office in Pretoria, Pieter Engelbrecht resuscitated Robert Huang's tab, which by then had more than doubled from the original R1 billion.

When SARS notified Lifman that it was proceeding with execution orders to seize his assets and auction them off to recover his tax debt, the gentleman gangster rushed to court to halt the action. He mentioned that SARS had undertaken to review his assessment and his claim that he had been improperly investigated. Judge Elizabeth Baartman would have none of it. She ruled in June 2019 that tax assessments by SARS are "undisputed, final, due and payable". She gave SARS the green light to collect R352 million from the tax delinquent.

Lifman attempted to appeal against the judgment, but in 2020 the Supreme Court of Appeal ruled that his attempts to stop the revenue service from seizing his assets were futile and had no prospect of success. SARS started selling the preserved properties while sequestrating Lifman. The revenue service hoped to collect around R100 million from his estate.

Lifman associate and bouncer boss André Naudé also felt the wrath of the IEU when SARS swooped on his Bellville and Durbanville properties in Cape Town to attach all his moveable assets after a writ of execution was issued by the Western Cape High Court. His construction company owed SARS R50 million while his personal tax bill amounted to R14 million.

At around the same time, the sheriff raided five properties belonging to Robert Huang and his wife, Shou Fang. The raid followed two judgments that SARS obtained against them to recover R236 million, a portion of the couple's long-outstanding debt to the taxman. The judgments were only for personal income tax owed by the Huang couple and did not include assessments raised against their company Mpisi Trading. That process of recovering unpaid taxes is still under way.

The IEU attempted to revive SARS's earlier campaign against illicit cigarettes, and the unit immediately made an impact. According to research by the University of Cape Town's Research Unit on the Economics of Excisable Products, the illicit market had risen from 17 per cent of all sales in 2014 – Moyane became commissioner in October of that year – to more than 30 per cent in 2017. But in the 2019/20 tax year – the first of the unit's existence – tax revenue from locally produced cigarettes rose by 19.2 per cent from R12.1 billion to R14.4 billion. The reported revenue was 14 per cent higher than the targeted revenue. Researchers at the research unit said the government was "winning the war against illegal tobacco products and the once rampant lawlessness in the industry may be coming to an end".

Days after the publication of the UCT paper, the president declared the Covid-19 lockdown, which was followed by Nkosazana Dlamini-Zuma's inane banning of tobacco products. The illegal trade again flourished, and vital revenue from the tobacco industry was lost.

* * *

Just as Judge Nugent had presented the heads of Luther Lebelo, Refiloe Mokoena and Mmamathe Makhekhe-Mokhuane to SARS on a plate, evidence before the State Capture Commission provided a list of probable tax delinquents. One was facilities management company Bosasa, implicated in the capture of the Department of Correctional Services (DCS). In return for scoring state contracts worth R12 billion, Bosasa allegedly bribed everyone from the DCS commissioner and a host of top officials to several Cabinet ministers and politicians. The rewards included cash in envelopes and bags, cars, holidays, air tickets, security upgrades and birthday parties. Among the beneficiaries was

South African Airways board chair and Zuma crony Dudu Myeni, who allegedly received R300 000 monthly on behalf of the Jacob Zuma Foundation. It is doubtful that Bosasa paid donations tax for the millions it siphoned off to officials and beneficiaries, but, more than that, criminal enterprises engaged in fraud, money laundering and racketeering are never tax compliant. In 2020, SARS slapped Bosasa and a host of its companies with a tax bill of R849 million, while informing them that it was in the process of raising further assessments.

✔ Pauli Van Wyk @PaulivW, 22 Feb. 2019
#Sars' Illicit Economy Unit knocked on #Bosasa's door in Krugersdorp today just after noon. They're sharing info with the liquidator. Further legal procedures are awaited.

✔ Yusuf Abramjee @Abramjee, 21 Sept. 2020
SARS hits Guptas with major tax bill and unearths R105m in mystery payments

With the Guptas long gone from the country and nothing left but the bare bones of their string of companies, there wasn't much for SARS to investigate – until its tax hounds probed a company called Linkway Trading, a subsidiary of Islandsite Investments 180, the company that owned the Gupta family's luxury properties, jet and other assets in South Africa. The four directors of Islandsite are two of the Gupta brothers, Rajesh and Atul, and their wives, Arti and Chetali.

AmaBhungane claimed that Linkway Trading was nothing but a money-laundering conduit and was used on one occasion to pay for the infamous Gupta wedding at Sun City in 2013. That money, in turn, came from the equally shameful R288 million Estina farm project in the Free State, the proceeds of which the Guptas and their associates laundered and routed to companies in Dubai. Through creative bookkeeping, the Guptas had the gall to declare the wedding a business expense and claimed back VAT to which they were not entitled. As part of their audit, SARS found another R105 million in earlier payments via Linkway that the Guptas had falsely put down to business expenses.

It is never a good idea to flaunt your illicitly gained riches on social media or in public. In May 2020, businessman Hamilton Ndlovu posted a video on Facebook boasting about a fleet of luxury vehicles – among them three Porsches, a Jeep and a Lamborghini – he had purchased after bagging a R172 million personal protective equipment (PPE) contract during the Covid pandemic. SARS conducted a search-and-seizure operation at Ndlovu's residence in September 2020, a day after the North Gauteng High Court issued a provisional preservation order and placed his assets under curatorship. The revenue service had discovered that from 2017 to 2021 Ndlovu enjoyed a gross income of nearly R73 million but submitted no tax returns. SARS presented Ndlovu with a tax bill of R36 million. In March 2021, the High Court in Pretoria found that the Gauteng-based businessman had no defence for his outstanding tax bill and had to find a way to pay back the money.

In the meantime, following an inquiry by the Special Investigating Unit (SIU) into Ndlovu's PPE contract, another court ordered him to repay R158 million to the government.

🐦 News24 @News24, 18 July 2022
Big blow for Chinese rail giant as court dismisses its bid against SARS

In December 2020, SARS successfully interdicted the transfer of R2.76 billion destined for Chinese rail conglomerate CRRC. It is a complicated story and dates back to 2014 when Transnet struck a deal to buy 1 064 new locomotives from CRRC for R38.6 billion. Enter the Guptas and their money-laundering associate Salim Essa. As a result of their manipulation of Transnet top management and state-capture enablers on the Transnet board, the deal ballooned from R38.6 billion to R54.4 billion. The Guptas and their cronies bagged almost R16 billion in the biggest state-capture deal on record.

SARS found that CRRC had overstated the price of its locomotives sold to Transnet and that the company owed a tax debt of more than R3.6 billion. The High Court rejected a bid from CRRC in July 2022 to have SARS return the money taken from its accounts.

* * *

Tax Justice South Africa @TaxJustice_SA, 29 Aug. 2022
Illicit cigarette giant Gold Leaf Tobacco is pleading innocence after being taken over by @sarstax. But investigations show it ran a transnational plunder network involving billions in illicit tobacco and gold cash.

The case against the biggest independent cigarette manufacturer in southern Africa indicates how far SARS has come in the four years since Edward Kieswetter was appointed to revive the revenue service and turn it again into the feared and revered tax beast it once was. This case is colossal and complex and holds the promise of billions for the fiscus.

Eight years after a multi-layered SARS investigation into Gold Leaf Tobacco Corporation (GLTC) had ground to a halt because of Tom Moyane's disembowelment of SARS, tax sleuths pounced on Simon Rudland's vast tobacco empire for alleged tax evasion, money laundering and fraud. Rudland has cigarette factories in South Africa and a tobacco-processing plant in Zimbabwe. He also owns farms, a logistics company, a bus company, and mines in Zimbabwe and the Democratic Republic of Congo. In August 2019, he was shot in the neck when gunmen ambushed the Porsche in which he was driving.

SARS approached the North Gauteng High Court in April 2022 with an application to launch a full-scale tax audit of GLTC, founder and co-owner Simon Rudland, and several associates and companies. A tax audit is a formal and secret process that compels the audited entity to reveal all to SARS. The revenue collector brought the application *ex parte*, which means that it applied for the order in secret to avoid warning GLTC or Rudland about its impending court action. Judge Colleen Collis granted the application and specified in her order that the relevant period for assessment was from 1 March 2013 to the current tax year.

Rudland is one of the pioneers of "cheapies" – illicit ciggies that have flooded the South African market but that dodge annual excise taxes and VAT. In a 2021 study, market research company Ipsos found that brands registered to GLTC constituted half of all products selling below the minimum collectible tax rate (MCT) of R20.01, set by law. This means that a significant percentage of GLTC's cigarette sales are "off the books" and not declared to SARS.

GLTC was on SARS's radar in the early 2000s when the tax collector launched Operation Honey Badger to curb the scourge of the illicit tobacco trade. Investigators were already probing GLTC for tax evasion and money laundering before Moyane arrived at SARS and shut down the project. When Kieswetter became commissioner, his tax sleuths dusted off the remnants of Honey Badger as they returned to their investigation and audit.

The tax inquiry into GLTC revealed that Rudland and co-director Ebrahim Adamjee allegedly failed to declare more than R2.5 billion in income from illicit cigarettes for the years 2017/18 and VAT of more than R356 million from September 2016 to July 2017. SARS rushed to the High Court for another *ex parte* application to obtain a preservation order to freeze the assets of Rudland and Adamjee.

As illicit cigarettes are traded in cash, smugglers are burdened with the problem of getting rid of mountains of money. SARS claimed that Rudland and Adamjee initiated a transnational money-laundering scheme to move more than R3 billion in undeclared money to the laundromat of international financing, Dubai. According to the *Daily Maverick*, they allegedly conspired with bank officials at Sasfin to conceal their financial footprints by deleting transactions, creating fake documentation, and wiping foreign exchange movement reports to the

Reserve Bank. In a letter attached to the SARS court application, Sasfin admitted that bank statements for GLTC had to be "reconstructed" before being handed over to SARS.

🐦 **JvL** @JvanLogg, 4 Sept. 2022
SCORPIO: R3bn "fraudulent, intentional tax evasion": An in-depth account of how Sars busted tobacco & gold plunder network

Investigators told the court they had "reason to believe that GLTC, assisted by Mr Adamjee and Mr Rudland, is still involved in illicit money laundering and continues to dissipate its assets . . . It is evident that GLTC would not hesitate to make use of any means at its disposal to frustrate the collection of tax." The court appointed a curator to take control immediately of the assets, bank accounts, investments and property of GLTC, Rudland and Adamjee.

*   *   *

Former SARS executives Hope Gloria Mashilo and Tshebeletso Seremane did not report for duty at Lehae la SARS on 1 September 2022, following the ruling by Labour Court Judge Smanga Sethene that they had been unlawfully dismissed by Tom Moyane and should be reinstated at the tax collector. Two days after Sethene's ruling, SARS announced that it was going to appeal against the judgment because the court had made a "material error in arriving at its conclusion". In reaction to SARS's decision, Mashilo said to News24: "We had questioned the integrity of the restructuring. So, when that ruling was made in our favour, we felt vindicated. We thought that at last justice had been served. SARS was making a mockery of our pain."

It is difficult to understand the moral rationale behind Edward Kieswetter's response to Smanga Sethene's court ruling – especially as it comes from someone who claims to understand the pain and suffering that many employees endured during the state-capture project. Soon after becoming commissioner, Kieswetter had said: "When I walk around and talk to people, you see their trauma; you see the pain they have experienced. The actual situation on the ground is worse than even the Nugent report says – and I have seen that first-hand." Ironically, just days before Sethene's judgment, Kieswetter paid tribute to struggle icon Ahmed Kathrada where he spoke about efforts to rebuild SARS. "We have started a process of engaging with staff that have left, assessing the circumstances under which they left, and where we thought appropriate, we have brought them back."

Despite Kieswetter's achievements in rebuilding the tax collector's capacity, he has mostly failed to re-employ skilled and dedicated officials who were the victims of the state-capture project. Why has he not attempted to lure back to the revenue service the likes of Ivan Pillay, Johann van Loggerenberg, Pete Richer, Gene Ravele, Ronel van Wyk, and many other tax investigators and officials who became victims of state capture? They have between them a century of irreplaceable experience and expertise that will be invaluable in the rebuilding of the institution.

SARS has been treading very cautiously around the issue of employees who were forced out by Moyane and how to compensate them. In 2020, Kieswetter appointed SARS group executive for compliance risk and case selection William Mpye to investigate and report on the status of "affected employees" and of reparations to them. Mpye was assisted by an external firm of attorneys and interviewed 31 employees in January and February 2020. Many were still struggling with the trauma of victimisation. Some had been pushed out of key positions into superfluous roles and sat for two years in a boardroom with nothing to do. But Mpye failed to interview those who were central to the controversy at SARS and had suffered most, most notably Ivan Pillay, Johann van Loggerenberg, Pete Richer and former spokesperson Adrian Lackay. Mpye's report subsequently recommended that apologies be offered to the 31 employees, but it also seemed to explore every possible avenue to prevent such reparations from being financial in nature. It cautioned that the apologies should not expose SARS to civil or employment litigation.

SARS said in a subsequent statement that "substantial progress" had been made with the reparations process. It noted that Kieswetter had always intended "to manage the process with dignity and outside the public domain because it touches the lives of many of its current and former employees". The statement concluded by saying that "a process of reflection and healing" was necessary for both SARS and the individuals concerned.

CHAPTER 20

Simba and Pumbaa

ON 21 DECEMBER 2018 at 9.46 am, Facebook deposited a message in my inbox. I opened it. "Hi Jacques I want to spill the beans, about Malema and Mazzotti." I responded: "I would love to hear what you have to say. How do you know about the two?"

Since the publication of *The President's Keepers*, I have had numerous informers plying me with claims about an alliance between wealthy cigarette manufacturer Adriano Mazzotti, founder and director of the Carnilinx tobacco company, and protest warrior Julius Malema. Some were delectable but nothing but conspiracy theories. The decade-long bromance between the two has sporadically hit the headlines, captured the imagination of people and raised a host of questions. Why has the rabble-rouser politician embraced a pale-skinned capitalist who has confessed to evading his taxes and laundering the proceeds of his illicit tobacco business, and who counts apartheid assassin Craig Williamson among his former business partners? On the face of it, it's a courtship as peculiar as that of the young lion Simba and the warthog Pumbaa in *The Lion King*.

My new Facebook friend responded only the next morning. "Mazzotti have apartments at Raphael hotel in Sandton, 305, and 309. 309 that's apartment Malema used to go. They used to do some party . . . making a terrible mess. And some champagne called moet, I was used to pick some used condoms at the veranda and at the couch. And every month he's getting some cash from Mazzotti and their company . . . so every month he's receiving cash. They send one of their drivers to give him a big envelope written 'Ju'."

I messaged her back: "So you are saying that Mazzotti gives an envelope of cash every month to Malema?"

"Yes . . . they used to carry some large amount of cash put in the cooler box . . . and Mazzotti gave money to the lawyer of Malema the time when he went to the court, he came to the apartment, and he gave him large amount."

I have always regarded the president and commander-in-chief of the Economic Freedom Fighters (EFF) as a pseudo-revolutionary in a red beret whose ranting at white monopoly capital is as fake as Michael Jackson's plastic nose. Malema and Mazzotti are two sides of the same coin. It's about money: it seems to be little more than a monetary courtship. Mazzotti has it, Malema wants it. In turn, Malema wields enormous influence and can be good for business. Malema, as we will see, has no qualms about gorging himself on money that comes from the poor or was destined to improve the lives of the disenfranchised. So why would he refuse a slice of bacon from a self-confessed former tobacco smuggler? Business and politics are both mostly endeavours of scant morality in which power, wealth and influence count for everything.

I asked my informer: "Have you seen other members of the EFF at that apartment?

"Yes, they used to come and partying."

Malema – as well as other members of the top "command" of the EFF – is frequently seen in Mazzotti's company; and the politician and his family live (or have, until recently, lived) in a double-storey villa in an exclusive estate that Mazzotti owns in the upmarket Johannesburg suburb of Hyde Park.

As recently as July 2022, Malema and his wife, Mantoa Matlala-Malema, attended the wedding of Mazzotti's daughter on the party island of Ibiza. The three-day bash took place at several venues, inclu-ding the exclusive Experimental Beach, a seaside escape tucked away in the Las Salinas salt reserve on the island. The bride and groom were treated to a Dolce & Gabbana-inspired event. At the wedding meal, guests were seated at a 42-metre-long table perched in an olive grove and adorned with crystals, roses and vintage lace tablecloths.

The EFF was quick to announce that Malema had funded his own Spanish fiesta and that he was working hard and deserved the break. Twin brothers Bandile and Banele Mbere, known as Major League DJz, and disc jockey Black Coffee also attended the wedding and provided the music on day three at a pool party held at a boutique hotel in Ibiza. Video footage shows Malema DJing at the celebration with a shot glass of Avion Reserva tequila in his hand. It costs R3 600 a bottle at a liquor store.

I asked my informant: "And what do you plan to do with this information about Mazzotti and Malema?"

"You can publish the story."

I continued messaging her for several months before meeting her in April 2019. I knew by then that she was a Zimbabwean citizen who had come to South Africa in January 1998 looking for work. She said she had obtained a diploma in general secretarial work and a certificate in business management. She married a South African and, as a result, obtained a South African identity document and a spousal visa.

She said that she started working for Mazzotti in 2009. She was ostensibly employed as a domestic worker but performed many other duties as well. According to her, Mazzotti and Carnilinx kept a luxury apartment in Sandton from where they sometimes worked and entertained guests. Mazzotti and his family lived for three years in another apartment in the same hotel while their villa in Hyde Park was being renovated. For several months before she left the employment of Carnilinx in August 2018, she worked at the cigarette factory in downtown Johannesburg.

She said Malema frequented the apartment, either to come and collect money or to have debauched parties with friends that lasted all night. She had to clean up the mess afterwards. It was in the apartment that she saw the firebrand politician for the first time. "Come meet the president," Mazzotti had instructed her.

* * *

𝕏 **Telita Snyckers** @TelitaSnyckers, 20 May 2020
Illicit cigarettes are lucrative and low-risk, netting $2m profit on a black-market container. Cigarettes are easy to smuggle, easy to buy, drug dogs can't sniff out the difference between a licit or illicit pack, and you don't go to jail for 50 years if caught.

The tobacco trade has been dirty for centuries, in effect breeding an industry that has criminality embedded in its DNA. So says former SARS executive Telita Snyckers in her book *Dirty Tobacco: Spies, Lies and Mega-Profits*. Her book shows that tobacco companies in South Africa are doing their damnedest to find loopholes in the tax system to avoid paying the minimum collectable tax of R22.79 per packet of 20 cigarettes. They are prepared to engage in rampant smuggling, bribe politicians and officials, and dodge their taxes.

By 2011, tax evasion in the tobacco industry had gone through the roof and the South African fiscus was losing around R3 billion a year through smuggling, corruption, and money laundering. As a result, the South African Revenue Service (SARS) launched Project Honey Badger and targeted various tobacco industry players, including the multinational company British American Tobacco.

Thanks in large part to Honey Badger, contraband tobacco dropped from around 26 per cent of the total market in 2013 to 17 per cent in 2014. In the process, SARS extracted hundreds of millions of rand in unpaid taxes from cigarette manufacturers, closed several factories, sequestrated some companies, and raided a host of others. SARS's focus on criminality in the tobacco industry resulted in a 25 per cent increase in excise and VAT payments. In 2012, SARS had seized 54 million illicit cigarettes; by 2014 this had increased to 270 million cigarettes. And all of this was attributable to a single project, Honey Badger.

The tax collector's probe revealed mountains of malfeasance by the smaller and independent manufacturers, among them Mazzotti's Carnilinx. The company's tax affairs were probed under the name of Project Pandora. Documents reveal that SARS investigators obtained affidavits from implicated parties demonstrating how Carnilinx allegedly used dormant companies to operate a sophisticated scam whereby they effectively pretended to import tobacco into Swaziland, when the true destination was its Johannesburg factory.

The evidence was so convincing and devastating that it seems to have forced Mazzotti and his Carnilinx co-directors to plead with SARS for leniency. He was told to depose to an affidavit and admit his and his co-directors' complicity in tax evasion and a host of other crimes. He signed the affidavit on 6 May 2014 in the apparent hope of reaching a tax settlement with SARS. Mazzotti admitted in his affidavit: "Carnilinx accepts that it acquired tobacco unlawfully and wrongfully of two tonnes per week over a period of some 40 weeks. In its drive to promote its business, Carnilinx entered into a host of transactions, some of which were lawful, and others corrupt and unlawful."

After Mazzotti's affidavit, Carnilinx was down and just about out for the count. By August 2014, SARS had issued a notice of intent to Carnilinx that it was in the process of cancelling its licence. SARS said in its documentation that it was conducting lifestyle audits on the Carnilinx directors and calculating the company's tax liability. Tax experts say that because fraud was involved, SARS's penalty regime would have imposed penalties, forfeiture amounts and interest of up to 200 per cent, which could theoretically have pushed Carnilinx's total tax bill to over R600 million. In addition, Carnilinx would have lost its cigarette manufacturing licence and would have been criminally charged, hence Mazzotti's admission in his affidavit: "It is hoped that this process will culminate in the company accepting criminal liability in a criminal court."

Desperate to get Carnilinx out of its tax predicament, Mazzotti decided to bribe SARS investigations executive Johann van Loggerenberg and acting SARS commissioner Ivan Pillay. He described in his affidavit how his friend and attorney Ian Small-Smith kept mentioning that he had influence over Van Loggerenberg and Pillay. Said Mazzotti: "We have paid to Small-Smith R800,000 in cash. We made this large payment to him on the basis of a perception, on our part, that he was using part of these monies to pay off SARS officials, in particular Van Loggerenberg." But he accepted in his affidavit that neither Van Loggerenberg nor Pillay received any of the money, and he apologised to the two for doubting their integrity. Small-Smith had pocketed the R800 000. He also later apologised to Van Loggerenberg and said that if Carnilinx, Mazzotti and the other directors "were led to believe by my representations . . . that I had influence over Johann or any other official at SARS, this was wrong".

*　*　*

Mazzotti and Carnilinx have long buttered the egos, palms and bank accounts of civil servants, law-enforcement officials, journalists and politicians. The proceeds of tobacco smuggling took the form of cash, often boxes full of it. Mazzotti mentioned in his affidavit that Carnilinx took R8 million that was unaccounted for in Carnilinx's books or records and used it as "company expenses, engaging in expensive dinners, entertaining businesspeople, politicians and other people who we considered would be useful in advancing the business of Carnilinx". He admitted that it was "unlawful and morally wrong".

He described in his affidavit how he bribed a SARS official to obtain an official document that showed that SARS contemplated withdrawing Carnilinx's manufacturing licence. He handed the document to tobacco attorney Belinda Walter, who in turn appointed top Johannesburg senior advocate Mike Hellens to address SARS's concerns. Hellens was successful in sorting out the matter, and at a celebration bash at the

Houghton golf estate in April 2013, Mazzotti showed his appreciation by handing Hellens a bag containing R500 000 in cash. This was in addition to his full fee. The Johannesburg Bar Council found in 2016 that Hellens had breached its rules by not asking for permission to accept Mazzotti's "gift". The council reprimanded Hellens, who has acted in recent years for an odious mob: Jacob Zuma, Duduzane Zuma, the Guptas and Julius Malema. Belinda Walter pocketed an even bigger payola: R780 000 in cash. She failed to pay donations tax on the handout and Carnilinx had to pay an additional R156 000 to SARS.

Politics and illicit tobacco are cosy bedfellows. According to Telita Snyckers: "At the heart of the tobacco industry's success in thwarting regulation lies a simple truth: they are masters at playing politics. Any South African can tell you about the value of political patronage. Buying power may not be cheap but it makes you virtually Teflon."

🐦 Nickolaus Bauer @ NickolausBauer, 12 Mar. 2014
@julius_s_malema says #EFF used beret sales money to fund their IEC deposit. And will now struggle for money to campaign. @eNCAnews

Hours after the EFF had paid its R600 000 deposit to contest the May 2014 general election, Julius Malema addressed reporters outside the office of the Independent Electoral Commission of South Africa (IEC) in Centurion, south of Pretoria. "This money comes from these fighters you see here. We have done everything in our power to register," he said, and added that the money came from selling berets, T-shirts, posters, and donations from members. "We didn't sleep, we had to run all over asking members [for money]. The biggest donation of R100,000 came from a member who lives in Pretoria."

Malema lied. A third of the money came from Adriano Mazzotti's Carnilinx. This was revealed in the cigarette baron's May 2014 affidavit when he admitted: "Carnilinx has made a donation in an amount of R200,000 towards a political party, registered to contest the forthcoming National Election." The EFF admitted afterwards that the money came from Carnilinx but downplayed the donation. SARS revealed in its tax battle with Malema that the young politician also received a R1 million loan from Carnilinx director Kyle Phillips to pay his debt.

Mazzotti acknowledged in 2018 that he had also donated money to the ANC and said that it was more than his contribution to the EFF. According to ANC spokesperson Zizi Kodwa, the organisation was aware that in January 2018 Mazzotti participated in an ANC fundraising gala dinner in East London and bought a so-called platinum package for R250 000. This would have guaranteed him the presence of one of the top six officials of the ruling party at his table.

* * *

Belinda Sheila Gay Walter is the James Blonde of the tobacco industry and acted as attorney for Carnilinx until October 2013, though she was later reappointed. She resigned the first time because she developed a relationship with SARS executive Johann van Loggerenberg, which ended acrimoniously seven months later. During this time, she revealed herself to him as agent number 5332 of the State Security Agency (SSA). It later emerged that she also spied for tobacco giant British American Tobacco (BAT), which paid her monthly in British pounds in the United Kingdom. She also snooped for the Tobacco Task Team, which was made up of representatives of different law-enforcement agencies, excluding SARS, to counter tobacco smuggling. Instead of targeting illicit cigarettes, members of the task team engaged in criminal activities themselves. Walter shopped Carnilinx, BAT, the SSA and the task team. They all plugged her purse. At the best of times, professional eavesdroppers lack a moral compass; in her case, she flourished in a salacious cesspool.

Van Loggerenberg's hanky-panky with Wobbly Walter, as she was also known, was always going to end in a clusterfucktastrophe. Following a lovers' tiff in early 2014, Walter confessed to the Carnilinx directors in the presence of a senior advocate and a journalist that she was a spy

358

and had snooped on them for both the SSA and BAT. She withdrew her confession the next day. It was at that point that Van Loggerenberg should have done a Caster Semenya for the nearest hill. Instead, the relationship continued until May before he dumped her. Intent on revenge, Walter claimed that Van Loggerenberg had provided her with confidential taxpayers' information, which was illegal.

In February 2014, Walter made an affidavit about her relationship with Carnilinx. She said in the affidavit that "I became aware of considerable criminal activity conducted by the business". She mentioned that Carnilinx had set up foreign bank accounts, ostensibly for laundering money, and reported incidents of fraud and tax evasion.

Despite shopping her clients in 2013, she and Mazzotti were together again by October 2014, united by their antipathy towards Johann van Loggerenberg. On the one hand he had dumped Walter and exposed her as the Mata Hari of the tobacco industry while on the other he threatened the continued survival of Carnilinx.

As I was about to publish *The President's Keepers*, I received information that Mazzotti had bragged about meeting then state security minister David Mahlobo. The cigarette manufacturer also had contact with SSA secret agent Yekani Monde Gadini, who seems to have played a seminal role in the capture of SARS and who was the husband of Jacob Zuma's legal adviser. After publication, I asked Mazzotti about his meeting with Mahlobo and Gadini. He confirmed that he had met the minister with his attorney and Gadini "as a state security agent". He wouldn't elaborate, and neither would Mahlobo. But the incident raises the question: why had the state security minister and a top intelligence agent met a cigarette manufacturer implicated in smuggling and wrongdoing? Was it because of his friendship with Julius Malema? Or were they colluding to get rid of Van Loggerenberg?

Hidden in an affidavit by Van Loggerenberg in the application to set aside the findings of Public Protector Busisiwe Mkhwebane about the SARS "rogue unit" is a transcript of a tape recording made of a conversation between Walter and two Carnilinx directors. The tape recording is mentioned in another affidavit submitted to the High Court. I have also listened to a section of the recording, and there is no doubt about its authenticity.

On 20 October 2014, Mazzotti and his co-director Kyle Phillips met Walter in the office of attorney Ian Levitt, who was incidentally also Malema's lawyer. Without Levitt being present, the three discussed Carnilinx's problems with Van Loggerenberg, referred to as JvL, and its looming tax bill. Walter recorded the meeting. Said Kyle Phillips: "The next thing we want to do is obviously, JvL needs to go. We never want him back again. We want him embarrassed . . . and destroyed. Because he threatened us."

Several years later, Van Loggerenberg confronted Phillips and Mazzotti with the recording. Mazzotti said in a written apology in October 2019 that he and Phillips were led to believe by their "then-legal representative" that Van Loggerenberg was the mastermind behind a co-ordinated effort to close their business by any means possible.

Maybe the self-confessed tobacco criminal had forgotten about a letter that Walter wrote to Carnilinx's attorney and its senior advocate, Nazeer Cassim, on 2 February 2014. She said: "What I said to Johann van Loggerenberg was untrue and devoid of any truth. Johann conducts himself in such a manner as to always be beyond approach [sic]. Mr Cassim mentioned that too and it is so. He simply does not and will not cross the lines that Carnilinx so desperately hopes he has."

Many of the allegations around the "rogue unit" originated from a former SARS employee, Michael Peega, who was arrested for rhino poaching at the end of 2008. SARS fired him after he made a confession that he had shot a baby rhino (the criminal case against him disintegrated when the docket and evidence disappeared). Intent on revenge, he compiled a "dossier", which he released in 2010, among others to Julius Malema. He knew the then ANC Youth League leader because he freelanced for him and Fikile Mbalula as a bodyguard. SARS refuted Peega's allegations line for line at the time, but four years later rogue state intelligence agents revived the "dossier", presented it to the inspector-general of intelligence (IGI) and fed it to the new SARS commissioner, Tom Moyane, as evidence of the criminality of Van Loggerenberg, Pillay and others.

As the "rogue-unit" narrative was in full swing, Carnilinx inexplicably paid Peega in cash for "security-related services" he had rendered to the company. Why did Mazzotti and the company hire a self-confessed rhino poacher who was the bullshitter-in-chief of this falsehood? Early in 2015, the current affairs programme *Carte Blanche* concocted an insert on the "rogue unit" that was based on interviews with Peega, Walter and her state intelligence boyfriend. The interviews were conducted on the smallholding of the *Carte Blanche* journalist near Lanseria airport on the north-western outskirts of Johannesburg. Mazzotti was present on set. What was he doing there with Walter, Peega and a state intelligence agent?

However, in Adriano Mazzotti's sight was not just Johann van Loggerenberg, but also cigarette giant BAT, which had paid Walter to snoop on Carnilinx. She offered to the company to make an affidavit about her deceit, hand them the evidence about her relationship with BAT, and testify against the tobacco giant for having recruited and paid her for spying on Carnilinx. In May 2015, Mazzotti, Phillips and their lawyers flew to London and had a four-hour meeting with the UK police's national crime agency, which was investigating whether BAT's secret payments to Walter broke bribery laws in that country. When the British authorities refused to grant Walter indemnity from prosecution, she withdrew her co-operation. Without Walter, there was no case. She then disappeared from the face of the earth. She had left South Africa and was working for an American mercenary outfit in war-torn Somalia. She then had a relationship with a police colonel that served on the Tobacco Task Team who had left his wife and children for her. The relationship did not last. Carnilinx fired one of their attorneys for allegedly having an affair with Walter and shielding her.

In 2016, Carnilinx laid criminal charges against among others BAT South Africa, BAT United Kingdom, Walter and several members of the Tobacco Task Team. Carnilinx alleged that they had contravened sections of the Prevention and Combating of Corrupt Activities Act and defeated or obstructed the course of justice. Walter emerged from her hideout in the Horn of Africa and conveyed a threat to senior advocate Nazeer Cassim, who represented Carnilinx, to reveal all. She said in her letter: "I do not wish for a war, particularly [with] people I once held dear." She threatened to release to the media recordings, text messages and other information about Carnilinx she held, and said: "Unfortunately, as you well know, the information is intermingled with information of . . . personal cocaine and drug use, prostitutes, mistresses, partying in London and Dubai, sex machines, transvestites, threesomes with cage fighters, photographs of drug use on Emirates etc which the media would love. There are also numerous instances and mention . . . of relationships with politicians and ministers."

Carnilinx didn't pursue the criminal case against Walter and the others, and nothing came of it. Walter disappeared again. She has no social media profile, and the rumour is that towards the end of the Zuma era, the State Security Agency gave her a new identity and resettled her in a foreign country.

* * *

By the time Adriano Mazzotti and Kyle Phillips met Belinda Walter in October 2014, Jacob Zuma had parachuted his crony Tom Moyane into one of the most crucial positions in government: the head of the South African Revenue Service. Within months of becoming SARS commissioner, Moyane had eviscerated the tax service. Gone was Ivan Pillay, Johann van Loggerenberg and a host of dedicated tax experts. Moyane disbanded the five investigations units and gave birth to the "rogue-unit" narrative. Operation Honey Badger perished and, with it, the criminal and tax case against Mazzotti and Carnilinx. According to Snyckers: "Honey Badger had come too close to the truth, and people like tax detective Johann van Loggerenberg and others had to go.

Tobacco was the thin end of the wedge that pried open the door for their departure."

Despite his admission of criminality in his affidavit, the ever-opportunistic Mazzotti must have seen in the "rogue-unit" narrative a golden opportunity to torpedo his tax bill. Johann van Loggerenberg was gone and his units disbanded. Mazzotti approached SARS at the beginning of 2016 about the "alleged unfair treatment and criminal activities committed by [the] SARS enforcement team whilst they audited the affairs of Carnilinx and related entities".

Like a host of others before him – including Capeland gangster Mark Lifman (tax bill, R388 million) and Chinese immigrant, convicted murderer and money launderer Robert Huang (tax bill, R1 billion, though it reportedly ballooned to R3 billion) – Mazzotti employed the "rogue-unit defence" to evade his tax obligation. The Carnilinx lawyers told SARS that their client was "unfairly treated by virtue of certain SARS officials behaving in a manner which seems to indicate that they are biased".

SARS should have dissed Mazzotti and collected its taxes. There was no need to engage with the tax evader. The tax investigation had been so thoroughly conducted and above board that it ultimately forced Mazzotti and Carnilinx to the confession box to admit their complicity in smuggling, tax evasion and fraud. "This was not only improper conduct but immoral. This was unlawful and morally wrong. No records were kept of the manufacturing process. This was deliberate as to avoid any detection."

Yet, Moyane's henchman and second-in-command, Jonas Makwakwa, and SARS executive for investigations Patrick Moeng engaged in discussions with Carnilinx. The outcome was a March 2016 memorandum in which they agreed "to appoint a new audit team to investigate the matters presently under investigation by SARS. SARS has acceded to their [Carnilinx's] demand, and that all Letters of Finding issued against the clients will be withdrawn."

When former finance minister Nhlanhla Nene testified before the State Capture Commission, he mentioned the "disappearance" of Carnilinx's tax bill. Because it didn't relate to the state capture project, he wasn't allowed to expand on the matter.

🐦 **State Capture Commission** @StateCaptureCom, 14 Mar. 2019
Nene says another issue he would like the commission to look into is the issue of SARS. He says a gentleman by the name of Adriano Mazzotti was being investigated but Mr Tom Moyane stopped it.

Following Makwakwa and Moeng's intervention, all the criminal and tax investigations into Carnilinx and the lifestyle audits of Mazzotti and his co-directors were abandoned. Detained containers of smuggled tobacco were handed back to Carnilinx, the letters of findings were withdrawn, and they were allowed to make new customs declarations. It was as though Mazzotti never made his affidavit; as though three years of criminal and tax investigations never existed; as though the evidence of tax evasion and fraud was never unearthed. The Mazzotti affidavit gathered dust somewhere in SARS until it was leaked to me when I wrote *The President's Keepers*.

Since the publication of my book, Mazzotti's attorney, Nicqui Galaktiou, has bared her fangs at me several times. Her letters were speckled with accusations of "a continuous barrage of defamatory publications", "a persistent and continuous slander of our clients", a "personal vendetta against Mr Mazzotti", and "an abuse of journalistic freedom of expression to tarnish Mr Mazzotti's reputation to his detriment". Speaking on behalf of Mazzotti, she constantly repeated that it was unlawful to "possess, publish and/or disseminate" taxpayers' information and that I had made "reckless allegations" that either Carnilinx or Mazzotti owed R600 million in taxes.

In July 2018, Galaktiou wrote to News24: "Carnilinx paid what was due to SARS which was approximately R25 million. A far cry from the R600 million being sensationalised by Mr Pauw and other media.

Mr Pauw is invited to produce evidence to support this outrageous allegation." There you have it: despite all the criminality admitted to by Mazzotti and his co-directors, the Carnilinx tax bill was seemingly only R25 million.

I have even been accused of putting Mazzotti's life in danger. "Given the blatant and reckless allegations about Mr Mazzotti, his life and that of his family have been placed in danger and he is considering his rights in this respect. Please do not underestimate and disregard the seriousness of this statement."

Malema has come to his benefactor's defence. In February 2019, SARS had obtained a High Court warrant of execution to attach movable property to the value of more than R30 million from Mazzotti. The sheriff raided his Hyde Park property and seized Mazzotti's Mercedes-Benz Geländewagen (price around R3 million), a BMW M760Li (price around R2.5 million), an A-class Mercedes-Benz, and various pieces of modern art. Mazzotti said the matter was subsequently settled.

When I joked on Twitter that Mazzotti might lose his villa and that his neighbour, Julius Malema, was going to be a lonely man, the politician reacted with fury.

▼ Julius Sello Malema @Julius_S_Malema, 19 Feb. 2019
Replying to @Jaqqs
You can go f^*€£ yourself

* * *

After Tom Moyane's demolition of SARS and the disbanding of the investigation units, tobacco smuggling went through the roof. Telita Snyckers said that by 2017 – the last year for which sound estimates are available – illicit cigarettes held a market share of between 30 and 35 per cent, and in the space of only two years there was a steep drop of 26 per cent in the quantity of cigarettes declared to the taxman. This amounted to unpaid taxes of R7 billion a year.

It costs around R2.50 to produce a packet of 20 cigarettes. By avoiding tax, one can make a fortune – more so than by smuggling cocaine. If you are caught with illicit tobacco, you get a fine. If you smuggle hard drugs, you go to prison.

Illicit cigarette manufacturers hit the jackpot in March 2020 when South Africa was in the clutches of the Covid pandemic and Cyril Ramaphosa declared a state of disaster. After becoming president, he had appointed Nkosazana Dlamini-Zuma as minister of co-operative governance and traditional affairs, whose portfolio included responsibility for overseeing the Disaster Management Act. As head of the National Coronavirus Command Council, she banned the sale of cigarettes and tobacco, ostensibly to limit the severity of the illness and free up vital health resources. But she failed to produce a shred of evidence of a link between smoking and Covid.

Overnight, more than seven million smokers had their supply severed. This was any entrepreneur or capitalist's dream. The price of illicit cigarettes tripled and then increased five- and sixfold. Someone very close to the industry said to me that whereas some of the bigger independent producers were multi-millionaires before lockdown, they became billionaires afterwards.

The demise of normality, the loss of connection with others, the threat of an economic toll, and the fear of the unknown during lockdown were all hard enough. Taking away smokers' fags was outright cruel. All Dlamini-Zuma achieved was to drive the trade underground and to turn law-abiding South Africans into criminals. The ban also led to the cash-strapped fiscus losing R35 million per day in tobacco tax.

A study by the Research Unit on the Economics of Excisable Products at the University of Cape Town showed that Carnilinx's market share rose fivefold (from 2 to 10 per cent) during lockdown. Carnilinx rejected the findings, but the unit did a second survey a month later and found that Carnilinx had increased its market share further, to 14.3 per cent. Imagine a sevenfold increase in market share during the many months of lockdown. And that is not all. Whereas a packet of cigarettes ostensibly manufactured by Carnilinx cost R20 or R22 before lockdown, it now cost R100.

In contrast, BAT's market share plummeted from 48 per cent to less than 20 per cent. During lockdown, smokers were still merrily sucking on Carnilinx brands like JFK and Atlantic. And it was all in cash. Mazzotti denied that Carnilinx was smuggling during lockdown and said that SARS had watched them like hawks, but, as the UCT study suggested, supplies never seemed to dry up.

🐦 **Tax Justice South Africa** @TaxJustice_SA, 4 June 2020
It's Day 70 of #LockdownSA tobacco prohibition. @GovernmentZA has lost R2.45 billion in cigarette "sin" taxes. It has a duty to collect that money for citizens. But it's enriching smugglers, counterfeiters and other crooks in illicit trade.

With no scientific evidence to back Dlamini-Zuma's assertion that smokers were more at risk of contracting the Covid virus, the public, politicians, and civil society began to speculate about her motivation.

I had written in *The President's Keepers* that Mazzotti provided Dlamini-Zuma with clothing paraphernalia such as caps and T-shirts for her 2017 campaign to become ANC president. The allegations in the book were dusted off during lockdown and Mazzotti's support for Dlamini-Zuma's 2017 campaign was advanced as "proof" that he benefited from her ban and that the duo were in cahoots.

According to media reports, 117 000 South Africans discussed the tobacco ban 520 000 times on social media within the first 60 days of lockdown. Much of the debate centred on Dlamini-Zuma's links to Mazzotti. She again reiterated during lockdown that she was not Mazzotti's friend, while Mazzotti said: "I have stated on record on numerous occasions that there is no relationship between myself and Minister Dlamini-Zuma and I did not fund her presidential campaign as has been maliciously alleged."

After publication of my book, Mazzotti said they had met only once, briefly and by accident. He lied. Days later, the *Sunday Times* published a second photograph of the two, taken in London. According to Dlamini-Zuma's spokesperson: "She has never approached him for any assistance, nor has he approached her and offered assistance with her campaign. The two occasions she met him were chance meetings, where there were other persons at the same event."

* * *

🐦 **Sunday Times** @SundayTimesZA, 10 June 2020
Adriano Mazzotti says if there is one thing he will regret for a very long time, it is asking Dr Nkosazana Dlamini-Zuma to pose for a picture with him. Especially because she turned him down – twice.

In June 2020, Mazzotti sat down with *Sunday Times* assistant editor Nicki Gules in his attorney's plush boardroom in Illovo, Johannesburg, for a rare interview. He was on a public relations drive to restore his image. The 50-something South African-born Italian, his face crease-less with a tint of toast, was, as always, dressed in his monochrome attire of black – understated but crafted by deft designer fingers. With a photographer clicking away to capture the essence of South Africa's most controversial cigs manufacturer, he remarked that he shouldn't have worn the outfit "lest readers believe that I am every bit the gangster many claim I am".

When his picture adorned the "Table Talk" page of the *Sunday Times* a few days later, the words "Justice at any cost" and "Law-abiding citizen" were inserted next to the photograph. This article made scant mention of Mazzotti being a self-confessed fraudster, tax evader, money launderer, smuggler and corruptor. But when asked about his confession to SARS, he said the affidavit emanated from a "voluntary disclosure on his tax affairs he made to SARS when he was naïve".

Did Mazzotti want *Sunday Times* readers to believe that a shrewd businessman who has risen to the top of the cutthroat cigarette industry didn't realise what he was doing when he declared under oath how he and his fellow directors connived to commit "ghost exports", "round-tripping" and import deceptions to dupe tax investigators? In fact, Mazzotti deposed to the affidavit because the revenue collector had caught him with his grubby paw in the Amaretti cookie jar and he then attempted to save himself from complete financial annihilation.

He told the paper that he was an avid gatherer of selfies with celebrities. He had bagged one with Winnie Madikizela-Mandela, "whom he loved spending time with", numerous ones with Julius Malema, and one with British boxer Lennox Lewis, to whom he sold T-shirts. He said he could not believe his luck when he saw Dlamini-Zuma in a hotel in London in 2017. It was selfie time, and he begged her for one until she said: "Yes, okay." The second picture of Mazzotti and Dlamini-Zuma was taken in a Houghton hotel when he and fellow Carnilinx director Mohammadh Sayed were having drinks. He said he again nagged her for a picture.

During the selfie opportunity in London he apparently told Dlamini-Zuma's group that he could help them obtain electioneering clothing like T-shirts for a good price. He said he had "pitched business for his brother-in-law". And therein lies the key to the liaison between Mazzotti and Dlamini-Zuma. The brother-in-law he referred to was Martin Wingate-Pearse; they are married to sisters. Martin Wingate-Pearse is a director of Carnilinx and, although he is not involved in the day-to-day running of the company, he holds the majority shares – 33.3 per cent – while the other directors (including Mazzotti) hold 16.6 per cent each.

* * *

In the early 2000s, SARS former head of criminal investigations Ronel van Wyk conducted a corruption investigation into a senior tax official.

The probe revealed links between the official and Johannesburg's "King of Diamonds", Serbian-born George Mihaljević, who was also a close associate of Czech mobster Radovan Krejčíř. When Van Wyk further investigated, she found business links between Mihaljević, Adriano Mazzotti and Martin Wingate-Pearse. Mihaljević was later assassinated.

In a submission to the SARS Commission, Van Wyk described how the police's Crime Intelligence asked the revenue collector to assist in an investigation into one of the world's most wanted fugitives, Cuban drug trafficker Nelson Pablo Yester-Garrido, and a South African syndicate to which he was linked. The Cuban was arrested in 2002 in South Africa, but the state's efforts to extradite him failed and he continued living here. Using the name Antonio Lamas, he came in 1997 to South Africa where he reportedly continued his trafficking in narcotics. Yester-Garrido was linked to the drug operations of Colombian drug baron Pablo Escobar and became famous for attempting to sell a Russian diesel submarine to the Cali cartel to smuggle cocaine into the United States.

SARS registered Project Dunlop Roller Bearing and discovered that Yester-Garrido had close contact with convicted drug dealer Glenn Agliotti, Martin Wingate-Pearse and Adriano Mazzotti, among others. Notorious security boss Clinton Nassif, one of the killers of mining magnate Brett Kebble, was also a member of the group. Agliotti was later charged for Kebble's murder and the killers – Nassif, Mikey Schultz, Nigel McGurk and Faizel Smith – turned state witnesses. Agliotti was acquitted and the killers, except for Nassif, got indemnity from prosecution. There is a photograph that has been widely published on social media in which Mazzotti and Malema can be seen in a bar with their arms around each other, drinking whisky or brandy with Schultz.

Van Wyk said in her submission: "Yester-Garrido was arrested whilst driving a motor vehicle owned by Wingate-Pearse and had a falsified passport in his possession, containing the details of Wingate-Pearse, but displaying Garrido's photo. Garrido also had official documents in his possession which related to the business dealings of Wingate-Pearse.

It was confirmed that during this period Garrido resided at a property belonging to Wingate-Pearse."

According to Van Wyk: "The taxpayers that were identified through Project Dunlop Roller Bearing were allegedly involved in drug smuggling, contraband second-hand clothing, money laundering and corruption." In April 2005, 250 SARS agents raided the business premises of 11 people and 26 business entities linked to Wingate-Pearse and Mazzotti. The investigators seized 230 tons of contraband clothing which were later destroyed.

It appears that SARS slapped Wingate-Pearse with a tax bill of R41 million, which was later reduced to R9.2 million. He applied for tax amnesty and, when that failed, he launched two review applications. It seems that the two brothers-in-law conferred about their tax woes and decided on the "rogue-unit defence". In August 2015, Wingate-Pearse asked the High Court to make a declaratory order that the "rogue unit" had abused its power and resources by engaging in activities it had "no lawful authority to perform". The High Court rejected his application in 2018.

You may well ask why nobody has ever been arrested or convicted for complicity in corruption, smuggling and fraud. The answer lies in the arrest of Yester-Garrido in 2011 following a 166-kilogram cocaine bust, worth R400 million, in Port Elizabeth (now Gqeberha). The cocaine, concealed in a shipping container, was directly linked to the Cuban. He was arrested and charged with drug trafficking.

In February 2013, the National Prosecuting Authority (NPA) withdrew all charges against Yester-Garrido because no one was available to translate official Brazilian documents into English. An NPA spokesperson said: "We are sure that as time goes on we will be able to reinstate the charges when we have done the necessary preparations."

So, there are 300 000 Portuguese-speaking South Africans, and the NPA couldn't get one of them to translate a Brazilian document into English? Of course, the charges were never reinstated. And you know what's the worst about this? Nobody cared. At the time Nomgcobo

Jiba was the acting national director of public prosecutions and was probably so busy protecting Richard Mdluli and hounding Johan Booysen, Anwa Dramat and Shadrack Sibiya that she didn't even notice the botched prosecution of a multimillion-rand cocaine seizure. It goes beyond incompetence. I'm willing to bet that if you venture deeper into the case, you will find that the confiscated cocaine also disappeared. It was probably sold back to Yester-Garrido, who was finally arrested in Rome in 2017 and extradited to the United States.

*   *   *

The involvement of Wingate-Pearse in the supply of electioneering paraphernalia to Dlamini-Zuma made a mockery of her reported assurance that she would not do business with the tobacco industry. And despite Mazzotti's profession of innocence that he simply "pitched business for his brother-in-law", he had in all probability a direct hand in supplying the electioneering caps and T-shirts to the Dlamini-Zuma camp. The two brothers-in-law share or have shared directorships in several clothing companies. Company records show that Mazzotti and Wingate-Pearse are or have been co-directors in the South African agency of the American hip-hop apparel collection Fubu and a company called Clothing Cave. Besides Carnilinx, they also share or have shared directorships in Hempco, AMK Properties, AMK Mining Projects, Real Time Investments 535, Fair-Trade Independent Tobacco Association, Branded World, Dithabeng Mining, Alrode Storage and several others.

Mazzotti's direct involvement in the deal to supply campaign clothing to Dlamini-Zuma lies in what he told Van Loggerenberg: "Yes, we played around and posed for photos wearing the hats and stuff, being silly."

Nkosazana Dlamini-Zuma's idiocy in banning tobacco had not just cost the South African fiscus billions in revenue but was, above all, illegal. The Supreme Court of Appeal ruled in June 2022 that the ban of tobacco was unconstitutional. If you have any doubt about what life might be like under the presidency of Dlamini-Zuma, think about lockdown. It would be a nanny dictatorship from hell.

Despite the lifting of the state of disaster and South Africa's return to normality, the illegal cigarette trade has continued to boom. Independent market researcher Ipsos found in a 2022 study that tobacco smugglers are continuing to flood South Africa's market with illicit cigarettes. "Four out of five stores in the Western Cape now sell cigarettes below the minimum collectible tax (MCT) rate of R22.79 per pack, as do almost 70 per cent of outlets in Gauteng, a significant increase compared to previous research."

The research found that packets of 20 cigarettes now sell for as little as R7, despite the MCT rate of R22.79. In simple terms, these cigarettes are illicit, and its manufacturers have not paid taxes or excise to SARS. Ipsos found that many of the brands were coming from either Zimbabwe-based Gold Leaf Tobacco or Carnilinx.

CHAPTER 21

Never leave an enemy behind

BEFORE JULIUS MALEMA celebrated his thirtieth birthday in 2011, he had converted the assets he had built up, from political acquaintances and factional sway, into Gucci shoes, Breitling watches, French champagne and Range Rovers. He was then at the crest of his popularity in the ANC after assisting Jacob Zuma to take occupation of the country's highest office. The porky young politician lived opulently and flaunted an aura of indestructibility.

His path from township boy to political prodigy has the elements of a fairy tale, were it not for the gluttony and greed with which it was riddled. Yet, there is something inexplicably amiable about Malema: his wittiness; his sharp intellect; his outrage about inequality; his eventual destruction of a crooked president whom he once helped into office. He is, after all, just a boy from a dusty Limpopo township that was raised by his granny after his mother died from an epileptic fit. His academic marks at school were dismal and, although he scraped through matric, he could so easily have faded into yet another nondescript existence of subsistence and survival. Instead, he rose to become one of South Africa's most forceful politicians.

And let us not fool ourselves. He is fundamentally right when he says that most money and power still reside with whites and that political freedom is meaningless without economic emancipation. The problem is that he uttered these wisdoms while his cronies were paying millions into networks of trusts and businesses for his personal benefit. The biggest beneficiary of Malema's brand of politics appears to have been Malema himself, not the poor and disenfranchised South Africans whom he says he represents.

His ascent to power in the ANC came in the mid-2000s when president Thabo Mbeki fired Jacob Zuma as his deputy president. Mbeki must have thought that his rival was down and out. Zuma was under investigation for fraud and, a few months later, he was charged with the rape of a friend's daughter. "Never leave an enemy behind because it will rise again to fly at your throat," was the maxim of the great Zulu king Shaka kaSenzangakhona. Although Mbeki gravely wounded his enemy, Zuma did exactly what Shaka had predicted. He rose from the ashes and retaliated with populist bluster, claiming to be the wronged son of the soil. He gathered behind him those that had been hurt and wounded by the paranoid and distrustful Mbeki and flew at his throat.

By then, it was clear to everyone that as a government the ANC had failed to stem the tide of unemployment and poverty in the country, close the tap on crime, and bring substantial foreign investment to the country. Corruption was on the rise, local government was unravelling, and cadre deployment and black economic empowerment were failing to redistribute wealth. This was the ideal breeding ground for the rise of populists like Zuma and Malema, who was elected as ANC Youth League president in April 2008. As his speeches grew more extreme, so his standing and popularity in the ANC seemed to swell. The echoes of his terrorisations, threats and menaces were everywhere. Offensive statements make headlines – and the more intolerant, vulgar and reckless, the better. As Malema saw it, behind virtually every problem he identified, be it poverty or unemployment, lurked a single scapegoat: white supremacy, or whiteness, or racism, or white monopoly capital. Malema later spoke about the two nations that Thabo Mbeki had identified and helped create in South Africa – the one white and rich, the other poor and black.

Malema and his (then) allies – the Congress of South African Trade Unions (Cosatu), the South African Communist Party (SACP), the ANC Youth League and a motley bunch of local businesspeople who sniffed the low-hanging fruit of his future presidency – crushed the ANC presidency of Mbeki and triumphantly carried Jacob Zuma on their shoulders into Luthuli House. Malema vowed that the ANC Youth League would take up arms if the prosecution of Zuma for fraud and corruption continued. He said: "Let us make it clear now: we are prepared to die for Zuma. Not only that, we are prepared to take up arms and kill for Zuma."

*   *   *

In 2009, the Limpopo Department of Roads and Transport invited bids for a new project management unit. The bid committee received sixteen applications, among them one from Aurecon, global management and engineering specialists with an impeccable track record. Its bid was thrown out because of a technicality. Another six were disqualified for submitting a bid in one rather than two envelopes. Three more bids were disqualified for lacking experience, skills and qualifications. This left a nonentity, On-Point Engineering, as the last one standing. The bid committee failed to do any vetting of On-Point's claims. The company lied about its experience and expertise and had no employees, no assets, no turnover, and no tax clearance certificate.

On-Point had one shareholder, Guilder Investments, which in turn had two equal shareholders: the Gwangwa Family Trust and the Ratanang Family Trust. The Gwangwa Family Trust belonged to Limpopo businessman Lesiba Cuthbert Gwangwa and the Ratanang Family Trust to Julius Sello Malema. The firebrand politician had set up his trust in May 2008, five weeks after he was elected as president of the Youth League. His son Ratanang was the only beneficiary.

By then, Malema lived large and way above his Youth League salary of around R20 000 per month. Sporting a R250 000 Breitling watch on his wrist, he reportedly had two houses to the value of R4.6 million. He owned a black Mercedes-Benz AMG and, according to an investigation by *The Star*, he also drove around in an Aston Martin and a red Range Rover Sport.

According to Fiona Forde, author of the biography *An Inconvenient Youth: Julius Malema and the "New" ANC*: "He developed a taste for nice shoes and good clothes and before long an attachment to designer labels. And that was also when the waistline began to bulge as he feasted off his new lifestyle. Malema was becoming a new man." She asked him where the money came from to fund his lifestyle. He told her that he belonged to an "important clique of key players – leading politicians and high businesspeople in the province – who opened doors for him in all directions". He added that they "lived like a family" and took care of one another.

One of Malema's properties, bought for R3.6 million in cash, was in the upmarket Johannesburg suburb of Sandown. YFM DJ Oskido provided the music for the housewarming bash where guests were treated to Johnnie Walker Gold Label whisky and Moët & Chandon French champagne. A police reservist who attended to a neighbour's complaint about the early-morning noise alleged that Malema assaulted him.

Not long into the Jacob Zuma presidency, the great ANC friendship with benefits landed on the rocks. Following the infamous incident in April 2010 in which Malema expelled a British journalist from a press conference after calling him a "bastard" and a "bloody agent", Zuma described the Youth League leader's conduct as "alien to the ANC". Malema was charged with bringing the organisation into disrepute and found guilty of "sowing discord". He was fined R10 000.

Two men who had so much in common became intent on destroying each other. Both Zuma and Malema were intoxicated with power and sowed disorder and revolt through a mixture of charisma and populism. The two once relied on each other to cement and expand their authority and influence, but after they raised their assegais, it became a duel to the death. Malema's rise to the top happened perhaps too quickly. He acquired the status of kingmaker when he led from the front to dethrone the feared Mbeki. Suddenly, no one would be king again unless they had Malema's backing and blessing. His pronouncements, however outlandish, became gospel.

Malema became drunk with power, which made him arrogant and disrespectful. And we all know that power corrupts. In many ways he dug his own grave by violating a fundamental African value: respect for your elders. He affronted people old enough to be his grandparents and showed no reverence for the office of the president. Many of his statements made a mockery of the conciliatory policy of the ANC. He told an enthusiastic crowd in Kimberley that white people should be treated as "criminals" for "stealing" land from black people. He said: "We must take the land without paying. They took our land without paying. Once we agree they stole our land, we can agree they are criminals and must be treated as such."

🐦 **Max du Preez** @MaxduPreez, 29 July 2011
Malema: "They [white people] must pay for making us slaves. We must punish them. And now they must pay." Reckless, dangerous stuff

Towards the end of 2011, the ANC threw the book at Malema for allegedly bringing the organisation into disrepute after pleading for regime change in peaceful Botswana. He even threatened to send in a Youth League team to overthrow the democratic government in Botswana.

🐦 **Julius Sello Malema** @Julius_S_Malema, 27 Feb. 2012
I humble myself before thee, ANC. My ANC. You're my trust, my hope, my life, the air I breathe, my father & mother.

The man who once claimed that the blood in his veins were the ANC colours of black, yellow, and green was now in the political wilderness. In addition, he faced two formidable opponents in the days to come: Public

Protector Thuli Madonsela and the revered and feared investigations units of the South African Revenue Service, which were after him for tax evasion. He ultimately faced financial ruin and jail time.

But Zuma had made the same mistake as Mbeki seven years earlier. He did not heed the great king Shaka's warning and left a wounded enemy on the battlefield. And exactly what Zuma had done to Mbeki, Malema would do to him. He would ultimately rise to fly at Zuma's throat – and rip it open.

* * *

In May 2012, a 36-year-old financial and human resources manager took the stand at a tax inquiry in Polokwane, Limpopo, into businessman Lesiba Cuthbert Gwangwa, a childhood friend and benefactor of Julius Malema. Over the next three days, the evidence of Nicolette Honeycomb, supported by twelve lever-arch files of financial data, a copy of the hard drive of her computer, and her personal diaries and notebooks, blew the lid off what seemed to be a financially beneficial and corrupt relationship between Gwangwa, the chief executive of On-Point Engineering, and the young firebrand politician Julius Malema.

SARS had launched an inquiry into eighteen of Gwangwa's companies and was probing fifteen suspected breaches of tax evasion. SARS discovered that Gwangwa had made cash payments of millions of rand into the Ratanang Family Trust account. Gwangwa provided for the young politician's every whim and fancy, from fitting out his car with new tyres to sending him off in a chartered jet – at a cost of R88 000 – on an all-paid holiday at an exclusive resort.

Gwangwa also paid the architects' bill that would have converted Malema's Sandown property into a sumptuous retreat and ordered that all payments relating to the building works should be invoiced to On-Point. He bought R135 000 worth of furniture for the house. Gwangwa purchased for Malema a Mercedes-Benz Viano worth a million rand and cars for Malema's bodyguards in Polokwane and Johannesburg.

Gwangwa paid R500 000 towards Malema's bodyguards, his gardener and his housekeeper. And to keep his poodle happy, Gwangwa footed the bill for Malema's designer clothing. The bill for one shopping trip to boutique outlet Vigano amounted to R100 000. Gwangwa also paid Malema's electricity bills, his auditors and his attorney, who received two payments of R600 000.

🐦 Julius Sello Malema @Julius_S_Malema, 26 Sept. 2012
The trick is 2 remain strong when everybody else expects u 2 breakdown, we remain resolute. The camp of the enemy is confused . . .

The expelled ANC Youth League leader appeared alongside Lesiba Gwangwa and four other accused in the Polokwane Regional Court in September 2012 on charges of fraud, racketeering and money laundering. Malema had consistently said that he was an indirect shareholder in On-Point and played no role in the company's securing of the R52 million contract with the Department of Roads and Transport or in any act of fraud or money laundering. He said in a 2015 affidavit – quoted in the *Sunday Times* – that there was no difference between the conduct of his Ratanang Family Trust, which bankrolled his lavish lifestyle, and that of Jacob Zuma's trusts. The charge sheet suggested that Malema played a direct role in managing the criminal enterprise and that between January 2009 and November 2011 On-Point paid altogether R6 453 382.33 into the Ratanang account. More than half the amount was by cash deposit.

The case was from the outset beset by delays and postponements. In August 2015, Judge George Mothle said the case had dragged on for too long, and this was "prejudicial" to Malema and the other accused. "For now, the case is over, you are free to go," the judge announced. He did add, however, that the youth leader had not been acquitted and that prosecutors could reinstate the charges.

* * *

Julius Malema's run-ins with SARS exposed him as a politician at the mercy of his keepers. SARS had started investigating the young politician back in 2009 and discovered that he had failed to submit tax returns for several years. The revenue service warned the young politician about a series of outstanding tax returns and told him that he was not tax compliant. Malema undertook to attend to the matter, but nothing happened. In July 2011, Malema lied at a press conference that he was fully tax compliant, and said he was in no way involved in corruption and would never exchange favours in return for money.

When Malema eventually sat down to settle his tax affairs, he underdeclared and misreported his income for several tax years and attempted to transfer his assets to third parties to place them outside the reach of SARS. The investigation showed that as Malema was cast into the political wilderness following his suspension from the ANC, he relied heavily on cash deposits into the ABSA bank account of his Mazimbu Investment Trust. In just one month from 23 July 2012 to 22 August 2012, more than 150 cash deposits, ranging from R70 to R14 000, were paid into the account.

The deposits into his accounts continued for years. For example, according to Malema's personal ABSA bank statement for 8 January 2014 to 7 February 2014, there were 20 cash deposits into his account, ranging from R1 000 to R50 000. Even after Malema became the leader of the third-biggest political party in Parliament and earned a substantial salary with vast perks, he continued to receive cash deposits into his account.

Yet, in an affidavit to SARS submitted in November 2012, Malema pleaded poverty. He said his net asset value was only R1.356 million. He had three cars that he leased to a taxi operator, and his monthly income was between R28 000 and R41 000. He claimed he could not pay his tax bill, but that "benefactors" were prepared to "lend" him R5 million. He said he would make an initial payment of R2 million and thereafter six payments of R500 000.

In January 2013, SARS chief officer for tax and customs enforcement Gene Ravele told Malema that the revenue service rejected his compromise offer because he had failed to make a "full and frank disclosure" and said that his tax debt was, at that point, R16 million, which would "substantially increase".

🐦 **Julius Sello Malema** @Julius_S_Malema, 22 Feb. 2013
I was baptized with fire at an early age, it will not be easy but it will be worth it. Let me die without nothing but with my soul intact . . .

🐦 **Nigel Cupido** @FrankieNigel, 22 Feb. 2013
You're kinda f**ked now, Chief . . . Eish! They're going for u!

Malema was in trouble. His newly formed Economic Freedom Fighters (EFF) was ready to contest the May 2014 general election and due to win seats in Parliament. However, if SARS sequestrated him, he would become an unrehabilitated insolvent and would not be allowed to take up his position in Parliament. The EFF persuaded almost 1.2 million South African voters to cast their ballots for the new army of red, which meant they won 25 seats in Parliament. Just days after Malema was sworn in, and with the final sequestration date looming, he approached SARS with yet another settlement offer. The fiery politician was as docile as a lamb when he said: "I wish to state unequivocally that I accept the liability . . . and that the penalties and interest imposed was due to my failure to fully declare income."

He said the curator of his estate held R4 million after the sale of his assets. He offered to pay an additional R4 million to SARS. He said his parliamentary salary as EFF leader was R1.3 million per year. He was willing to pay R30 000 per month for six months. He said if SARS did not accept his offer, "I will in all probability be sequestrated and my eligibility for public office will cease and I would not be able to earn income. That would cause me hardship and would effectively exclude me from the pool of taxable individuals."

In his settlement proposal Malema revealed the existence of a trust that was established to help him settle his tax liability. An amount of R3 million was paid in monthly instalments of R500 000 into the trust. He admitted that a further R2.4 million in donations was paid into the account of his erstwhile firm of attorneys, Brian Kahn Inc., over ten days in September 2012. He said he suspected the payments had been made by "my supporters but whose identity is yet to be established". According to Malema's submission, R584 140 in cash deposits was paid into his account between May 2013 and May 2014. The amounts ranged from R1 000 to R40 000.

🐦 **EWN Reporter** @ewnreporter, 26 May 2014
#Malema EFF leader has reached a compromise with SARS to pay his taxes.

Following the settlement agreement with SARS, Malema said: "I did not attend to my tax affairs in the manner that I was required to by law. Where I may have made public utterances that may have suggested bias or wrongdoing on the side of SARS, I unreservedly apologise. I accept the bona fides of SARS and its officials who have dealt with the matter."

* * *

In May 2014, Julius Malema and 24 of his fellow fighters, dressed in red overalls and wearing industrial hard hats, took their seats in Parliament. Gone were the days of monotonous and dire debates, members of Parliament slumbering in their green leather seats, and the president hiding behind the safety of the ANC numbers in the House. The EFF shattered the dignity of Parliament and broke the twenty-year dominance of the ANC in the house. They refused to shut up and, when the Speaker ruled them out of order, they confronted Zuma head-on and rose to their feet to cause pandemonium. Zuma was at the crest of his popularity in the ANC and, although he was engulfed in scandal upon scandal, opposition parties failed to make a dent in the armour with which the ruling party clad him.

During the first question session of the new Parliament, Zuma had to answer a question about when he would respond to the Public Protector's report on the security upgrades at his residence in Nkandla. In typical Zuma fashion, he dismissed it with the one-liner that he had already submitted a report to Parliament the previous week. Malema got to his feet and went for the jugular: "We want a date when we will get the money," he bellowed. "We are not going to leave this House before we get an answer!"

Speaker Baleka Mbete failed to call Malema to order before threatening in a fit of rage: "I will throw you out if you don't listen!" This encouraged EFF MPs to join in and shout into the microphones that Zuma should answer. "Pay back the money!" they chanted repeatedly while hammering on their desks and chanting insults. In turn, ANC MPs threatened to storm the House to physically attack them.

Mbete announced an adjournment and summoned the riot police. They seemed uncertain what to do. According to Malema, there was also an attempt by ANC staff "to beat us up but we barked at them and they disappeared because they are cowards". The EFF MPs remained in their seats until the uproar calmed down and they left of their own choice.

This was the onset of a period of parliamentary chaos, broken rules and philistine behaviour on the part of the EFF that turned Zuma's presidential presence in Parliament into an embarrassing misery. The EFF introduced an era of commotion, walkouts and combative rhetoric in Parliament. Day after day and week after week, Malema and his fighters chiselled away at Zuma's moral authority and ultimately contributed greatly to bringing him down.

🐦 **Julius Sello Malema** @Julius_S_Malema, 3 Oct. 2014
We will equally stop at nothing to ensure that President Zuma is brought to full account, and has his day in court.

CHAPTER 22

Flies on the wall

IN APRIL 2019, I met a cheery and convivial woman, wrapped in African cloth and sporting deftly knotted braided hair, in a Johannesburg township. It was late on a Sunday morning, and she had just come from church. This was my Facebook friend who had sent a message in October 2018 to "spill the beans" about the relationship between tobacco tycoon Adriano Mazzotti and EFF president Julius Malema.

In the preceding months, we had exchanged more Facebook and WhatsApp messages. By then I had a clear picture of what the relationship between Mazzotti and Malema seems to have entailed. Over a period of several years, claimed my source, Mazzotti plied Malema with cash, and his or Carnilinx's apartment in the Raphael Penthouse Suites in Sandton became a party venue where Malema, members of the EFF top command and their guests partied with expensive alcohol and food.

My informant was officially employed by Carnilinx although she mainly worked at the apartments at the Raphael and, more specifically, in the apartment rented by Carnilinx. She also helped at Mazzotti's villa in Hyde Park before and after he renovated the property, which took three years. In addition, she worked for several months at the Carnilinx cigarette factory in Salisbury Street in downtown Johannesburg, where she said that she witnessed piles of money being counted with money machines and taken away in boxes. She saw how envelopes were stuffed with cash.

I asked her why she left Carnilinx. She said a company manager falsely accused her of stealing groceries. When he confronted her, she swore at him. She was charged with disobedience and fired two days later.

Journalists love people who have suffered an injustice or have a gripe to settle. But such sources also come with their own problems, as their motives can cloud their objectivity and may cause them to exaggerate, manufacture events or manipulate facts. This is particularly the case where a source may have something to gain. I was therefore extremely circumspect in dealing with this person.

Soon after we had met, I asked her if she was talking to me because she wanted to take revenge for having been fired by Carnilinx. No, she said, she got justice when the Commission for Conciliation, Mediation and Arbitration (CCMA) ordered Carnilinx to pay her out for her unfair dismissal. She later handed me documents that confirmed her version.

During our first meeting, I asked her why she was talking to me. I reminded her that Malema was an extremely powerful man, and that Mazzotti was prepared to throw vast amounts of money about to get what he wanted. She said Malema was "arrogant" and did not treat the staff in the apartment particularly well. He was also, in her estimation, a liar when he claimed to have received money from Mazzotti only once – the EFF election deposit of R200 000 – and nothing ever again.

She has never asked me for a cent, and I have not offered or paid her any money for her testimony. She hasn't received anything else from me, except for the odd simple meal and a cooldrink on the occasions we met.

I typed up everything that she told me about her knowledge of the relationship between Mazzotti and Malema, and she then deposed to an affidavit on 29 July 2019. We stayed in contact and, more than six months after our first meeting, I interrogated her again. We wrote another affidavit which she signed on 7 February 2020.

The affidavits are under her real name, and she had verified her identity by providing me with her ID and passport. We stayed in touch, and I saw her again a few months before the publication of this book. I again questioned her about certain aspects of her story, and her answers remained consistent with her earlier versions.

I have decided to withhold her name, although she has given me permission to use it and there is no doubt that Mazzotti and probably Malema will know who she is. True to their style, they will probably embark on some dirty-tricks campaign and deny, deny, deny.

I have decided to call her Margaret for the purposes of this book. I submitted the chapters about Malema and Mazzotti to her before publication and, after reading them, she agreed with the content. Should it become necessary, Margaret has given me permission to release her affidavits and other documentation. They contain far more explicit descriptions of what happened in Mazzotti's apartment.

Mazzotti also employed two Malawian chefs who worked in the apartment from time to time and cooked for Malema and the others. There are thus other potential witnesses who could confirm at least some of Margaret's allegations.

The position of household workers as onlookers and observers of happenings and exchanges like those between Mazzotti and Malema is fascinating. Obviously, the apparent exchange of money and favours between a prominent politician and a controversial businessman is meant to be secret, but by then the workers were part of the furniture and completely trustworthy.

I asked Margaret about it, and she said that when the EFF partied in the apartment, she was told to leave after they and their guests arrived, but then had to come back to clean up the mess they left behind. She was often present when money exchanged hands, and nobody seemed to care. As she put it: "We were just like flies on the wall. Nobody paid attention to us."

* * *

🐦 **Julius Sello Malema** @Julius_S_Malema, 6 Oct. 2019
Tshepo, Tsubi and Ronny's brother. Rati, Zhedzi and Pano's father and Mantoa's husband. The grandson of Koko Sarah and the only child of Mahlodi Malema. And indeed Adriano Mazzotti's Friend.

Julius Malema mentions Adriano Mazzotti in the same breath as his brothers, his children, his mother, his grandmother and his wife. It doesn't get much closer than that. Mazzotti family members frequently published photographs of Malema at their bashes. They showed the firebrand politician cuddling Adriano's youngest son on his lap while posing with him and his wife. I have no reason to doubt that the two really like each other and have struck up a close friendship. I am, however, not sure what values a self-confessed tobacco smuggler and tax evader shares with a champion of the poor and disenfranchised.

In a statement Mazzotti sent to me in December 2018, he said: "It is no secret that Mr Malema and I have been friends for over a decade." Their friendship thus dates back to his earlier days as ANC Youth League leader. Carnilinx's contribution to the EFF's registration fees for the 2014 general election and the subsequent R1 million "loan" for Malema's tax bill have long been the subject of reports.

What's in the friendship for Malema seems to be clear: money. But what is in it for Mazzotti? He admitted in his 2014 affidavit to splashing out on politicians and people in power. He said that he and the other Carnilinx directors spent millions on "expensive dinners, entertaining businesspeople, politicians and other people who we considered would be useful in advancing the business of Carnilinx. I accept, and so does Carnilinx and all its directors, that this was unlawful and morally wrong."

One would assume that because he regarded this as morally wrong, he would have stopped doing it. But he did not. It simply continued. Mazzotti mentioned several examples in his affidavit where he bribed or attempted to bribe officials while Malema is no novice when it comes to collecting handouts. Both saw the transaction as commonplace, an everyday occurrence. And both saw nothing wrong with it.

Mazzotti and Carnilinx have seemingly spent a fortune on Malema's upkeep of his luxury lifestyle. I have little doubt that Mazzotti was forking out for the honour of having the commander-in-chief at his table. Or maybe he saw Malema as a future investment. Malema is ambitious and suffers from an almost ballistic quest for power. Although the EFF will probably never garner enough votes to become the majority party in Parliament, Malema might eventually find his way back into the ANC and into a top ministerial position. He might eventually be in line for the presidential throne. Many analysts and commentators have predicted that when the ANC slips under 50 per cent in the polls, South Africa will enter an era of coalition politics, which may elevate Malema and the EFF to the role of kingmaker.

In *The President's Keepers* I revealed that in February 2017 Mazzotti became a founder member and director of Dithabeng Mining, an open-cast chrome mine in Mphahlele, 45 kilometres south-east of Polokwane in the Limpopo province. The area is rich in chrome, iron and vanadium. The other director was Carnilinx's Mohammadh Sayed. Dithabeng described itself on its website as "progressive, trailblazing, socially conscious" and claimed that it had consulted widely with the community, whereafter an agreement was reached with the latter in 2017.

🐦 **amaBhungane** @amaBhungane, 18 July 2019
There have been allegations that businessman Adriano Mazzotti has leveraged his friendship with Julius Malema – who has been living in Mazzotti's luxury complex in Hyde Park – to defuse opposition to the Dithabeng mine

🐦 **News24** @News24, 18 July 2019
LATEST: One killed amid protests over disputed mine owned by Malema ally Adriano Mazzotti

In July 2019, amaBhungane reported that violent protests had erupted around the mine after the traditional leadership of the area was accused of hijacking the community trust and striking an illegal deal with Dithabeng Mining. The mine was accused of operating unlawfully and of being in cahoots with the chief, his mother and a faction of the traditional leadership.

AmaBhungane said that there were allegations that Mazzotti had used his friendship with Malema to diffuse opposition to the mine. A local EFF leader, Topa Mphahlele, said local community leaders opposed to the mine asked him and the party for support at a February 2017 meeting with Dithabeng. Mphahlele said that at the meeting Mazzotti called Malema and passed the phone to him. Malema told Mphahlele to leave the meeting and not do anything to frustrate Dithabeng. AmaBhungane said it spoke to three other EFF members who claimed to have been present at the meeting and who confirmed the phone call to Malema and his message.

In September 2017, community members sent a letter to EFF Limpopo leader Jossey Buthane, accusing the EFF of meddling in the community's affairs and siding with the mine. The letter claimed that Mphahlele, who has in the meantime joined the Action Transformation Movement (ATM), led a group of supporters to the mine to "bully" protesting security workers, demanding they resume work because "Malema will not like the delay in production".

According to Mphahlele, Buthane had said it was their mine and that they must protect their interest. Buthane instructed him to lead a group to protect the mine. The EFF has denied Malema's involvement: "He has never done any of these things. We really have no idea what amaBhungane is talking about." Mazzotti has, through his attorney, denied making the call, saying that "Mr Mazzotti's friendship with Mr Malema is not abused for personal gain."

* * *

Margaret started working for Adriano Mazzotti and his wife in 2009 at their villa in Hyde Park. She informed me that Malema and his family moved into the estate much later and became Mazzotti's neighbours. This she told me before it was revealed in the media that the Malema family was Mazzotti's tenant.

Margaret said she worked in Mazzotti's villa until around 2011 before being assigned to a plush apartment in the DaVinci Hotel and Suites in Sandton, which Carnilinx kept to entertain guests. She said the apartment became too small and in October 2013 they rented a bigger apartment in the upmarket Raphael Penthouse Suites, a stone's throw from the DaVinci and with a view over Nelson Mandela Square. Both properties belong to Legacy Hotels, which promises a life of absolute luxury in the most sough-after living space Johannesburg has on offer.

According to Margaret, in October 2013 renovations commenced at Mazzotti's Hyde Park estate and the family moved into a multi-bedroomed apartment in the Raphael, where they stayed for three years until September 2016. The family lived in one apartment, while Carnilinx kept the other. She said she mainly worked in the Carnilinx apartment.

As rumours swirled around Nkosazana Dlamini-Zuma's links to Adriano Mazzotti during the Covid lockdown, I asked the tobacco tycoon in June 2020 if the minister had ever visited him in his apartment at the Raphael. He replied: "The Raphael Penthouse Suite was me and my family's place of residence, which was leased by me for a period of approximately three years. I vacated the premises in 2016. Neither Minister Dlamini-Zuma nor anyone representing her met with me at my apartment." He thus confirmed what Margaret had stated almost a year earlier in her affidavit about the family relocating to the Raphael for three years.

Margaret said she met Malema in May 2014 when he arrived at the Carnilinx apartment with his driver, whom she named as Nhlanhla Mbatha. This was days after the general election in which the EFF participated for the first time and won 25 seats. Before his arrival, Mazzotti told the Malawian chef, John Mbewe, to prepare food for Malema. "Mazzotti called me and John over to greet Malema. He said: 'Come and greet the president.' He always called him the president," she said in her affidavit. "Mazzotti handed Malema a cooler box that was half-filled with money. The money was for a celebration party for the EFF for doing well in the elections." Margaret said she had seen the money herself.

She said that Malema regularly fetched envelopes, on which was written the name "Ju", from the apartment in the Raphael. When she later worked in the Carnilinx factory in downtown Johannesburg, she saw how these envelopes, with the name "Ju" on them, were stuffed with cash. "I saw several times how Malema, accompanied by Mbatha, came to fetch the 'Ju' envelopes. I don't know how much money was in the envelopes . . . it was R100 and R200 notes. It was full and bulging. The handing over happened at least once a month. Sometimes they would come more often."

During January and February 2018 Margaret had to help at Mazzotti's villa in Hyde Park. "Malema came to fetch money there as well. He waited downstairs while Mazzotti went upstairs to fetch it."

Margaret said that at the beginning of 2017 an attorney acting for Malema arrived at the Raphael to collect money from Mazzotti. She identified him as "Tommy Mokoena". Malema's attorney was Tumi Mokwena, who acted for him during the On-Point criminal case and his tax problems with SARS. He has since been suspended from practising as an attorney.

While speaking to Margaret, I asked her who could confirm her story. She mentioned three names: Agrippa Khumalo, who was Mazzotti's driver, and two chefs, John Mbewe and Bright Kumwembe, both Malawian. She said Mbewe worked for Mazzotti for several months in 2014 before he went back to Malawi. She had lost contact with him, but she gave me telephone numbers for Kumwembe and Khumalo.

I spoke to both, and they initially agreed to see me. Khumalo kept postponing our meeting and eventually said it was too dangerous to speak to me. Bright's wife contacted me a few days later on WhatsApp and said I must stop bothering Bright as I might be endangering his life.

I traced Mbewe on Facebook, messaged him and received from him his cellphone number in Malawi. I asked him if he would talk to me about Mazzotti and Malema. He responded: "OK Jacques I can give you what I know of him, but not on the phone, I know lots trust me."

* * *

Malawi's capital of Lilongwe can best be described as unmemorable; a scuzzy, bland and spread-out metropolis named after the river that runs through this city of a million people. Most tourists land at the drab Kamuzu International Airport but skip through the city on their way to one of Africa's true natural wonders: Lake Malawi.

After navigating customs at the airport – when I had last visited Malawi about ten years previously it was a building site, and in August 2019 it was still under construction – I jumped into a taxi and headed into the city. It was peak hour, and the road was also under construction. Although Lilongwe is not a city like Nairobi, Accra, Lagos, Kinshasa or Khartoum that has reproduced itself many times over in a few decades and is now gasping for air, life on the street resembles a palpitating heart that propels cars, buses and taxis through its clogged arteries. And like everywhere else in Africa, the pavements are choked with people that milled around seemingly with nowhere to go. In one the world's poorest countries where half of the population lives in poverty, many of the pavement brooders are people who have abandoned their villages in the countryside and journeyed to the city in the hope of scoring a job or something meaningful to do.

"And what are you doing in Malawi?" the taxi driver wanted to know.

"I am here to see someone. I have to talk to him."

"You came all the way from Johannesburg to speak to one person?"

"Yes," I said. "I have to ask him questions to make sure that another person is telling me the truth."

"Are you a lawyer?"

"No, I am a journalist."

After I booked into my hotel – a characterless three-star establishment with a view over a dusty carpark – I called Mbewe's cellphone number. A voice creaked on the other side: "Yes, hallo."

"Hi, John, I have arrived in Lilongwe. I am at the hotel."

"I will see you in half an hour."

Like most Malawians, 41-year-old John Mbewe came with a warm heart and a wide smile. A stubble beard framed his lean, handsome face. We settled in the bar – a hive of activity on this early Friday evening – and ordered two local Castel beers. After we exchanged niceties and I told John about the book I was writing, he wanted to know: "So, have you ever met Adriano Mazzotti?"

"No, I haven't."

"And have you ever met Julius Malema?"

"No, I haven't."

"Well, I have, and I saw a lot."

* * *

John Mbewe came from Malawi in 2005 to South Africa, where he worked as both a chef and a driver. He was later employed by the Italian consul-general in South Africa, Dr Enrico De Agostini. He honed his Italian cuisine skills and cooked up delicacies such as spaghetti alla carbonara, vitello al limone and risotto alla Milanese. When De Agostini returned to Rome, Mbewe accompanied him and worked for him in his luxury apartment near the Vatican where he continued to cook and learned to speak some Italian.

In early 2014, when De Agostini was appointed as ambassador to Zimbabwe, Mbewe returned to South Africa and advertised his attributes and skills in a local newspaper. The Mazzottis were probably attracted by his Italian cooking skills and his knowledge of their native language. He landed a job as what he calls a "house person" and a chef. He worked for Mazzotti from early in 2014 until the second half of that year. "Mazzotti is a smart man. We communicated mostly in Italian and, as a result, he trusted me. He was almost always dressed in black, was fit, relatively quiet and often didn't eat."

Mbewe said he had been working for a few weeks when he saw Julius Malema for the first time. "Malema was accompanied by [Floyd] Shivambu and two men that I understood were their bodyguards or drivers. Mazzotti was not there, and I served them drinks while they waited for him to arrive. He [Malema] asked me where I am from and when I said Malawi, he said: 'Ah, so you are from the British empire.' I left when Mazzotti arrived."

Mbewe told me he witnessed one more meeting between Malema and Mazzotti before the EFF leader arrived for a third time, accompanied by his bodyguard or driver. He said Margaret (he mentions her real name in his statement) was also present. "At this meeting, Mazzotti called her and I and said: 'Come and meet the president.' Mazzotti always called Malema 'president'." According to Mbewe, "Malema and Mazzotti discussed something about an event at a stadium. Mazzotti gave Malema a bag. There were lots of money in the bag. Both [Margaret] and I saw this."

He said when he saw Malema again, he accompanied Mazzotti to the parking garage of the Raphael. The latter carried a bag that was about half a metre by half a metre. He assumed the bag was full of money. Mazzotti handed the bag to Malema's driver/bodyguard.

Mbewe told me that one afternoon at about two, Mazzotti called him. "He said that I must do something urgent for him. I had to go to his bedroom. Under the bed was the same kind of bag that I previously handed to his bodyguard/driver. Mazzotti said I must open the bag. I unzipped the bag. It was full of money. He said I must close the bag and hand it to Malema's bodyguard/driver. I had to take it down to the parking basement where I handed the bag to this person. He was then driving a dark-coloured Mercedes-Benz."

Mbewe was prepared to confirm his allegations under oath and agreed to his name being used. I did not pay him for his evidence. After writing a statement, we went to the Lilongwe Model police station in the Malawian capital to have it affirmed. Policemen told us that unlike their counterparts in South Africa, they were not commissioners of oath, and to make an affidavit Mbewe would have to find an attorney or go to court. He signed his statement on 20 August 2019 at the police station.

* * *

In Carnilinx's apartment in the Raphael Penthouse Suites were cracked bottles of French Moët champagne that Julius Malema and his cronies had forgotten to take out of the freezer, empty booze bottles strewn across the lounge, dirty plates with the remnants of a flame-grilled chicken-and-chips dinner piled in the kitchen, and used condoms and female underwear in the bedrooms. This was the scene, said Margaret in her affidavit, that greeted her when she had to clean up in the aftermath of a bash held by Julius Malema and his cronies in the apartment. She said she spotted EFF deputy leader Floyd Shivambu with Malema several times while spokesperson Mbuyiseni Ndlozi joined them once. There were other partygoers she did not know and to whom she was never introduced.

"These parties usually took place on Friday nights, when they also slept in the apartment. Their bodyguards/drivers arrived at the apartment with consignments of alcohol. There were Castle Light beer, Savanna cider, Johnnie Walker Black Label and lots of bottles of Moët champagne. The champagne came in boxes of six. The bodyguards would drop Malema and his friends at the apartment with alcohol. The bodyguards then left to fetch girls and women. I was told to leave. I know Malema's wife and she was not one of them. Malema would say to his bodyguard: 'The auntie to go.' That was a reference to me," she said in her affidavit.

Although Mbewe had worked for Mazzotti for only a few months, he also witnessed Malema and his friends partying at the apartment. In his statement Mbewe said: "There were lots of alcohol, amongst it whisky and wine and champagne. They also had food like chicken and chips. They started drinking as soon as they arrived. There was a knock on the door. Mazzotti ordered [me] to open for them. I opened the door and there were two girls. I was then ordered to leave."

He said he also afterwards helped to clean up when Malema, his friends and the women had gone. "There were used condoms in the toilet and the place was very, very messy. There were some of the underwear of the girls left in the apartment. I washed it and gave it to [Margaret] that Monday."

Mbewe said that in the second half of 2014 he decided to leave Mazzotti's employ. "I became aware of all the cash in the apartment and [Margaret] told me this was the mafia." He said he told Mazzotti that he needed to attend a funeral in Malawi. He didn't return and changed his telephone number. He was replaced by Bright Kumwembe.

Margaret said the parties in Mazzotti's apartment continued until she left in 2018. She said in October 2016 she arrived at the apartment to clean up. "The apartment was a complete mess. There were lots of empty bottles of Moët. They even put some of the champagne in the freezer to cool. The glass bottles burst in the freezer. There were used condoms all over the apartment. There were condoms in the toilet, but it wasn't even flushed. There were traces of white powder on a DVD cassette. There was a rolled-up note next to the cassette." Margaret asked Kumwembe what it was. "He said it was cocaine. There was still some white powder stuck to the note."

If you wonder how Malema, Shivambu and their friends explained their all-night escapades in Mazzotti's apartment to their spouses and partners, the answer may lie in a speech that the EFF president made in 2017 at the wedding of his second-in-command, Floyd Shivambu. Addressing the bride, Siphesihle Pezi, Malema had this to say: "Floyd also has a family which is the EFF, so sometimes he will be forced to go to meetings at night. There are some of the meetings that our wives must not question." Are we to believe that in the lotus land of the Republic of Malemastan the elected have meetings that last through the night where the top command strategises the downfall of Cyril

Ramaphosa until way past midnight and the protection of Public Protector Busisiwe Mkhwebane until the sun rises in the east?

* * *

The three-storey Carnilinx cigarette plant in Salisbury Street hides behind iron fencing and locked gates. Urban renewal projects have transformed many drab and dreary downtown Johannesburg precincts into hip and artsy centres of creativity. They now pulsate with a post-industrial vibe and are abuzz with restaurants, coffee shops, clothing boutiques and art galleries. However, the area around Carnilinx remains untouched by urban renewal. It is a place of broken pavements, auto graveyards, Pentecostal churches, and nondescript factories and warehouses.

Carnilinx claims on its website that its state-of-the-art production facility has the capacity to produce more than 300 million "sticks" monthly. That is 15 million packets of twenties. It also claims that its reputation is built on a "solid management team having over 100 years' experience in the industry."

In February 2018, Margaret was transferred from the Raphael to the Carnilinx plant, where she worked until her dismissal in August 2018. Here she performed general housekeeping duties. She said in her affidavit: "Every day, Mazzotti and/or one of his co-directors, Mohammadh Sayed, and/or another Carnilinx employee brought bags of cash into the factory. The bags were about one metre by one metre in size. They brought up to eight of these bags into the factory every day."

I asked Margaret how she knew about the money. She said: "This money was counted in the boardroom at the factory. The door was closed when they counted the money. I however had to take them food and I saw them counting the money. They used money machines to count the money. As far as I could establish, this money was never taken to the bank. It was locked away in the factory."

Margaret said one of the workers at Carnilinx, a man called Ayanda, showed her a packet of Derby cigarettes. It was in a blue and red packet, and he told her: "This cigarette is for Malema." Said Margaret: "I understood this to mean that the money that Mazzotti made out of Derby was going towards Malema. While working in the factory in 2018 I became aware that on a weekly basis Mazzotti and/or the directors and/or other employees stuffed A3-size envelopes full of money. They wrote 'Ju' on the envelope – a reference to Malema." These were the envelopes that Malema would eventually fetch at the Raphael apartment.

* * *

In August 2018, Carnilinx fired Margaret. She explained in her affidavit: "I was accused by a Carnilinx employee that I had stolen groceries. I told him that it was untrue and that my husband had given me R500 to buy groceries. I was nonetheless dismissed as an employee." According to the documentation she showed me relating to her dismissal, she faced two charges of "disrespect/insolence" after she allegedly told her Carnilinx manager who wanted to search her bag: "Fuck you it is my groceries and you have no right to ask me." She allegedly insulted the same manager again two days later. She was found guilty of disrespect/insolence at the disciplinary hearing and dismissed. There was no theft-related or dishonesty charge against her.

Margaret laid a complaint of unfair dismissal with the Commission for Conciliation, Mediation and Arbitration (CCMA). CCMA documentation shows that Carnilinx did not attend the hearing and again failed to appear a few weeks later. The CCMA upheld her complaint and ordered the company to pay her R20 000 in compensation. She received the money several months later.

* * *

When I wrote *The President's Keepers*, our lawyers advised us not to approach any of the implicated characters – Arthur Fraser, Tom Moyane,

Richard Mdluli, Berning Ntlemeza, Jacob Zuma, Shaun Abrahams, Nomgcobo Jiba, David Mahlobo, Roy Moodley – or any of the so-called keepers for comment as they could have launched a legal challenge to prevent the publication of the book. Given what I'd uncovered when researching the book, we felt that the information was too important to risk being tied up in a court battle that could have lasted for years.

We were proven right when Fraser and the State Security Agency tried to ban *The President's Keepers*, the Hawks raided my office, and Moyane and the SA Revenue Service took legal action against me. NB Publishers and I are once again confronted with the same dilemma.

The South African Press Code requires that journalists give a person who is the subject of critical reportage the right of reply. There is, however, an exception: "This need not be done where the publication has reasonable grounds for believing that by doing so it would be prevented from publishing the report or where evidence might be destroyed or witnesses intimidated."

This is one of the main reasons why we have decided not to approach Adriano Mazzotti, Julius Malema or Floyd Shivambu for comment.

We are fearful that Margaret could become the victim of intimidation. She is vulnerable and to a certain extent, exposed. She is just an ordinary person speaking out about wrongful behaviour that she had witnessed, and we need to protect her as far as we can.

Both Malema and Mazzotti have been less than forthcoming with the truth before.

A week before the release of *The President's Keepers*, I prepared an article for the *Sunday Times* that coincided with the publication of the book on the last Sunday of October 2017. Because it was a news article for a newspaper, I had to ask Mazzotti for comment about the allegations contained in the book. He didn't know at that stage that I had a copy of his May 2014 confession and affidavit to SARS.

I sent him a series of questions, among others: Have you attempted to bribe Johann van Loggerenberg and Ivan Pillay when they were still at SARS? Did you pay an attorney to bribe the two said officials? Did the attorney pocket the money himself? Did you pay an "unlawful" gift of R500 000 to a senior advocate?

Regarding every question, Mazzotti said: "No."

He lied in his answers.

And he will no doubt continue to do so.

* * *

𝕏 Daily Maverick @dailymaverick, 3 July 2019
HYPOCRISY, SQUARED: Revolutionary trash sometimes requires trash journalism, literally By Marianne Thamm @MarianneThamm

When the residents of Cape Town woke up on a chilly winter's day in 2019, the remnants of the high life of the EFF were on public display in front of a guest house in Camps Bay. Here a party delegation had stayed for eight days while attending the president's State of the Nation address and the subsequent parliamentary debates. After paying their R60 000 bill, they left their garbage in fourteen rubbish bags on the street, which made it public property. Intrepid and seasoned *Daily Maverick* journalist Marianne Thamm collected seven of the bags (she did not have space for the rest) and dissected the revolutionary trash – to the dismay of many.

𝕏 THE HITTA @lordmodiba, 3 July 2019
Replying to @dailymaverick and @MarianneThamm
You are trash journalist in a trash media

𝕏 PhumzaN @nicollecious_Y, 3 July 2019
Replying to @dailymaverick and @MarianneThamm
This is the most racist shit I have seen from a publication

Said Thamm: "And so it came to pass that I found myself on the morning of Friday 29 June elbow-deep in uneaten food, used condoms, boxes of discarded unused condoms, discarded deposit slips with bank account numbers, slips of paper from purchases from H&M (yes, the store the fighters trashed), Zara as well as slips and packaging from other fast-food restaurants."

She packed out the 40 or so booze bottles on the pavement and took a picture. Much of it was French champagne Veuve Clicquot, silver Veuve Clicquot Rich and Moët Nectar Imperial at between R600 and R900 a bottle. The red wine of choice was Meerlust Rubicon (around R450 per bottle), eighteen-year-old Glenfiddich whisky (R1,500 per bottle) and Tanqueray gin (R280 per bottle). Thamm reckoned that the stash must have cost in the region of R25 000.

The booking for the fighters at the villa with its panoramic sea views was made by Larry Mavunda, Julius Malema's bodyguard. Thamm also found a South African Airways business class boarding stub in the name of EFF spokesperson Dr Mbuyiseni Ndlozi.

🐦 **Secretary Of Black Twittter** @Prince_S_A_, 3 July 2019
I don't care if EFF leaders fvck with condoms or not. But I do care if they rent a 60k 4bedroom apartment in Camps Bay, splash on alcohol then pitch up in Parliament in red overalls & kitchen clothes like our mothers who were helpers & lived in poverty. Wat a paradox. Hypocrisy.

When Thamm wrote to Ndlozi to seek his response, she said there was the "not so small matter" of R40 000 worth of damage to the property. She asked: "I would like your comment in relation to purchases made at H&M at the Waterfront as well as your views on the young women who were seen leaving the house." She said to Ndlozi that what she was doing was "policing hypocrisy" and that he had to bear in mind "the constituency that has trusted you with its vote". She added: "You are an elected official and are entitled to spend your money whichever way you please. But if this is not out of your own pocket then you do have a case to answer."

The doctor replied: "This is laughable and typical trash journalism. Well, am not scared of you and the rouge [*sic*] unit! I have given you my response, so go on and publish whatever satisfies your rouge [*sic*] investigative interests."

A day later, Malema addressed supporters and joked: "After they've gone through used condoms, they're going to start peeping through windows to see how many rounds you last in bed. You know, a used condom, wrapped in a packet, can you imagine opening that?"

Thamm's piece had flaws, among them that she did not tell her readers how many EFF members slept in the guest house, which had five bedrooms. Was there only one EFF official per room or more per room? Only then can one determine if an amount of R60 000 for eight days was excessive. Apart from Ndlozi, we do not know who else slept in the establishment, although we have a good idea. We know who the champagne-swigging coterie of the EFF is.

The value of Thamm's exposé lies in the picture it paints of the debauchery of the top echelons of the party, and the same goes for what Margaret told me. The simple point is this: the EFF command are public servants, voted in because they portray themselves as champions of the poor. But we've all seen the Range Rovers, houses, farms, Breitling watches, Gucci shoes and holidays on chartered jets, which would seem to be well beyond the salary of a South African politician.

Thamm's trash story came several months after Margaret had first confided in me about the EFF's festivities in Mazzotti's apartment. Her story thus came as no surprise and was just one more example of the extravagance of those who profess to fight for the upliftment of the disenfranchised.

CHAPTER 23

A brotha from anotha motha

THEY ARE MORE than just bros, fighters, comrades, a brotha from anotha motha. They are two sides of the same coin; paypals of each other. Julius Malema and Floyd Shivambu are also glued at the hip by their mutual complicity in wrongdoing and hypocrisy. And like Malema, virtually every time Shivambu opens his mouth, he blows smoke.

In the Republic of Malemastan, where the commander-in-chief and his deputy smoke the regal pipe, an array of bountiful benefactors have shelled out for much of their needs, ranging from Moët, Gucci and Breitling to Range Rovers, Sandown villas and exotic holidays.

When Malema and Floyd Shivambu were exposed from 2019 onwards for benefiting from millions looted from VBS Mutual Bank, it was with money deposited by the poor and vulnerable, often through stokvels and burial societies. Many had invested their total life savings in VBS. Later, in contravention of the Municipal Finance Management Act, ANC municipalities also invested money in the bank. When they were ordered to withdraw the funds, most had already been stolen.

Originally known as the Venda Building Society, VBS Mutual Bank was a nondescript lender in Limpopo before it emerged from obscurity in 2016 by granting Jacob Zuma a controversial loan to repay the state for improvements to his Nkandla homestead. It was the first time most people had heard of the bank. It then grew rapidly and advertised itself as a champion of the poor and of black advancement.

Following a liquidity crisis in March 2018, the Reserve Bank placed VBS under curatorship. Forensic investigators said in a 148-page report that between March 2015 and June 2018, 53 persons gratuitously received R1.89 billion from VBS. The alleged kingpin of the heist was Tshifhiwa Matodzi, chair of VBS and the bank's holding company, Vele Investments. He has been accused of siphoning R325 million from VBS depositors and investors. VBS CEO Andile Ramavhunga apparently helped himself to R28.9 million while executives Robert Madzonga and Phophi Mukhodobwane are thought to have bagged R30.3 million and R30.5 million respectively. The suspected looters splashed the loot on ski holidays in Alaska, fleets of cars, holiday farms, and mansions in the most exclusive suburbs. Matodzi, for example, had twelve cars, ranging from Porsches to Ferraris.

According to the forensic report, one of the beneficiaries of the heist was Brian Shivambu – brother of Floyd Shivambu – who netted a cool R16.1 million from VBS. The money was deposited into the account of one of his companies, Sgameka Projects. The company offered no services, paid no taxes, and employed no staff. It had no operational expenses and did not function as a business. In addition to the R16.1 million, VBS reportedly allocated an illegal home loan of R1.46 million and a possibly fraudulent business loan of R4 million to Sgameka.

Both Malema and Shivambu have denied any complicity in the looting of the VBS bank and asked why they have not been arrested? "I've never spoken to VBS people. I have never had any dealing with the VBS people. I've got no one close to me who benefited from VBS bank," said Malema at a press conference in June 2020.

The *Daily Maverick*'s Pauli van Wyk and other journalists have, however, traced the flow of the illicit funds and found that Brian Shivambu and Sgameka were nothing but fronts through which millions of rand were laundered to Floyd, Malema and the EFF. Said the *Daily Maverick*: "Apart from the many laws that were broken, Pauli van Wyk's exposé has blown to smithereens the myth of a corruption-fighter and exposed a naked hypocrite who's in it for power and money."

After the VBS money landed in the Sgameka account, Brian Shivambu paid R4.8 million in several tranches into the bank account of Mahuna Investments. The *Daily Maverick* obtained the bank statements of Mahuna, which belonged to Malema's cousin Matsobane Phaleng. The publication analysed around 470 transactions effected in 2017 and 2018 in Mahuna's bank statements.

🐦 **Kenny Motai** @MelatoMotai, 27 May 2019
Vbs or no vbs pauli can go to hell Satan.

Sgameka was seemingly also a slush fund for Floyd Shivambu and the EFF. The company paid R5.16 million into Grand Azania, a small wine bar and distribution company controlled by Brian Shivambu, and R1.3 million into the EFF's bank account. Grand Azania, in turn, paid a further R500 000 into Mahuna's bank account, bringing the total of VBS money deposited into this account to R5.3 million.

The money in Mahuna's account paid for, among other things, Malema's eldest son's school fees, his house and pool in Sandown, an array of designer suits and outfits, the EFF's birthday celebrations, and the commander-in-chief's own political campaigning. The *Daily Maverick* then showed how a bank card linked to the Mahuna account followed Malema around the country, paying for his lavish lifestyle. Van Wyk matched Malema's diary as documented on social media with the point-of-sale bank card transactions. She also analysed Phaleng's social media accounts, which suggested that he was present at locations where the money from the Mahuna bank card was spent.

🐦 **Julius Sello Malema** @Julius_S_Malema, 9 Sept. 2019
You are welcome to open a case, no one will stop you.

🐦 **Gibson!!!!!!** @GibsonBaby1, 13 Sept. 2019
This Pink Girl is so very Obsessed with Julius Malema . . . Hands of our President you witch Devil

For example, from 17–19 July 2018, the Mahuna bank card followed Malema to the North West province where he attended the land debate in three towns. The card paid for R6,200 worth of fuel and accommodation in Christiana and Rustenburg, a purchase at a Mmabatho pharmacy, and another at Nando's in Vryburg. The social media accounts of Malema, the EFF and their followers place Malema in each town on the dates the point-of-sale payments were made.

In the same month in 2018, Malema used the Mahuna Investments bank card to spend R27 094 on Gucci and Le Coq Sportif in Sandton City, R30 860 on the Durban July, R11 560 on the Hampshire Hotel in Ballito and R416 900 on the Polokwane party venue of Mekete Lodge.

In December 2018, Malema splurged another R367 000 on Mekete Lodge, R59 000 on tailored suits from designer Linda Makhanya, R10 200 on Gucci and R29 233 on @Home. The Mahuna Investments account reflected an internet payment of R50 000 for fireworks.

Between 2017 and 2018, Malema spent almost all the VBS money in Mahuna's account. This included altogether R415 087 paid in ten tranches to the Standard Bank business account of Linda Makhanya. Gucci was paid R67 800, Lacoste R15 760, Louis Vuitton R35 100 and the cosmetics boutique Skins R34 695. More than R200 000 was spent on school fees for Malema's children, and R458 056 on renting a Sandown home for the commander-in-chief.

The *Daily Maverick* found that besides the VBS money, fifteen highly questionable sources paid an additional R8.74 million into Grand Azania's bank account. According to the online publication: "Highly questionable transactions worth about R28-million washed through Shivambu's slush funds between 2016 and 2018." The loot in this account paid R1.8 million in cash for a new Range Rover Sport for Shivambu and R2.38 million towards three properties where he and his parents live.

Confronted by the *Mail & Guardian*'s investigative team about the purchase of his Range Rover, Floyd Shivambu was adamant: "I never got any money from VBS and bought the Range Rover Sport long before

I even knew there's a bank called VBS." A week later, the journalists again challenged Shivambu's denial when they revealed a R680 000 payment from Sgameka Projects for the purchase of the vehicle – and the company only ever received money from VBS. With smoke billowing from his ears, nose and mouth, he then suddenly remembered the sale of a 2012 BMW 7 Series which partly funded the Range Rover in his possession.

𝕏 Daily Maverick @dailymaverick, 14 Oct. 2019
SCORPIO: The Chronicles of Grand Azania, Part Two: Floyd Shivambu's time of spending dangerously

Much as with the Mahuna Investments bank card that followed Malema through the country, the *Daily Maverick* detailed how the Grand Azania bank account card accompanied Shivambu through southern Africa. Pauli van Wyk analysed around 260 point-of-sale payments captured in the company's bank statements. She linked the places and times of the payments to Shivambu's movements and appearances detailed on his and the EFF's social media accounts.

Shivambu had the bank card in his purse when he went on a shopping spree at Sandton City on 28 December 2016 and paid R20 300 for new clothes at Gucci, R3 579.96 for Nike and R7 600 for Louis Vuitton. About to undertake a trip to the Victoria Falls in Zambia, he spent R3 495 at Moda Luggage & Leather. He celebrated his birthday on New Year's Day 2017 at the falls, where the card paid R8 429.42 at the Royal Livingstone Hotel, situated on the edge of the Zambezi River. The next day, as Shivambu returned home, the bank card made a payment at a Zambian airport shop for R1 034.39.

The *Daily Maverick* showed that Grand Azania also paid R583 000 for renting a house for Shivambu in Bryanston in Johannesburg. Between 2016 and 2018, Shivambu spent hundreds of thousands of rand in VBS money as well as other dodgy cash on clothing from Burberry (R52 770), Gucci (R82 900), Louis Vuitton (R16 450), groceries from

Spar (R13 635) and Shoprite (R13 923), and technology from Dion Wired (R13 329), iStore (R33 637) and Esquire Technology (R172 978). Sgameka Projects also paid R180 000 in VBS money directly into Shivambu's personal bank account.

The looting of VBS has implicated Julius Malema and Floyd Shivambu in a host of crimes. They received what appears to be fraudulently acquired monies, which they must have known about. And did any of them report their VBS booty to SARS?

Malema's and Shivambu's strategy was one of deny, deny, deny. When Pauli van Wyk fired off a series of questions to Malema and Shivambu in May 2019, this was Malema's reply to her: "I won't be answering any questions from this moloi [Setswana for 'witch']; she can write anything she wants. I have responded to all her questions before and won't be doing it going forward. She [gets] extraordinarily personal and I am not answerable to white madam. She can go to the nearest hell."

Everyone in the chain of money laundering and fraud has denied their complicity. It started with Matsobane Phaleng, Malema's cousin, denying that his account ever received any money from VBS bank. However, R4.8 million worth of payments in nine tranches into his account were clearly marked "Vbscredits*shivambu". Buti Brian also denied receiving stolen money from VBS and said he had done "consulting", this time for VBS investor Vele Investments.

Why then did VBS pay Sgameka and Grand Azania? The answer may lie in a WhatsApp message that former VBS chairperson Tshifhiwa Matodzi sent to VBS executive Phophi Mukhodobwane at the end of December 2017: "Nndaa can we do 350k for sgameka. Those are lobbying fees."

🐦 Pauli Van Wyk @PaulivW, 12 Oct. 2020
The VBS money was always only one of Julius Malema & Floyd Shivambu's illegal income streams. Neither declared "interventions" & "gifts" to Parliament, because it is proceeds of crime. In doing so, & by continuously denying the facts, the MPs seemed to have defrauded parliament.

* * *

In February 2019, EFF MP Thembinkosi Rawula took to Facebook to vent his anger with Julius Malema and Floyd Shivambu. Rawula was a member of the party's highest decision-making body, the central command team (CCT), and the chairperson of the EFF's national disciplinary committee.

In his Facebook post, Rawula said that Malema and Shivambu were the "antithesis" of everything they claimed to stand for and accused them of hiding behind the "slogans of economic freedom for dejected African masses" to commit corruption. Despite Malema's and Shivambu's public assurances that neither they nor the party ever took any VBS money, Rawula said it was a lie. "The political overview of Julius Malema in the most recent CCT meeting admitted to EFF taking VBS money to finance the revolution. In fact he said, 'sometimes we are forced to kiss dogs or [the] devil to get funding'. The VBS money was done under the full knowledge of the leadership."

Rawula revealed that the 61 EFF members of Parliament and provincial legislatures each paid a "levy" of R6 800 per month to the EFF. The EFF had 852 councillors in metros and district and local municipalities who each paid R2 000 a month to the party. That's around R2.2 million in "levies" from its elected officials every month. He said the EFF also received around R25 million per quarter from Parliament and the provincial legislatures.

"All these [monies] are centralized in the EFF under the control, abuse and dictatorship of Julius Malema and Floyd Shivambu. [The] pair have made it clear, this is their organization and all of you have come to join us, not the other way round. We have never had a Financial Report and, when occasionally we find courage to ask about it, we are chastised as spouses and treated with disdain and threatened to be removed from Parliament."

Referring to Rawula as a "position-monger", then EFF spokesperson Mbuyiseni Ndlozi said: "How can you sit for five years at the highest echelons of the organisation but also sit in its different parliamentary organisations and also campaign for it and when you lose the position in an open, democratic process, you throw your tantrums and you lie about the organisation?"

Rawula failed to make it onto the EFF's parliamentary list for the May 2019 general election. He claimed he had been victimised for speaking out and asking questions about VBS money, among other things. He said: "I am poor, [I] live like a church mouse despite the fact that I have been a member of Parliament for the past 4 years. The pair has milked every cent I worked for in Parliament but despite that, my integrity remains intact. Bloody crooks."

🐦 City Press @City_Press, 10 Apr. 2019
Malema says he is suing Rawula for R1 million. "I am taking him to the cleaners."

Malema is cautious about whom he legally crosses swords with. He has never attempted to sue the *Daily Maverick* and Pauli van Wyk or any other media outlet for defamation for accusing him of pocketing poor people's money in the VBS scandal. He would never survive a discovery process that would allow the respondents insight into his financial affairs and bank accounts.

But he gunned for Rawula, who was jobless and forced to represent himself in court. In contrast, Malema was armed with a set of attorneys and an advocate.

To avoid a trial in which Rawula could subpoena bank accounts and documents, call witnesses and cross-examine Malema, the EFF leader applied for a final interdict and damages.

High Court judge Nick Mullins said Malema's application was misguided and bad in law. In rejecting Malema's application, the court said that Rawula had a defensible case based on truth and public interest.

🐦 Thembnkos Rawula, Former MP @trawula, 14 Nov. 2019
Victory is when you walk free after being sued for R1 Million Rand by a
Party Leader of the 3rd biggest organisation represented by 3 white law
firms led by Advocates and you stand alone by truth and public interest.

Not happy, Malema appealed against the judgment and roped in one
of the finest senior counsels in the country, Tembeka Ngcukaitobi. In
argument before a full bench of the Supreme Court of Appeal (SCA),
Malema dropped his claim for R1 million in damages as well as the
demand for a retraction and apology and an interdict against further
publication of the Facebook post. He asked the court to declare Rawula's
Facebook post unlawful and defamatory.

The evidence against Malema was mounting. The five judges were
confronted by a handwritten affidavit of another former EFF MP,
Zolile Rodger Xalisa, who recalled the CCT meeting at which Malema
admitted that the EFF had received VBS money. He further claimed
that Malema "confirmed that they could not receive the donation with
[the] EFF account of theirs (him and Floyd Shivambu) but had to devise
other means, he said sometimes you must kiss dogs or the devil to get
money . . ."

The SCA rejected Malema's application for an interdict because
Rawula had laid a "foundation for a defence of truth to be asserted".

* * *

Twitter has a glum underbelly that is loud, divisive, intolerant, fanatical
and racist. It twists and reinvents reality, and there are no checks and
balances. It is also the ideal social media platform from where a fanatic
like Julius Malema can spew his racial poison and hatred. He has dispatched his tweets like drones armed with missiles at journalists who
have exposed his racism and debauchery. He has declared investigative
journalists "enemies of the revolution" and warned the media: "We are

in a war here. If you think we are playing, you must stand aside." When Malema fires off in public, he does so with fury and incandescence.

He has banned publications like the *Daily Maverick* and investigative teams like amaBhungane from EFF media events. In a society engulfed in violence against women, he has verbally attacked, diminished and condemned female journalists. Malema must know that his vociferous tweets spur his bots and trolls into action, yet he relentlessly continues with his cowardly behaviour.

🐦 Pauli van Wyk @PaulivW, 24 Nov. 2018
#JuliusMalema has to take responsibility for violence meted out to journalists. He is stoking the flames of a campaign against journalists whose work he disputes . . . and ultimately endanger the lives of journalists.

🐦 Julius Sello Malema @ Julius_S_Malema, Nov 24, 2018
You are sick, go to hell satan.

🐦 Micky @micky_radio, 24 Nov. 2018
But you 'on't talk to a woman in such manner

🐦 Julius Sello Malema @Julius_S_Malema, 24 Nov. 2018
I just did, so what?

🐦 VacancyMail.c–m - Jobs in South Africa @vacancymailsa, 24 Nov. 2018
She's not a woman. She's a devil

🐦 Khawuta Ka Gcaleka @Jonguyise2, 24 Nov. 2018
This thing is not even a woman. Caucasian piece of dead meat.

Although Pauli van Wyk was at the forefront of the EFF's cyber-misogyny directed at journalists, she is by no means the only one.

Many more female journalists have suffered the brunt of the vulgarity and crudeness of Malema and the EFF leadership and their supporters.

The *Daily Maverick* associate editor Ferial Haffajee wrote: "Every morning, I pick up my phone and check WhatsApp messages. Then, I open my Twitter feed. 'Bitch!' reads a response to something I've posted or written or reported. I block. 'Cunt,' reads another. Block. 'Racist, go back home,' says another. As I reflected, I realise that when reporting, I walk with a stoop now, bent from the world as if to protect myself. It's not like me. At news events, like EFF media conferences, I make myself small and will ask questions in a way that sounds to me, as I reflect, almost obsequious."

And it is not just journalists that have been at the receiving end of Malema's and the EFF's hatred. They refer to public enterprises minister and Ramaphosa confidant Pravin Gordhan as "Jamnadas", which is his middle name. In the cloak-and-dagger world of gangsters and prison numbers, "jananda" is a deliberate racial insult and a slang word for an Indian person. By doing so, they have labelled Gordhan as an outcast, a foreigner and a native from the Indian subcontinent who does not belong in South Africa.

🐦 Sunday Times @SundayTimesZA, 29 July 2019
Malema: "Jamnadas, while you are enjoying your curry at home, you must know that the #EFF has pronounced on you. We are only scared of God, we are not even scared of death. How can we be scared of Pravin?"

🐦 Floyd Shivambu @FloydShivambu, 31 Oct. 2019
The DOG OF WHITE MONOPOLY CAPITAL, Founder of the Rogue Unit, Grand Master of the CABAL, god of STRATCOM, the nepotist who's destroying State Owned Companies Jamnadas Gordhan was defeated and should pay cost for his frivolous application.

Malema and the EFF have revolutionised their social media accounts to advance their revolutionary war. In the process, the EFF has turned into a quasi-military organisation in which Malema has become the "commander-in-chief" who controls "ground forces", a "military wing" and a "student command". Malema's tweets are not mere cheap political rabble-rousing; they have consequences. He has several times ordered an army of red-clad supporters into action in cases where he detected elements of racism. Several stores have been trashed and looted by his supporters, among them Clicks and H&M.

✔ Floyd Shivambu @FloydShivambu, 13 Jan. 2018
That @hm nonsense of a clothing store is now facing consequences for its racism. All rational people should agree that the store should not be allowed to continue operating in South Africa. Well done to Fighters who physically confronted racism.

✔ Julius Sello Malema @Julius_S_Malema, 6 Sept. 2020
@Clicks_SA see you tomorrow. Fellow fighters and ground forces; ATTACK!!!

It is not as though Julius Malema has led any of these attacks himself. He was nowhere to be seen as his ground forces descended on their targets.

* * *

VBS was by far not the only benefactor of Floyd Shivambu and Julius Malema. As Shivambu was about to tie the knot in 2017, Grand Azania had less than R1 000 in its account. Other grooms would have knocked on a family door or paid the bank manager a visit. Not Shivambu. The investigative journalists at amaBhungane revealed how Shivambu fired off a WhatsApp message to connected businessman Lawrence Mulaudzi in March 2017, just a month before his wedding. Mulaudzi was in the spotlight at the Mpati Commission, which was tasked with probing allegations of wrongdoing at the Public Investment Corporation (PIC).

Mulaudzi's companies received loans of altogether R3.6 billion from the PIC.

Shivambu said in his WhatsApp message to Mulaudzi: "Heita . . . Please don't forget to activate that intervention. Am in great need." If there was any doubt whether "intervention" was a code word for money, Shivambu also sent him details of the FNB account of his slush fund, Great Azania. Two days later, Mulaudzi paid R200 000 into Grand Azania's bank account. He was honoured with a wedding invitation to the Shivambu wedding.

After the wedding, Shivambu sent this message to Mulaudzi: "Thank you very much for the assistance towards the success of the wedding. We had a very fulfilling event to welcome Makoti [the bride] wa ka Shivambu and all who partook are very happy and satisfied. I really appreciate." Mulaudzi paid another R100 000 into Grand Azania's account in August 2017 and a further R100 000 a month later.

According to amaBhungane, the payments to Shivambu were part of a pattern in which Mulaudzi made "interventions to decision-makers and powerful people to keep the funding pipeline going". The *Daily Maverick* discovered that when the businessman pocketed a R47.5 million advisory fee from a R1.37 billion PIC deal in 2018, he paid R6 million into an attorney's account for an upmarket townhouse bought by the family trust of ANC treasurer-general Zweli Mkhize.

Shivambu and Mulaudzi seem to have gone to some trouble to conceal their communication. Between December 2016 and May 2017, they met at several restaurants, bars and hotels. In the end, though, Shivambu seems to have been overcome with greed and need, and furnished the businessman with his details over the phone. Referring to the payments to Floyd Shivambu, Mulaudzi told amaBhungane: "I have a contractual obligation with a number of companies including Grand Azania, which I pay from time to time for consulting and advisory services."

Shivambu has failed to declare his income from "consulting and advisory services" to Parliament, as he was legally obliged to do. In the

2017 Parliamentary Register of MPs' Interests, Shivambu said that his salary as an MP was his only income for the year.

As Shivambu tied the knot with Siphesihle Pezi at a lavish traditional wedding, Malema had this to say: "Floyd, you must look after this lady. We don't want divorce. If you divorce this lady, you must go to the magistrate and sign on your own." The marriage didn't last long, and in 2020 *Sunday World* reported that celebrity chef Lorna Maseko, who was incidentally Shivambu's chef previously, "has moved her culinary exploits to his bedroom". A year later, she reportedly gave birth to their first child. It was Shivambu's fourth.

* * *

🐦 **amaBhungane** @amaBhungane, 5 May 2021
Politically-connected businessman Thulani Majola's company LTE Consulting made regular headlines for its role in a water project in Giyani which failed to bring water, but cost taxpayers R3-billion . . .

For decades, areas around Giyani in Limpopo, once the capital of the apartheid-era Gazankulu homeland, have been crippled by a water shortage. Residents and villagers have been forced to wash and drink from polluted and infested rivers and the area became prone to outbreaks of water-borne disease. In 2009, it was declared a disaster area and it was only in 2014 that water and sanitation minister Nomvula Mokonyane announced a billion-rand project to bring water to the area.

LTE Consulting, a company owned by tenderpreneur Thulani Majola, was awarded a R3 billion contract to deliver water to Giyani and to more than 50 villages in the region. Majola had a long-standing relationship with Mokonyane, and during her reign as Gauteng premier between 2009 and 2014, LTE bagged various large contracts.

Over three years between 2013 and 2016, Majola donated R14 million to the ANC, which might explain why he has been awarded so many government contracts in a diverse range of fields. Ahead of the 2016 municipal elections Majola donated around R10 million to various ANC entities in the months preceding the August vote. Over half the amount went to the ANC in Gauteng – Mokonyane's political home ground. According to amaBhungane: "This leaves the question of whether the payments were general sweeteners to keep politicians onside. Either way, the conflicts of interests for the politicians who accepted money from Majola – and then acted in ways that advanced his interests – appear undeniable."

Majola's motivation for giving money to the ruling party is easy to grasp, but why fund Malema and the EFF? In the run-up to the 2016 local elections, Malema campaigned in the Giyani area and said he was there "to see if the water had been delivered". At the time, *City Press* ran an exposé titled "R170m and still no water". Majola's Limpopo water project was faltering and beset with delays and escalating costs. Mokonyane's Department of Water and Sanitation claimed it had run out of money while the Treasury was said to be investigating. Billions of rand were at stake for Majola and LTE.

So, guess what happened next? Four months later, Malema became a beneficiary of Majola when the businessman deposited R500 000 into the bank account of Santaclara, owned by another Malema cousin, Jimmy Matlebyane. He is a DJ who boasted a Sandown address that was owned by Malema through his Munzhedzi Family Trust. Santaclara funds Malema's personal expenses and some EFF activities. Between 2016 and 2019, Majola paid altogether R3 million into the Santaclara account. Majola has also donated R250 000 to a company connected to EFF secretary-general Marshall Dlamini, who was a member of Parliament.

By October 2016, just two months after the municipal elections, the EFF made a U-turn and condemned the Treasury for what it said was a decision to terminate the water project. Floyd Shivambu wrote to then finance minister Pravin Gordhan, saying: "We write to demand that the process to deliver water to the people of Giyani should not be discontinued because for a very long time, the people of Giyani have [been] promised water."

Between 15 and 23 December 2016, Malema phoned Mokonyane eight times to demand that service providers be paid. A day after Malema's last call to the minister, LTE paid another R100 000 into Santaclara's account. Malema's explanation for the call was that he wanted to ensure that the workforce of the contractors got paid in December.

As the department started falling behind in payments, the EFF took its campaign to Parliament. An EFF letter, addressed to president Zuma, demanded that the contractors be paid.

Both Malema and Majola have denied any wrongdoing. The Hawks raided Majola's office in November 2020, but at the time of the writing of this book, no charges had been brought against him. The Special Investigating Unit (SIU) launched civil proceedings to recover more than R2 billion from Majola and LTE.

* * *

Early on a Wednesday morning in June 2020, eight suspects who had allegedly pillaged VBS Mutual Bank into bankruptcy were netted in Hawks raids in Gauteng and Limpopo. Among the accused were chairperson and alleged kingpin Tshifhiwa Matodzi, treasurer Phophi Mukhodobwane, chief financial officer Philip Truter, CEO Andile Ramavhunga, KPMG auditor Sipho Malaba, two non-executive directors, and a former lieutenant-general in the SAPS. They were hauled before court and charged with racketeering, theft, fraud and money laundering. They were released on R100 000 bail each.

A few months later, Philip Truter pleaded guilty in a plea agreement to all the charges and was sentenced to seven years' imprisonment. In return for a lesser sentence, he agreed to assist the state in determining how the funds from the defunct bank were plundered. Truter had control over the bank's financial system and had a fiduciary obligation to protect the bank's interest, yet he was instrumental in creating a web of fabricated deposits to expedite the looting of the bank.

✈ Pauli Van Wyk @PaulivW, 11 Mar. 2021
#VBS fixer #KabeloMatsepe was arrested along with Danny Msiza & 6 others today. Matsepe was the link between the bank & municipalities – for this, he received R35m in "fees".

According to the state, ANC Limpopo treasurer-general Danny Msiza's grubby paws were all over the plunder of VBS bank. As the looting intensified and the liquidity crises mounted, he was at the heart of a plot to cajole municipalities into investing in VBS. Standing with him in the dock was his protégé, Kabelo Matsepe, a former ANC Youth League leader in Limpopo. A former ally of Julius Malema, Matsepe allegedly received R28.9 million for his role in fleecing the bank. Both denied any unlawful conduct and pleaded not guilty.

These arrests brought to fourteen the number of former bank executives, chartered accountants, politicians, lawyers and businesspeople who face 188 counts of theft, fraud, money laundering, corruption and racketeering. Twenty municipalities had illegally invested more than R1 billion with the bank and have been able to recover only small amounts. Since then, several more people have been bagged by the Hawks. Several municipal officials and managers have also been arrested.

Why have Julius Malema, Floyd Shivambu and their frontmen and proxies not been arrested for fraud, corruption and money laundering? There is no doubt that the EFF leaders received millions through a money-laundering scheme that they used to fund their sparklicious lifestyle and advance their political aspirations. If there was any doubt whether they were knee-deep in the cesspool of malfeasance, SARS brought it to an end.

SCORPIO: VBS scandal: SARS demands R28.2m from Brian Shivambu, displays clear connection to Floyd

For years before the collapse and capture of SARS, it was the revenue service and its tax sleuths that financially crippled some of the country's most notorious gangsters. Tom Moyane brought this to an end when he destroyed SARS's ability to extract taxes from the so-called criminal economy. Since his suspension and firing in 2018 and the appointment of Edward Kieswetter as the new commissioner, SARS has attempted to rebuild its investigative ability.

In August 2021, the criminal and illicit economic activities division of SARS presented Brian Shivambu and two of his companies, Grand Azania and Sgameka Projects, with a tax bill of R28.2 million. He had not paid tax for 2016, 2017 and 2018 and incurred a host of penalties.

SARS said in two liquidation applications against Sgameka Projects and Grand Azania, filed at the High Court in Pretoria in July 2022, that the two companies "have been utilised by its director and only shareholder, Brian Shivambu, as the vehicles through which he defrauded the VBS Mutual Bank of approximately R16-million".

* * *

How many legal lives does Julius Malema have? Seldom has any politician or public figure succeeded in circumventing so many legal, financial and political difficulties. Hate speech and criminal charges against him have gone nowhere, he wriggled himself out of his tax dilemma, and for several years the National Prosecuting Authority (NPA) did not bother to put the On-Point case back on the roll.

🐦 **AfriForum** @afriforum, 19 Apr. 2018
Adv #GerrieNel: We will privately prosecute #Malema and co-accused for fraud and tender corruption.

🐦 Julius Sello Malema @Julius_S_Malema, 19 Apr. 2018
Bring it on bloody racists, you don't scare me at all. I'm born ready! No white man will decide my destiny, the poor masses of our people will . . .

Eighteen months after AfriForum's legal head Advocate Gerrie Nel threatened to privately prosecute Malema and his former co-accused for the On-Point fraud, the NPA announced that it would re-charge Limpopo businessman and Malema benefactor Lesiba Gwangwa and On-Point director Kagiso Dichabe for fraud. The acting director of public prosecutions in Pretoria, George Baloyi, said he would not charge Malema – "for now".

The role of Baloyi in the resurrection of the On-Point case evoked no confidence. He has been implicated in the hounding of and illegal arrest of forensic investigator Paul O'Sullivan and his attorney Sarah Jane Trent in 2017, which I write about in an earlier chapter. Instead of charging Malema, Baloyi added a shareholder of On-Point, Thomas Rasethaba, to the charge sheet. The only problem was that Rasethaba was dead.

It is ludicrous that Malema was not charged. The original indictment stated that Malema played a direct role in managing the criminal enterprise and that between January 2009 and November 2011 On-Point paid altogether R6 453 382.33 into his Ratanang account. In typical NPA fashion, the current case also went nowhere.

🐦 Eyewitness News @ewnupdates, 3 June 2022
Malema claims assault case against him emanates from white supremacy

Malema's tactic is consistent: deny everything, claim victimisation and racism, intimidate the complainant, and employ the best lawyers that money can buy. Not only has the NPA disregarded its constitutional imperative to charge Malema with serious crimes, but state prosecutors are also scared to take him on.

🐦 **Ferial Haffajee** @ferialhaffajee, 2 Mar. 2022

EXCLUSIVE: Malema prosecutor said to have resigned over fears of being "branded a racist"

State prosecutor Elna Smit asked her superiors to remove her from a case against Julius Malema and his bodyguard Adriaan Snyman for illegally discharging a firearm. It is said she feared that Malema would call her a racist and attempt to humiliate her during cross-examination. She was reportedly hesitant from the outset about prosecuting Malema, but the final straw was a hate speech court case that AfriForum brought against him. Malema called their advocate, who was white, the weakest lawyer he had ever dealt with and said the case was driven by racism. The case was dismissed. But the NPA refused to remove Smit, forcing her to resign.

The state alleged that Snyman passed an assault rifle to Malema during a rally in the Eastern Cape in July 2018. He then fired several shots in the air. Caught on camera, Malema was charged with the unlawful possession of a firearm, unlawful possession of ammunition, discharging a firearm in a built-up area or public place, and reckless endangerment to people or property. Snyman faced one count of contravening the Firearms Control Act.

The EFF's first reaction was (once again) one of total denial. Said then EFF spokesperson Mbuyiseni Ndlozi: "It's not a real firearm, and no bullets were fired . . . it's a toy gun, it's a toy." However, cleaners afterwards found a cartridge near the spot where Malema pulled the trigger. According to evidence in court, the cartridge matched the firearm, a Chinese-manufactured Norinco assault rifle. The EFF was forced to hand over the Norinco to police but its breechblock had been changed.

Malema's advocate Laurence Hodes SC argued that the spent cartridge could have been planted there six months before the event took place and that the gun could be a replica or an air pistol firing blanks. A police expert testified that there was a distinct difference in sound between an airgun and a real rifle. The sound on the video was that of a real gun.

The case continues and, although Malema must still testify, this might be the case that strips the rabble-rouser politician of his legal armour and make him, like the rest of us, subject to the rule of law.

Epilogue

News24 @News24, 31 July 2022
Thuli Madonsela: Do we want a mafia state?

A FRIEND WHO had read the whole manuscript of this book commented that it is "the definitive guide to how irreparably fucked up this place is". This is not how I had wanted it to be.

I am penning the final words to my book on Saturday, 8 October 2022. Before me on my computer screen, the News24 home page tells of another bloody, dark (as in no lights) and politically tumultuous week in our beloved Mzansi.

A tourist from Germany, South Africa's largest trading partner in the European Union and our third-biggest tourism market, was shot dead in an ambush as he and his compatriots were about to enter the Kruger National Park in Mpumalanga. It created another photo opportunity for police minister Bheki Cele, while tourism minister Lindiwe Sisulu held a press conference, having had to interrupt her campaign to become the candidate of the ANC's radical economic transformation (RET) faction for the party's December presidential election. She said that South Africa was safe for tourists and that only three had been killed in the country since 1994. This is a lie because there were many more.

Thirteen people were gunned down in a week of gang warfare that raged across Cape Town. Two senior gang members were shot dead in their Mercedes-Benz at a busy intersection in the city. Along the famous beach and restaurant strip in the tourism spot of Camps Bay, two men were assassinated in taxi-related violence. In the Eastern Cape, three men were killed and another three wounded in a tavern. This was just the latest in a series of tavern shootings across the country in 2022. The corpse of a 67-year-old retired banker was found next to an athletics field in Johannesburg after she left home for a jog and went missing. And in the Western Cape town of Paarl, a small white coffin draped in pink flowers was lowered into a grave, containing the body of a four-year-old girl who had gone missing two weeks earlier and who was found brutalised and dead in the veld.

There was also a message for those (few and useless) criminals who haven't acquired a gun yet. You can get one at your friendly corner police station. Three badsters walked into the Devon police station in Mpumalanga, disarmed policemen on duty, and made off with seven pistols and three rifles, which I presume were R1 or R4 assault rifles. The low-scale civil war raging in South Africa is fought with police guns on both sides.

The man who would give Cyril Ramaphosa a run for his money for filling the toughest job in the country, Eskom CEO André de Ruyter, doesn't move without bodyguards because of death threats. And it ain't because unhappy South Africans want to lynch him in the aftermath of the worst bout of load shedding yet, but because he is the driving force behind probing and exposing crime syndicates in Eskom. The criminals, operating hand in glove with corrupt officials, sabotage operations and sell the stolen goods back to the energy supplier. Operating on the fringes of Eskom are a coal mafia, a trucking mafia and a fuel-oil mafia, to name but a few.

And what did our president have to say about Eskom in the first days of October 2022? He had a lot on his plate with the ANC elective conference looming large in December. He needed the support of the ANC's Eastern Cape provincial structures and therefore opened a crèche in Mbizana's Qungebe village where he cuddled pre-schoolers and, in another photo opportunity, read them a story about Nelson Mandela.

The Cabinet had in the same week approved a new board for Eskom and Ramaphosa said he was confident that it had the right mixture of expertise and experience to solve the country's energy problems. He has promised the fixing of Eskom since 2015 when Jacob Zuma appointed him as the head of the government's "war room" to oversee the turnaround of Eskom. He infamously announced in September that year that "in another 18 months to two years, you will forget the challenges at Eskom ever happened".

After clinching the presidency of the country in February 2018, Ramaphosa has repeatedly said that his government is urgently addressing the energy crisis. Almost five years on, South Africa has experienced from January to October 2022 already 1 949 hours (81 days) of load shedding, compared with 1 153 hours over 48 days in 2021, and 844 hours over 35 days in 2020. I have no doubt that Ramaphosa genuinely wants to fix Eskom and accepts that the solution lies in renewable energy, but what boggles the mind is his unwavering faith in a coal fundamentalist like energy minister Gwede Mantashe, who exists somewhere in an parallel coal galaxy. In the past year, he has suggested setting up an Eskom 2 (I kid you not, another Eskom, run by the government) and a nuclear power reactor in the Eastern Cape (it will take at least ten years to build).

Gauteng, the heartbeat of our economy, has also become the victim of water restrictions. Even some hospitals have run dry. At one Johannesburg hospital, doctors and staff were told to bring water to work to flush toilets and help prevent infections. This happened against the background of the ANC's seizure of power from a Democratic Alliance-led coalition in the Johannesburg metro. It brought the city's mouthwatering R70 billion budget and its accompanying procurements yet again within the grasp of the ruling party's deployed cadres.

While Jacob Zuma had brought us to the edge of the abyss where lurked the mafia and a criminal state, Cyril Ramaphosa initially managed to pull us back from the brink. Much happened in the first year of his rule. Spy boss Arthur Fraser went, and the High-Level Review Panel into the State Security Agency uncovered a rat's nest of fraud and corruption. The president fired SARS commissioner Tom Moyane and appointed Edward Kieswetter in his place, while the Nugent Commission delved into Moyane's reign of misconduct and identified a host of malfeasant officials who had to go. Prosecutions boss Shaun Abrahams became part of state-capture history after South Africa's highest court ruled that he had been unlawfully appointed; while a retired Constitutional Court judge found that his henchmen, Nomgcobo Jiba and Lawrence Mrwebi, were unfit to hold office. Ramaphosa booted them out. To much acclaim, Shamila Batohi was appointed as head of the National Prosecuting Authority, Godfrey Lebeya as the head of the Hawks, and Peter Jacobs as divisional commissioner of police Crime Intelligence. Ramaphosa strengthened the powers and capacity of the Special Investigating Unit and announced the setting-up of the Investigating Directorate within the NPA to prosecute high-level corruption. The first hearings of the State Capture Commission under the chairmanship of Judge Raymond Zondo commenced in August 2018.

But the president failed to remove his Zuma-appointed police commissioner, Khehla Sitole, despite being aware that he was implicated in the attempted grabber procurement in the run-up to the ANC elective conference in 2017. It took Ramaphosa four years to give the commissioner a pat on the shoulder and allow him to retire early with full benefits.

Ramaphosa pussyfooted Arthur Fraser into the job of Correctional Services commissioner despite knowing that the former spymaster faced allegations of serious crimes committed during his reign at the State Security Agency. While he was in charge of prisons, Fraser unlawfully (as it stands, pending an appeal) granted medical parole to Zuma after the Constitutional Court had sentenced the former president to fifteen months' imprisonment. More recently, Fraser laid criminal charges against Ramaphosa and others that emanated from the theft of a pile of US dollars at the president's Phala Phala farm in Limpopo.

In his first term, Ramaphosa also failed to deal decisively with the SSA, which had been captured during the Zuma years. And, most damningly, he appointed as his minister of police Bheki Cele, despite the latter being implicated in possible fraud and corruption when he was Zuma's commissioner of police. These lamentable decisions came back to haunt Ramaphosa when police and law enforcement, starved of adequate intelligence and a coherent strategy, looked on as the violence and looting of the July 2021 unrest set KwaZulu-Natal and Gauteng alight.

Is South Africa a mafia state? And are we becoming a failed state? When your two top Treasury officials warn that this is where the country is heading, you should sit up and take note. Treasury director-general Dondo Mogajane warned in March 2022 that South Africa was beginning to show the signs of a failed state, in part because of a culture of greed and entitlement among the country's politicians and public servants. I referred earlier in the book to the warning by acting Treasury director-general Ismail Momoniat that South Africa might be emerging as a mafia state.

Surging crime in South Africa has now reached levels where it poses an existential threat to our democratic institutions, economy and people. The country has a thin veneer of order and stability but underneath lurks a dark web: a self-sustaining, self-protecting and self-expanding criminal economy. Left unchecked, organised crime will continue to seriously impair South Africa's reputation and development, undermine the rule of law and the integrity of the state, exacerbate inequality and discourage investment.

So said the director of the highly respected Global Initiative Against Transnational Organised Crime (GI-TOC), Mark Shaw, in a September 2022 report on the state of organised crime in South Africa. In assessing the levels of organised crime in the 193 member states of the United Nations, GI-TOC found that it had spread like wildfire across the globe. In South Africa, government institutions that are supposed to fight organised crime have been infiltrated because of corruption and state capture and, as a result, criminal networks are flourishing.

South Africa now ranks 19th on GI-TOC's global criminal index out of 193 countries. The Democratic Republic of Congo tops the list, followed by Mexico, Nigeria, Iran, Kenya and Turkey. We have surged ahead of all our neighbours and countries like Tanzania, Uganda, Ghana, Angola, Zambia, Russia, China and Brazil.

The Global Initiative says South African organised crime is connected, diverse, embedded, entrepreneurial and violent. The organisation assessed fifteen criminal markets in the country, ranging from illicit drugs, illegal firearms, extortion and organised robbery to wildlife smuggling, illegal mining, cybercrime and financial crimes. Ten of the categories are increasing while five are stable, three at a high level. None is declining. According to Shaw: "It is not an insurmountable challenge: the problem can be tackled. With the right leadership, long-term strategic vision and resources, and with a systemic institutional overhaul of its crime-fighting agencies, South Africa can and will defeat organised crime."

I think it is premature to label South Africa a criminal or failed state. But the next few years will be telling. If the candidate of the RET faction – whether it's Nkosazana Dlamini-Zuma, Zweli Mkhize or Lindiwe Sisulu – comes to power, the corruption taps that Ramaphosa closed in the aftermath of Jacob Zuma's debauched rule will be reopened. An RET president will throw the findings and recommendations of the State Capture Commission out of the window, and we might see the likes of Arthur Fraser, Brian Molefe and Lucky Montana appointed once again in positions of great power and influence in the public sector.

If Ramaphosa survives the RET onslaught and the fallout from the Phala Phala catastrophe, he faces a challenging few years. He needs to get rid of Bheki Cele, revive police Crime Intelligence, ensure the State Security Agency fulfils its mandate of safeguarding the Republic and its people, boost the ranks and budget of the Investigating Directorate, and recruit top legal minds into the NPA. And we cannot have the Hawks operating at less than half its capacity.

Ramaphosa lacked courage and urgency in his first term as president. He now needs to change the course of this poisoned land. If he fails, we will again be at the mercy of the keepers.

Author's note

THIS IS A book I never thought I'd write. In fact, there was a time when I thought I'd never write anything ever again.

What happened in a rather posh Belgian restaurant at Cape Town's V&A Waterfront on 6 February 2021 was inexcusable. I messed up, became toxic, and devastated those I love and hold dear.

For those that missed the sorry episode, this is what happened. On that day, I had lunch at the Waterfront. It was a boozy affair that left me with a bill for several bottles of wine and twenty shots of tequila. When it came to paying, my credit card was declined. I had R1 000 in my pocket, but the restaurant manager wanted payment in full. I went off to look for an ATM and was arrested, charged with theft and thrown in the cells for the night. I was released the next morning – minus the R1 000. I was incensed about my arrest because an inability to pay a restaurant bill is not theft or a criminal offence (the state subsequently withdrew the case). I decided to write a story for the *Daily Maverick*. I should never have done this, as my memory was muddled. I believed the police had stolen the R1 000. It was wrong and I lied. The *Daily Maverick* investigated the incident and found that I had lied about various other things as well. I accept this and deeply regret misleading the public and damaging the *Daily Maverick*'s journalistic integrity.

In the days thereafter, I went off to lick my wounds. I was convinced my career was over. I sat for days feeling sorry for myself. I was too ashamed to show my face. If only I had a delete button in my life to erase those few hours at the Waterfront. How do you get up and carry on after something like that – especially if you are a journalist who has just violated the trust and faith the public have put in you?

Amid the madness came a voice from journalist Unathi Kondile called "The curious case of journalist Jacques Pauw". This is an extract:

431

"The first time I heard his name was in the early '90s, when my grand-mother relived the story of how she came to learn of her son's (uncle Sizwe) death. It was the *Vrye Weekblad's* reporter, Jacques Pauw, who narrated the details of how Dirk Coetzee's Vlakplaas unit abducted, tortured, shot and burnt Uncle Sizwe's body to an ash before scattering it over the Komati River.

"'If it was not for Jacques, we would have never known what happened to Sizwe!' she would say. They kept in touch. Met once or twice. Pauw held a special place in my grandmother's heart.

"The Jacques Pauw my grandmother knew and the one on Twitter did not reconcile in my mind. Things really fell apart for Jacques Pauw last week, when the *Daily Maverick* published his lie-laden opinion piece. We have since learnt that his version of events was not entirely accurate. He has since apologised. But where he overstepped the line was in using a media platform that trusted him to advance his lies.

"In journalism, we are often taught that you are only as good as your last story. Is this how Jacques Pauw will be remembered? I have often wondered about the likes of Pauw . . . journalists who were active during the height of apartheid, who also contributed to the TRC. Some journalists never recovered from working with that kind of content. Some, like Pauw, by way of catharsis, wrote books like *Into the Heart of Darkness: Confessions of Apartheid's Assassins*.

"I cannot begin to imagine what Pauw is going through and has been through. It is easier to be engulfed by a sense of entitlement and vengefulness when you have gone through hell and back, using your pen for justice. Writing that fake opinion piece was spurred on by a similar kind of anger? "How dare they put me in a police cell!", "How dare they treat me like apartheid police did?" and so on.

"Make no mistake, I am not speaking for Pauw. I am trying to under-stand how someone who has experienced police brutality at its worst can pull out the most vindictive story from a mere drunken misunder-standing. Think about it. What is the image of police authority in the mind of someone like Pauw? What does it trigger? Add alcohol. Rethink.

"Be that as it may, I write this to express my sadness in seeing one of the best go down like this. It is no wonder the good die young, to prevent us from ever seeing what they might have turned out to be. Let us not celebrate the downfall of Pauw."

*   *   *

It was, among others, this piece by Unathi that made me realise that it wasn't yet time to fade away, but that I had to stand up and continue writing. Much of what I had written in *The President's Keepers* was proven true at the State Capture Commission, but it was just the beginning, and I was not nearly finished yet.

I went for therapy, vowed to drink less, and started writing. The result is this book. I trust that the facts speak for themselves.

Acknowledgments

I AM GRATEFUL to the Henry Nxumalo Fund, in partnership with Wits Journalism, for a generous grant that enabled me to do extensive research for this book. The vast bulk of my information and material came from a host of officials, officers and administrators in our law-enforcement agencies. Some were former employees; many were still employed. Many spoke to me on condition of anonymity, and they will remain unnamed.

For those who have read the manuscript or advised me – Anneliese Burgess, Max du Preez, Jessica Pitchford and Riaan de Villiers – thank you so much. Many friends encouraged and invigorated me with their support, love and understanding.

I had a tried-and-trusted team at Tafelberg: thank you to publisher Erika Oosthuysen and her troop. A special word of thanks to editor Russell Martin, who once again brought clarity and elegance to the script.

I acknowledge the dedicated contribution of attorneys Willem de Klerk and Charl du Plessis – whose work might not yet be over!

I have relied heavily on the published work of some of this country's most distinguished journalists, among them Sam Sole, Marianne Thamm, Pieter-Louis Myburgh, Pauli van Wyk, Thanduxolo Jika, Ferial Haffajee, Pieter du Toit, Kyle Cowan, Caryn Dolley, Greg Ardé, Stephen Grootes, Marianne Merten, Mandy Wiener, Jessica Bezuidenhout and Sipho Masondo – to name a handful.

I couldn't have written this without the understanding and love of my wife, Sam. Thank you for giving me, once again, the space and time to write this.

Bibliography

CHAPTER 1

TimesLIVE
- Book reveals Zuma's 'darkest secret', 29 October 2017
- The President's Keepers will not be retracted, publisher tells SSA, 6 November 2017
- President's Keepers compromises the security of the state says spy agency, 3 November 2017
- Steer clear of 'pirated and hacked' copy of book, publishers of The President's Keepers urge, 4 November 2017
- State Security Agency tries to block Jacques Pauw's book again, 9 November 2017
- We won't withdraw anything says The President's Keepers publisher, 7 November 2017
- Axe these listeriosis legionnaires, 11 March 2018
- 'The President's Keepers': SARS to consider laying charges over exposé, 3 November 2017
- Pauw book launch cancelled after power outage, 8 November 2017
- Jacob Zuma 'spooked' Cyril Ramaphosa's campaign, 10 March 2019

Daily Maverick
- The Principal Agent Network (PAN) dossier, Part 1: Zuma and Mahlobo knew about Arthur Fraser's rogue intelligence programme, 5 December 2017
- The Principal Agent Network (PAN) dossier, Part 2: Bugging the auditors – dumb and dumber, 6 December 2017
- Spooks and spies: The PAN progamme, Arthur Fraser and eight years of investigations, 9 November 2017
- President's Keepers: Why Tom Moyane might have a legal duty to publish President Jacob Zuma's tax records, 8 November 2017
- The President's Keepers: South Africa's fastest-selling book ever, 8 November 2017
- President's Keepers' Jacques Pauw raided – but why now?, 28 February 2018
- Scorpio: The curious case of ANC benefactor Robert Huang, a never-ending investigation and billions owed to SARS, 23 January 2018
- Trainspotter: Keeping the president – Securocrats on the rampage, 10 November 2017
- Jacques Pauw: SARS' court application against writer 'conceded the truth' – NB Publishers, 20 December 2017
- South Africa: President's Keepers – Why Tom Moyane might have a legal duty to publish President Jacob Zuma's tax records, 8 November 2017
- Analysis: ANC leadership race – still not about hearts and minds, but political alignments and vested interests, 30 October 2017
- Celebrate the good while addressing the bad in journalism, 10 November 2017

News 24
- Jacques Pauw wrong about my family – Arthur Fraser, 6 November 2017
- I won't be silenced: Kasrils hits back at 'intimidation' by security agency's Fraser, 7 December 2017
- Video: Hawks raid home of author Jacques Pauw, 28 February 2018
- As it happened – Jacques Pauw's #ThePresidentsKeepers launch interrupted by power cut, 8 November 2017
- Pirate copy of President's Keepers goes viral on social media, 4 November 2017

Mail & Guardian
- Sunday Independent editor defends paper's probe into Jacques Pauw's sources, 8 December 2017
- State security agency says Zuma book must be recalled, 3 November 2017
- Hawks leave with 'insignificant' papers after raid on Pauw's property, 28 February 2018
- Ramaphosa loses court bid to halt publishing of potentially damaging story, 2 September 2017
- The President's Keepers: State capture, white vindication, 14 December 2017

The Guardian
- South African security services move to ban exposé of Jacob Zuma government, 7 November 2017

Business Day
- Cyril Ramaphosa reads The President's Keepers to see if SSA's action is 'credible', 16 November 2017

SABC News
- DA calls for an investigation into the book the President's Keepers, 4 November 2017

Polity
- Principal Agent Network created to get ANC back in power in Western Cape – Pauw, 7 November 2017

eNCA
- First 20,000 'The President's Keepers' books sold, 5 November 2017
- The President's Keepers: Arthur Fraser's family considering legal action, 6 November 2022
- Newspaper alleges Gordhan is behind Pauw's explosive book, 10 December 2017
- Detective removed from Zuma book case – Pauw, 12 December 2017
- Watch: The President's Keepers launch abandoned, 8 December 2022

Al Jazeera
- Are South Africa's anti-corruption crusaders racist?, 13 November 2017

Politicsweb
- Sunday Independent planning to expose Jacques Pauw's alleged sources, 8 December 2012
- Pirate copy of President's Keepers goes viral on social media, 4 November 2017

Independent Online
- Pauw facing lawsuits over book, 10 December, 2017
- Moodley says Pauw's book is a sham, 19 November 2019

Huffington Post
- The President's Keepers: South Africa's fastest-selling book ever, 8 November 2017

CHAPTER 2

Business Day
- Cabinet's newcomer, Bongani Bongo: a relative unknown from Mpumalanga, 17 October 2017

News24
- Who is the new state security minister Bongani Bongo?, 17 October 2017
- South Africa: State security minister-designate Bongani Bongo to be sworn into office, 18 October 2017
- Zuma appoints Inspector-General of Intelligence, 13 March 2017
- Newsmaker: The snake that eats other snakes, 4 December 2016
- Dintwe can't be trusted with state secrets – Fraser, 15 April 2018
- Spy watchdog's oversight powers undermined by SSA and Arthur Fraser, Zondo Commission hears, 21 April 2021

Mail & Guardian
- Arthur Fraser vs Inspector General of Intelligence in court over security clearance, 17 April 2022

Business Day
- A full plate for David Mahlobo in the Department of Energy, 17 October 2017
- Arthur Fraser knew he was being investigated, says intelligence inspector, 17 April 2018

Daily Maverick
- Dr No: Inspector-General Setlhomamaru Dintwe, silent sentinel who stood his ground against state capture, 25 April 2021
- When guardians refuse to be guarded, or, the curious case of one Arthur Fraser, 16 April 2018

Sunday Times
- Top spy's own rogue network exposed, 3 December 2017

City Press
- In hot water for trying to keep the office of the Inspector-General going, 12 Nov 2016
- SSA boss Arthur Fraser threatened me, says Inspector-General of Intelligence, 11 April 2018

eNCA
- Inspector General of Intelligence's security clearance reinstated, 19 April 2018

CHAPTER 3

Mail & Guardian
- Many gifts, but no Guptas or payments declared by Zuma, 13 November 2017

News24
- Security company paid Zuma over R1.5m, Zondo Commission hears, 11 March 2021
- Exclusive: How a crooked cop tried to lock me up, by Jacques Pauw, 3 May 2018
- Officer, magistrate in Pauw case probed for suspected misconduct, 14 December 2017
- Pauw 'relieved' by no further threats of arrest, 12 December 2017

Politicsweb
- Docket has been opened against Jacques Pauw – NPA, 8 December 2017

Daily Maverick
- Dons have KZN in their grip – and don of dons Jacob Zuma has the tightest grip, 18 April 2022
- The hands that rocked the securocrats' cradle, 13 December 2017
- The public protector's quest for Zuma tax records is a farce – here's why, 20 November 2019
- Analysis: Why are South Africa's securocrats so jumpy over Jacques Pauw & Ronnie Kasrils?, 13 December 2017

The Citizen
- Metrorail collapses despite billions spent, as 'Zuma ally' Roy Moodley threatens legal action, 16 November 2018
- Zuma's 'pet cop' has been taken off case against Jacques Pauw, 12 December 2017

Independent Online
- #ThePresidentsKeepers: A taxing time for Zuma, 9 November 2017

AmaBhungane
- New twist in Durban's 'unending contract' security tender saga, 15 November 2017

TimesLIVE
- Durban cop removed from the Jacques Pauw probe, 12 December 2017
- Rage against moneyed cop, 22 August 2010

CHAPTERS 4 & 5

News24
- Exclusive: ANC delegate and Zuma 'keeper' Moodley scores Prasa millions, 15 December 2017
- Roy Moodley was like Prasa's own Gupta, Zondo Commission hears, 12 March 2020
- Lucky Montana threatens Pieter-Louis Myburgh with possible beating, 4 May 2018
- Popo Molefe explains perils of Prasa locomotive deal, maintains trains were 'too tall', 15 July 2021
- I intend to lay criminal charges against Zondo, says former Prasa boss Lucky Montana, 27 June 2022
- Zondo calls for new inquiry into how SA's passenger rail was left on brink of collapse, 22 June 2022
- High court sets aside R4.5 billion Prasa security contract with Siyangena Technologies, 8 October 2020
- Lawyer forks out R25m for Montana's mansions, 4 October 2015
- SARS to grab Lucky Montana's property, 20 November 2019
- Legal team at Prasa had no control over certain contracts, commission hears, 17 March 2020
- Lucky Montana withheld contracts from Prasa board, inquiry told, 13 March 2020
- Resignations, dismissals and suspensions as Prasa nabs staff linked to dodgy contracts, 20 July 2022
- Off the rails: Prasa loses over R4bn to vandalism and sabotage, CEO aims to boost security, 6 July 2021

TimesLIVE
- Lucky Montana blames 'corrupt' Popo Molefe for collapse of Prasa, 17 April 2021
- Zuma, Ramaphosa and ANC stood by while Prasa was plundered, says Zondo, 22 June 2022
- Hawks failed to follow the money in Prasa-Siyangena tender, says whistleblower, 25 August 2022
- Hawks must answer for inaction over looting at Prasa – Zondo, 30 June 2020
- Popo Molefe: 'ANC top six ignored widespread corruption at Prasa', 29 June 2020
- Justice Malala: Now Zuma and his cronies want to crush those who speak out, 6 November 2017
- Prasa Group CEO Zolani Matthews placed on precautionary suspension, 19 November 2021

Mail & Guardian
- Zondo: Prasa and SAA whistleblowers needed protection, 9 January 2022
- Prasa eyes iced company for its billions, 12 July 2019
- Prasa waiting for court order to secure return of 23 tall locomotives – Ramatlakane, 30 March 2022

Open Secrets
- Unaccountable 00023: How Prasa was looted and left for scrap
- Unaccountable 00029: Roy Moodley – Mr Prasa?
- Unaccountable Case File 00030: Sfiso Buthelezi: The board chair who derailed Prasa
- Unaccountable 00026: Vossloh: The German railway giant that derailed Prasa
- Unaccountable 00024: Auswell 'tall trains' Mashaba: The middleman who derailed Prasa
- Unaccountable 00010: Jacob Zuma: comrade in arms
- The enablers: The bankers, accountants and lawyers that cashed in on state capture

Daily Maverick
- It's now Lucky Montana against the world: Ex-Prasa CEO defies mountain of evidence against him, 20 April 2021
- Brian Molefe's tall tales of state capture, 13 March 2021

- Commission hears sorry tale of ministers ignoring MPs, papering over Prasa cracks – and the late AG Makwetu's damning affidavit, 2 February 2021
- Prasa's ex-CEO Lucky Montana joins the state capture commission conspiracy club, 17 April 2021
- The full story: Zondo Commission testimony fills key gaps in Lucky Montana's R45m 'bribery' scandal, 3 July 2020
- Lucky Montana questions Zondo on bias during this week's Prasa testimony before State Capture Commission, 3 July 2020
- Chief Justice calls for special commission to investigate Prasa's implosion, 23 June 2022
- Gravy trains: R500m from failed Prasa locomotives deal 'fraudulently' funnelled to trust, private accounts and properties, 3 March 2020
- Come on baby, do the locomotion: Prasa's too-tall trains under the hammer, 23 July 2019
- 'Hawks' wanted R500m from me, claims former Prasa boss Lucky Montana during commission testimony, 10 May 2021
- Following the money: Lucky Montana, Prasa and a R25m question, 3 May 2020
- Prasa chair Leonard Ramatlakane gets the facts wrong, 5 February 2021
- Matshela Koko cries conspiracy over Gupta-links charge, 4 December 2020

Sunday Times
- Prasa 'wasting millions' to sack executives after court rulings, 24 April 2022
- Prasa chair embroiled in fallout from unlawful R4.5bn contract, 14 September 2022

Engineering News
- PRASA audit identifies 3 000 ghost employees, 1 February 2022

Independent Online
- Molefe manufactured facts to make Prasa look dysfunctional – Montana, 16 April 2021

The Citizen
- Popo Molefe explains perils of Prasa locomotive deal, maintains trains were 'too tall', 16 April 2021
- Fired whistleblower tells Zondo how she was hounded out of Prasa, 23 February 2021

EWN
- Popo Molefe: Montana misled Prasa board about R2.4bn Braamfontein project, 7 May 2019

Public Protector
- *Derailed*: Public Protector investigation report, 24 August 2015

State Capture Commission
- Testimony of Transnet board chairperson, Dr Popo S Molefe, 7 May 2019
- Testimony of Transnet board chairperson, Dr Popo S Molefe, 12 March 2020
- Testimony of Transnet board chairperson, Dr Popo S Molefe, 13 June 2020
- Testimony of forensic auditor Ryan Sacks, 16 July 2021
- Testimony: Former Minister of Transport, Ms Dipuo Peters, 22 February 2021
- Testimony of Prasa head of legal risk Martha Ngoye, 22 February 2021
- Testimony: former Prasa CEO Lucky Montana, 16 April 2021
- Testimony: former Prasa CEO Lucky Montana, 20 April 2021
- Testimony: former Prasa CEO Lucky Montana, 3 May 2021
- Testimony: former Prasa CEO Lucky Montana, 10 May 2021
- Testimony: Director of Swifambo Rail, Mr Auswell Mashaba, 24 February 2021
- Testimony: former Prasa manager Tiro Holele, 1 June 2021
- Affidavit submitted to commission: Roy Moodley
- Affidavit submitted to commission: Popo Molefe
- Affidavit submitted to commission: Lt-Gen. Godfrey Lebeya
- Final Report on Prasa, 20 June 2022

City Press
- Zuma buddies score R80 million, 31 January 2016

GroundUp
- #PRASALeaks: Werksmans reports (2018 leak)
- #PRASALeaks: Treasury reports (2017 leak)

Business Day
- Zuma and Ramaphosa stood by while Prasa was plundered, says Zondo, 22 June 2022

Moneyweb
- Prasa malfeasance and maladministration go back a long time, 27 June 2022

Amluxury.co.za/am-lodge-luxury-safari-lodge/
- Website of AM Lodge, Hoedspruit

SABC News
- State capture inquiry hears about Montana's alleged spending spree, 3 July 2020

CHAPTERS 6, 7 & 8

News24
- Adriaan Basson: Connecting the dots of the Zupta fightback, 19 August 2019
- Analysis: Big political battle lies ahead as the outline of a 'new Scorpions' unit takes shape, 11 August 2020
- 'Porn-cop', who once sent graphic videos to detectives, to head Hawks in North West, 18 December 2018
- Steinhoff submitted 'malicious' report to Hawks, 13 March 2018
- Steinhoff: Parly hears why the Hawks can't interrogate Jooste, 30 August 2018
- 'The honeymoon is over', warns impatient Hawks head Lebeya, 15 June 2018
- R73.5m spent on 'Operation Clever' probe into medical school admissions, UKZN reveals, 8 February 2021
- 'Unlawful occupation': Prince Mokotedi calls for Hawks boss Godfrey Lebeya to retire, 31 January 2020
- Analysis: Captured and constrained: Ramaphosa goes from ruthless to rudderless, 14 February 2020
- Analysis: The fightback: Ramaphosa's enemies within the ANC, 31 January 2020
- Crime stats: More than 6 400 people murdered in SA in just three months, over 40% killed by guns, 19 August 2022
- Top cop looking into PPE procurement 'definitely' poisoned – Files, laptop 'removed' after his death, 13 December 2021
- Senzo Meyiwa murder: Bheki Cele says there's 'much more to come', 27 October 2020
- State capture inquiry: 'All hell broke loose' when Ntlemeza took over as Hawks head – Booysen, 3 May 2019
- Victory for General Shadrack Sibiya as court orders police to reinstate him, 16 May 2022
- Exposed: Barry who? The Zambian man behind SA's 'Black Twitter CIC', 18 January 2019
- Ace Magashule's charges are 'very serious' and he should not trivialise them – court hears, 26 May 2021

Daily Dispatch
- Anger over raid on top Hawks cop, 17 August 2017
- Top cop told to give up R500m fraud dockets, 6 January 2018
- Hawks officers face probe, 22 August 2017

Sunday Times
- Cut the deadwood from senior police ranks urgently, Mr President, 5 December 2021
- SA has been brought to its knees by a tired, soulless government that shows no signs of stopping the rot, 22 May 2022

Daily Maverick
- South Africa is not (yet) a failed state, and the downward slide can be halted, 20 April 2022
- What Zuma's supporters tell us about where the #FightBack faction is at, 6 February 2020
- Anwa Dramat will be remembered for being on the right side of history, 13 April 2019
- Operation Clean Audit: Scopa hears directors-general are not reporting corruption, 13 March 2018
- Sexual offences unit head tells Cele of bullying and humiliation by senior officer, 7 February 2019
- South Africa owes those who paid a great personal price for fighting against state capture, 1 October 2019
- To rebuild South Africa's investigative capacity, disband Hawks, 24 June 2019
- State capture inquiry: 'All hell broke loose' when Ntlemeza took over as Hawks head – Booysen, 3 May 2019
- #StateCaptureInquiry: Ntlemeza was central to state capture project – Gordhan, 20 November 2018
- The full slight of the law: South Africa's demise is enabled by rot from the top, police inertia and ceaseless tides of violence, 22 September 2021
- Death squads & covert units: Nathi Nhleko's not-so-hidden hand in state capture to be revealed, 27 March 2019
- McBride to tell Zondo Commission about police 'death squad', 6 September 2018
- Want an illegal gun in Western Cape? Not a problem, 21 February 2021
- Battle lines have been drawn between SAPS factions, and we are the casualties, 6 July 2021
- To serve and endanger: Corrupt cops are South Africa's greatest security threat, 29 July 2021
- Police are still arming criminals, despite 'plans' to stop the scourge, 7 February 2022

- Inside a police smuggling scandal: 175 missing firearms, increased inspections and a suicide, 23 February 2022
- Clear and present danger: Rogue cop unit could subvert Western Cape police service unless shut down, 24 June 2022
- Criminal cases involving R1.5-trillion: Hawks take stock under Godfrey Lebeya's watch, 23 August 2022
- Shadrack Sibiya has a right to justice against the state capture enablers still jammed in the system, 8 November 2018
- Johan Booysen confirms the nightmare reign of Berning Ntlemeza, 3 May 2019
- The case against Ace: Why Magashule may not end up behind bars soon, 26 February 2022
- Ace Magashule's corruption case offers hints of the challenges to prosecuting state capture crimes, 21 February 2022

TimesLIVE
- Wanted: Finance sleuths to rebuild Hawks arsenal, 16 September 2018
- Former Steinhoff CEO Markus Jooste 'relaxing in Hermanus' as Hawks dither, 31 August 2018
- Hawks officers face probe, 22 August 2017
- Zandile Gumede pleads not guilty as R320m corruption trial gets under way, 22 August 2022

Business Day
- Editorial: Finally, a taste of justice over state capture, 22 November 2019
- Editorial: The end of accountability, 6 August 2020
- Editorial: While Germany tackles Steinhoff, SA drags its feet, 9 March 2021
- Editorial: Your game, Shamila Batohi, 11 June 2020
- Fred Khumalo: Corruption knows no pigmentation, 29 October 2020
- Gareth van Onselen: The age of stupid ANC money, 22 September 2021
- Hawks 'don't have the budget' for Steinhoff probe, 4 March 2021
- Hawks await information from abroad in Steinhoff probe, MPs told, 6 July 2021
- Hawks firing on half its cylinders, says Godfrey Lebeya, 16 March 2021
- Letter: Crooks abound as cops sleep, 30 January 2020
- Markus Jooste guns for secret PwC report, 17 September 2020
- PIC to take legal action to force Steinhoff to release PwC report, 3 September 2019
- Steinhoff bankrolls Hawks probe into itself, 11 July 2020
- The state's slow dance with Markus Jooste, 5 November 2020
- This is why the Hawks have been the 'least effective' of all the Steinhoff regulators, 30 August 2020
- Why SA's most wanted have nothing to fear from the justice system, 15 July 2021
- Politics Live: Let's go through the three charges the Hawks want Gordhan to face and his defence, 25 August 2016
- Anthony Butler: Rating Ramaphosa, 9 September 2021
- Justice Malala: How Ramaphosa can save himself – and maybe even SA, 24 November 2021
- SA 'in danger of being a mafia state,' says Momoniat, 24 October 2021

Mail & Guardian
- Hawks colonel: 'My own people are plotting against me', 30 November 2016
- Latest crime statistics: Murder, kidnapping and commercial crimes increase, 18 February 2022
- Molefe, Singh released on R50 000 bail in Transnet R93m corruption case, 29 August 2022
- Panday's close family bailed as World Cup case heads to high court, 7 May 2021
- Jacob Zuma and the untouchable Mr Panday, 1 October 2015
- Panday indictment for Fifa fraud becomes a family affair, 9 February 2021
- Hawks boss: I was 'set up' to silence corruption investigations, 29 April 2015

Parliamentary Monitoring Group
- DPCI: Turnaround strategy on high profile cases, 15 August 2018
- Hawks current cases, 13 March 2018
- Report of the Portfolio Committee on Police on the 2021/22 budget vote, 12 May 2021

Politicsweb
- Named, shamed: MPs who killed the Scorpions, unlocked gates for Zuptas, 19 July 2017

Biznews
- Paul O'Sullivan: Lucky Montana: a professional criminal & a liar – And what of Major General Khana?, 15 January 2021
- Why Hawks are beyond symptomatic treatment – Paul Hoffman, 20 September 2018

Financial Mail
- Rob Rose: The bats on Markus Jooste's tail, 6 September 2018

- Analysis: Jooste hit with R122m fine for warning ex-Springbok prop, chauffeur to sell Steinhoff, 30 October 2020
- Rob Rose: If 8-million pieces of evidence can go missing . . ., 8 March 2021
- Forget Zuma, it was Gary Porritt who pioneered Stalingrad, 15 July 2021

ISS Today (Institute for Security Studies)
- South Africa's Hawks are preparing to fly, 1 October 2019
- ISS Today: How to free South Africa's police after state capture, 6 March 2018
- SAPS needs freedom from interference and streamlined management to address critical failures, 28 July 2021

Independent Online
- Ex-Hawks boss tried to protect his rape accused 'daddy' Timothy Omotoso, 20 December 2020
- Hawks head confident staff shortage challenges will not hinder investigations, 4 October 2021

The Citizen
- I was never involved in Meyiwa murder investigation – General Sibiya, 27 February 2018

City Press
- Former Hawks head guilty of disregarding witness' rights, 24 October 2021

Helen Suzman Foundation
- Illicit financial flows – Part III: Laws and institutions, 19 October 2018

eNCA
- Nigerian pastor had senior Hawks member in his pocket, court hears, 4 May 2017

SABC News
- Tonight with Jane Dutton: Interview with General Khana, 16 December 2018

EWN
- Lebeya: Hawks need more investigators to deal with its 20 736 cases, 4 October 2021

Businesstech
- These crimes are worse than ever in South Africa, 19 August 2022

State Capture Commission
- Testimony of Maj-Gen. Johan Booysen, 17 and 18 April 2019 and 3 May 2019

CHAPTERS 9, 10 & 11

State Capture Commission
- Final report: Crime Intelligence, 22 June 2022
- Testimony by Colonel Dhajanaya Naidoo, 30 September & 1 October 2019
- Testimony by Colonel Kobus Roelofse, 17–20 September 2019

News24
- Grabbing at thin air: Politics, internal squabbles cripple SAPS Crime Intelligence, 29 March 2019
- Crime Intelligence: Night of the long knives sees Peter Jacobs fall, 4 March 2021
- Crime Intelligence's decade of crisis, 18 January 2021
- Questionable intelligence reports had potential to 'destabilise the country' – Zondo report, 23 June 2022
- Exclusive: Cops splurge R100m on spy technology they cannot use, 15 June 2021
- Exclusive: Standoff in Crime Intelligence: Factionalism, racism and 'untouchables', 21 December 2018
- Peter Jacobs scores court victory in battle for the heart of Crime Intelligence, 17 March 2021
- Police in crisis: Inside Bheki Cele's stunning dressing down of top cop Khehla Sitole, 6 May 2021
- Suspended Crime Intelligence boss Peter Jacobs warns of shadowy spy 'plot', 10 February 2021
- The fight for control of Crime Intelligence: Jacobs and Sitole in labour court showdown, 11 March 2021
- Zuma's Crime Intelligence cash-splashing looters at 2012 Mangaung and 2017 Nasrec conferences to be arrested, 22 November 2021
- Crime Intelligence: Peter Jacobs heads to court to halt disciplinary action amid claims of criminality, 25 February 2021
- Exclusive: Crime Intelligence spent R112m on spy tech they can't use, and criminal charges could follow, 11 April 2021
- Jacobs vs Sitole: Treasury note allowed for emergency PPE procurement from slush fund, confirming suspended CI boss' claim, 16 December 2020
- SAPS members of rogue Crime Intelligence division are being protected by the Tactical Response Team, 5 November 2020
- Top Crime Intelligence boss loses court bid to overturn suspension over Covid-19 PPE scandal, 8 January 2021

- There's something wrong with SA where killing police officers is the norm – Cele, 6 September 2021
- Police were hung out to dry after President Ramaphosa's 2018 Anti-Gang Unit launch fanfare, 18 November 2021
- Jeremy Vearey defends Afrikaaps 'moer hulle' post, alleges discrimination, 4 June 2021
- Unfriended: The 'moer hulle' Facebook post, which could see top cop Jeremy Vearey fired, 29 May 2021
- Unrest SA: How police operations should have unfolded, according to these experts, 26 July 2021
- Western Cape top cop Jeremy Vearey fired, 31 May 2021
- July unrest: One year on, SA still doesn't know who masterminded the chaos, 8 July 2022
- From president to prisoner: Jacob Zuma taken to Estcourt prison after day of high drama, 8 July 2021
- Cops fear gun battle as Jacob Zuma's high noon approaches, 7 July 2021
- Mandy Wiener: Lies upon lies: The Trumpism of Jacob Zuma, 6 July 2021
- Police commissioner fails to recall Phoenix death toll at Human Rights Commission hearing, 30 November 2021
- Charl Kinnear murder: Zane Kilian in fresh attempt to secure bail, 5 May 2021
- Widow of slain detective Kinnear furious over bid to withdraw security again, 20 May 2022
- Father of Hawks detective shot dead in car outside his Cape Town home, 9 July 2019
- The shocking price of a hit that killed a policeman's dad: R25K, split five ways, 14 April 2022
- Cape Town man sentenced for killing Hawks detective's father in botched hit, 11 April 2022
- Targeting AGU Team C: How Zane Kilian tracked anti-gang cop Charl Kinnear and his team, 15 December 2020

Mail & Guardian
- Zondo's report on intelligence agency is important but flawed, 14 July 2022
- Looting and violence wasn't only in July 2021, it's a fact of daily life, 12 July 2022
- July unrest was designed to overwhelm police – Sitole, 22 November 2021
- Phase two: Looting was just the start say investigators and intelligence, 15 July 2021

Daily Maverick
- State pushes for start of former top cop Richard Mdluli's corruption trial after 'endless delays', 12 May 2022
- 'I am asking for mercy from the court' – Richard Mdluli pleads at sentencing hearing, 11 March 2020
- Bheki Cele steps in as Crime Intelligence boss Peter Jacobs takes 'flawed' disciplinary debacle to labour court, 25 February 2021
- Cops confirm probe under way into police boss's 'Covid' death as poisoning and exhumation suspicions swirl, 1 September 2021
- Crime Intelligence head Peter Jacobs is told he can return to work after months of fighting 'suspension', 8 February 2021
- Crime Intelligence: Musical chairs continue with trusted Zuma ally appointed to act in top job, 24 August 2017
- Déjà vu as Peter Jacobs transferred out of Crime Intelligence, suspension lifted, 3 March 2021
- Former Crime Intelligence secret fund head is facing corruption probe; he is also the new acting divisional commissioner, 8 June 2021
- Good morning, Colombia: Kidnappings, assassinations and corruption – SAPS is a systemic threat to SA, 19 November 2021
- Millionaire top cop at centre of feud between police minister and national commissioner, 20 August 2021
- South Africa's crime intelligence is politicised, riddled with nepotism and factionalism – and broken, 5 September 2021
- South Africa's Insecurity Cluster: Anatomy of a cock-up foretold, 25 July 2021
- ANC's persistence with the National Democratic Revolution, cadre deployment at the root of SA corruption, 14 August 2022
- 'National security threat' reference and technical glitches mark former detective chief Jeremy Vearey's dismissal hearing, 18 August 2021
- Crime Intelligence head Peter Jacobs recommends WC rogue CI unit be disbanded and members criminally investigated, 28 January 2019
- Crime Intelligence: Who is Major-General Peter Jacobs?, 29 March 2018
- Disgraced police boss Khomotso Phahlane ordered 2017 investigation into Jeremy Vearey and Peter Jacobs, hearing told, 17 August 2021
- Top cop Peter Jacobs heads to court again to stop police bosses from holding disciplinary against him, 12 May 2021
- General Feroz Khan's business interests and unlawful secret service account sign-offs are indeed a matter of grave public concern, 14 September 2021
- A year after top cop Charl Kinnear's murder, the SA Police Service is more chaotic than ever, 20 September 2021

- Anti-Gang Unit was not properly formed, had no adequate resources, failed to protect Charl Kinnear – SAPS watchdog, 12 November 2021
- Hawks officers did nothing to prevent Charl Kinnear assassination, should be criminally charged – SAPS watchdog, 12 November 2021
- Rogue cop unit in the Western Cape 'exists' and drove divisions in the province's police – SAPS watchdog, 12 November 2021
- Crime Intelligence: Axing Mdluli will allow cops to 'release state power' on crime while new Hawks head sought – Mbalula, 17 January 2018
- A defiant Jeremy Vearey strikes back over his dismissal by SAPS national commissioner Khehla Sitole, 3 July 2021
- Axed detective boss Jeremy Vearey's dismissal 'is fair', bargaining council rules, 16 November 2021
- Two Crime Intelligence cops launch R15m defamation claim against axed detective Jeremy Vearey, 13 September 2021
- Top cop Jeremy Vearey should be fired over 'threatening' Facebook posts that 'degraded' boss Khehla Sitole – disciplinary finds, 28 May 2021
- Police Commissioner Khehla Sitole: 'It's not necessarily a gross dereliction of duty, it was a shortcoming of intelligence', 30 November 2021
- Kinnear suspect, Zane Kilian, believed to have played a key role in assassination plot, charged with murder, 25 September 2020
- Nafiz Modack deeply implicated in assassinations in Cape Town, appears in multiple courts, 9 June 2022
- Jailed Nafiz Modack loses bid for tastier food, more showers and quicker lawyer access, 21 July 2022
- Rogue, rogue-er, rogue-est: Dissecting (real/fake) claims of cops colluding with criminals, 7 July 2022
- Kinnear assassination: Top brass knew, 27 September 2020
- Nafiz Modack, Mark Lifman and the spread of protection gangs from Cape Town's CBD to Khayelitsha, 2 May 2021
- Heads are yet to roll over murder of top cop Charl Kinnear, 18 September 2022
- Gang leader charged alongside Nafiz Modack over attempted murder of lawyer William Booth, 3 June 2022
- Nafiz Modack 'a violent personality with mysterious financial means' – state contends in closing arguments to oppose bail, 30 December 2021
- Associate of Nafiz Modack charged with corruption, fraud and money laundering, 27 January 2022
- Igor 'the other Russian' Russol's journey from Cape Town underworld power to murder conspiracy accused, 3 August 2022
- RET social media influencer Sphithiphithi Evaluator 'unmasked' in court over July insurrection, 31 August 2021

City Press
- 'Liar' Chris Ngcobo gets post as ambassador, 23 November 2015

Sunday Times
- All expenses paid, 22 April 2012
- Inside SA's police assassination problem, 4 October 2020

Parliamentary Monitoring Group
- Crime Intelligence turnaround strategy; SAPS restructuring, 22 August 2018

TimesLIVE
- SSA and Crime Intelligence 'peddled fake intelligence reports for Zuma and allies', 22 June 2022
- Editorial: Unqualified and clueless, police chief must cop it for July riots disaster, 2 December 2021

EWN
- SAPS top cop lied about qualifications, 21 August 2015

AmaBhungane
- 'Mdluli cops bugged Cele': Security chiefs slug it out, 13 April 2012

Security.co.za
- R4m to spy on the EFF, 23 Sept 2019

ISS Today (Institute for Security Studies)
- South Africa's damaged intelligence system is at a crossroads, 17 April 2018
- SAPS needs freedom from interference and streamlined management to address critical failures, 28 July 2021

The Conversation
- South Africa's deadly July 2021 riots may recur if there's no change, 9 July 2022

CHAPTER 12

State Capture Commission
- Final report: Crime Intelligence, 22 June 2022
- Affidavit: Brig. Tiyani Hlungwani, DCI
- Affidavit: Humbulani Innocent Khuba, IPID

Sunday Times
- Cut the deadwood from senior police ranks urgently, Mr President, 5 December 2021
- 'It's war now': Cele and generals clash over R138m in crime funds, 12 December 2021
- Justice Malala: It beggars belief that Cele and Sitole are still in office, 5 December 2021

Daily Maverick
- The real state of South Africa's police under Sitole: Reading between the crooked blue lines, 15 November 2021
- End of the legal runway for Khehla Sitole and his top officers as Supreme Court of Appeal sides with suspension, 3 November 2021
- Police commissioner Khehla Sitole: 'It's not necessarily a gross dereliction of duty, it was a shortcoming of intelligence', 30 November 2021
- Public order policing should be run as specialised unit to curb SAPS-related deaths, says panel, 29 March 2021
- Public order policing: SAPS demands more muscle, 3 September 2014
- R45m 'Nasrec grabber' was Fikile Mbalula's idea, claims national police commissioner Khehla Sitole in court papers, 22 February 2022
- SAPS embarked on procurement before 2017 Nasrec conference to protect and benefit the ANC and not South Africa, court finds, 19 January 2021
- Sitole and fellow top police brass in breach of statutory obligations, court finds in R45m 'Nasrec grabber' scandal, 3 March 2021
- Sitole vs Jacobs: what lies behind the top-level rupture at the SAPS?, 7 December 2020
- Nasrec plot: IPID targets senior SAPS members and former ministerial adviser in ANC vote-buying scandal, 7 January 2019
- Khehla Sitole and the case of the disappearing national security threat, 11 April 2021
- Khehla Sitole was felled by an ethical compass inclined towards blind loyalty, 7 March 2022
- Police commissioner Khehla Sitole bows out after mutual agreement and 'in the best interests of the country', 25 February 2022
- Minister of police Bheki Cele tells Parliament he was unaware of Sitole 'grabber' court case finding, 30 July 2021
- Appeal court confirms Khehla Sitole's 'breach of duty': His job as head of SAPS now untenable, 29 July 2021

TimesLIVE
- R598m spent improving public order policing unit that responds to protests, 29 March 2021

ISS Today (Institute for Security Studies)
- More public order police is no easy answer for South Africa, 5 August 2021

Mail & Guardian
- R45m 'grabber' case from 2017 haunts cop top Sitole, 7 October 2021
- How Masemola became police commissioner, 31 March 2022

News24
- 'I have no skeletons': Career cop takes over top job, 26 November 2017
- Critical Crime Intelligence systems under threat of shutdown, 7 April 2018
- Top cop Khehla Sitole's Nasrec 'grabber' splurge and the 'non-existent' threat, 25 March 2021
- Investigating Directorate probes top cop Khehla Sitole and the dodgy Criminal Intelligence splurges, 2 October 2021
- Investigating Directorate probes top cop Khehla Sitole and the dodgy Criminal Intelligence splurges, 3 October 2021
- Exclusive: 'Don't fire me' country's top cop tells Ramaphosa – and blames McBride, 15 September 2021
- National Treasury calls top cop Khehla Sitole to heel over R100m spy tech splurge, 3 July 2021
- Strained relationship with Sitole not responsible for 'dysfunction' in police operations – Cele, 7 March 2022
- Police, intelligence failed to stop July unrest – but executive also to blame, report finds, 7 February 2022
- Exclusive: Bheki Cele instructs outgoing top cop Khehla Sitole to reveal 'high-profile' cases, 9 March 2022

- The issues that led to Ramaphosa announcing the early termination of Khehla Sitole's contract, 25 February 2022
- Axed Khehla Sitole 'was not there' to deal with July unrest, police issues – Bheki Cele, 28 February 2022
- Fannie Masemola named new national police commissioner, 31 March 2022

The Citizen
- IPID confirms it opened a case against police boss Khehla Sitole, 27 January 2022

Politicsweb
- Police a 'matrix of corruption' – Robert McBride, 31 March 2018

CHAPTER 13

State Capture Commission
- Final report: Crime Intelligence, 22 June 2022
- Testimony by Colonel Dhajanaya Naidoo, 30 September & 1 October 2019
- Testimony by Colonel Kobus Roelofse, 17–20 September 2019

News24
- Thuli Madonsela must stop acting like she is God – Bheki Cele, 7 April 2014
- Moloi's report biased, unethical – Cele, 6 July 2012
- Court sets aside 2012 decision to fire Bheki Cele as police commissioner, 9 April 2019
- Businessman Roux Shabangu welcomes Bheki Cele judgment, 10 April 2019
- Magashula wants answers, 9 October 2016
- Caught on tape: Tax boss and drug dealer, 24 March 2013
- List: Bheki Cele names 19 people for allegedly instigating July's devastating unrest, 19 March 2022
- Drug dealer was paid to 'influence' Cele, 14 April 2012
- McBride vs Cele: Police committee to comply with court deadline, 13 February 2019

BBC
- South Africa police chief Bheki Cele fired by Jacob Zuma, 12 June 2012

SA Police Service
- Strategic Plan 2020–2025

AmaBhungane
- SAPS wars, Part 3: Bheki Cele, Robert McBride and the mysterious Mr Marimuthu, 8 April 2019
- Tax boss trapped by spying, 19 July 2013

Business Day
- SAPS can be effective only if Cele is replaced by an honest technocrat, 18 September 2018
- Go after the high-up apples and don't just pick fallen fruit in corruption hunt, 11 February 2019
- Prosecution service can start going after bigwigs among the corrupt, 30 July 2019
- Bheki Cele is trying to foster 'false narrative' against me, Robert McBride says, 21 February 2019

Independent Online
- Roux Shabangu loses R340 million lawsuit for dodgy police head office lease, 3 October 2020
- Madonsela wants answers from Cele, 4 March 2011
- Cele takes judge to High Court, 8 July 2010
- Listen: Bheki Cele's 'adviser' caught on tape, 1 July 2021
- McBride heads for a showdown with Cele over non-renewal of contract, 22 January 2019

Daily Maverick
- Op-ed: #DontBringBackBhekiCele, 6 November 2014
- Bheki Cele's last hurrah – that actually isn't, 13 June 2012
- Bheki Cele is unfit for office and has been so for more than a decade, 14 July 2022
- Bheki Cele case shows the criminal justice administration is toothless in cases of serious corruption, 14 September 2022
- Wake up and smell the McBride: How the state capture project corroded essential law enforcement cogs and wheels, 12 April 2019

Sunday Times
- Khalipi 'Jake' Moloi: Interpreter who became a respected judge, 13 August 2017
- The drug lord who took Oupa down, 14 July 2013
- Moodley denies being at Marimuthu's party, 15 October 2012
- Marimuthu in row with SARS over 'influence', 29 April 2012
- How cop spies looted slush fund, 22 November 2015

TimesLIVE
- Judge takes Cele to task, 9 March 2012
- Court sets aside Jacob Zuma's 2012 decision to axe Bheki Cele as top cop, 2 April 2019
- Bheki Cele rubbishes 'assumptions' he took bribe to protect 'corrupt' official, 30 September 2019
- Lying tax czar ousted, 14 July 2013
- Drug dealer 'Timmy' implicated in state capture, wanted by taxman, 1 December 2019
- Bheki Cele rubbishes 'assumptions' he took bribe to protect 'corrupt' official, 30 September 2019
- ANC MPs back Bheki Cele in his battle with Robert McBride over IPID job, 25 February 2019

Biznews
- Cyril's shocking side-step of Cele's impunity – Paul Hoffman, 2 May 2019

Mail & Guardian
- Mystery millions burglary, 18 June 2010
- Teflon Cele has survived decades of tender allegations, 7 July 2021
- Cele must answer police committee over McBride's job, 14 February 2019

EWN
- Cele slams Madonsela, 2 February 2014

Legalbrief Today
- Criminal probe of Cele actions recommended, 12 October 2022

CHAPTER 14, 15 & 16

State Capture Commission
- Affidavit: Paul O-Sullivan: Forensics for justice
- Affidavit: Thereza Heather-May Kunneke, for the Commission
- Affidavit: Gladstone Sella Maema, NPA
- Affidavit: Karen Helen van Rensburg, NPA
- Affidavit: Helen Elizabeth van Jaarsveld, NPA
- Affidavit: Ntebo Jan Mabula, retired, DPCI
- Affidavit: Robert John McBride, former head IPID
- Affidavit: Johan Wessel Booysen, retired, Hawks
- Affidavit: Dr Jacobus Petrus Pretorius, NPA
- Affidavit: Khulekani Raymond Mathenjwa, NPA
- Affidavit: Sarah-Jane Trent, Forensics for Justice
- Affidavit: Humbulani Innocent Khuba, IPID
- Testimony: Humbulani Innocent Khuba, 29 September 2019
- Testimony: Robert John McBride: 11 & 12 April 2019 and 15 & 16 April 2019
- Testimony: Ntebo Jan Mabula, 20 August 2020
- Testimony: Johan Wessel Booysen, 17 & 18 April 2019 and 2 and 3 May 2019

Open Secrets
- Unaccountable 0031: National Prosecuting Authority
- Unaccountable 0033: Andrew Chauke
- Unaccountable 0034: Sello Maema
- The De Kock Report, 27 June 2019

Daily Maverick
- Deliverance: NPA's Shaun Abrahams and the incredible shrinking case against Pravin Gordhan, 20 October 2016
- The fixers (3) – Shamila Batohi: Slowly, slowly catchy capture, 19 December 2019
- Paul O'Sullivan targets NPA & SAPS 'rogues' after charges withdrawn. 2 August 2018
- Disgraced Khomotso Phahlane loses labour court appeal against dismissal from SAPS, 12 August 2012
- Only God can help the state's case, says World Cup graft-accused Thoshan Panday, 4 May 2022
- State adds five more accused to Panday racketeering case, 17 December 2017
- The SAPS deals: Inside the Thoshan Panday indictment, 17 January 2012
- Toshan Panday and the many ways implicated people avoid accountability, 23 September 2020
- In control and close to tears: Study in contrasts as Thoshan Panday's co-accused family appear for World Cup graft case, 7 May 2021
- 'Untouchable' Thoshan Panday loses battle to avoid prosecution for World Cup SAPS fraud, 17 September 2020
- Retired Hawks colonel details how investigation into Thoshan Panday was squashed, 16 January 2020
- NPA is finally reaching solid ground to deliver justice, 7 July 2022
- Why the NPA is misfiring on high-profile corruption cases, 19 March 2022

- It's now or never for the National Prosecuting Authority, 20 June 2022
- The National Prosecuting Authority is in crisis and is failing in its core business – the prosecution of suspects, 18 January 2022
- Why has Sello Maema, the NPA's deputy prosecutions boss in North West, not been suspended? 31 August 2022
- After Zondo, the National Prosecuting Authority dare not fail the nation, 30 June 2022
- Daily roll call of arrests, NPA prosecutions and convictions, 17 February 2022
- Lawfare: Priority Crimes Litigation Unit refuses to give undertaking regarding Gordhan arrest, 6 September 2016
- Lesotho's chief justice castigates SA's Shaun Abrahams and bars him from prosecuting high-profile trial, 30 January 2022
- Analysis: After NPA's epic loss, Glynnis Breytenbach must return to all her cases, 28 May 2013
- Breytenbach tells of days of darkness at NPA, 30 January 2019
- House of cards: O'Sullivan vs Phahlane – who will outwit, outlast, outplay?, 14 February 2017
- House of cards: Paul O'Sullivan's arrest masks 'hidden agenda', 17 April 2016
- Corruption-accused ex-top cop Khomotso Phahlane tells public protector of SAPS's 'destructive battle against him', 27 July 2022
- Former acting national police commissioner Khomotso Phahlane sacked, 30 July 2020
- Paul O'Sullivan: National police commissioner slayer strikes again, 9 February 2018
- House of cards: Phahlane heads for a showdown with IPID amid detention of a lawyer working for O'Sullivan, 13 February 2017
- Charges against me and assistant are 'trumped up' – O'Sullivan, 14 February 2017
- House of cards: Gloves off as head of IPID alleges police minister protects corrupt cops, 15 February 2017
- House of cards: IPID to charge national police commissioner over R8 million mansion, 23 November 2016
- SARS wars: 'Rogue unit' prosecutor Sello Maema compromised, but NPA is keeping mum, 19 March 2018
- Fourteen years later, former SAPS North West deputy commissioner to face trial for apartheid-style torture, 23 November 2020

News24
- Paul O'Sullivan seeks damages following withdrawal of umpteenth 'fake' case, 2 August 2018
- Moipone Noko writes to NPA colleagues: I am 'made to feel like I am parading naked in public', 31 October 2020
- Former KZN police boss instructed Booysen to shut down 'Panday investigation', state capture inquiry hears. 17 April 2019
- NPA official who dropped charges against Zuma friends resigns after Ramaphosa orders inquiry, 18 February 2021
- Cloud of political interference still hangs over NPA – Pikoli, 22 November 2016
- Lawyers in former North West top cop's 'torture' case get more time to consult with witnesses, 11 May 2022
- 'Go to hell' – Paul O'Sullivan, accused face off at top cop's kidnapping, torture and assault trial, 11 May 2022
- Kidnappings, beatings and torture: Prosecution of ex-Hawks general stalls, 7 October 2020

Corruption Watch
- Hawks, NPA are failing the country on state capture prosecutions, convictions, 26 August 2022

Sunday Times
- The seasoned veteran leading Gordhan fraud prosecution, 23 October 2016

Business Day
- Shaun Abrahams denies targeting Pravin Gordhan, 24 February 2019
- Natasha Marrian: Thanks, Zuma, for a job well done in wrecking SA's core institutions, 15 February 2019
- Steven Friedman: No easy task for Cyril Ramaphosa to restore security services, 13 February 2019

TimesLIVE
- NPA investigating its own for state capture allegations, report reveals, 25 August 2022

CHAPTER 17

State Capture Commission
- Affidavit: Loyiso Jafta, SSA
- Affidavit Lloyd Mhlanga, SSA
- Affidavit: Mr Y, SSA
- Testimony: Ms K, SSA
- Affidavit: Ms K, SSA
- Affidavit: Fholisani Sydney Mufamadi

- Testimony: Fholisani Sydney Mufamadi, 25 January 2021
- Testimony: Loyiso Jafta, SSA, 16 January 2021
- Testimony: Setlhomamaru Isaac Dintwe, IGI, 12 May 2021
- High-Level Review Panel Report on the State Security Agency, December 2018
- Final Report, SSA, 22 June 2022

News 24
- Spy vs spy at state capture commission: Zondo allows Miss K to give evidence, 27 January 2021
- SSA declassified: Networks which looted R1.5bn from spy agency still in place as investigations collapse, 21 February 2021
- State capture inquiry: Zondo dismisses state security minister's bid to block spy boss from testifying, 26 January 2021
- SSA declassified: Spy boss Arthur Fraser's R225 million covert spying bill – and how he seized power, 23 February 2022
- SSA denies maintaining criminal networks – 'reappointed suspended officials are being kept in check', 21 February 2022
- SSA declassified: Spy boss Arthur Fraser got top-secret clearance using 'fake' documents, 28 February 2022
- Adriaan Basson: Why does Arthur Fraser still hold sway over the SSA?, 16 February 2022
- Exclusive: Arthur Fraser's 'right-hand man' appointed to top SSA job, 15 March 2021
- SSA denies aiding Arthur Fraser in battle with Jacques Pauw over 'classified' files, 17 February 2022
- Zondo report: Hawks should reopen criminal investigations into Arthur Fraser, 22 June 2022
- Fraser confirms he did not graduate from 'London University', 21 February 2022

TimesLIVE
- State capture: Minister Ayanda Dlodlo's attempt to stop SSA evidence falls flat, 26 January 2021
- State capture: State Security Agency splurged millions on Zuma's upkeep, 25 January 2021
- Spy boss Fraser says he is victim of 'malicious' investigation, 14 April 2018

Daily Maverick
- Spy vs spy: Cloned phones, break-ins and rogue agents – all in a day's work at the State Security central, 4 March 2020, 24 June 2020
- Evidence indicates Mkhwebane's office a virtual 'branch' of State Security Agency, remarks committee, 18 August 2022
- Ramaphosa wants the SSA where he can see it – but is that good for the country?, 18 January 2022
- How Jacob Zuma's spies trampled on national security and citizens' rights to change SA's trajectory, 25 June 2022
- Investigate Arthur Fraser, David Mahlobo and Thulani Dlomo – State Capture Commission, 23 June 2022
- Zondo affidavit: Spooks aligned with Zuma enabled state capture. 30 January 2022
- Commission hears of alleged covert ops in media, judiciary, civil society, academia and unions, costing taxpayers 'hundreds of millions', 26 January 2021
- Arthur Fraser's attorneys push NPA for update over perjury complaint against Sydney Mufamadi and others, 30 May 2022
- Arthur Fraser: How did he get in there – report reveals dodgy backdoor vetting for spy boss, 23 June 2022
- State intelligence mess: How the SA spy watchdog's teeth have been pulled, 23 January 2022

CHAPTERS 18 & 19

SARS Commission
- Evidence: Barry Hore, 27 June 2018
- Evidence: Tshebeletso Seremane, 27 June 2018
- Evidence: Keith Hendrickse, 22 August 2018
- Final report, 11 December 2018

State Capture Commission
- Final report: SARS, 4 January 2022
- Final report: Bosasa, 1 March 2022

Daily Maverick
- Fired mothers take former SARS commissioner Tom Moyane to court and win, 24 August 2022
- Paid to read the paper: Court victory for SARS execs fired under Moyane, 24 August 2022
- 'I performed sterlingly' – former commissioner Tom Moyane's take on the historic gutting of SARS, 26 May 2021

- Five things to know about the State Capture Commission's findings and recommendations on SARS, 4 January 2022
- Mr Moyane, you failed. Then you lied. Time to tell the truth, 13 August 2018
- Scorpio: The Moyane dossier, Part 1: How SARS boss disregarded the law to pay Guptas' VAT refund, 16 March 2018
- The Gospel of Truth according to Tom Moyane – a rich work of impure fiction, 2 October 2018
- The 'vexatious and abusive' Tom Moyane's big loss, 12 December 2018
- Tom Moyane solicited views on SARS from Bain & Co before appointment, 31 August 2018
- SARS wars: End of the road for Tom Moyane, one of state capture's most loyal foot soldiers, 20 March 2018
- Analysis: The case against Tom Moyane, 1 May 2018
- Analysis: Charges against Tom Moyane – serious, detailed, devastating, 7 May 2018
- Tom Moyane accused of costing SARS, and South Africa, at least R142-billion, 28 June 2018
- With Moyane's dismissal, Ramaphosa's slo-mo revolution claims a crucial scalp, 2 November 2018
- For Moyane and Zuma, Bain was a team player, 4 September 2018
- Hamilton Ndlovu's opulent empire implodes as he's ordered to pay back the millions, 7 June 2022
- SARS targets Hamilton Ndlovu's Porsches, freezes bank accounts, 22 September 2020
- The people and businesses the State Capture Commission recommends for prosecution by the NPA, 3 March 2022
- Brazen assassination attempt as SA tobacco war gets deadlier, 16 August 2019
- R3bn 'fraudulent, intentional tax evasion': An in-depth account of how SARS busted tobacco & gold plunder network, 29 August 2022
- R3-billion: SARS swoops on Gold Leaf Tobacco over transnational plunder network, 26 August 2022
- Simon Rudland's Gold Leaf Tobacco used Sasfin Bank officials to launder its dirty cigarette money – here's how, 12 September 2022

TimesLIVE
- Court orders reinstatement of SARS executive who blew the whistle on Bain, 24 August 2022

News24
- Zondo report guns for SARS under Moyane as 'a clear example of state capture', 5 January 2022
- SARS intentionally captured and SSA involvement: 7 things to know from Zondo's report, 6 January 2022
- Top SARS officials 'neutralised': Tom Moyane, Bain blasted by State Capture Inquiry, 4 January 2022
- SARS to appeal ruling reinstating employees axed during Bain restructuring, 25 August 2022
- Zuma, Myeni and Molefe: The nine cases from the Zondo report that the NPA can move on now, 17 January 2022
- Exclusive: Tom Moyane wanted to collapse the ANC, say party vets, 19 May 2019
- Gordhan vs Mpofu: Heated exchanges on arrogance, jealousy and racism didn't help – Zondo, 7 Jan 2022
- Tom Moyane's 10 biggest blunders at SARS, 20 March 2018
- SARS' Tom Moyane suspended with 'immediate effect', 19 March 2018
- SARS denies Moyane acted unlawfully in Gupta VAT repayments, 16 March 2018
- Bain 'ashamed' of mistakes in SA, but fails to reach out to SARS, 13 August 2022
- Exclusive: 'Akin to treason' – Treasury boss wants SA firms to stop doing business with Bain, 4 August 2022
- 'Hearsay' – SARS wants court to disregard Zondo, Nugent findings, 1 September 2022
- Wrap: Bosasa directors Leshabane, Gumede must be prosecuted for 'corrupt' ANC 'war room' deal, 1 March 2022
- How flashy businessman Hamilton Ndlovu scored close to R172 million in irregular PPE tenders, 27 January 2022
- Court freezes Gold Leaf Tobacco assets amid SARS tax evasion probe, 26 August 2022

City Press
- 'Corruption, exodus of skilled staff' – SARS is still reeling from Moyane's legacy, 2 September 2019
- Businessman's R11m luxury cars boast sparks Hawks' interest, 21 September 2020

Business Day
- Return of the taxman, 2 April 2022
- Zondo: ANC watched as state coffers were plundered, 5 January 2022

Mail & Guardian
- Apology be damned, Bain colluded with Tom Moyane to capture the South African Revenue Service, 26 August 2022
- Is taxman massaging the numbers?, 10 March 2017

AmaBhungane
- SARS hits Guptas with major tax bill and unearths R105m in mystery payments, 21 September 2020
- At a minute to midnight SARS tries to secure R4bn state capture loot, 4 December 2020
- Multibillion-rand gold VAT scheme: The Rudland connection, 9 February 2022

CHAPTER 20

Daily Maverick
- SARS wars: Massive data leak alleges British American Tobacco SA's role in bribery and corruption, 16 August 2016
- The saboteurs (4) – Julius Malema: Ka-ching!, 19 December 2019
- No country for appeasers as fascism rises in South Africa, 18 December 2019
- Mazzotti's smoke 'n mirrors: A matter of taxes, fraud, smuggling and cigarettes, 11 December 2018
- Scorpio: The curious case of ANC benefactor Robert Huang, a never-ending investigation and billions owed to SARS, 23 January 2018
- Sheriff raids Adriano Mazzotti's home and premises to pay taxman, 19 February 2019
- I am not an 'illicit tobacco kingpin' and am opposed to the illicit tobacco trade, 11 August 2020
- Mazzotti: It's Mrs Malema's property and she pays rent, 4 December 2018
- R3bn 'fraudulent, intentional tax evasion': An in-depth account of how SARS busted tobacco & gold plunder network, 29 August 2022
- BAT's UK headquarters oversaw and financed a South African corporate spy ring, 1 October 2021
- Public protector & 'rogue unit': How a big lie became a bigger and bigger lie, 8 December 2020
- Tobacco wars: Illegal cigarette trade kingpins rub shoulders with ANC brass, 18 August 2022
- US jails Nelson Pablo Yester-Garrido, the Cuban drug lord who operated from South Africa, 8 December 2020
- Escobar man's 'Narcos'-styled life: How a Cuban drug lord ran a global cartel from the safe haven of South Africa, 28 November 2020

Mail & Guardian
- Who is Nelson Yester-Garrido?, 29 June 2007

TimesLIVE
- Malema's family lives on estate owned by cigarette kingpin, 3 December 2018
- 'Allegation I influenced tobacco ban is outrageous,' says cigarette trader, 5 May 2020
- Picture with Dlamini-Zuma 'used to suit a certain narrative' – Mazzotti, 3 June 2020
- 'I am not Mazzotti's friend' – Nkosazana Dlamini-Zuma to MPs, 26 May 2020

The Citizen
- Moyane killed Adriano Mazzotti investigation, says Nene, 14 March 2019

Independent Online
- Malema guns for Jacques Pauw over Mazzotti loan claim, 5 July 2018
- EFF scrapes together election deposit, 12 March 2014

Sunday Times
- Smoked out! NDZ hanging out with cigarette smuggler and gambling tycoon, 5 November 2017
- Adriano Mazzotti says he had 'no relationship' with Dlamini-Zuma but is good friends with Malema, 7 June 2020
- Smokes and mirrors, 4 July 2021

Business Day
- Telita Snykers: The rogue unit that never was, 8 December 2020

City Press
- Malema denies he asked SARS 'rogue unit' boss for help, 4 October 2019

AmaBhungane
- Malema buddy's mine leaves community reeling, 18 July 2019
- How disinformation, propaganda and manipulation shape our online discourse (Chapter 1), 18 May 2020

News24
- Tobacco wars: More footage emerges, this time showing attempted hit on cigarette baron Adriano Mazzotti, 18 August 2019
- SARS moves against controversial businessman Mazzotti over multi-million rand tax debt, 19 February 2019
- Malema's wife, kids live in house owned by 'tobacco smuggler', 3 December 2018

- Malema's Spanish fiesta with the Mazzottis, 9 July 2022
- Malema defends trip to the Mazzottis' Ibiza wedding: 'I am not fighting to live in Alexandra', 27 August 2022
- Adriano Mazzotti denies 'outrageous' claims he influenced NDZ, govt to ban tobacco sales, 4 May 2020
- Businessman Adriano Mazzotti apologises to former SARS exec Johann van Loggerenberg, 1 November 2019
- Malema: Arrest Adriano Mazzotti if he is engaged in illicit cigarette smuggling, 18 July 2019

Politicsweb
- Carnilinx paid R25m to SARS – Adriano Mazzotti, 7 July 2018

Financial Mail
- Tobacco sales: Smoked out, 17 February 2021
- The mystery of how SA's cigarette 'exports' soared after lockdown, 13 July 2021
- Telita Snyckers: Tobacco companies and the politicians who love them, 27 July 2020
- Telita Snyckers: With the ban lifted, what's next for dirty tobacco?, 17 August 2020
- Telita Snyckers: Countering illicit trade: where's the strategy, SARS?, 15 January 2021

CHAPTER 21

Daily Maverick
- Mangaung: Malema, Shivambu, Magaqa appeal to come back to ANC and ANC Youth League, 17 December 2012
- Madonsela's report on Malema's manufactured money hits hard and deep, 11 October 2012
- ANC Youth League goes to bat for Malema against Broederbond media, 25 July 2011

TimesLIVE
- Malema's secret trust fund revealed, 24 July 2011
- Malema blasts Zuma on eve of hearing, 11 September 2011
- ANC dismisses Malema lifestyle report, 19 February 2010
- Where did Malema get the money? SARS reveals why deal collapsed, 12 April 2015
- Malema loses gagging bid, 24 July 2011
- Push for Julius Malema probe, 25 July 2011

Independent Online
- Uproar over Malema's R16m playboy mansion, 18 July 2011
- 'My money is none of your business' – Malema, 21 July 2011
- Malema: White people are criminals, 8 May 2011
- 'Kill for Zuma' gets life of its own, 30 June 2008
- Juju's confidant in SARS accord, 6 June 2015
- Court rejects Malema's interdict bid, 24 July 2011

News24
- Jacques Pauw open letter to Julius Malema, 6 July 2018
- Politics: The rise and fall of a youth league, 24 August 2020
- Malema's sugar daddy, 6 November 2011
- Malema forks out R78 000 in cash for 5-star break, 11 July 2011
- A tale of two Jonahs: Malema and 'that' lifestyle, 25 April 2016
- Malema: I don't have ambitions to become a president, 25 April 2016
- We have Winnie Mandela's blessing to continue fighting – Malema, 24 April 2016

BBC
- South Africa's Julius Malema in his own words, 21 September 2012

Sunday Times
- Malema: I know who gave cash to Zuma, 26 April 2015

Mail & Guardian
- ANC demands apology for Malema report, 20 February 2010
- Malema dares revenue service to conduct lifestyle audit, 19 July 2011
- Malema's lifestyle 'sponsored by govt tenders', 21 February 2010

AmaBhungane
- How Juju's Mauritius wedding host made his millions, 4 November 2011

CHAPTER 22

Daily Maverick
- Protests at Malema buddy's mine turn deadly, 18 July 2019
- Revolutionary trash sometimes requires trash journalism, literally, 3 July 2019

Business Day
- Tom Eaton: In detritus veritas – as well as hypocrisy and H&M, 5 July 2019

CHAPTER 23

Daily Maverick
- VBS bank heist: EFF's family ties and moneyed connections, 21 November 2018
- For too long now, the state of South Africa has been malfunctioning. It's time for the choking apparatus to cough back into life. The truth is, South Africa doesn't have much time left and it had better happen. Now, 10 September 2019
- 'Cruising nicely' on VBS: EFF's parties, lies and looted money, 27 May 2019
- Along with the R16.1m in illicit payments, VBS approved Brian Shivambu's R1.46m home loan, with a little help from uBhuti ka Brian, 9 December 2018
- Eight key takeaways from 'Julius Malema's time of spending dangerously' story, 9 September 2019
- It wasn't me, says Malema . . . it was my brothers, 10 September 2019
- Twitter and the rest of social media are a rising threat to media freedom – and I am part of their roadkill, 6 August 2019
- Malema: Journalists must not be 'crybabies', 7 August 2019
- Julius Malema and the looted VBS funds: The devil's in the detail, 10 September 2019
- The great VBS heist: How the Shivambu brothers benefited even more, 3 April 2019
- The chronicles of Grand Azania, Part 2: Floyd Shivambu's time of spending dangerously, 13 October 2019
- The chronicles of Grand Azania, Part 3: Floyd Shivambu's four strikes, 26 November 2019
- The VBS aftermath: 'If we speak, they will kill us', 9 September 2019
- VBS bank heist: EFF's family ties and moneyed connections, 21 November 2018
- VBS theft, money laundering & life's little luxuries: Julius Malema's time of spending dangerously, 8 September 2019
- With echoes of Adolf Hitler, Julius Malema makes his move to establish an African reich, 18 December 2019
- No country for appeasers as fascism rises in South Africa, 18 December 2019
- EFF's new top leadership: Malema and Shivambu tighten their grip over SA's third biggest party, 15 December 2019
- EFF land dream: Turning South Africa into one big Bantustan – for the impoverishment of the people, 16 December 2019
- VBS bank heist arrests: Who's next?, 8 June 2020
- EFF violence up – but popularity ratings way down, 5 September 2019
- Beyond reasonable doubt: VBS scandal exposed Julius Malema and Floyd Shivambu's corrupt dealings, 18 August 2021
- The grim prospect of the EFF governing SA looms, 3 October 2022
- Julius Malema: The one man who can bring down the republic, 8 February 2022
- A further eight VBS Mutual Bank looting kingpins to stand trial, 12 March 2021

AmaBhungane
- Brian Shivambu rocks up with R3m after pleading poverty, 13 September 2019
- Toilet tender stinks, 20 September 2019
- Tender comrades, Part 2: Tshwane tenderpreneur's R15m 'EFF tithe', 29 September 2019
- Tender comrades, Part 1: Trailing the Juju tractor, 19 September 2019
- Tender comrades analysis: When it looks like a duck, swims like a duck and quacks like a duck, 30 September 2019
- Firm that won R1bn Jo'burg fleet contract paid Malema-EFF 'slush-fund', 29 November 2018
- Malema ally has the world in his hands, 28 June 2019
- Statement: Why Malema should not get away with banning us, 13 September 2019
- WhatsApps expose Floyd and the 'Red Boys', 6 May 2019
- Update: Brian Shivambu finds another R1.5m to settle VBS debt, 26 September 2019
- Brian Shivambu rocks up with R3m after pleading poverty, 13 September 2019

TimesLIVE
- Floyd Shivambu asked me to stop VBS going into curatorship – Nhlanhla Nene, 14 March 2019
- How VBS loot helped Julius Malema get a R5m house, 24 November 2019

- Julius Malema claps back at man who posted snap of him in business class, 26 August 2019
- Traumatised black voters perpetuate their own poverty, 11 August 2019
- SCA dismisses Julius Malema's appeal on statements by former EFF MP about VBS money, 23 June 2021
- Editors tackle EFF over 'hate speech' towards journalists, 5 August 2019
- The EFF is tapping into vile sentiments in its attacks on journalists but free political choice is fundamental, 10 March 2019
- Sanef charges Malema, EFF with hate speech and intimidation of journalists, 19 December 2018

Mail & Guardian
- Juju's cousin also linked to VBS, 26 October 2018
- Outrage greets VBS bank report, 12 October 2018
- PIC, VBS, Floyd and his baby brother, 12 October 2018
- Shivambu blames 'weapons of mass deception' for alleged VBS links, 13 October 2018
- VBS bounty buys Floyd a Rover, 20 September 2019
- Shivambu apologises for scuffle with journalist, 20 March 2018
- Rawula resigns, calls on EFF to produce financials, 10 Apr 2019
- Shivambu used VBS money for flat, 30 November 2018
- Malema: Floyd brought us his financial statements, 16 October 2018

News24
- Ralph Mathekga: VBS could shatter EFF leadership at December elective conference, 12 November 2019
- Opinion: On Malema, free speech and going against the grain of our cultural biographies, 7 September 2019
- Probe Gucci-wearing Malema for perjury for pleading poverty in R500K hate speech claim – AfriForum, 14 June 2022
- Malema: Twitter is 'entirely divorced from reality', 6 July 2019
- SACP slams intimidation, threats against journalists, 15 December 2018
- VBS bank saga: Corruption-accused former municipal official arrested in hospital bed, 25 May 2022

Business Day
- Malema loses VBS money defamation case in appeal court, 23 June 2012
- Rob Rose: The hypocrisy of Malema's 'march to save lives', 21 June 2021
- Gareth van Onselen: The state of the EFF, 1 April 2021
- Justice Malala: Habib, Malema and the creeping fascism of the EFF, 17 March 2021
- Gareth van Onselen: Mapping the evolution of the EFF threat, 19 November 2020
- Red faces all around for the EFF, 10 June 2021
- Editorial: EFF had better make sure its hands are clean, 19 October 2020

City Press
- Malema loses R1m defamation case against former EFF MP, 6 April 2019

The Citizen
- Malema tells 'sick' Pauli van Wyk: 'Go to hell satan', 25 November 2018

BOOKS

- Greg Ardé, *War Party: How The ANC's Political Killings Are Breaking South Africa*, Tafelberg, 2020
- Caryn Dolley, *The Enforcers: Inside Cape Town's Deadly Nightclub Battles*, Jonathan Ball Publishers, 2019
- Caryn Dolley, *To the Wolves: How Traitor Cops Crafted South Africa's Underworld*, Daily Maverick, 2021
- Kaveel Singh, Jeff Wicks and Qaanitah Hunter, *Eight Days in July: Inside the Zuma Unrest That Set South Africa Alight*, Tafelberg, 2021
- Telita Snyckers, *Dirty Tobacco: Spies, Lies and Mega-Profits; A SARS Insider Spills the Beans on Global Crime*, Tafelberg, 2020
- Johann van Loggerenberg, *Death and Taxes: How SARS Made Hitmen, Drug Dealers and Tax Dodgers Pay Their Dues*, Jonathan Ball Publishers, 2018
- Jeremy Vearey, *Into Dark Water: A Police Memoir*, Tafelberg, 2021

Index

456

JACQUES PAUW has been a journalist since 1984 and has written for some of the country's most esteemed publications before becoming a documentary filmmaker in 1994, specialising in investigating criminality and the abuse of power on the African continent. He produced documentaries on i.a. conflicts in Rwanda, Burundi, Algeria, Liberia, Sudan, the Democratic Republic of Congo and Sierra Leone. His work has been shown around the world and he has received several national and international awards, including the Media Institute of Southern Africa's award for investigative journalism, the Vodacom Journalist of the Year Award and the Nat Nakasa Award for bravery and integrity in journalism. Internationally, he has won CNN's African Journalist of the Year twice; Italy's Ilaria Alpi television award; and in the United States, the Daniel Pearl Award for Outstanding International Investigative Reporting. He is also a recipient of the Ahmed Kathrada Excellence in Leadership award.

Apart from journalism, Pauw has also authored several books: *In the Heart of the Whore: The Story of Apartheid's Death Squads* in 1991; *Into the Heart of Darkness: Confessions of Apartheid's Assassins* in 1997; *Dances with Devils: A Journalist's Search for Truth* in 2007; the novel *Little Ice-Cream Boy* in 2009; *Rat Roads: One Man's Incredible Journey* in 2012 and *The President's Keepers: Those Keeping Zuma in Power and out of Prison* in 2017. It became the fastest-selling book since Nielsen BookData started auditing South African book sales in 2004 and has sold more than 205 000 copies. This book became part of a social movement, and a shorthand for opposition to corruption and cronyism. In 2018, Pauw and NB Publishers were awarded the Association of American Publishers' prestigious International Freedom to Publish Award for the publication. The book also received the Nielsen Booksellers Choice Award.